Sewing Machine Skills FOR Beginners

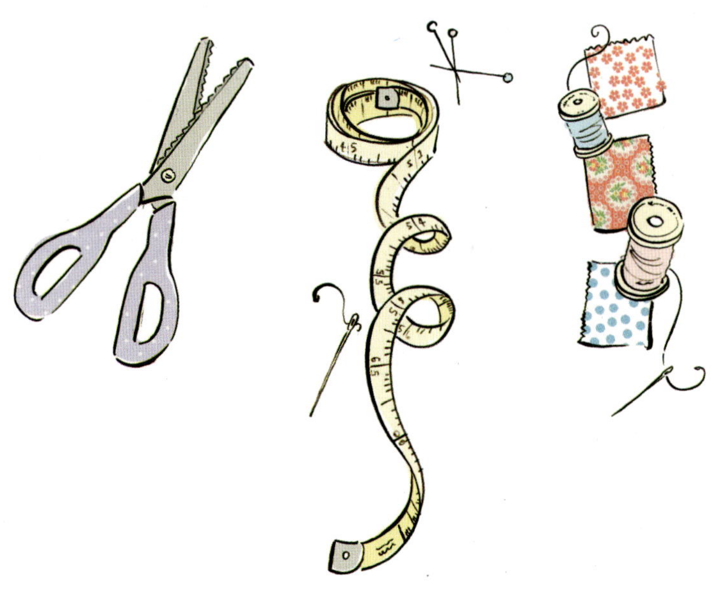

LOS ANGELES

Sewing Machine Skills FOR Beginners

EASY-TO-FOLLOW GUIDES FOR FIRST-TIME STITCHERS

Includes 7 full-size pull-out patterns

Jane Bolsover

CICO BOOKS

For Jan Dabbous,
a very special friend

This edition published in 2025 by CICO Books
An imprint of Ryland Peters & Small Ltd
20–21 Jockey's Fields
London WC1R 4BW

1452 Davis Bugg Road
Warrenton, NC 27589

www.rylandpeters.com
Email: euregulations@rylandpeters.com

10 9 8 7 6 5 4 3 2 1

First published in 2010 as *Sewing Machine Basics*.

A CIP record for this book is available from the British Library.
US Library of Congress CIP data has been applied for.

ISBN: 978 1 80065 469 3

Printed in China

Design: Roger Hammond
Technical illustrations: Stephen Dew
Decorative illustations: Hannah George
Copy editor: Sarah Hoggett
Project photography: Penny Wincer
Stylist: Sania Pell
Equipment and fabric swatch photography: Martin Norris
Production manager: Gordana Simakovic

The authorised representative in the EEA is
Authorised Rep Compliance Ltd.,
Ground Floor. 71 Lower Baggot Street,
Dublin, D01 P593, Ireland
www.arccompliance.com

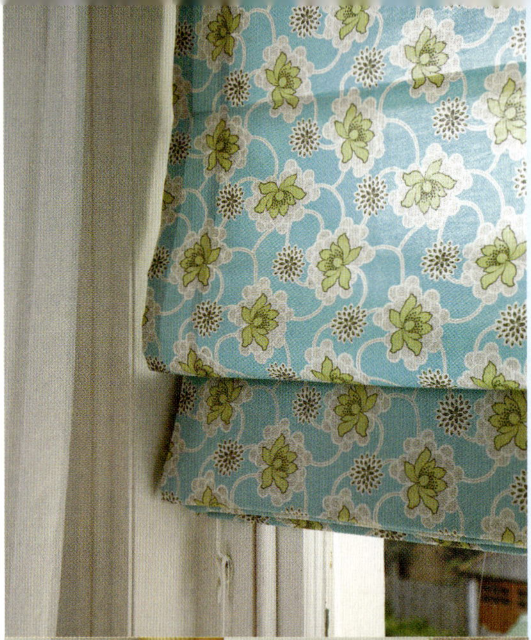

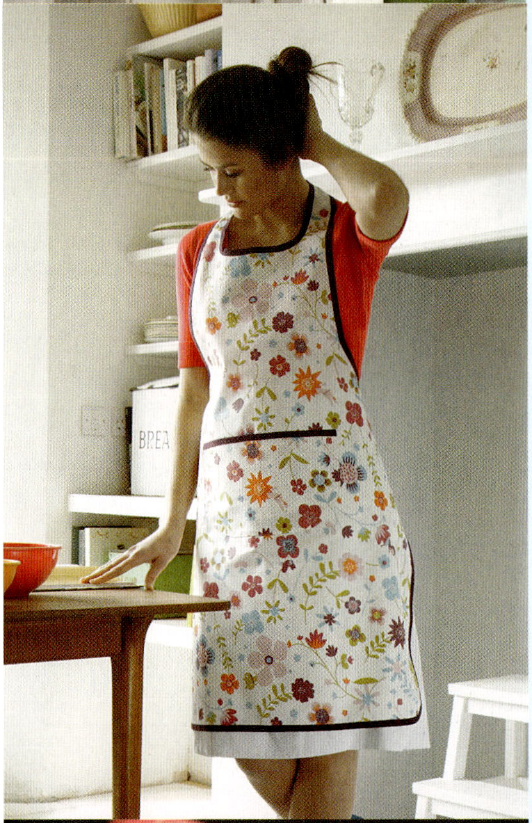

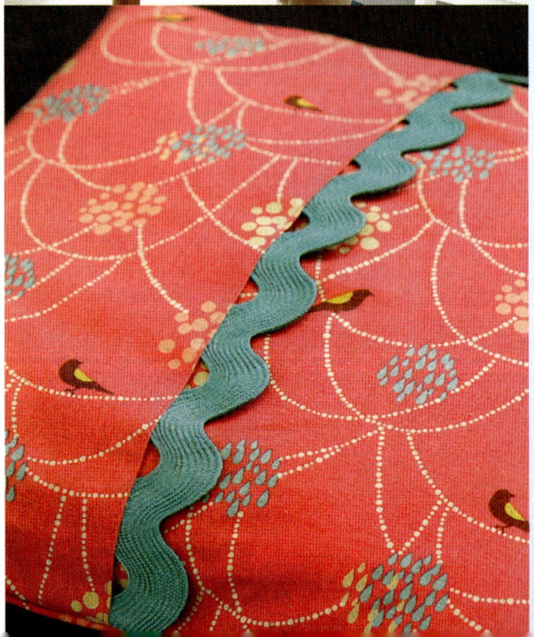

Contents

Introduction

Why another book on sewing? In recent times, sales of sewing machines have suddenly gone through the roof—which, as far as I am concerned, is great news!

I am lucky enough to be of a generation where my grandma was able to light my passion for sewing. We sat for hours lovingly making clothes for my dolls, which later turned into clothes for myself, and then into an exciting career as a fashion designer and beyond. Young people today are not so fortunate; their grandma probably didn't know how to sew and, as sewing was even dropped from the school curriculum, it became something that wasn't cool to do.

In recent years I have had the opportunity to teach "Learn to sew" workshops at major department stores, and have been thrilled by the response and keenness of the young people who came along. This book is intended to help those who have become excited by the new wave of "make do and mend"—those have not been able to get to a workshop, but have gone out and purchased a sewing machine only to get it home and then realize that they don't really know what to do with it. Maybe you've bought your first home and are excited at the prospect of making some simple curtains, or are expecting your first baby and would like to make some clothes for both baby and yourself? I hope to be able to take your hand and show you step by step how to create unique and beautiful things; not only that, I want to show you the joy and satisfaction that comes with being able to say, "I made that!" I promise you, it's a much better feeling than simply passing a credit card over the counter!

I wish you many happy days of sewing ahead!

Jane

Jane Bolsover

How to use this book

This book is designed for absolute beginners, or as a refresher course for those who have not sewn for many years and need to regain their confidence.

Section 1: **Getting started**

This part contains a wealth of information on how to get to grips with your sewing machine. Although your instruction manual will tell you how to use the controls on your particular machine, manuals are sometimes a bit vague about the reasons why you might need to make adjustments, or exactly which needle or machine foot you should use in a particular situation—but once you understand the basic principles, you'll be in a much better position to make decisions for yourself.

This section also introduces you to basic sewing equipment, different types of fabric, and how to prepare your fabric prior to sewing.

Take the time to read through this section before you begin, ideally when you're sitting in front of your own sewing machine, and practice basic sewing machine techniques such as changing needles, machine feet, stitch length, and stitch tension until you feel confident.

Section 2: **Workshops**

This section consists of eleven workshops, covering fundamental sewing techniques from simple seams and hems to buttonholes and zippers, darts, and tucks, and working with patterns.

At the end of each workshop is an easy-to-follow step-by-step project, ranging from a simple pillow and scarf that require nothing more complicated than the ability to stitch in a straight line to stylish garments that you will want to wear time and time again.

Full-size patterns for all the projects are included on pull-out sheets at the back of the book. Throughout, the information is presented in an easily accessible way, with clear step-by-step instructions and diagrams explaining every stage of the way.

Work through the workshops consecutively, as they have been designed to move your sewing skills on to another level each time.

At the very end of the book, you will find some helpful reference material, including a chart on selecting the right needle, thread, and stitch length for particular situations, tips on maintaining your sewing machine so that it runs smoothly, and a glossary of common sewing terms to help you make sense of the jargon.

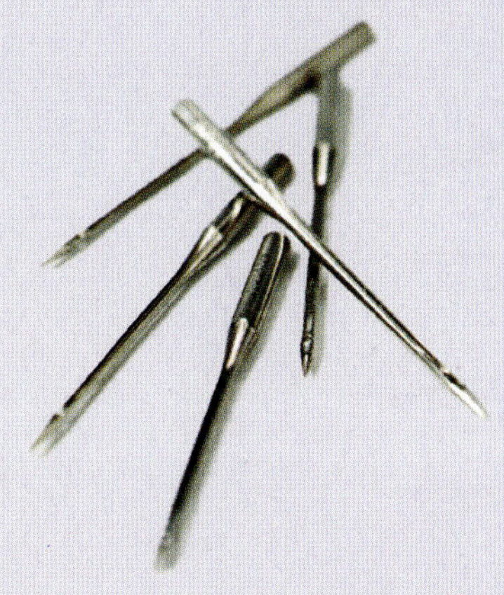

SECTION 1

Getting started

This section sets out everything you need to know to choose the right sewing machine for your needs, get to grips with the technicalities, select fabrics, and—finally!—embark on your first sewing project. Although it's tempting to rush out and buy lengths of gorgeous fabric straight away, take the time to read through this section first—ideally when seated in front of your own machine. This will allow you to familiarize yourself with the controls and all the things that your machine can do, and to build up the confidence to start stitching.

Sewing machine know-how

How do you go about choosing a sewing machine, or get to grips with the one that you have? It isn't as scary as you might think. In this chapter we will unravel the mysteries, explaining the different types available and how they work. We'll soon have you up and stitching!

Choosing a sewing machine

There are so many brands of sewing machine available, each one offering a wide range of stitch options, that it can be difficult to decide what to buy. The first thing you need to know is that there are three basic types of sewing machine: mechanical, electronic, and computerized.

Mechanical This type of machine can do straight stitching, zigzag, satin stitch (close-up zigzag), and decorative stitches that can be made with zigzag, such as four-step buttonholes and simple forms of embroidery. They are great for beginners, as they are competitively priced; you may even find a good second-hand one.

Electronic Mechanical with computerized features, these machines can do straight stitching, zigzag, and satin stitches, plus an automatic buttonhole, blind hemming, and some decorative stitches. They cost more than mechanical models, but they are still great for beginners and some features, such as the automatic buttonhole, give a very professional finish.

Computerized These machines are fully computerized with touch-button controls and a screen. They are more expensive and can do all of the above at the touch of a button, plus a wide range of fancy stitches.

There are also specialist embroidery machines that can be linked directly into your computer to create your own embroidered motifs; alternatively, you can slot "cards" into the machine to create designs from a catalog. However, they are not recommended for the novice.

Flat-bed machine

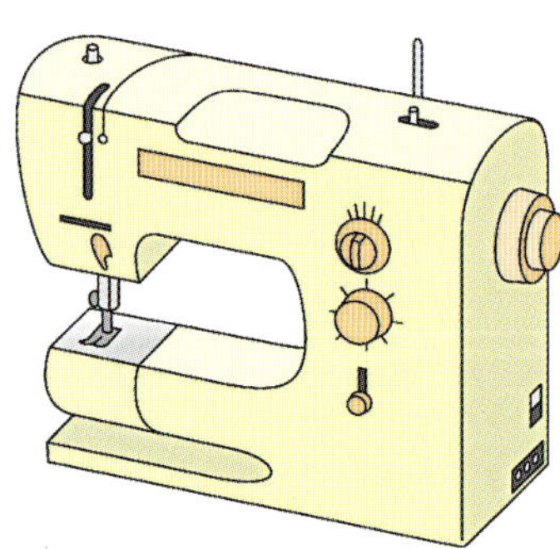

Free-arm machine

Flat-bed, free-arm, or portable? A flat-bed machine can be built into a special sewing cabinet and folded away, meaning that you always have a built-in sewing table on which to work. Free-arm machines are generally more useful, as the free-arm allows you to do tubular sewing and to get into awkward little places without having to undo the side seams. With a special clip-on table, free-arm machines can also convert into a small flat-bed.

If you're planning to make mainly clothing, a free-arm machine is the best choice. For home furnishings such as curtains, opt for a flat-bed, as it has a large, sturdy surface for supporting the fabric.

Portable machines are lightweight, so you can store and carry them around more easily. Most important, make sure that the machine is stable and will sit firmly on your table.

Sewing machine features

Whichever type of machine you choose, remember that all machines are basically similar. The operating parts shown in this photograph are common to any average sewing machine that can do straight and reverse stitch (for sewing straight seams) and zigzag stitch for neatening and working buttonholes—which are the stitches that, as a beginner, you will probably use most for basic dressmaking and home furnishings.

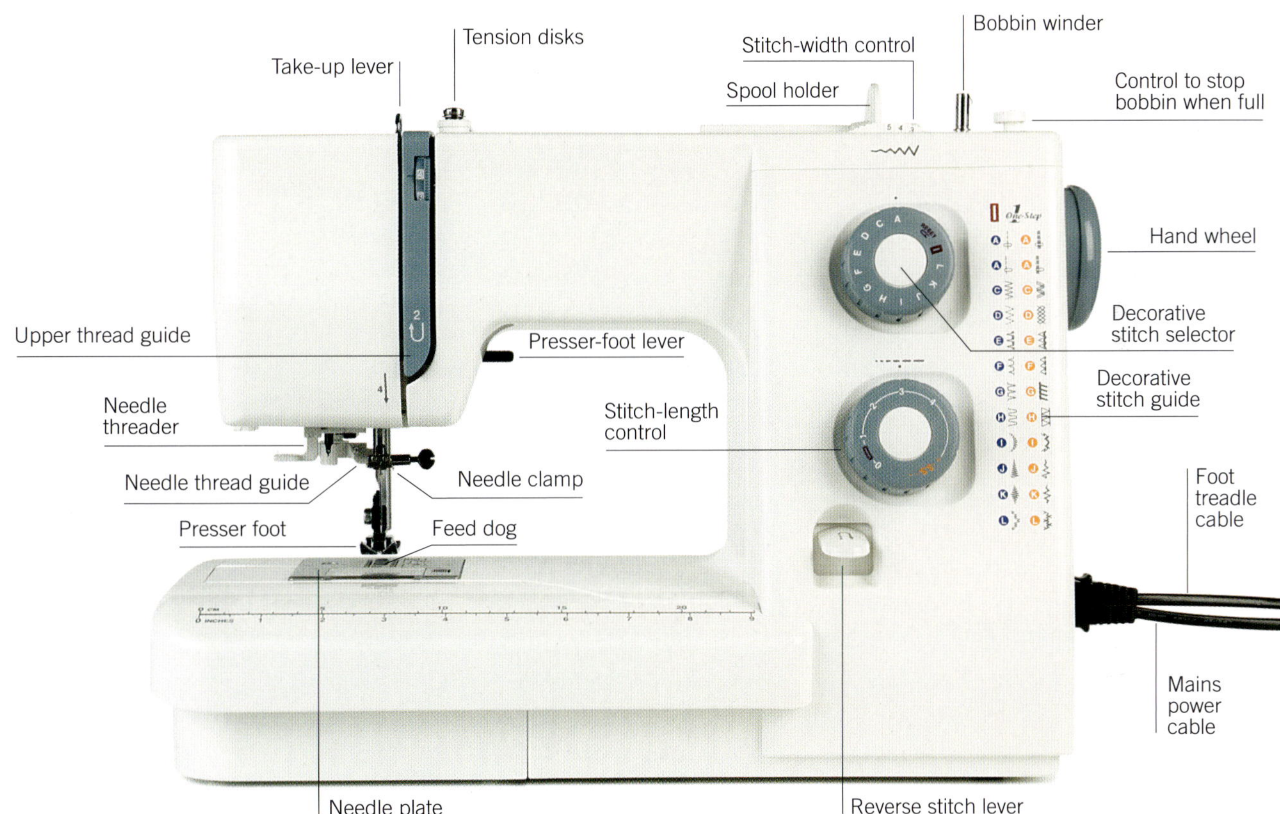

Other things to consider

Guarantees When you purchase a machine, you are protected by the warranties and conditions laid down by law. However, some stores offer additional benefits, so do remember to ask. Most sewing machines come with a standard 12 months' guarantee, so be sure to keep a record of your machine's serial number, model number, and date of purchase.

After-sales service Choose a well-known brand, as the availability of replacement parts during the lifetime of your machine is important. Most distributors have agents or stores in large towns, which will carry a range of spare parts and can do some servicing. Problems may occur if you have a second-hand machine that is no longer in production; however, by using the Internet you should be able to track down a dealer somewhere who specializes in parts for old machines.

Free lessons Some sewing machine manufacturers offer free sewing lessons with their distributors. The number of lessons usually depends on the type of machine you have bought and the price that you have paid. Do not worry if there are no lessons on offer—you have this book to guide you! But it is always advisable to read your instruction manual carefully in order to get to know your own machine and its controls.

How stitches are formed

Basically, all machines work on a timed sequence: the needle moves up and down, taking the upper thread with it to link around a second thread that is wound onto a separate bobbin housed in the lower part of the machine, thus forming a stitch.

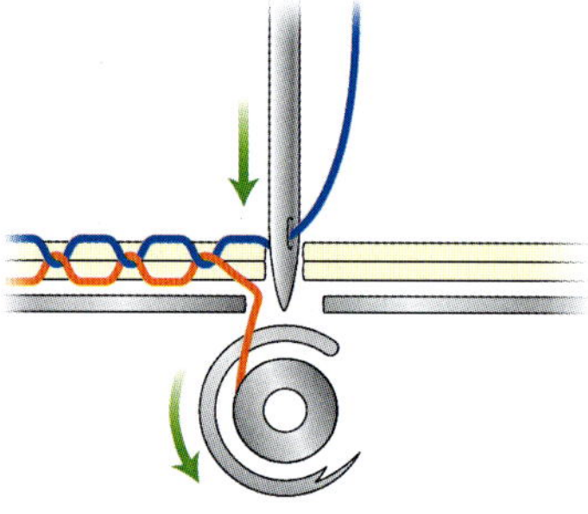

1 The needle moves down to penetrate the fabric and bring the top thread into the bobbin area.

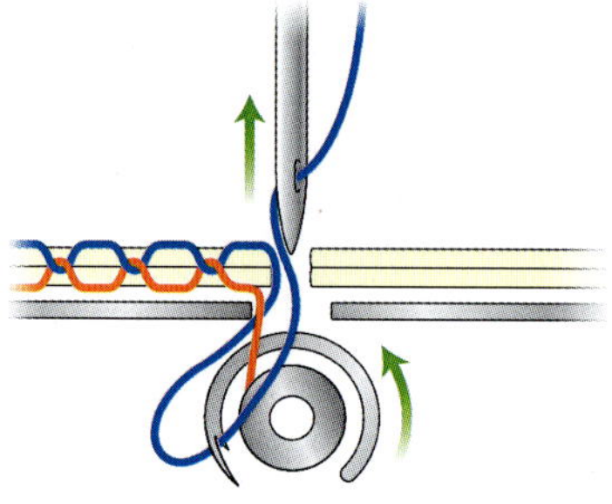

2 As the needle starts to rise, the top thread forms a loop for the shuttle hook (located on the bobbin housing) to catch.

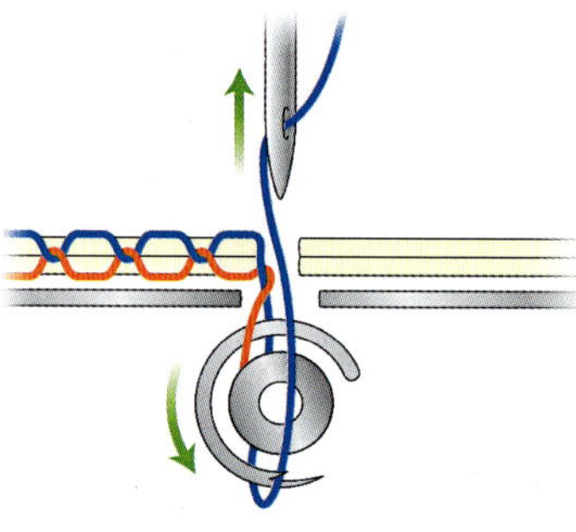

3 The shuttle hook carries the thread loop around and under the bobbin case.

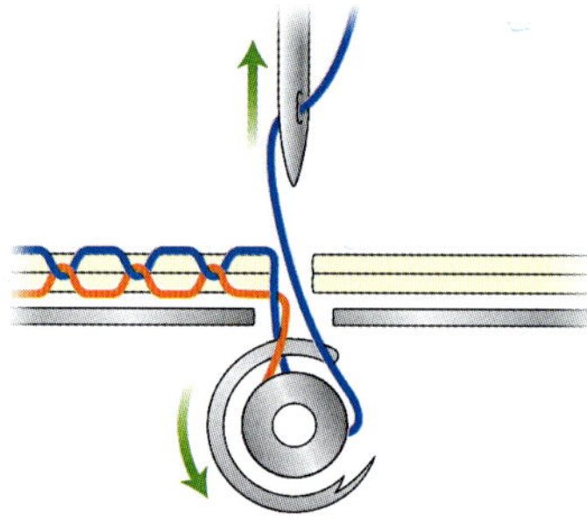

4 The loop slides off the hook and bobbin case, to go around the bobbin thread.

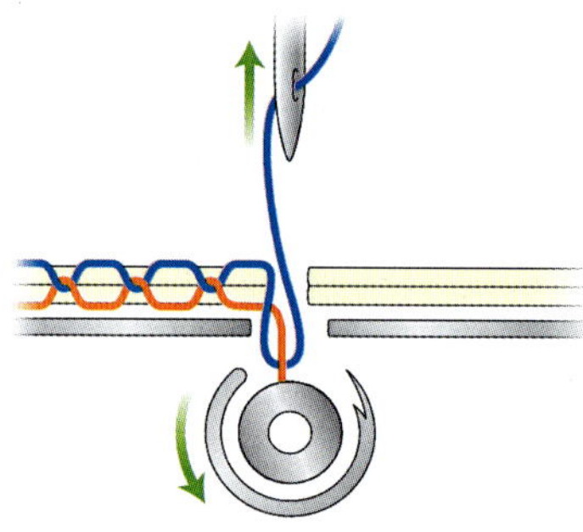

5 The threads are pulled up and into the fabric layers as "locked stitches"—hence the name, "lockstitch."

Another important function of your machine is the interaction between the presser foot, needle, and feed. The presser foot holds the fabric in place and the needle goes up and down through the fabric to form stitches, while the "toothed" feed, which is located under the presser foot, moves the fabric along ready for the next stitch. This feed is able to move forward and back in order to work reverse stitches. To form a zigzag stitch, which is used to neaten seam edges (see page 44), your needle must also be able to move from side to side.

Threading your machine

Both the top and the bottom (bobbin) threads need to be fed through a series of tension disks and thread guides to ensure a constant control of the threads and to form perfectly balanced stitches.

Top threading

Most new models have a numbered sequence with arrows marked on the machine, which makes threading the needle very simple. If you are not sure, always refer to your machine instruction manual. Although the location and appearance of the parts involved differs between models, the process is basically the same.

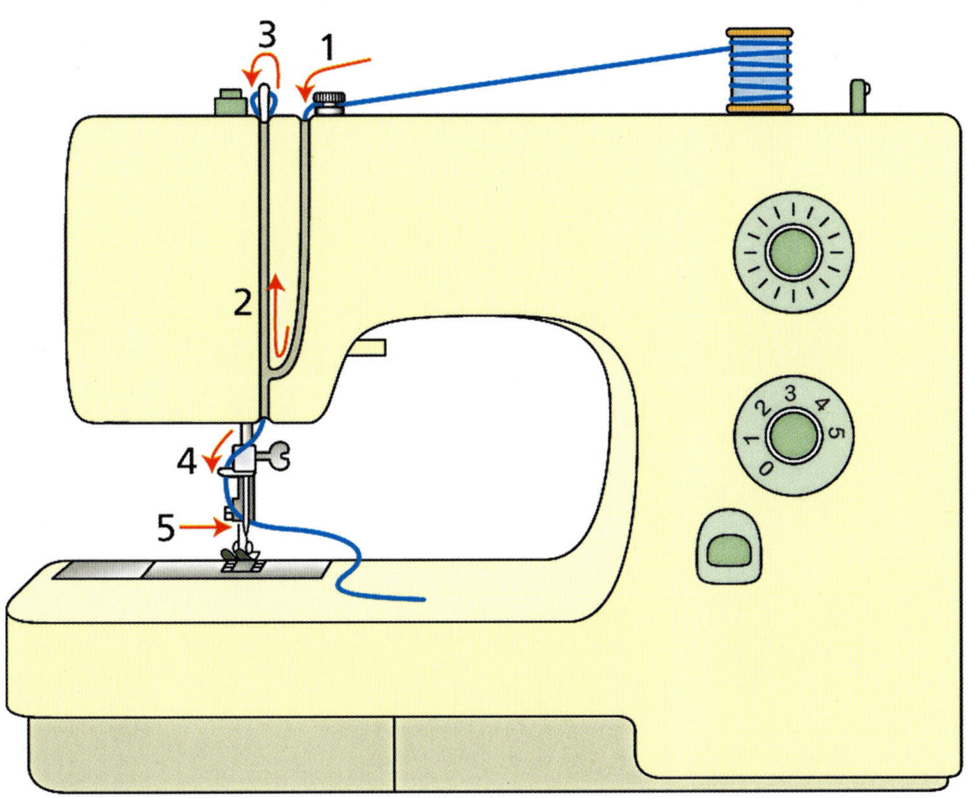

TIPS

- If the eye of your needle faces the side of your machine, thread it from left to right; if it faces the front, thread it from front to back.
- Use a pair of sharp scissors to cut the thread at an angle before you insert it through the eye of the needle.

1 Place the reel of thread on the spool holder (this may be in a horizontal or vertical position depending on the model of your machine). Unwind the end of the thread from the reel and take it around the tension disks.

2 Take the thread end down and around the thread guide, following the direction of the arrow.

3 Bring the thread up and pass it, from the right, though the eye or slot on the take-up lever.

4 Take the thread down through the needle thread guide.

5 Finally, pass the thread through the eye of the needle. You may find that your machine has a built-in needle threader. If it does, refer to your instruction manual to see how this works; normally the needle should be in the highest position, with the presser foot down.

Before you thread any machine, remember to do two things:

- Lift the presser foot. This will allow the tension disks to release, so that the thread can be pulled through easily.
- Raise the needle to its highest point, so that it will not come unthreaded on its first stitch.

Bobbins

The thread for the lower part of the machine is always wound onto a separate bobbin, which is stored in a case located in an area under the needle and needle plate. Bobbins are made to an exact size and specification for your machine and are therefore not normally interchangeable. Make sure that you use only the ones recommended for your machine and replace any that are worn, cracked, or chipped, as these can cause sewing problems.

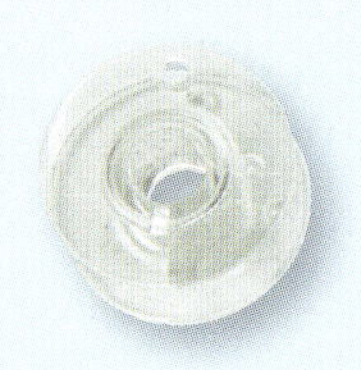
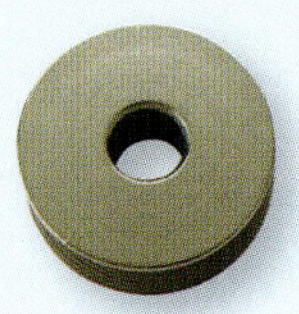

Bobbin types
Bobbins can be made of metal or plastic and vary in size and design. Make sure you use only the type designed for your machine.

Removing the bobbin

Before you attempt to remove a bobbin, make sure that the needle is up at its highest point and that the presser foot is lifted.

Open the cover plate to gain access to the bobbin area. Where this is located varies depending on the type of machine that you have. On mechanical versions it will probably be set in vertically at the side or front of your machine. On electronic and computerized versions, it will probably be dropped horizontally into the front of the machine. Refer to your manual if you are unsure.

Mechanical machines normally have removable bobbin cases, which must be lifted out by means of a little latch before the bobbin itself can be removed (see below). On electronic and computerized machines the bobbin is usually simply lifted out of its fixed casing.

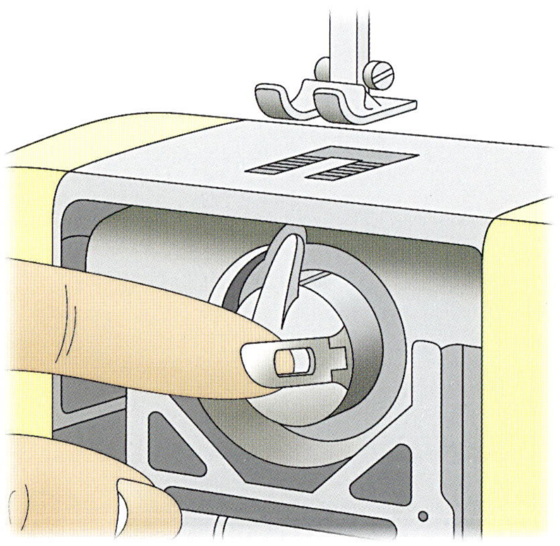

Mechanical machine bobbin
With index finger and thumb, take hold of the latch on the side of the case. Still holding the latch, pull the bobbin case free from the machine. Let go of the latch and the bobbin will drop out.

Winding thread onto the bobbin

On mechanical and electronic sewing machines, you have to manually deactivate the up-and-down motion of the needle before winding a bobbin can commence. On computerized versions, this deactivation is done automatically. Check your instruction manual to find out exactly how this needs to be done for your brand of machine.

1 Place the empty bobbin on the bobbin winder and your reel of thread on the spool holder.

2 Take the thread end from the reel, pass it around the upper thread guides, and wrap it around the bobbin several times (the direction will depend on your machine).

3 Slide the bobbin on the winder across the top slot to engage the bobbin-winding operation.

4 Press the foot treadle on your machine and the bobbin will start winding; it will automatically stop when the bobbin is full.

5 Slide the filled bobbin back across the top slot to the normal position and cut the thread.

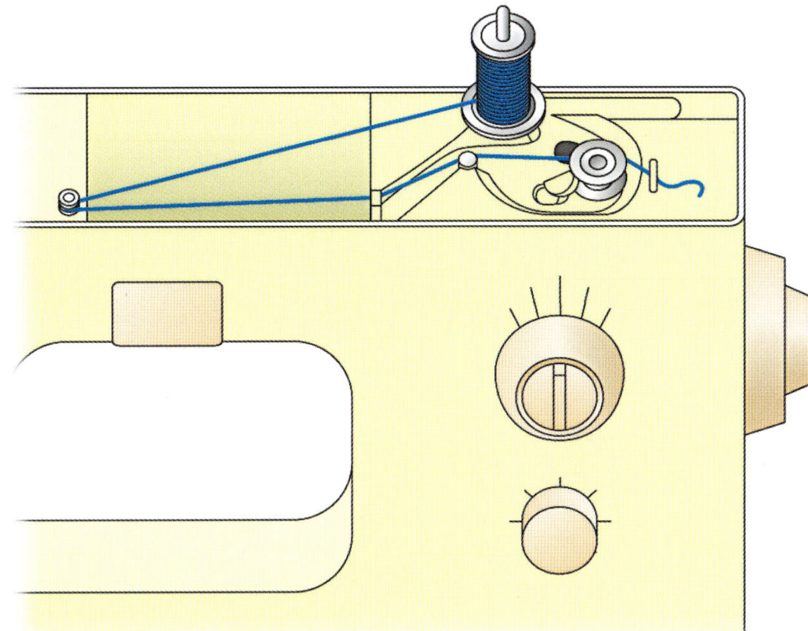

Raising the bobbin thread

After the bobbin has been inserted and the top of the machine threaded correctly (see pages 13 and 16), the bobbin thread has to be raised up above the machine needle plate. Take hold of the end of the upper thread with your left hand; with your right hand, rotate the flywheel backward to make the needle go down and up. Raise the bobbin thread, as shown below right.

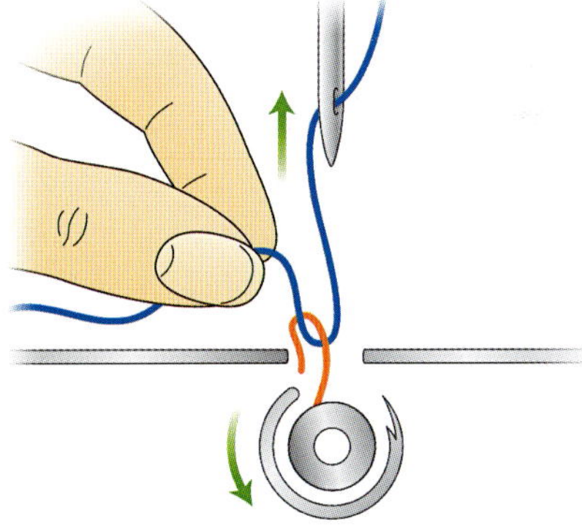

As the needle rises, a loop of bobbin thread will come up with it. Pull on the loop and draw the thread through.Pass both the upper and bobbin threads under the presser foot and bring them back toward the right. The thread ends need to be around 4 in. (10 cm) long.

Even bobbin winding

The thread needs to be wound evenly onto the bobbin. If it is not, you may encounter problems when stitching, or find unevenness with the stitch tension.

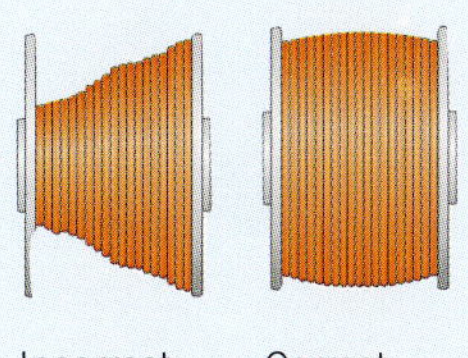

Bottom threading

Threading the lower part of the machine involves feeding the bobbin thread out of the bobbin case correctly. How this is done depends on whether your machine has a fixed or a removable bobbin case. Once again, it is best to refer to your instruction manual for the exact threading for your machine.

For proper stitch formation, the flow of the thread needs to be constant—so it is controlled, like the upper thread, through a tension device.

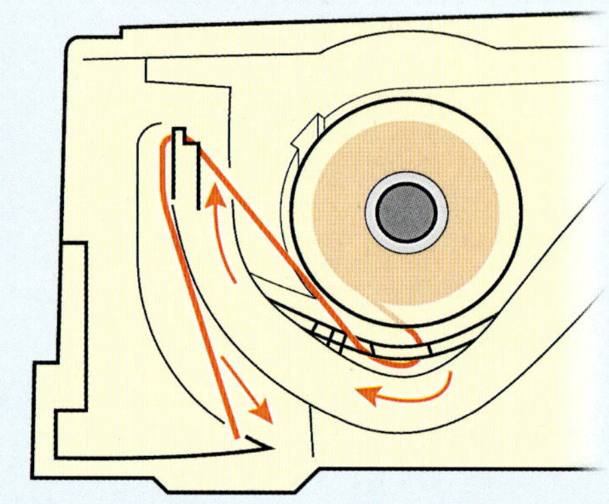

Fixed bobbin case
On most modern electronic and computerized machines, a diagram printed on the clear plastic bobbin cover shows how the thread should be fed through the tension device.

Removable bobbin case

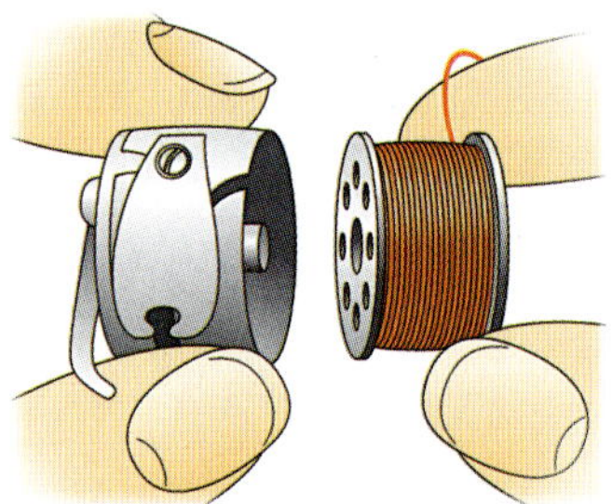

1 Hold the case and bobbin, making sure that the thread comes off the bobbin in the same direction as the slot in the case.

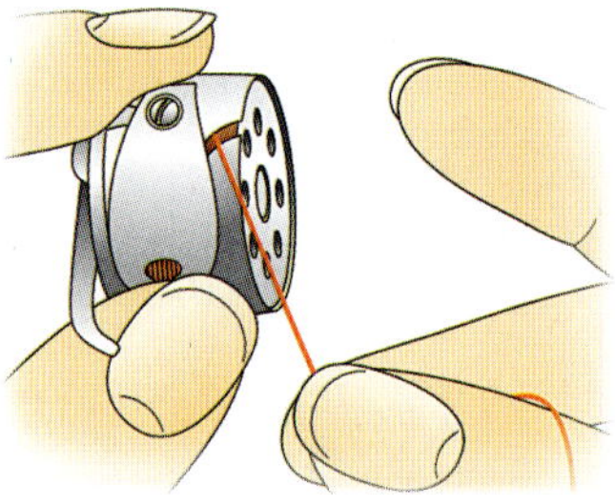

2 Place the bobbin in the case. Holding the end of the thread, bring the thread into the slot opening.

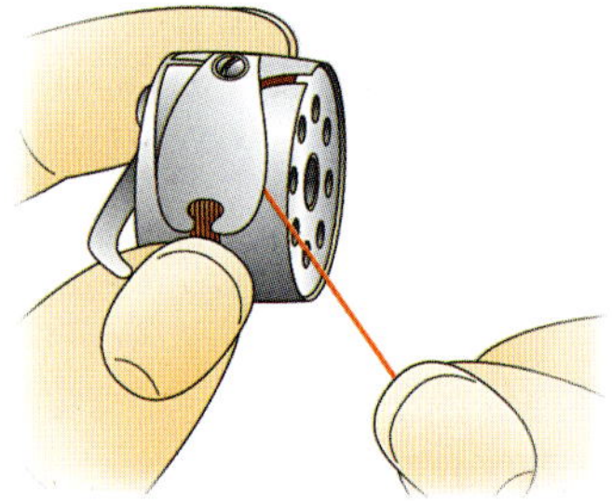

3 Hold the bobbin still with your fingertip and then pull the thread down under the tension plate.

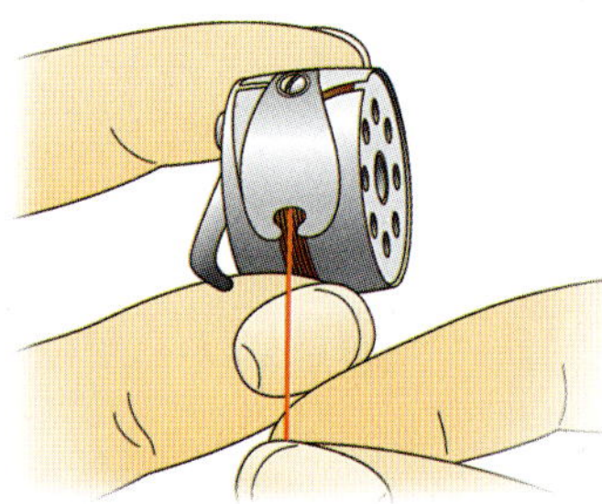

4 Pull the thread right over until it comes out into the slot. The case is now threaded.

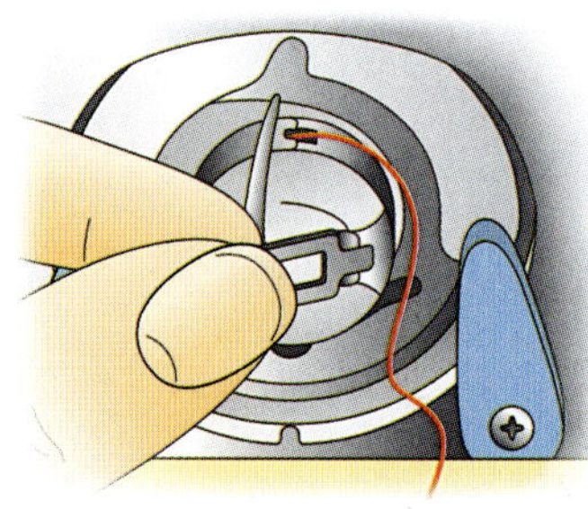

5 Grasp hold of the latch on the side of the case and insert the case into the housing.

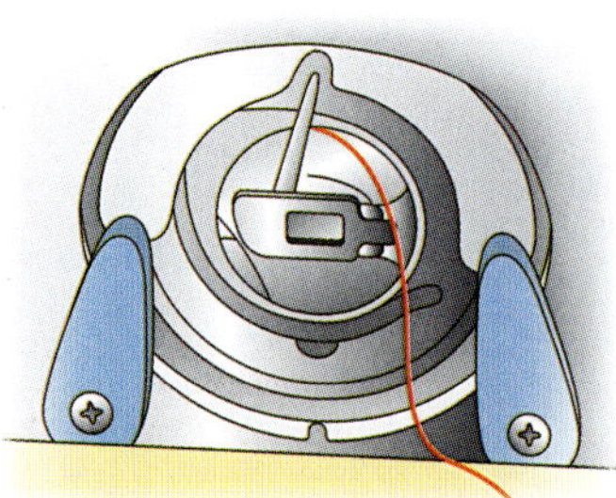

6 Line the shuttle hook up with the slot and make sure that it clicks in place. Then release the latch.

Machine needles

The sewing machine needle plays an important role in successful sewing. When you buy a new sewing machine it will come with a pack of needles of various sizes and types to suit your machine. You will be able to purchase more needles from good sewing machine stores and notions (haberdashery) departments. It is important to change them regularly, as needles blunt surprisingly quickly, especially when you are sewing man-made fibers. Remember, blunt needles can cause skipped stitches, uneven tension, pulled or tight seams, and damaged fabrics.

Needle sizes

You must choose a needle that is the right size for the fabric that you are going to be using. The lower the number, the finer and thinner the needle. A needle sized 11 (70) is thin and fine for lightweight fabrics; while a 16 (100) is coarse and suitable for heavyweight fabrics.

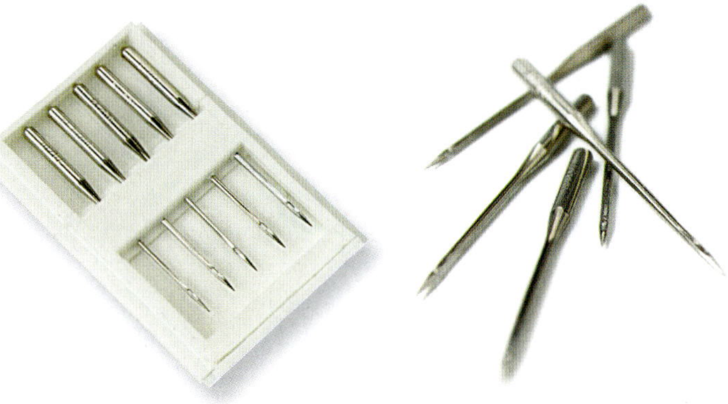

TIPS

- If your bobbin goes into the machine from the side, then the flat part of your needle faces the right-hand side of the machine.
- If the needle goes into the front, the flat part of the needle faces away from you. If the needle is not inserted in the correct way, you simply won't be able to sew.

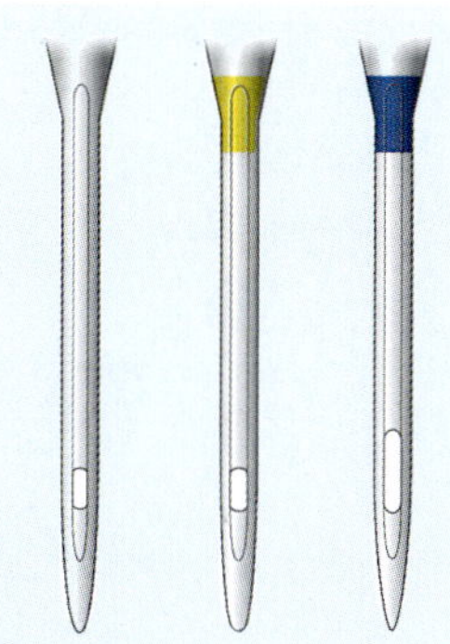

Needle points

Needles also have different points, each designed for a certain type of fabric. The most common types are the sharp-point (left), which is for woven fabrics, and the ball-point for knitted fabrics (center); there are also extra-fine points (right), for twill, denim, and heavy linen and wedge points for leathers and imitation leathers, as well as special "jeans" needles designed, as the name suggests, for working on denim and canvas-type fabrics.

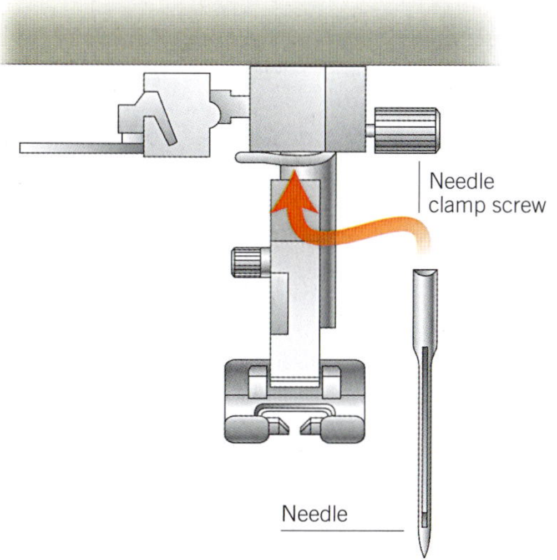

Replacing a needle

Using a small screwdriver, loosen the screw in the needle clamp and remove the old needle. Push the new needle up into the needle clamp until it will go no further, then use the screwdriver to tighten the screw firmly.

Looking at stitches

Machine stitching has several distinct advantages over hand sewing. The first, and probably greatest, is speed—but machine stitching also creates a clean look because the stitches are straight and uniform in length, a technique that can take experienced seamstresses and tailors years to perfect.

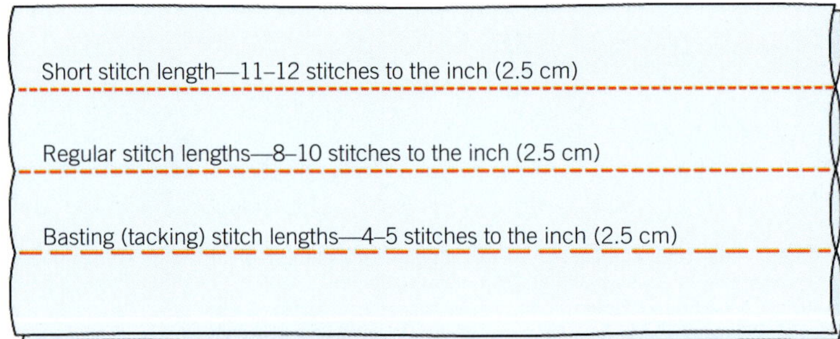

Stitch lengths in straight stitching

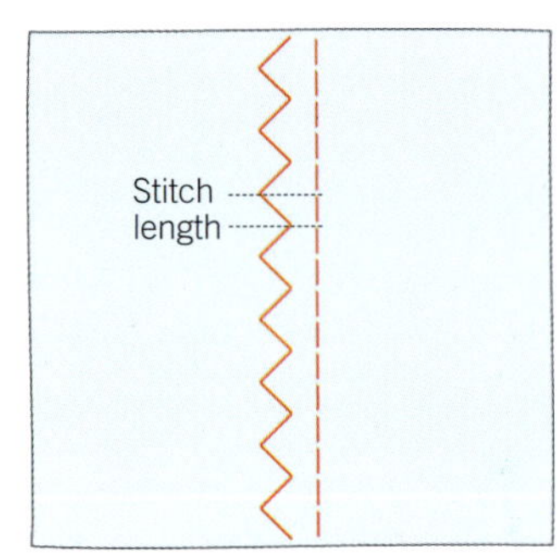

Stitch lengths in zigzag stitching

Stitch length

All sewing machines have a control that allows you to alter the stitch's length for different sewing situations (see chart on page 156). Usually, the higher the number, the longer the stitch. Most machines also have a reverse control which, when activated, makes the machine stitch in reverse at around the same stitch length as it did going forward. Check your manual for the position of your controls.

Stitch width

Zigzag stitches are lockstitches with a side-to-side width, as well as a stitch length. The stitch length is selected in the same way as for straight stitch, but when you look at the stitches, the length is the distance between the points, and not the actual stitch measurement.

The actual stitch measurement, or how far the needle moves from side to side, is operated by a separate width control. As with the stitch-length control, normally the higher the number, the wider the stitch. A "0" setting will revert the machine back to straight stitch.

Zigzag stitches have more give than straight stitches, and so are less subject to breaking. This is particularly useful when you are sewing knit or stretch fabrics. The stitches lie diagonally across the fabric, which means that the stress on the seam is spread out, making them more flexible than straight stitches; however, zigzag stitch does use up more thread.

Needle position selector

If your machine will do zigzag stitch then it will also have a needle position selector, which places the stitches to the left or right of the central position. This is helpful when stitching four-step buttonholes, sewing on buttons, and positioning stitches closer to or further away from an edge.

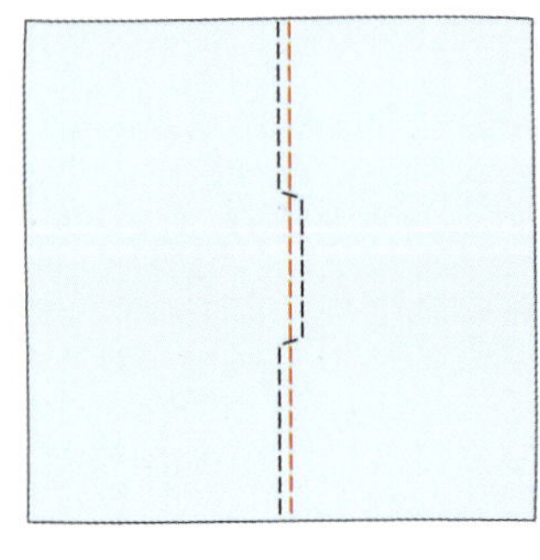

The needle position selector allows you to place stitches to the left or right of the central position.

Stitch tension

Every sewing machine has a tension control for the top thread; most machines have one for the bobbin thread, too. These controls increase or decrease the pressure on the threads as they are fed through the machine. Too much pressure creates too much tension and your stitches will be tight, causing the fabric to pucker up as you sew; the stitches may even break. Too little pressure and the tension will be loose, allowing too much thread through and forming loopy stitches.

If the tension is correct on both the top and the bobbin thread, then the connecting link between the two threads will sit centrally between the layers of fabric (see below).

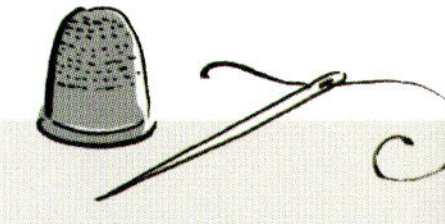

TIP

Check your stitch tension on a scrap of doubled fabric before you start to sew. Use a different-colored thread on the bobbin so that you can see the links more evenly. Then wind the correct color onto the bobbin when you are ready to start sewing properly.

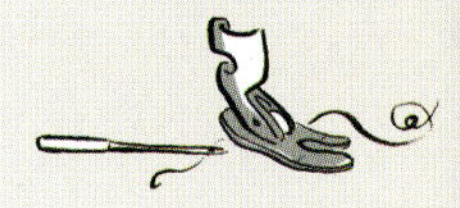

Checking your machine for the right stitch tension

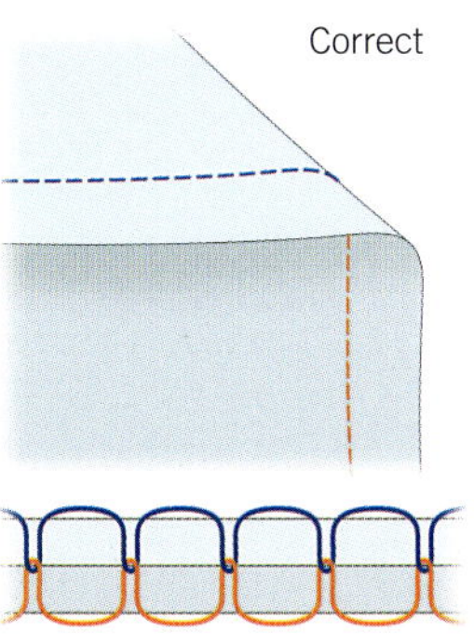

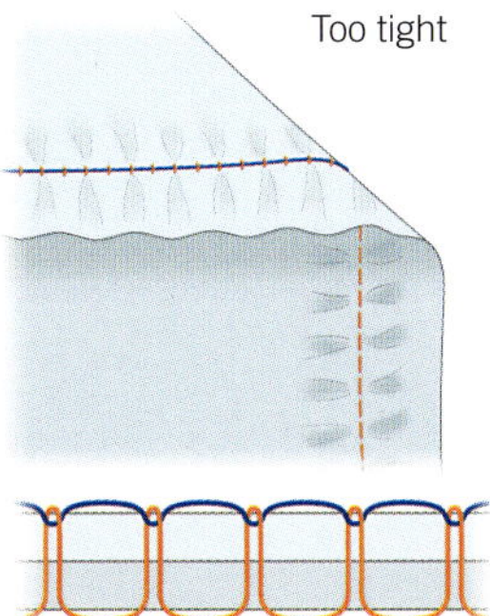

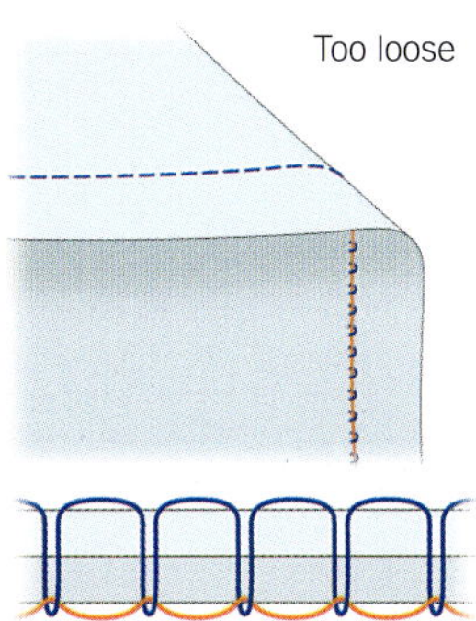

Before you adjust your tension dial, check that you are using a scrap of the same fabric you will be using for your project, have inserted the correct needle and thread (see page 156), and that the pressure foot is down; when the foot is up, then the tension disks are open, so you won't get an accurate result.

The tension dial will be situated close to the tension disks. Double-check your instruction manual for details of how to adjust the tension on your individual machine. Generally, to decrease the tension you need to turn the dial to a lower number; to increase it, turn the dial to a higher number.

Bobbin tension

If the stitch tension is not corrected by the top-tension adjustment, then you may have to adjust the bobbin thread tension, too—but only do this as a last resort. If your bobbin has a tension control, it is adjusted by means of a small screw situated on the tension plate.

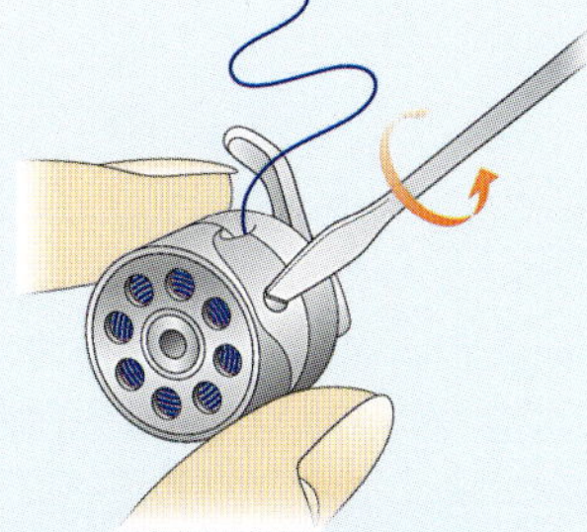

Turn counter-clockwise to decrease bobbin tension

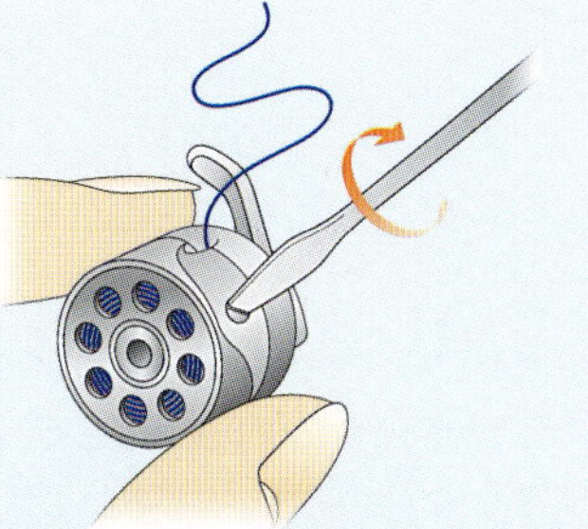

Turn clockwise to increase bobbin tension

Adjusting the bobbin tension

Use a small screwdriver to turn the screw counter-clockwise to decrease the pressure or clockwise to increase the pressure. Note that you do not need to turn it very far in either direction to make a big difference.

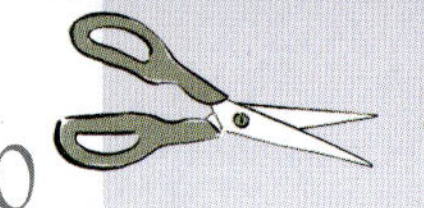

Machine feet

Most stitches can be performed with a basic sewing foot, but there are times when it helps to use a foot designed specifically for the job.

New sewing machines come with a selection of feet, which might include a multipurpose or zigzag foot, a zipper foot, a narrow hemming foot, and a blind hem foot. As a general rule, the more expensive your machine, the more feet and attachments will be included.

If a specialist foot is provided for your machine, it really is advisable to use it to ensure the best results. The recommended foot for the technique will be listed in your manual and they are often numbered or lettered for identification.

When using any type of foot, it is important to know what stitches can be sewn with it. This will depend on the needle hole. If it is small and round, the foot can only be used for straight stitches; if it is wide with a slot, then it can be used for both straight and zigzag stitching.

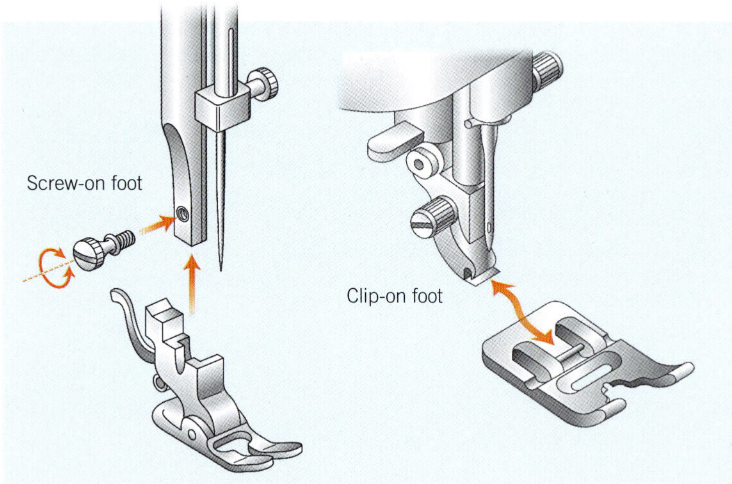

Attaching machine feet

Today most machines have feet that clip on and off, so it is not such a chore to keep changing them. However, on some older machines you may have to screw them in place. Check your instruction manual to find out how to attach your machine feet.

Basic machine feet

Here is a round-up of the basic range of sewing feet that you will need for "everyday" sewing, most of which will be provided with your machine. We have shown both the top and the underside of each one, to make it easier for you to identify them.

Straight stitch foot

A straight stitch foot has a small round central hole; often, one side of the foot is wider than the other. Using this foot will give you a better stitch quality for seams and topstitching, especially on harder-to-stitch fabrics (see page 28).

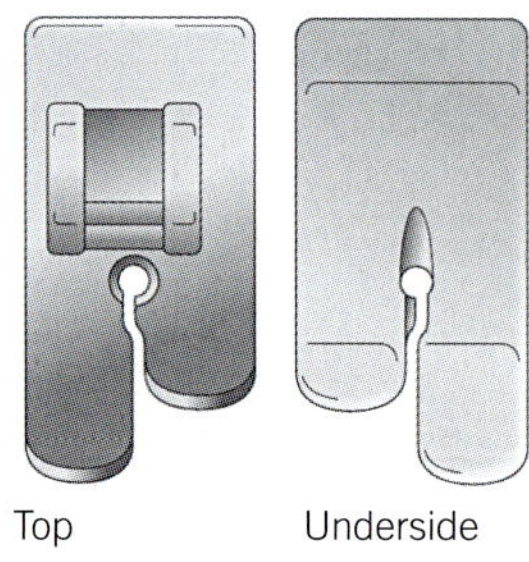

Zigzag foot

The width of the slot in the foot that allows for the needle to swing depends on the maximum stitch width of your machine. If you have to buy or replace this foot, make sure that the slot is wide enough to allow for your needle swing.

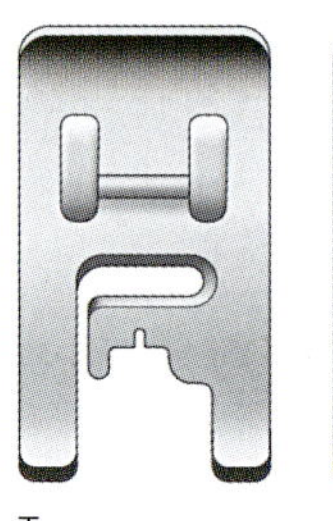

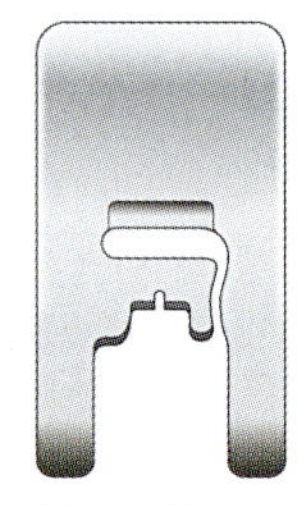

Overcast foot

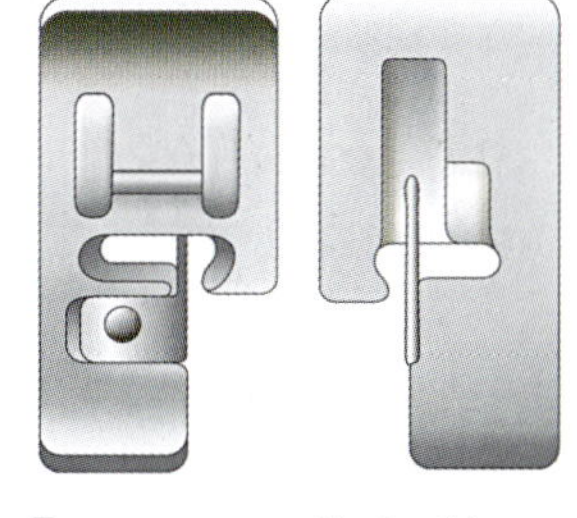
Top Underside

When you stitch over the edges of a fabric—for example, when neatening seams (see page 44)—you will find there is quite a pull on the sewing thread that can cause puckering, especially on fine and soft fabrics. An overcast foot has some means of reducing the pull, usually with a built-in pin that you stitch over.

Rolled hem foot

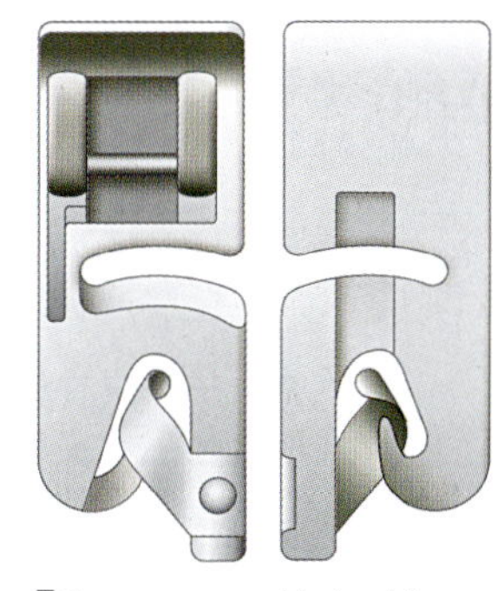
Top Underside

By inserting the fabric into the corkscrew shape on the front of the foot, the fabric will "roll over" during stitching, forming a narrow hem.

Zipper foot

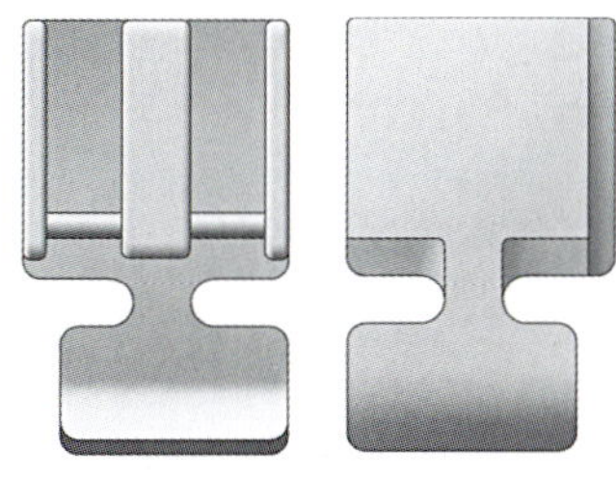
Clip-on zipper foot—top Clip-on zipper foot—underside

Screw-on zipper foot

There are various types of clip-on zipper feet available (right); essentially they all do the same job, which is to help you stitch right on the outside edge of the foot, ensuring you are pressed snugly up against the zipper teeth or piping cord that you are applying (see pages 78 and 82). However, for stitching on heavy-duty zippers and thicker piping cord you will find a screw-on foot (above) works better, as they allow for more depth and thickness. These screw-on feet usually also have a slider that allows you to move the foot across to the exact position required, making them more accurate. When using a zipper foot, remember to adjust the needle position so that you stitch in the exact spot required.

Blind hem foot

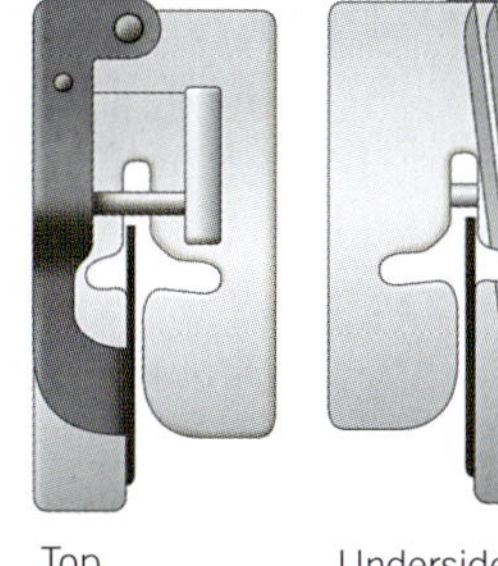
Top Underside

Blind hems are straightforward to stitch; however it is the folding of the fabric that takes a bit of practice. It is vital to fold the fabric back on itself so that the stitching is done on the hem allowance and the sideways stitch takes the tiniest piece of the main fabric (see page 90).

Buttonhole foot

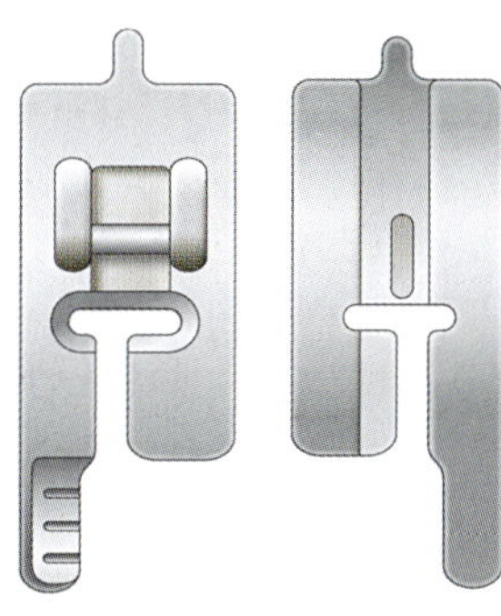
Clear buttonhole foot—top Clear buttonhole foot—underside

These can be small clear plastic ones that allow you to see where you are stitching, metal ones with measurements marked, as shown right, or slider feet that help you stitch a four-step buttonhole to the right size. Check your manual to find out how yours works.

Automatic buttonhole foot

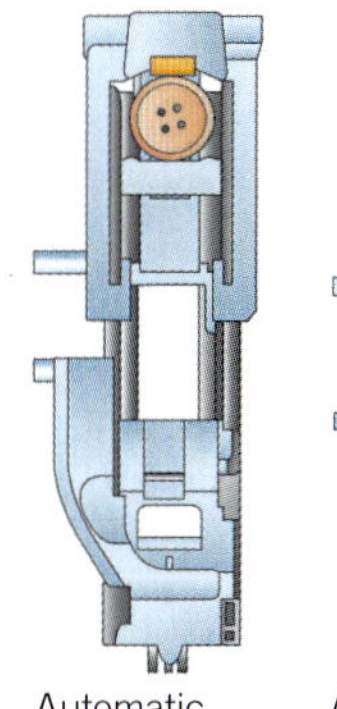
Automatic buttonhole foot—top

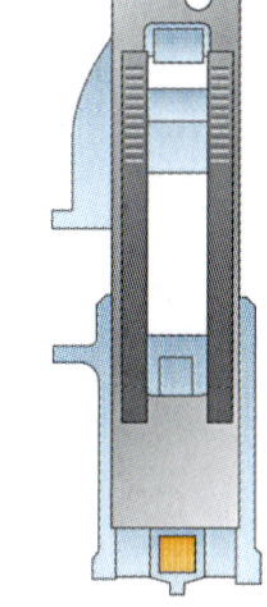
Automatic buttonhole foot—underside

The back of this plastic foot extends to accommodate your button. The machine will then stitch a buttonhole automatically to fit its size using a special sensor.

Button foot

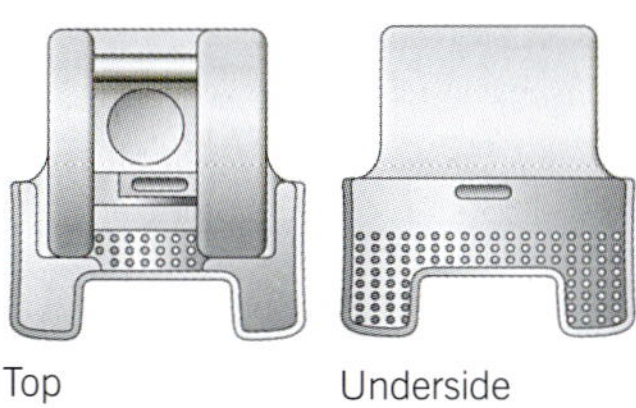
Top Underside

These hold sew-through buttons in place for attaching with a zigzag stitch, set at stitch length 0. There is usually a 1/8 in. (3 mm) clearance between the holes; so you will need to make sure that you set the stitch width just right to allow the needle to go down and across into each hole.

Tools & equipment

Having the right tools for the job can, like everything, make your sewing more successful and enjoyable—but there is no need to go out and spend a fortune. This chapter takes you through all the basic equipment you will need to get you started, from pins and needles to scissors and seam rippers.

Basic sewing kit

One of the nice things about sewing is that you need very little in the way of specialist tools. Apart from a sewing machine, there are only seven basic pieces of equipment, plus some optional extras.

Dressmaker's shears

These have bent handles, which allow the fabric to lie flat on the surface while you are cutting out your pieces. Go for the best quality that you can afford, ones with blades that are at least 7–9 in. (18–20 cm) long. Treat your shears well and never use them to cut anything other than fabric—especially paper, as it blunts them very quickly.

Small-pointed scissors

These are useful for clipping into seams and trimming thread ends after stitching.

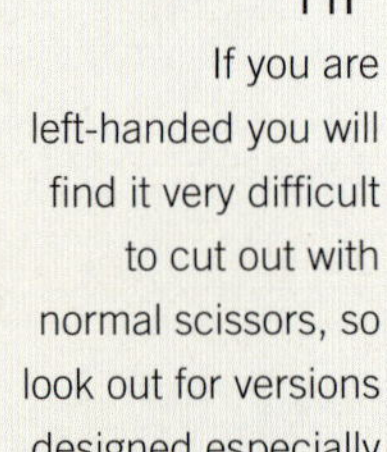

TIP

If you are left-handed you will find it very difficult to cut out with normal scissors, so look out for versions designed especially for left-handed people, where the blades are reversed so that you can get a cleaner cut.

Pins

Pins come in a range of sizes and lengths to suit different fabric types. For general sewing, glass-headed pins are the easiest to handle. Make sure you buy plenty of them, and store them preferably in a pincushion to keep them safe and accessible.

Tape measure

This is essential for most measuring jobs, from lining up your pattern pieces on the fabric to measuring the hems and positioning buttonholes. Make sure that you buy a new one made from a flexible non-fraying material with metal ends. Using granny's old one may seem a nice idea, but the chances are that it may have stretched over time, so your measurements will not be accurate.

Hand-sewing needles

Hand-sewing needles should be fine enough to slip through the fabric, yet strong enough not to bend and break. Sharps are the needles most commonly used for hand sewing. They are available in a variety of sizes and points, numbered 1 to 12—the larger the number, the shorter and finer the needle. Generally, a No 9 is the most useful for basic hand sewing. When choosing a needle size, consider the type of fabric you'll be using. Normally, the lighter the fabric, the thinner the needle. If you are unsure what to use, try passing a few different sizes through the fabric in an inconspicuous place and ask yourself which one passes through the fabric most easily and which one leaves the smallest hole.

Chalk

Chalk is ideal for marking around your pattern pieces on to the fabric. It can be bought in wedge form called tailor's chalk, which is very economical; the edges can be sharpened with a knife.

Alternatively, go for a chalk pencil, which is perfect for marking dart points and buttonholes. Avoid wax, as it often leaves greasy marks on your fabric, which you might find difficult to remove.

Steam and spray iron

Whether you are ironing out fabric creases or pressing seams, the combination of steam and heat in an iron is indispensable. If you don't have a steam iron, then place a damp muslin cloth or a clean damp dish towel on top of the fabric. It is essential to press your seams as you work to ensure a professional crisp finish. Please remember though, that not all fabrics can be ironed—so check the recommended pressing instructions for your fabric and, as a safeguard, test a sample piece of your fabric first.

Useful extras

The following sewing aids are worth investing in, once you gain a little more experience; they are useful, but not totally essential.

Needle threader

A needle threader makes it easy to thread hand or machine needles. Its wire loop is inserted into the eye of the needle and the thread fed through the loop. The wire loop is then pulled out of the needle, bringing the thread with it and so threading the needle.

Stitch ripper

This can be used to unpick incorrect stitches and seams quickly. It can also be used to cut buttonholes, once they are stitched. Also called a seam ripper.

Thimble

Using a thimble helps to avoid a punctured middle finger when hand sewing. It can take some getting used to, but it is worth the effort, especially when hand sewing thicker fabrics. Try several to find one that is comfortable for you.

Tracing wheel

This is a simple tool for transferring patterns and their markings from a pattern sheet. The metal-pronged wheel rotates as you follow the pattern lines. However, it may ruin the surface of your worktable, so you will need to protect the surface.

Metre stick

This long rule is handy for dressmaking and for measuring up and making home furnishings.

TIP

Always keep the face of your iron really clean. Special cleaning sticks are available from good notions/haberdashery stores.

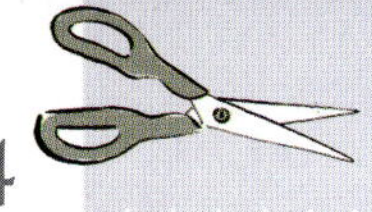

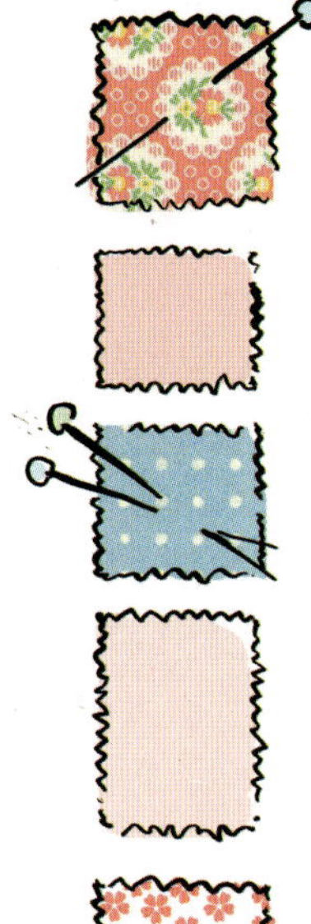

Understanding fabrics

Choosing a fabric for your project is exciting and it is easy to get carried away with the wide variety available. Understanding the way a fabric is made and behaves will help you to make the right choice and is an important part of achieving a successful result.

Natural and man-made fabrics

Fabrics are made from yarn, which is spun from threadlike structures called fibers. Fibers can come from a natural source such as wool or cotton; they can be man-made, such as polyester or nylon; or they can be a blend—a mixture of the two. Each fiber has its own properties, and this is what gives each fabric its own unique characteristics and determines its use and care. The dominant fiber in a blend usually appears first on the fabric label and has the greatest influence on the character and look of the fabric.

Natural fibers

Fiber	Properties	Fabric types	Care
Cotton	Cotton comes from the seedpods of the cotton plant, which is grown in India, Israel, Australia, and Egypt. Egyptian cotton is known for its fine, even quality. Strong and increasing in strength when wet, cotton is absorbent and cool to wear, but it does tend to crease and shrink unless treated.	Denim, corduroy, poplin, gingham, and organdie.	Most cotton can be washed—colorfast cotton in hot water and others in warm or cold water. You can use bleach if color instructions permit. Cotton irons best when damp.
Linen	Linen comes from the fibers of the flax plant, which is mainly grown in Western Europe. It is strong, absorbent, and is valued for its exceptional coolness and freshness. It can crease badly unless treated and has a tendency to shrink. It can stretch during wear and doesn't always dye well.	Handkerchief linen (the name often used for fine, lightweight linen), dress-weight linen, and suit-weight linen.	Usually dry-cleaned to retain its crispness. It can be washed to soften it, but it may shrink. Use a hot steam iron to remove creases from dry fabric, but iron while still damp after washing for best results.
Silk	Silk is obtained by unraveling the cocoon of the silkworm and comes primarily from China and India, where there are huge silkworm farms. Strong, absorbent, and warm to wear, it is crease resistant and dyes well, but the colors may run if washed. Sunlight and perspiration will weaken the fabric.	Lustrous, luxury fabrics that feel beautiful: brocade, satin, crepe, chiffon, tweed, and jersey.	Silk is usually dry-cleaned, but if it is washable, use mild soap flakes, cool water, and handle gently. Iron on a low setting when damp; do not use steam, as it can create watermarks.
Wool	Wool is spun from the fleece of sheep, but there are other animal fleeces and fur whose fibers have much the same properties as wool. These tend to be more luxurious and expensive, such as cashmere and mohair from goats, angora from rabbits, and alpaca from alpacas. Wool is very absorbent and not very strong; it loses more of its strength when wet. It is crease resistant, but it attracts moths and can shrink when washed, unless it is treated.	Flannel, gabardine, tweed, jersey, and crepe.	Wool is usually dry-cleaned, but there are many woolen fabrics nowadays that you can wash by hand or machine, using a gentle soap. Use a steam iron on a low setting.

Man-made fabrics

Fiber	Properties	Fabric types	Care
Polyester	Polyester is strong, crease resistant, has a low absorbency, and is warm to wear. It can collect static electricity and tends to "pill" (small balls of fiber form on the fabric surface when it is rubbed during wear). It can be permanently pleated, pressed, and embossed.	Crepe, satin, organza, double knit, and lining.	Very easy to care for, it can be hand- or machine-washed in warm water and drip- or tumble-dried on a low setting. It dries very quickly and needs minimal ironing.
Acrylic	Acrylic has many of the same properties as polyester, in that it is strong, crease resistant, and warm to wear. It is non-absorbent and dyes well but, like polyester, has a tendency to collect static and to pill.	Double and single knits, fake fur, felt, and fleece.	Acrylic can be machine washed and tumble-dried on a warm setting. Iron at a low temperature: it melts on a high setting.
Viscose	Viscose is soft and absorbent, but not very strong. It retains body heat and dyes well. It is usually treated to reduce its tendency to crease, stretch, and shrink.	Jersey, crepe, and linings. Often mixed with rayon, which has more or less the same properties, for dress fabrics.	Although many viscose fabrics are dry-clean only, some can be gently hand- or machine-washed in warm water. Iron on a moderate setting.
Lycra™ (Elastaine)	Lycra™ is strong, lightweight, non-absorbent, and very elastic. It is often mixed with other fibers to add some elasticity.	Usually knitted, it is used for sportswear, leisurewear, and lingerie, and as a fashion fabric for body-hugging garments.	Lycra™ can be hand- or machine-washed on a gentle cycle and drip dried, or tumble dried on a low setting. It needs little or no ironing.
Acetate	Acetate is relatively weak and tends to crease. It dyes well and does not usually shrink or stretch but it will melt at a high temperature.	Silk-like fabrics that drape well, plus linings.	Acetate is usually dry-clean only, but some fabrics may be washed by hand or machine on a gentle cycle. Iron on a synthetics setting.
Nylon (polymide)	Nylon is very strong, non-absorbent, and crease resistant. It is warm to wear, tends to pill, and collects static electricity.	Lining fabric, jersey, fake fur, ciré.	Nylon can be gently hand- or machine-washed on a warm setting. Drip dry or tumble dry on a low setting. Iron at a low temperature if necessary; it melts on a high setting.
Metallic	Metallic fiber is weak, non-absorbent, and can tarnish unless it is coated with a protective film. It is very sensitive to heat.	Often mixed with other fibers and made into glittery fabrics.	Follow the care instructions provided. Many metallics have to be dry cleaned, but some may be washed at a low temperature. Iron on a low setting if permitted.

Fabric types

Fabrics can be divided into three main groups—woven, knitted, and non-woven, with woven and knitted being the most common. These groups indicate the way in which the fabric is made and, together with the fiber and finish, determine the characteristics of the fabric.

Woven fabrics

Woven fabrics are produced by passing lengthwise and crosswise yarns under and over one another on a loom (see below). The lengthwise yarns are called the warp and the crosswise yarns are called the weft. Every woven fabric has firm, self-finished edges called the selvages, which run lengthwise along each side of the fabric, parallel to the warp, and prevent it from fraying. There are three basic weave types—plain, twill, and satin—which form the basis for more complicated weaves such as dobby, a geometric pattern, and jacquard, usually a more flowing floral design. Pile weave is a variation on a plain or twill weave, which has a surface of raised yarn.

Plain weave

Plain weave is the simplest weave construction. Each weft yarn goes alternately over and under each warp yarn. It is the basis for most printed fabrics. Examples of plain weave include lawn, chambray, gingham, challis, and dupion.

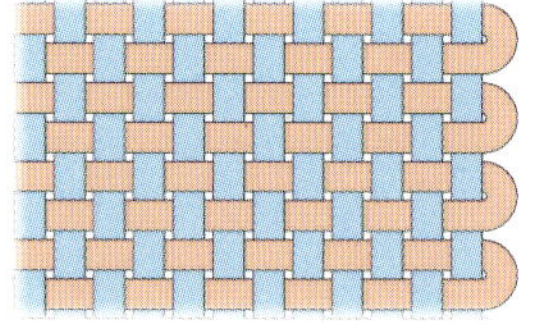

Twill weave

Twill weave is formed by the weft yarn passing over a few warp yarns in a staggered pattern, forming a fine diagonal rib across the fabric. Twills are more hardwearing than plain weaves. Fabric types include gabardine, denim, drill, and tartan.

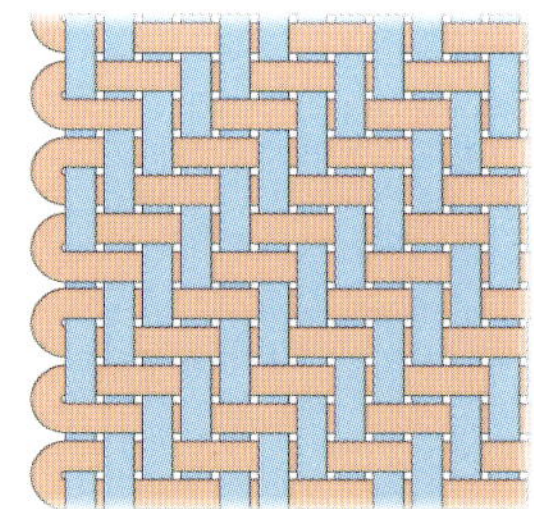

Satin weave

Passing the weft yarn over a number of warp yarns in a similar way to twill produces satin weave. The exposed surface yarns give satin its sheen, but it can easily snag or pull. Crepe-backed satin and duchess satin are both satin weaves.

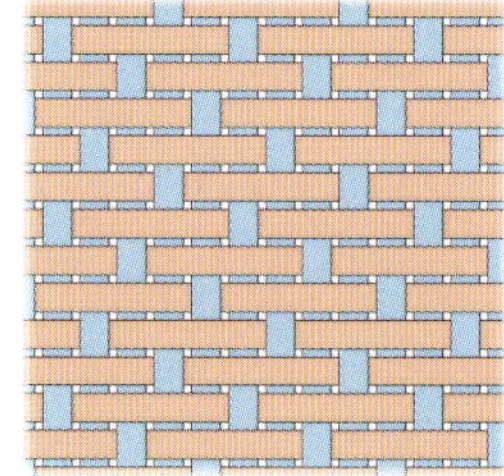

Pile weave

Adding an extra warp, or filling, yarn to a plain or twill weave creates a pile weave. This is drawn into loops on the fabric surface, which are cut for plush, sheared for velvet, or left as loops for toweling.

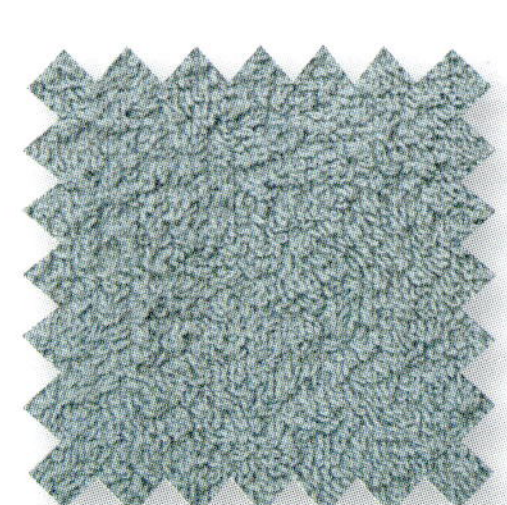

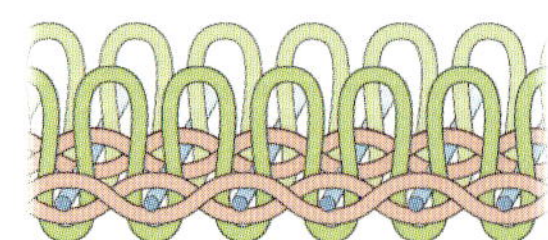

Knitted fabrics

Knitted fabrics are made up of a series of interlocking loops, which form a supple fabric. The vertical rows of loops are called ribs and the crosswise rows are called courses. The amount of stretch depends on the yarn and structure of the knit, but it is always greatest in the width.

There are two categories of knitted fabrics—single knits, which stretch the most, and double knits, which are much firmer. Single knits, as the name implies, are produced on a single set of needles and a single yarn. The most popular patterns are plain jersey knit and purl knit, which are ideal for lingerie, sport, and leisure wear. Double knit is made by two yarn and needle sets, which work simultaneously, producing a fabric that is used to make more structured garments such as pants and jackets. More complex variations of both single and double knits produce a wide range of ribbed and patterned knits.

Knitted fabrics can be flat or tubular. Flat knits have selvages, which are unfinished but structurally sound. Some have a perforated edge similar to a number of woven fabrics. If it is hard to tell whether a fabric is woven or knitted, pull a thread from the crosswise edge. If loops show, the fabric is knitted; if a fringe is formed, then you know the fabric is woven.

Plain jersey knit
Plain jersey knit is smooth on the face (front) with vertical ribs. There are horizontal rows of half circles on the reverse side, formed by the loops being pulled to the back of the fabric.

Purl knit
Purl knit is formed by the loops being pulled alternately to the front and back of the fabric, so purl stitch is formed on both sides. It has more stretch than plain jersey knit, with almost the same amount of stretch in the length as in the width.

Double knit
Double knit has stability and body (substance) similar to a woven fabric and a limited amount of stretch.

Non-woven fabrics

There are several other types of fabric construction that cannot be classed as either woven or knitted. One of these is felt, which is probably the very oldest recorded method of making fabric. Other methods include netting, fusing, bonding, and laminating.

Felt

Felt is made traditionally from wool fibers, which have a tendency to naturally mat together (as anyone who has shrunk a jumper during washing knows), but modern versions are also made from acrylic. The short fibers are laid out in a layer, and then moisture, heat, and pressure are applied, which mat them together. Felt does not unravel and can be cut or blocked or shaped, as in hat making.

Fused fabrics

Fusing is similar to felting, but is done using fibers that do not naturally mat, so a bonding agent is added to hold them together. A good example of a fused fabric is non-woven interfacing (see page 134), which is used for stiffening parts of garments such as collars and cuffs.

Netting

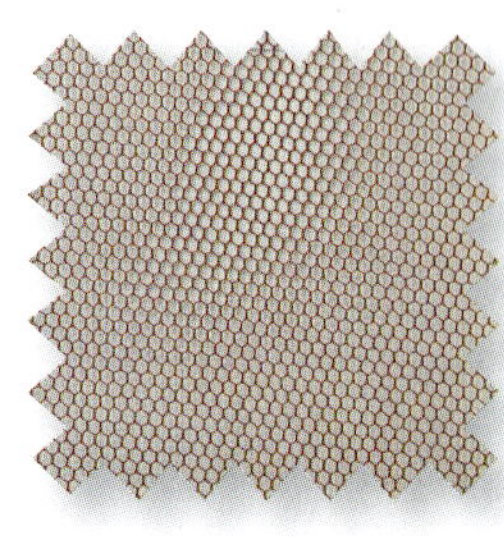

Netting has an open, meshlike appearance and is created by knotting the yarns together where they intersect. This type of fabric can be produced in many weights, from heavy industrial fishing nets through to delicate silk tulle for bridal veils.

Bonding

This type of fabric is formed when two different fabrics are joined together with an adhesive. Combinations that you may come across are loosely woven fabrics backed with jersey to make them more stable, or PVC leatherette backed with a fine jersey fabric.

Special-handle fabrics

Some fabrics, because of their structure and finish, need special handling. They require extra time and skill, so be aware of this when you are making your fabric choice. If you haven't worked with a particular fabric before, it is better to buy 8 in. (20 cm) and test it for yourself, rather than invest in a large quantity of fabric only to struggle and give up. For suggested needle, thread, and stitch sizes for different fabrics, refer to the chart on page 156.

Crepes

Most crepes tend to slip and stretch during sewing. To prevent slipping, use strips of tissue between the fabric and the feed dogs and tear it away after stitching. Stitch and tension adjustments are necessary and pressing needs a light touch.

Lace

On lace the seam finish is often visible, rather like sheer, so use enclosed seams (see page 88) and press it carefully.

Sheers

Soft sheers such as chiffon will slip and stretch during sewing; use strips of tissue paper between the fabric and the feed dogs (see page 11) and tear it away after stitching. Stitch and tension adjustments will probably be necessary. As you can see straight through sheer fabrics, they require seams that are neat and enclosed (see page 88).

Taffeta, satin, and brocade

These fabrics are stiff and therefore do not ease or gather well (see page 144). Like velvet, they can only be stitched once, as unpicked stitches leave holes. Press carefully and lightly, using a low, dry iron setting.

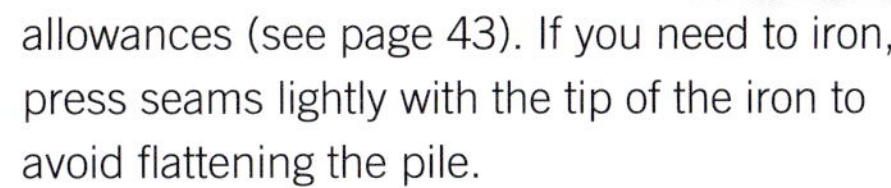

Velvet

The layers of velvet have a tendency to creep when stitching, as the two piles push against each other; so seams need to be hand basted (tacked) carefully (see page 38) prior to sewing. Use a fine machine needle and stitch in the direction of the pile as much as possible. Remember that you will only be able to stitch once, as unpicked stitches leave holes. It is also very difficult to press—the less the better. A steam-filled bathroom is the best answer, but do not work on the fabric until it has dried out. We really recommend that velvet is best left to the experienced stitcher.

Stretch knits

These require special needles and stitching techniques. Seams may need stabilizing and careful pressing is necessary. These also are better left to experienced stitchers.

Leather

Leather requires special needles (see page 17) and a special Teflon™-coated machine foot. It can only be stitched once, as unpicked stitches leave holes. If necessary, press it at a low, dry setting and use adhesive to hold the seam turnings in place.

Deep-pile fabrics

Fabrics that have a deep pile, such as fur fabric, will need stitch and tension adjustments. Stitch in the direction of the pile and trim away the bulk of the pile on the seam allowances (see page 43). If you need to iron, press seams lightly with the tip of the iron to avoid flattening the pile.

Metallics

Metallic fabrics can irritate the skin and may need lining. They do not ease well (see page 146) and can only be stitched once, as unpicked stitches leave holes. Use a fine needle and change it regularly to avoid "cutting" the metallic threads when stitching. Press it carefully and lightly, using a low, dry setting.

Reversible fabrics

Reversible fabrics require flat-fell seams (see page 89) for a neat finish on both sides and a pressing cloth to flatten them.

Choosing the right fabric

There is a huge range of exciting fabrics to choose from, but whether you are making home furnishings or clothes, it is important to make the right choice. If you are using a commercial pattern (see page 110), always follow the list of suggested fabrics on the back of the pattern envelope to achieve a good result. Do not pick an expensive fabric for your first attempt at sewing, and gain some experience with woven fabrics before you tackle knitted or specialty fabrics that require more expertise (see page 28). Avoid large checks and prints for the same reason; you want your first experience to be a labour of love and not a disappointment.

Buying fabric

Before your fabric length is cut from the roll, have a good look for defects that indicate poor quality and double-check its suitability for your project.

Choose a fabric whose qualities suit the type and style of the item you are making. Think about the way the fabric handles—whether it is lightweight or heavy, smooth or textured, firm or stretchy, whether it drapes in stiff or in soft folds. Unroll a length and drape it over yourself, preferably in front of a mirror, to see how it falls and whether it suits you. It is no good making a draped top in stiff, heavy cotton, as it simply will not look right. Squeeze a corner of the fabric to see if it creases or goes back to normal. Always read the label to see what fiber, or fibers, it is made from and whether it is washable or dry-clean only. Find out the recommended iron setting and whether it is easy to sew. If no information is provided, ask the salesperson.

If you are buying a fabric that has a one-way design, where the printed or woven motifs are not the same in both directions, or a fabric such as velvet, where the pile, or nap (see page 32), lays in one direction, all the pattern pieces must be laid in one direction and you will probably need to buy extra fabric. Commercial patterns give fabric quantities for napped fabrics if they recommend using them (see page 110). If you are not sure how much extra fabric you will need, then once again ask the salesperson, who should be used to making these calculations. You will soon become familiar with the qualities of various fabrics, but if you are uncertain, it is much better to ask for advice than to make an expensive mistake.

The weave

- It should be firm; if you can move the threads with your fingernails, they can separate with wear and develop weak areas or holes around the stitching; this is known as slippage. Some fabrics are designed to have an open weave and this is fine, as long as the threads do not shift.
- It should be uniform to ensure even wear; check for thick or thin areas by holding it up to the light.
- The weft yarns running across the width of the fabric should meet the selvages at a right angle, otherwise the fabric is off-grain (see page 26).
- If the fabric frays easily, it will be more difficult to work with. You will need to neaten the edges of the cut pieces before sewing them together.

The color

- Make sure the fabric is evenly dyed. Avoid fabrics if you can see that the color has faded on a central crease-line, or if the color can be rubbed off the fabric surface onto a white tissue.
- Print colors should be even, with no white spots on areas that should be dyed.
- Make sure you buy enough fabric,

because rolls can vary in color if they come from different dye lots.

The print design

■ Symmetrical and geometric prints should meet the selvages at right angles; otherwise it is very difficult to match corresponding seams or edges.

■ One-way designs or pile fabrics may mean you have to buy extra fabric.

The finish

■ Rub the fabric between your fingers; if fine powder appears there is too much sizing, which is often used to disguise poor quality.

■ Crush the fabric to see if it sheds its creases. If it doesn't, it will always look crumpled.

Basic considerations

■ Make sure that the weight and drape suit the item you are planning to make.

■ The width should correspond to the fabric details given with commercial patterns, or be wide enough to cut out any large pieces you may need.

■ You may need a lining fabric (see page 137) if you want to avoid stretch, ensure comfort and longer wear, or are using a fine or sheer fabric.

■ Fabric care is a big consideration; washability is a great advantage, as dry-cleaning costs can be huge.

Sewing threads

There are many types of threads on the market today. Each thread varies in fiber content, size, and intended use. A good-quality thread is a lot easier to work with, on both a sewing machine and by hand, and the results will be better than those you can achieve with a "bargain" thread. A good-quality thread is strong, smooth (not fuzzy) and consistent in thickness, does not tangle, and is colorfast.

Thread choice

Your fabric will mainly influence the type of thread that you select. The fiber content need not be the same as your fabric, but heavyweight fabrics will require a heavier thread and lighter-weight fabrics a finer one. Using the correct size thread may reduce puckering, a problem frequently encountered when sewing lightweight fabrics (see page 156).

Spun polyester thread is a good all-purpose choice, as it is strong, has stretch without fraying, snapping, shrinking, or rotting, and usually has a greater color choice. It is not always possible to find a thread that matches the color of your fabric exactly, so choose one that is a shade darker, or matches the main color on a printed fabric.

Thread reel sizes

Most thread designed for domestic use comes on 100 yd (100 m) reels, although black, white, and selected colors are available in larger sizes, which is useful when you are stitching larger jobs, such as curtains.

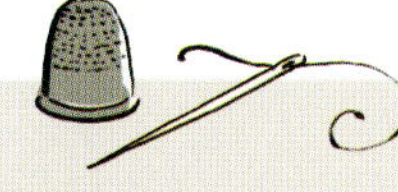

TIP

When you are buying thread, unwind the end of thread off the reel and lay it over your fabric; the color will look slightly different to how it looks on the reel.

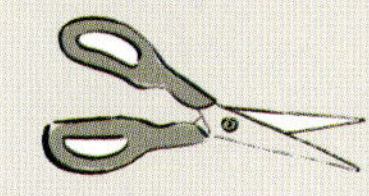

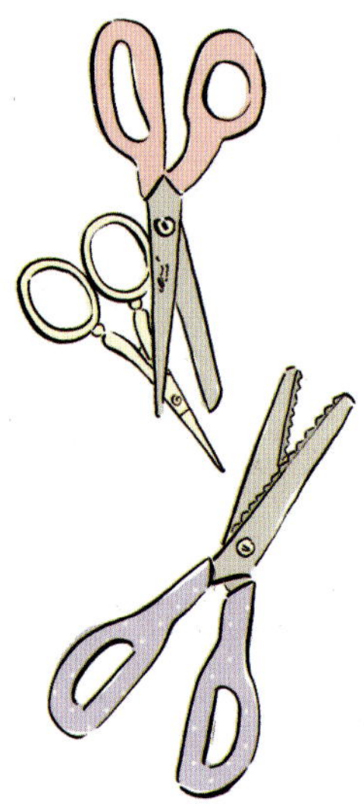

Get set for cutting

Cutting out seems a big hill to climb for most novice stitchers, but it will not be a problem if you take your time and prepare your fabric properly.

Key fabric terms

Before you start to lay out the fabric and pin on any pattern pieces, it is a good idea to familiarize yourself with some basic fabric terms.

Straight grain

The grain describes the direction of the threads in a woven fabric. Pieces are usually cut out on the "straight," or lengthwise, grain, following the warp yarn. The straight grain runs parallel to the selvage; see page 28.

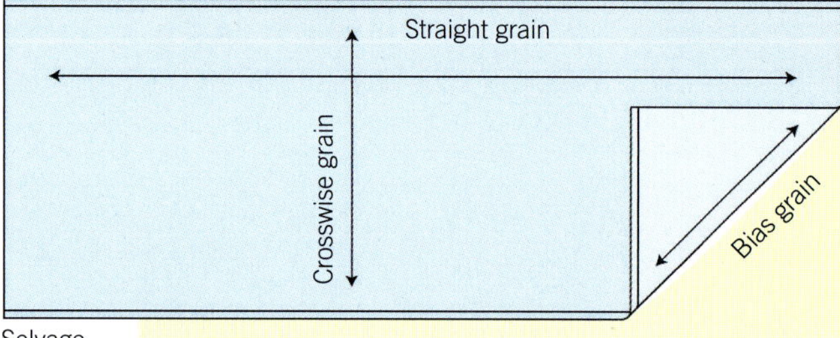

Crosswise grain

The crosswise grain, which follows the weft yarn, runs from one selvage to the other and has more give. If the weft yarn does not meet the selvage at a right angle, the fabric is off-grain. The crosswise grain is only used vertically for design features, such as placing a border print around a hemline.

Bias grain

The bias grain is an imaginary line that intersects the other two grainlines diagonally and stretches the most. The true bias lies at a 45-degree angle to the straight grain and the crosswise grain and has the greatest give of all. A bias-cut garment will drape softly, but will also tend to have an unstable hemline.

Nap

This refers to fabrics that have either a pile finish, such as velvet, or a printed one-way design, such as flowers pointing in one direction (see page 30). Dressmaking patterns often have "with nap" cutting layouts (see page 110) for this type of fabric to show you how to place the pattern pieces.

Fabric widths

Dress fabrics generally come in three widths: 36 in. (90 cm), 45 in. (115 cm), and 60 in. (150 cm). Furnishing fabrics are usually 54 in. (137 cm) wide. The fabric quantities chart that is printed either on the back of a pattern envelope or with the introduction to your pattern will indicate how much fabric to buy for that specific project (see page 110).

Straightening the ends

Proper fabric preparation is an essential preliminary to cutting out. After pressing your fabric to remove any folds and creases, you must straighten the ends; this must be done with every fabric you use to ensure that it can be folded evenly, and that the grain is aligned.

Woven fabrics

There are several ways to straighten the raw ends on woven fabrics, depending on the type of fabric and its construction.

Any woven fabric

Mark a line at a right angles to both selvages, using a set square or right-angled object such as a book, a metre stick (see page 23), and tailor's chalk (see page 22), then cut across it.

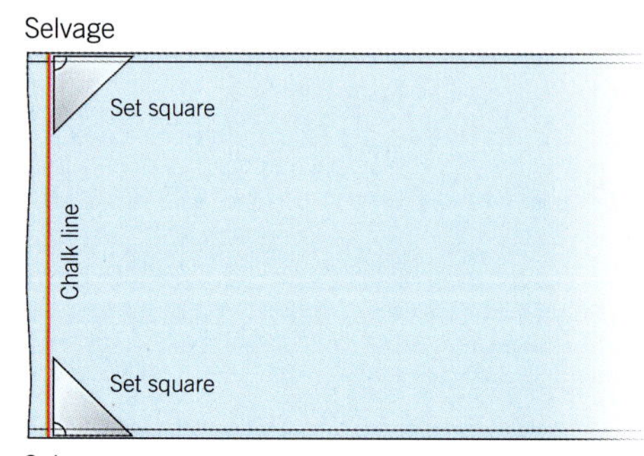

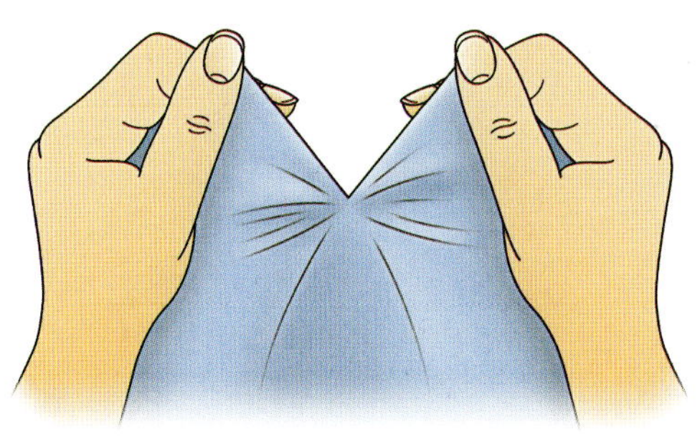

Firmly woven fabric
Snip into the selvage, grasp the fabric firmly on each side of the snip, then simply tear across. If the strip runs off to nothing partway across, snip further down and tear again.

Decorative striped or woven checked fabric
Cut along a crosswise line. If the design is printed, try tearing it first.

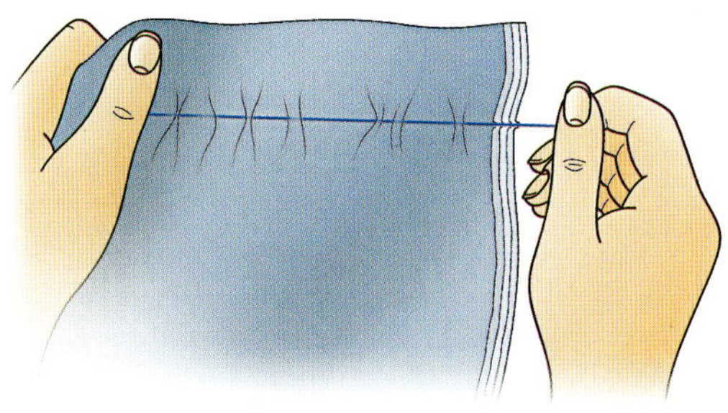

Loosely woven fabric
Snip into the selvage, take firm hold of a couple of threads, and pull gently, gathering up the fabric and sliding out the thread until you get to the other edge. Cut the pulled thread.

Coarsely woven fabric
Cut across the fabric from selvage to selvage between two warp threads.

Knitted fabric

We do not suggest you use knitted fabrics to begin with, but you may want to try them when you have gained more experience. As with woven fabrics, you must press your fabric to remove fold lines and creases before you can straighten the ends. Some tubular knits may also need to be cut open along a vertical row of loops called a rib, to flatten them out.

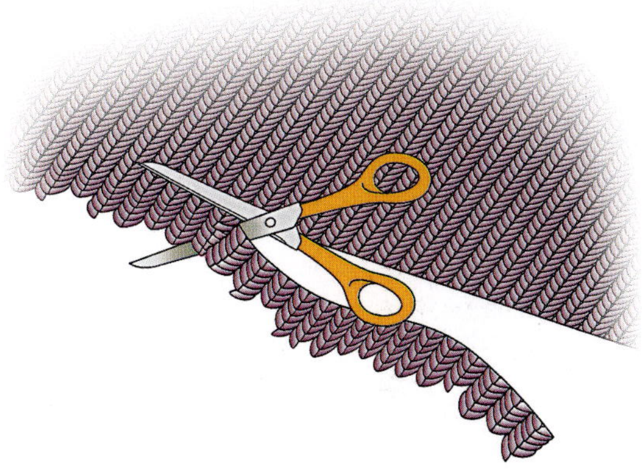

Flat knits
Trim along a crosswise row of loops, called a course. If it is a fine knit, you will have to rely on your eye or draw a chalk line at a right angle to the selvages and cut across it (see Any woven fabric, opposite).

Preparing to cut

Cutting fabric is an important step in the making-up process and one that you should take your time with, especially if you have paid a lot of money for fabric; one careless snip and you could be back to the drawing board. By following these basic steps, you will not only save yourself time and money, but you will find that your pieces stitch together much more easily.

Recognizing the right side of fabric

Make sure you know which is the right side of the fabric. Usually this is obvious —but if it is not, here are some clues:

- Smooth fabrics are shinier on the right side.
- Pre-folded cottons and linens are usually sold right side out; wools are wrong side out.
- Textures and prints are clearer on the right side.
- Noticeable nubs and yarn ends are more visible on the wrong side.
- The selvage is smoother on the right side.
- If you still are not sure, pick the side you like best and mark it with chalk, so that you remember.

Folding fabrics for cutting

Most pattern pieces are cut out on folded fabric. The fabric is usually folded lengthwise, along the straight grain (see page 32), with the right sides together, the selvages meeting or parallel, and the fold positioned as suggested on your cutting layouts (see page 116). Before you pin the pattern pieces in place, make sure that the fabric lies smooth and flat.

Selvages
Straight grain
Wrong side of fabric
Fold

Standard lengthwise fold

Made along the straight or lengthwise grain, with the selvages matching exactly along one edge. If the fabric is slippery and moves easily, pin the layers together at regular intervals.

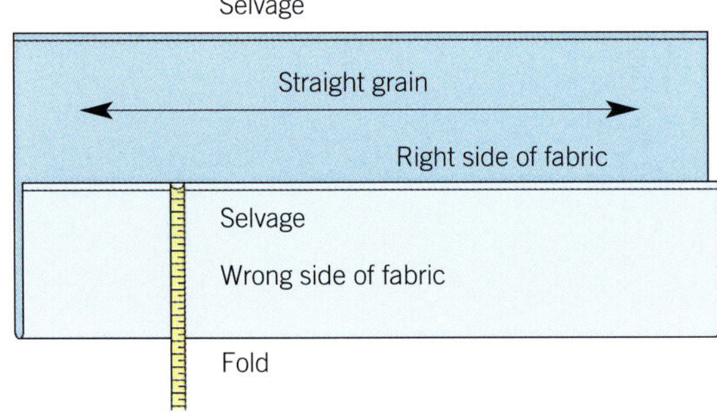

Partial or double lengthwise fold

When a partial or double lengthwise fold is made, measure the distance from the fold to the selvage at regular intervals to ensure that it remains uniform along the length of the fabric.

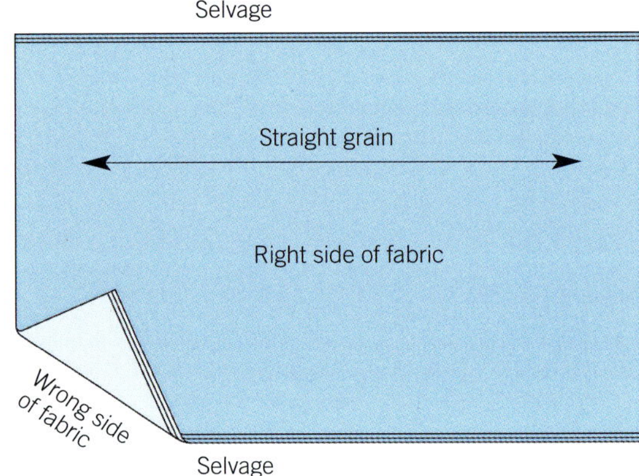

No fold required

When no fold is required, lay the fabric right side up.

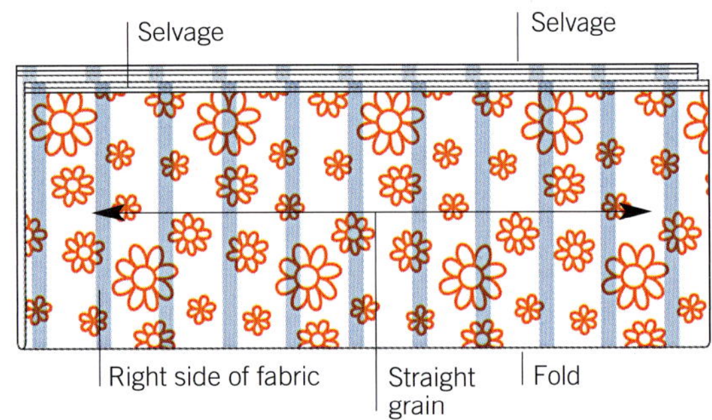

Napped fabrics

If you are cutting a pile fabric, a design that needs matching, or a design with large motifs, fold the wrong sides of the fabric together.

Let's cut!

After you have straightened your fabric ends and laid the fabric out, you are now ready to start cutting. To cut out any fabric pieces for making up, slide the scissors along the fabric, making long cuts on the straight pieces and shorter cuts on the curves. Take time and care to cut smoothly to avoid making jagged edges. You will find a good pair of bent-handled shears (see page 22) are best for the job; never use blunt ones, as they will make the fabric edges fray.

Smooth cutting

Place your left hand (or right hand, if you are left-handed) lightly on the piece, or layers of fabric, to be cut and hold the shears in your other hand. Open the blades and slide the lower blade under the fabric, making sure that the shears rest on the table and that the fabric is only slightly raised. Make one long smooth cut using the full length of the blades, re-open the blades, slide them under the fabric again, and move your other hand along, next to the blades, to stabilize the fabric. Carry on in the same manner until your piece is cut out.

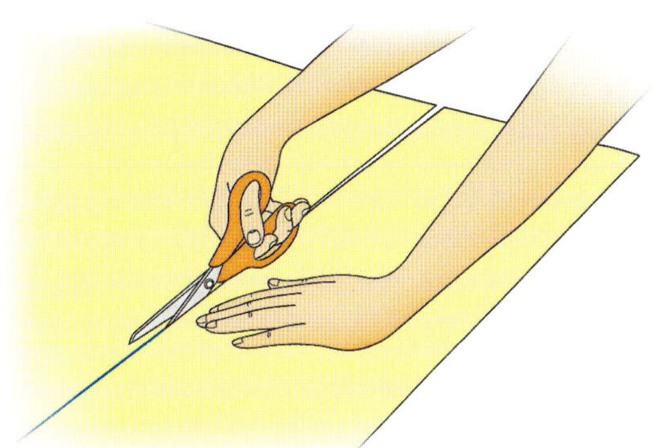

Using shears

- To get used to using bent-handled shears and cutting in a smooth way, buy yourself a piece of stripy fabric and practice cutting along the stripes. This can be a little bit boring, but it will certainly help you to cut out more accurately and your end projects will look more professional.
- Do not be tempted to lift up the shears or fabric as you cut, as this will move the fabric around and distort the piece you are trying to cut out.

Before you start to sew

- Familiarize yourself with the machine controls.
- Set your machine on a firm table and make sure your chair is the correct height for you to operate the controls and reach the foot treadle; the treadle should be facing you, flat on the floor.
- Check that the power lead can reach an electric socket safely. Use an extension lead if necessary.

Mastering speed control

Take a piece of firm, inexpensive fabric such as calico. Turn on the power, place the fabric under the foot, drop the foot onto the fabric, and grasp hold of the thread ends from your bobbin and needle with your left hand, to prevent them from being dragged down into the bobbin case.

Press down on the foot treadle—slowly at first, then faster as you gain confidence. Stitch across the fabric as many times as you like, raising the needle and lifting the foot each time to reposition the fabric.

Finding a cutting surface

You will need a large, flat, firm surface, such as a dining table or a clean area of floor, on which to fold and cut out your fabric. Pins and shears can leave scratch marks and present a danger to children, so make sure that the surface is protected, or is one that you are not worried about, and that the children cannot get near it.

Sewing straight lines

Now practice sewing straight lines on stripy fabric. Place your hands flat on the "table" section of the machine, one each side of the foot (keeping them well clear of the needle). Using both hands to steer the fabric, stitch along the stripes. Practice until you feel confident, as you will need to sew in a straight line for seams.

Moving on

Now you can move on to more exciting things! The workshops that follow are designed to develop your sewing skills step by step, so work through them consecutively. Take your time–and most of all, have fun!

SECTION 2

Workshops

The following workshops build up to a complete beginners' course in machine sewing. They gradually increase in complexity; designed to be worked through in sequence, so that you master each technique in turn before you move on to the next. At the end of each workshop is a sewing project that gives you a chance to put into practice the skills you have just learned. Fabric quantities, cutting layouts (where appropriate), and easy-to-follow step-by-step instructions are given for each one. All the step-by-step instructions are illustrated; the red stitching shows what you are working on at present and the black shows stitching completed in previous steps... so you'll soon be stitching your own beautiful home furnishings and clothes in next to no time!

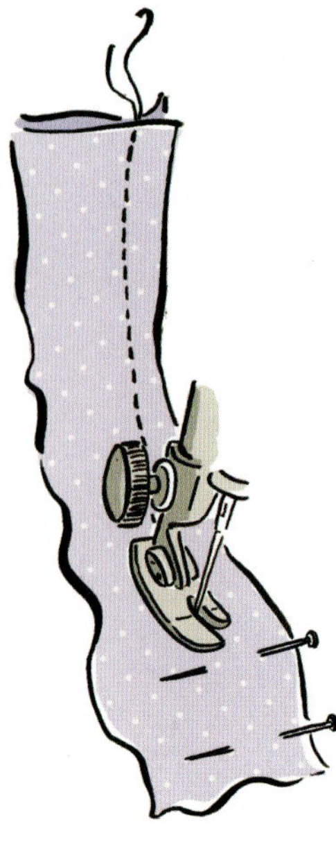

Simple seams & easy hems

From threading a needle to stitching a simple seam or hem, mastering a few basic techniques makes the sewing process a much more enjoyable experience. Workshop 1 guides you stage by stage through everything you need to know to make your first project—an envelope pillow.

Basting (tacking) a seam

Basting (tacking) stitches are temporary stitches that are used to hold two or more pieces of fabric together. Make easy work of basting by pinning your fabric pieces together and preparing your needle and thread properly before you start.

Pinning

Pinning the fabric layers together will prevent them from slipping out of position while you baste.

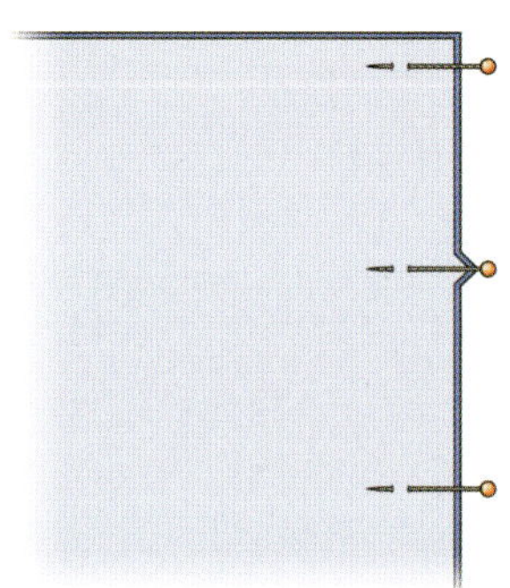

Place the fabric pieces right sides together (unless instructed otherwise) and match the raw edges and any corresponding pattern markings (see page 113). Check the width of the seam allowance (the distance between the seamline and the edge of the fabric) that you need to take, then insert the pins at a right angle to the seamline, with the pin heads close to the raw edge and the tips extending just beyond the seamline.

Securing stitching

At the start of stitching, most hand-sewn stitches are secured with a knot made at the end of the thread. It doesn't matter if the knot is visible in basting, because it is temporary and will be removed. The end of the stitching is secured with a couple of backstitches. If you prefer, you can work a couple of backstitches at the beginning instead of a knot.

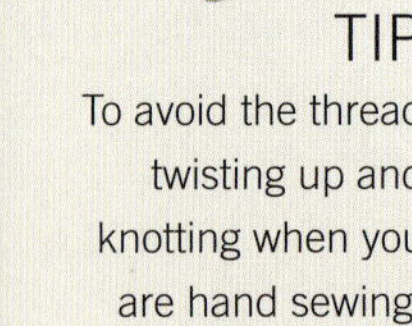

TIP

To avoid the thread twisting up and knotting when you are hand sewing, always thread the needle with the end coming off the spool, not the end just cut.

Knotting a thread end

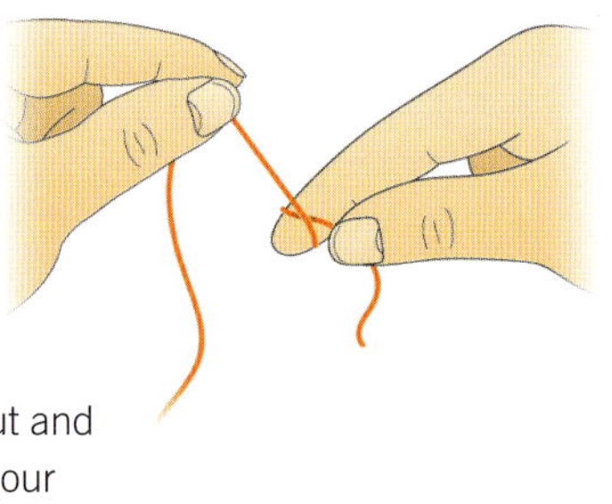

1 First, thread your needle. To knot the thread, hold the end of the thread between your thumb and index finger and, with your other hand, wind the remaining thread over and around your finger. Hold the remaining thread taut and slide your index finger firmly back along your thumb, so that the thread twists to form a loop.

2 Slide the loop off the top of your fingernail, but hold it firmly in place between your finger and thumb. Pull the remaining thread to tighten the loop and form the knot.

Securing with backstitch

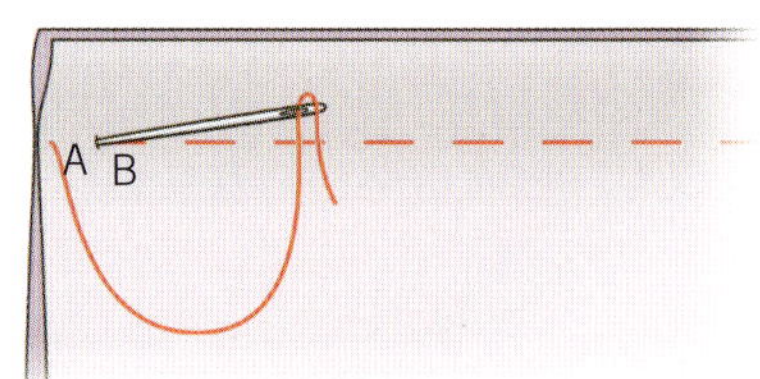

Bring the needle and thread to the upper side of the fabric at A. Insert the needle through all the fabric layers at B, one stitch length behind A, and bring it back up again at A. Repeat to form another backstitch in the same place. Trim the thread end.

Get basting

It is much easier to stitch seams if you have basted them together first. There are several types of basting stitch: the most common are even basting stitch, which maintains greater control of the fabric; uneven basting stitch, which is good for general use; and slip basting stitch, which enables stripes, checks, and some large prints to be matched exactly at seamlines.

Even basting This is best used on smooth fabrics that can slide or move against each other and for seams that need to be carefully controlled, such as curved seams, multiple fabric layers, and seams with ease-stitching or gathers (see page 144).

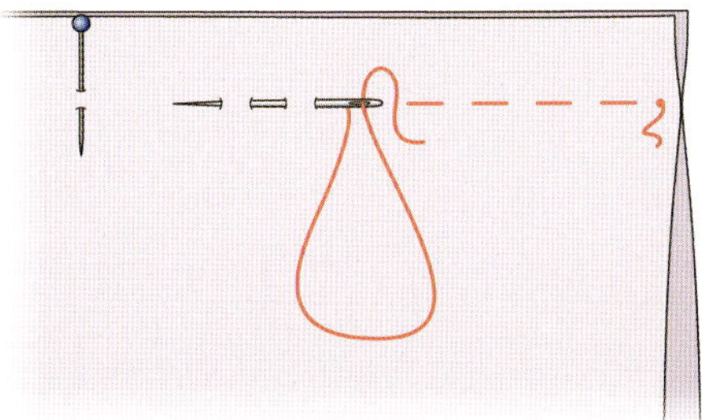

Working from right to left (reverse this if you are left-handed), take short, evenly spaced stitches about 1/4 in. (6 mm) long through the fabric layers, stitching close to the seamline but within the seam allowance. Take several stitches onto your needle at one time, before drawing the thread through the fabric.

Uneven basting This is the most frequently used basting stitch and is fine for edges where less control is required during machine stitching. It is also used to mark position lines such as stitch lines for pleats or large darts.

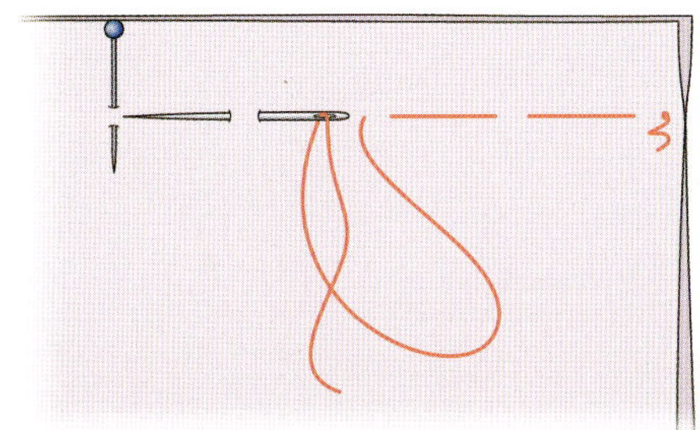

Working from right to left (reverse this if you are left-handed), take short stitches about 1/4 in. (6 mm) long and 1 in. (2.5 cm) apart through the fabric layers, stitching close to the seamline but within the seam allowance. You can use longer and more widely spaced stitches to mark a stitch line.

Slip basting This stitch is very useful when you need to match two pieces of patterned fabric, because it is worked on the right side of both pieces.

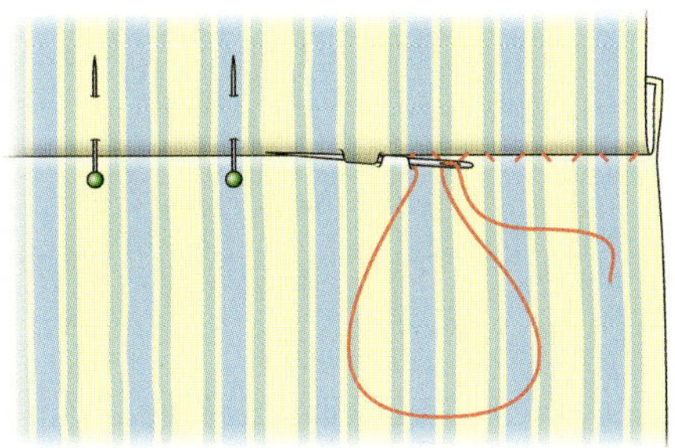

Press one edge of one fabric to the wrong side along the seamline. With the right sides up, place this folded edge along the seamline of the corresponding piece, so that the pattern matches exactly, and pin it in place as shown. Working from right to left (reverse this if you are left-handed) and keeping your stitches evenly spaced, take a 1/4-in. (6-mm) stitch through the lower piece on the seamline next to the fold, then take the next stitch through the fold of the upper piece. Continue alternating the stitches in this way, removing the pins as you go.

Choosing a basting thread

Use a contrasting colored thread to work your basting stitches to make it easily distinguishable from your permanent stitches when they are being removed.

However, although specialist basting threads are available, avoid inexpensive types, unless it is white, as you may find it is not colorfast, and deep colors can mark lighter-colored fabrics.

TIP

As you gain more expertise, you will find that you can dispense with basting on many seams. Just pin the layers together, then machine the seam, stitching slowly and carefully over the pins to avoid breaking the needle; alternatively, remove the pins as you stitch.

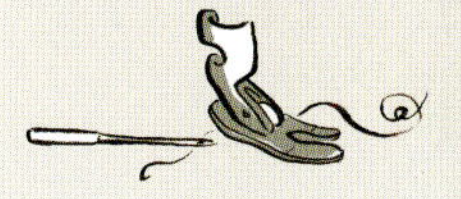

Plain seams

For self-enclosed seams, in which the seam turnings are enclosed within the finished seam, see page 88.

You form a seam when you stitch two or more pieces of fabric together with a seam allowance that is often neatened (see page 44) and usually pressed open. The most commonly used seam is the plain straight seam, but you will also come across plain cornered seams and curved seams. Before you sew your seam, using the appropriate needle and matching thread (see page 156), stitch on a double-folded scrap of your fabric to check that the stitch length, tension, and pressure are correctly adjusted. Check, too, the width of the seam allowance that you need to take; it is normally $^{5}/_{8}$ in. (1.5 cm) on most commercial patterns.

Plain straight seam

The first thing you need to know is how to secure the stitching at the start and end of any seam. There are two ways of doing this—reverse stitching (the strongest method) and tying the thread ends.

Reverse stitching

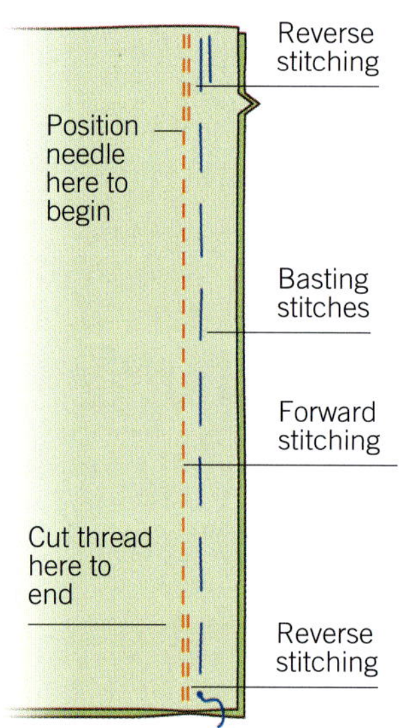

Place your basted fabric pieces under the machine foot, lining the raw edges up with the correct seam guideline. Position the needle about $^{1}/_{2}$ in. (12 mm) down along your seamline, then lower the presser foot. Set your machine to reverse and stitch backward, almost to the top edge. Don't stitch beyond the cut edge, as the fabric may then be pulled down into the needle plate hole. Change the setting to stitch forward, and stitch along the seamline to the lower edge, keeping the raw edges on the guideline. Set the machine to reverse once again and backstitch $^{1}/_{2}$ in. (12 mm) up the stitchline. Cut the threads close to the stitching.

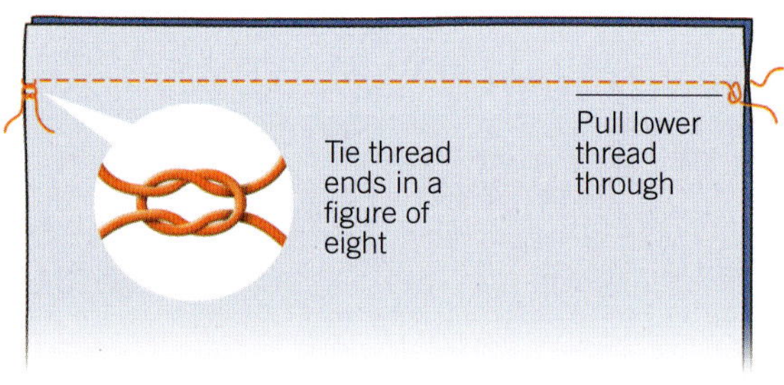

Tying thread ends

Tying the thread ends gives a neater, flatter finish. Leaving long thread ends at your top edge and using the correct seam guideline, stitch along the seamline from top to bottom. Cut the threads, again leaving long ends. Pull on the upper thread to bring a loop of the lower thread to the other side of the fabric. Pull the lower thread through completely and tie the corresponding ends together in a figure of eight to form a reef knot. Repeat at both ends of the seamline and cut off the excess thread.

TIP

Make sure your iron is on the correct setting for your fabric; if you are unsure, test on a scrap of the fabric before you start.

Pressing the seam

Pressing is important at every stage of sewing. It smoothes out seams, making it easier to piece garments together, and helps to give the garment a more professional finish. If you leave pressing to the very end, you will find it impossible to get inside the garment and press properly; if you press as you go along, everything is more accessible.

Pressing a seam

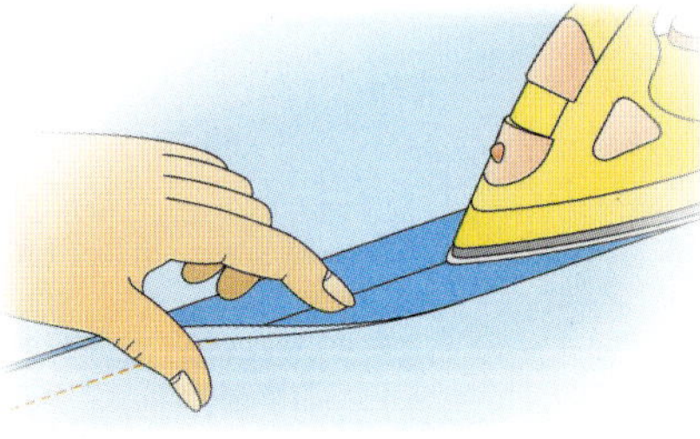

Unpick the basting stitches. Using an iron, press over the seam in the direction in which it was stitched to embed the stitches. Finally, press the seam open so that the seam allowances lie flat, using your fingers to open out the seam edges as you press.

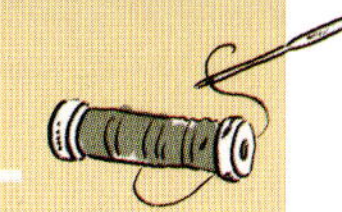

Using seam guidelines

Seam guidelines can be found on most needle plates and are a huge help in keeping your stitching straight. Practice using them and it will give you plenty of confidence to start your project. If your machine does not have them, masking tape or a magnetic seam guide that you can attach to the plate are useful alternatives.

Needle plate guidelines

Most sewing machines have a needle plate that is etched with measured guidelines. The guidelines can be positioned to the right, left, and front of the needle and are usually marked in eighths of an inch and millimetres, so you can select the correct guideline for any given seam allowance (normally 5/8 in./1.5 cm on most commercial patterns) or row of stitching. Line up the edges of your fabric against the guidelines and keep them aligned as you sew. Some bobbin covers are also marked with horizontal crosslines, which can be used as a pivoting guide for stitching corners (see page 42).

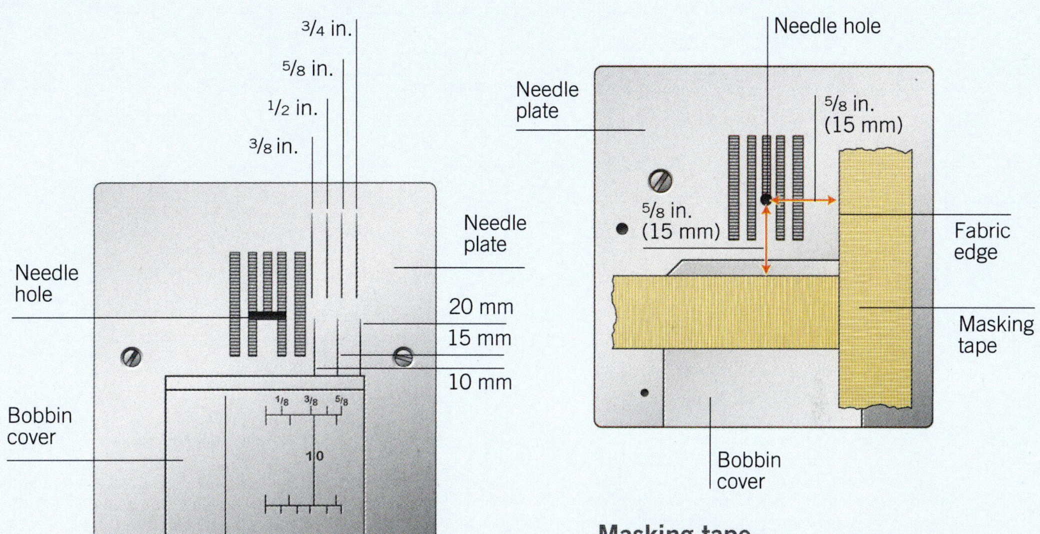

Masking tape

Stick a strip of masking tape 5/8 in./1.5 cm (or the width of your seam allowance) to the right and in front of the needle hole to use as a guide. Align the fabric edge with the left-hand edge of the tape when you stitch.

Magnetic seam guides

Magnetic seam guides are available from good notions/haberdashery stores. They are great for using with mechanical machines, but the magnets can interfere with electronic models; they obviously also need a metal surface to adhere to.

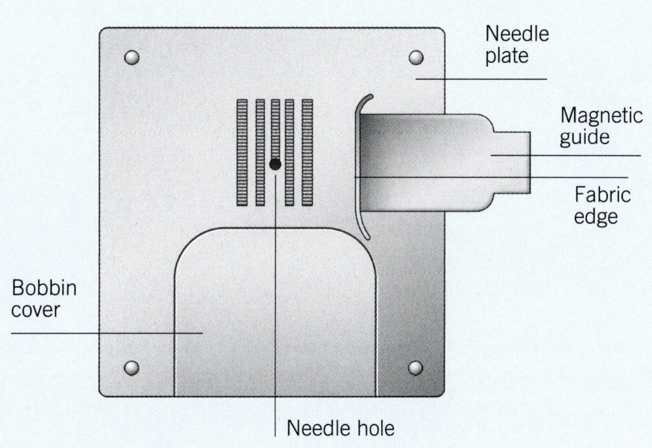

Curved seam

Curved seams are stitched in exactly the same way as plain seams, but you will need to take extra care when guiding the fabric under the machine needle, to ensure that the width of the seam allowance is consistent around the entire edge of the curve. To maintain control, use one of the seam guidelines as described above, set a shorter stitch length than normal (around 1/16 in./2 mm), and a slower machine speed.

Plain cornered seam

Cornered seams are stitched in the same way as plain straight seams, but you also need to know some simple handling techniques for turning the corner. If there is no cornering crossline on your bobbin cover, it's a good idea to stick a piece of masking tape the same distance in front of the needle hole as the width of the seam allowance.

Outward cornered seam

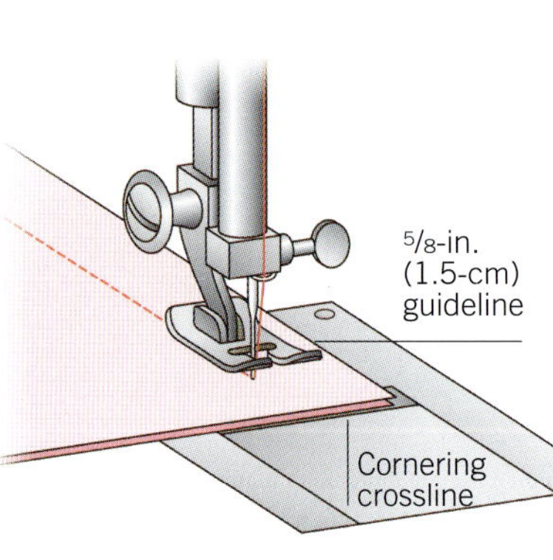

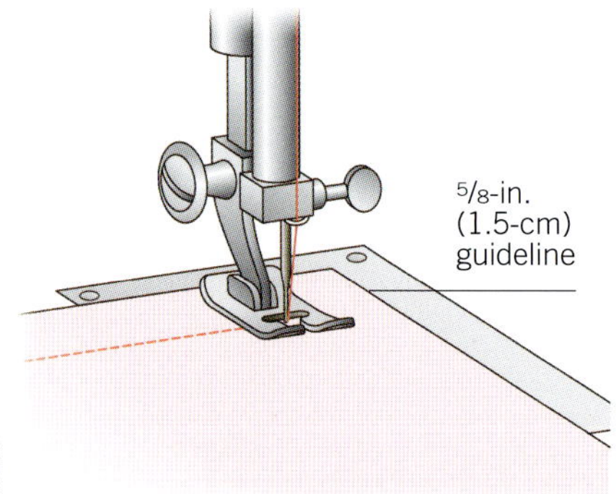

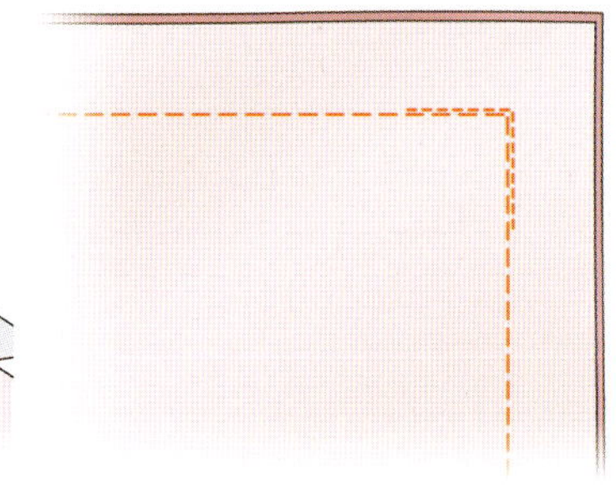

1 Taking a 5/8-in. (1.5-cm) seam allowance and reverse stitching to start, stitch the seam toward the corner, stopping with the needle down in the fabric when the bottom edge of the fabric reaches the cornering crossline on the bobbin cover (or the edge of your tape). Raise the presser foot.

2 Pivot the fabric on the needle through 90°, bringing the bottom edge of the fabric in line with the 5/8-in. (1.5-cm) guideline on the needle plate. Lower the foot and continue stitching to the end of the seam, reverse stitching to finish.

3 Strengthen the corner by reinforcing it with a row of small stitches, about 1/16 in. (2 mm) long, extending 3/4 in. (2 cm) either side of the corner, stitching and pivoting accurately on top of the existing stitchline.

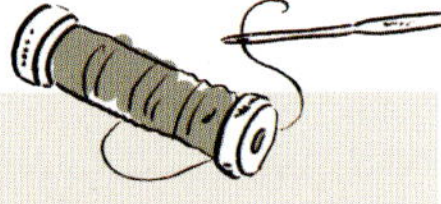

TIP

Wet the end of your chalk pencil for a clear mark.

Inward cornered seam

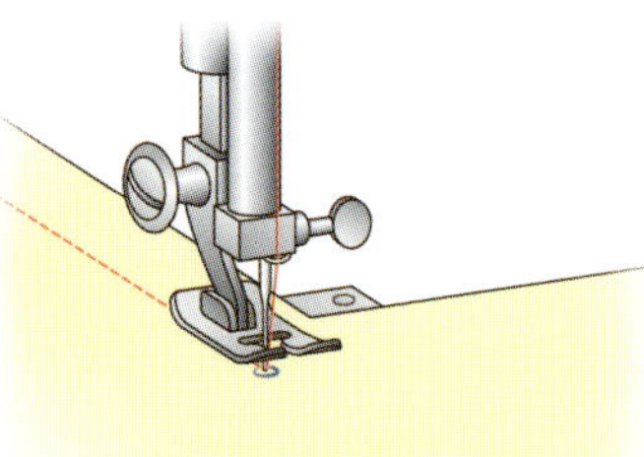

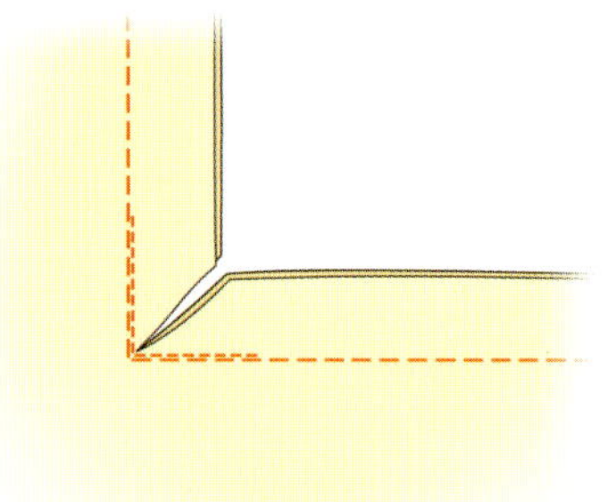

1 Using a tape measure and chalk pencil (see page 22), measure and mark the corner point of the seamline on the wrong side of the upper fabric. Reverse stitch to start, then stitch the seam to the marked corner point, stopping with the needle down in the fabric. Raise the presser foot and pivot the fabric on the needle through 90°. Lower the foot so that it sits parallel to the raw edge and stitch to the end of the seam, reverse stitching to finish.

2 Strengthen the corner by reinforcing it with a row of small stitches, about 1/16 in. (2 mm) long, extending 3/4 in. (2 cm) either side of the corner, stitching and pivoting accurately on top of the existing stitchline. Using a sharp pair of small pointed scissors (see page 22), clip into the corner close to the angle of the stitching, taking care not to cut through the stitches.

Stitching an acute corner

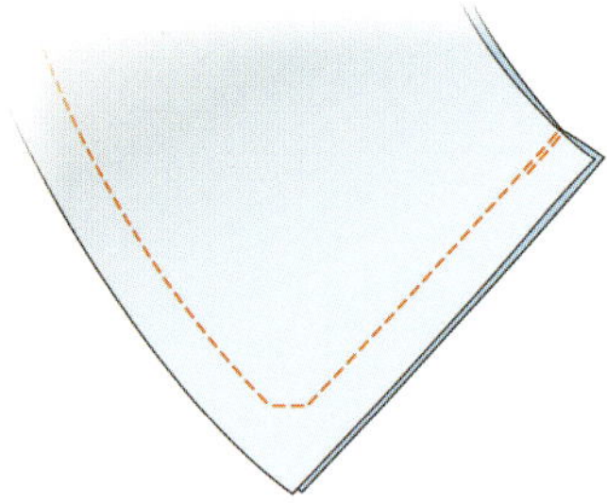

When you are stitching a corner that has a more acute angle, such as on a collar, the best way to create a neat, well-formed point is to take one or two stitches diagonally across the corner: take one stitch across on a fine fabric, two on a medium one, and three on a heavy or bulky fabric.

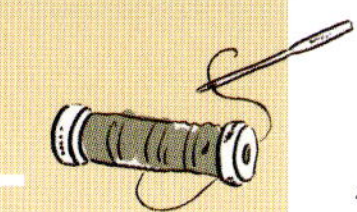

Reducing bulk

There is a simple trick to giving your garment a more professional finish—and that is to carefully trim away excess fabric from the seam allowances, where it will cause ridges and a lumpy finish. This is particularly important when the seam is going to be enclosed, such as in a collar, or where several layers of fabric have been stitched together. There are several methods of reducing bulk.

Trimming corners

Trimming the seam allowance at corners is essential for a neat point.

Right-angled corner

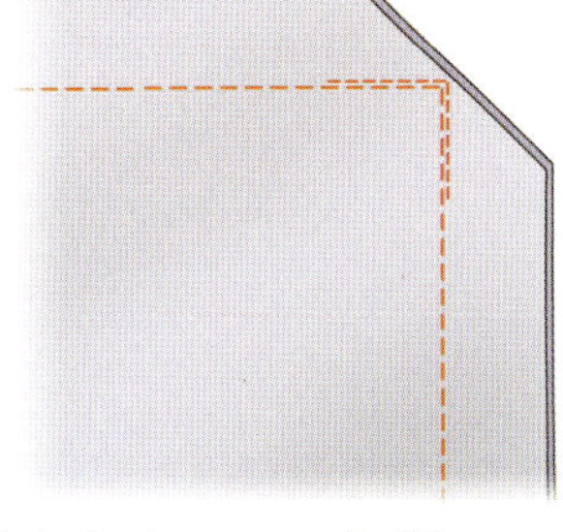

Simply cut across the corner of the seam turnings, as shown, close to the stitching but taking great care not to cut through the actual stitches. When turning your seam to the right side, use a pair of small pointed scissors or a knitting needle to carefully push out the point, making sure you do not push too hard and form a hole.

Acute corner

This type of corner needs to have a little more fabric trimmed away. Cut across the corner of the seam turnings close to the stitching, as for a right-angled corner, then trim away another slither of fabric from each side, as shown. The aim is to reduce the fabric in the seam allowances so that, when the corner is turned right side out, the seam allowances will have room to lie flat.

Trimming seam allowances

When several layers of fabric have been stitched together—when applying a waistband or a collar, or when seams are matched at the crotch or underarm, for example—you can end up with as many as four layers of fabric. Trimming the seam allowance reduces thickness.

Layering seams

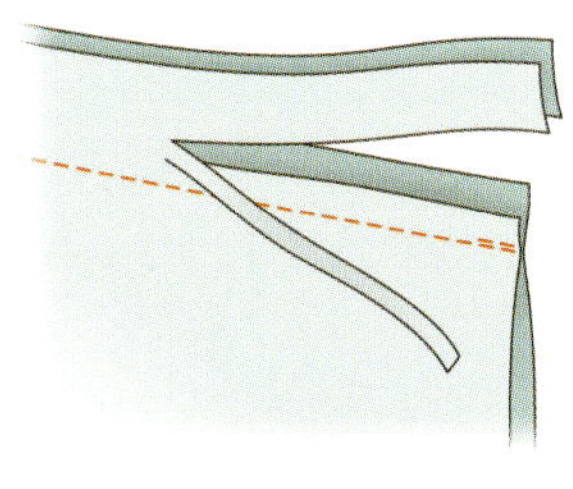

Trim the seam allowances to graduating widths so that the narrowest seam allowance is $^3/_{16}$ in. (5mm) wide and the widest lies next to the most visible seam edge—the top collar, for example. If you are using a fabric that frays, don't trim too closely.

Trimming matched seams

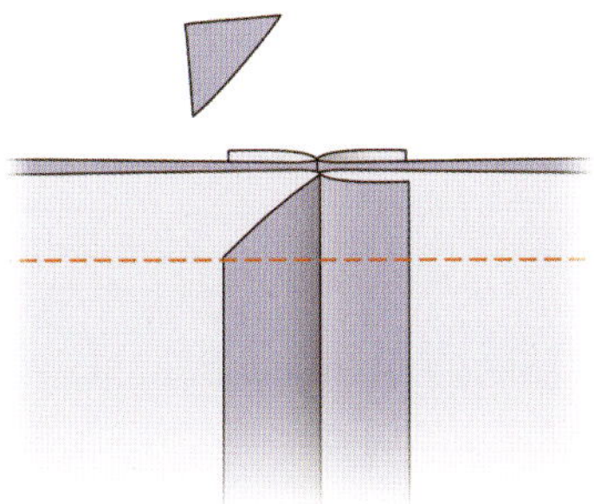

Trim away the fabric corners within the seam allowance after you have stitched the seam, as shown.

Notching and snipping curved seams

Notches are small wedges of fabric cut from the seam allowances of inward (concave) curves to allow them to lie flat. On outward (convex) curves, make small snips into the seam allowances. If the curved seams are to be visible on your project, neaten the seam allowances before notching or snipping (see page 44).

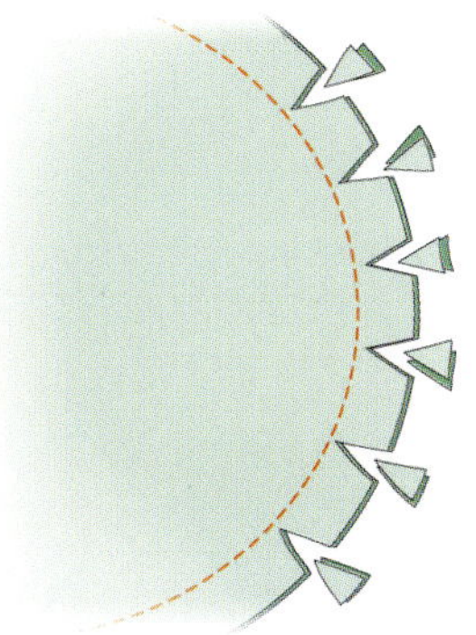

Using a sharp pair of small pointed scissors, notch the seam allowance around the curve at regular intervals, taking care to cut close to, but not through, the stitches.

Neatening seam edges

Neatening seam edges prevents them from fraying, helps them lay flat, and gives a neat, professional touch. There are many ways of doing this, but for a quick effective finish, you can machine overcast the edges using a zigzag or 3-step zigzag stitch.

Zigzag stitch

This stitch can be used on most woven fabrics. It is the fastest way to finish an edge, leaving it neat and flat. To achieve a neat zigzag stitch, use an overcasting foot if your machine has one. This foot has a special pin over which the stitches are formed, which stops them from pulling up tight and creating a lumpy edge (see page 21).

Plain zigzag using an overcasting foot

This stitch is best suited to firm natural fabrics and heavy or bulky ones.

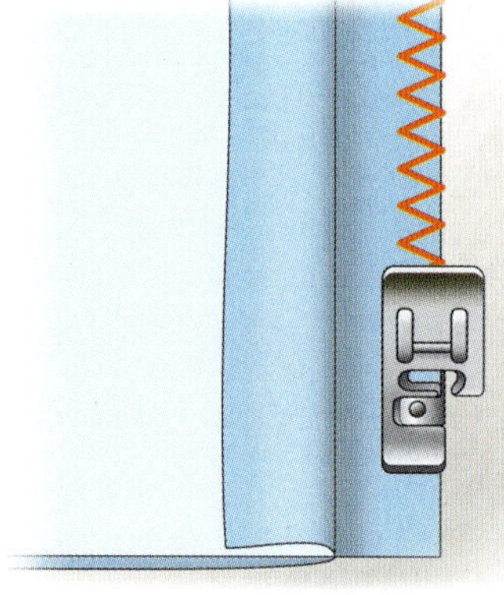

First, trim the edges to remove any fraying, then refer to your instruction manual for the correct stitch settings. Place the edge of your fabric under the overcasting foot, with the pin on the foot along the edge of the fabric, and stitch along the raw edge of the fabric to neaten.

Zigzag without an overcasting foot

Using the normal zigzag foot, stitch on a scrap of your fabric to check the tension.

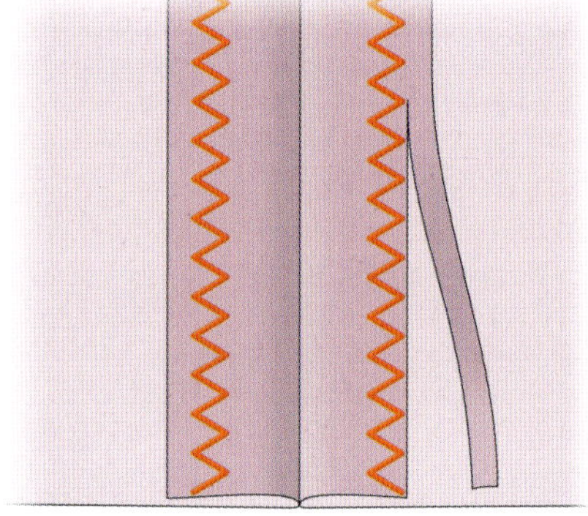

Set your stitch for a medium width and short length zigzag, then stitch 1/8 in. (3mm) from the edge of the seam allowance. Trim away the outer edge of the fabric, close to the zigzag stitching.

TIP

If your machine does not do zigzag stitch, then straight stitch along the edges using a short machine stitch, sewing 1/4 in. (6 mm) in from the edge of each seam allowance, then trim the edges with pinking shears; alternatively, overcast the edges by hand (see page 49).

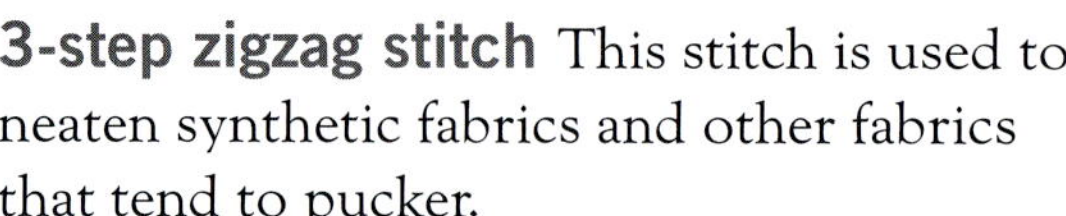

3-step zigzag stitch This stitch is used to neaten synthetic fabrics and other fabrics that tend to pucker.

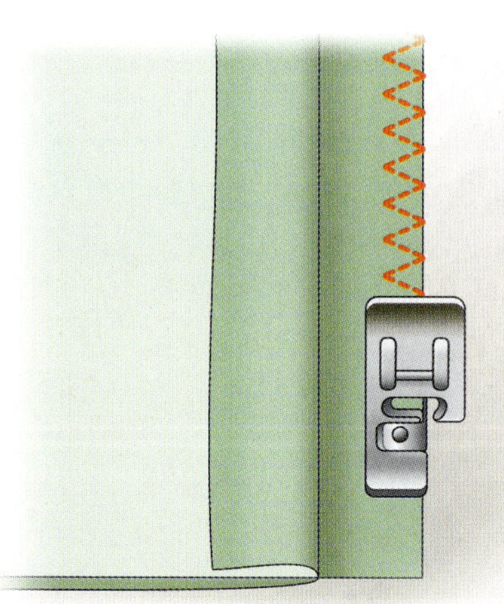

First, trim the edges to remove any fraying, then refer to your instruction manual for the correct stitch settings. Place the edge of your fabric under the overcasting foot, with the pin on the foot along the edge of the fabric, and stitch along the raw edge to neaten.

Stitching a double-turned hem

This is one of the simplest and most durable ways to finish an edge and it is frequently used on garments and soft furnishings. The hem edge is folded over twice, as the name implies, before it is machine stitched in place, enclosing the raw edge within the hem.

You can make the hem as narrow or as deep as you like, and the depth of the fabric enclosed within the hem can vary to suit the thickness of the fabric and the size of the hem. (For example, a narrow hem in a lightweight cotton fabric can have a double 3/8 in./1 cm fold, but on a deep hem the enclosed edge should be narrower than the hem depth as this will give a flatter, smoother finish.) Always take care not to stretch the fold of the hem when pressing.

Narrow double-turned hem

This is a neat, inconspicuous finish and it is often used on blouses, table linen, and sheer curtains.

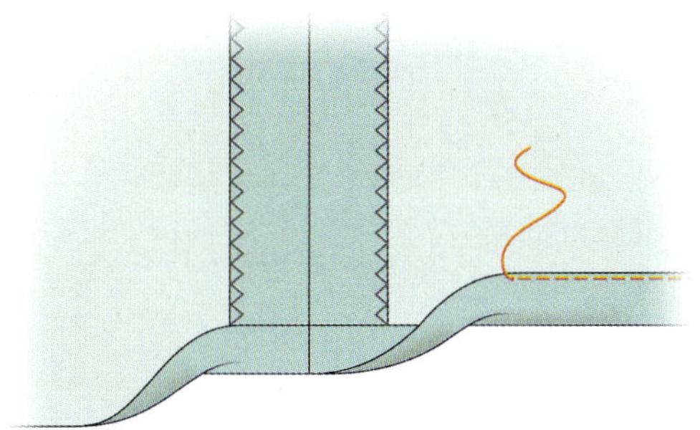

If the hem allowance on your project is for a deep hem, then trim the fabric down to 3/4 in. (2 cm). Fold the raw hem edge over to the wrong side by 3/8 in. (1 cm) and pin it in place. Press along the folded edge, taking care not to press on the pins and removing them as you go. Fold again on the hemline. Pin, then baste (tack) the pressed edge in place, keeping the grainlines aligned so that the hem doesn't twist. Press the hemline fold, then machine stitch the hem in place close to the first pressed edge. Unpick the basting stitches and give the hem a final press.

Deep double-turned hem

This hem can be used as a more decorative finish, where the stitching becomes a feature. It works best on a straight hem edge. Before you begin to cut out your project, calculate the hem allowance required, decide how far in from the hemline you want your stitchline to be, and add 1/2 in. (12 mm) to this measurement. Adjust the hem allowance to the calculated depth and cut out your project.

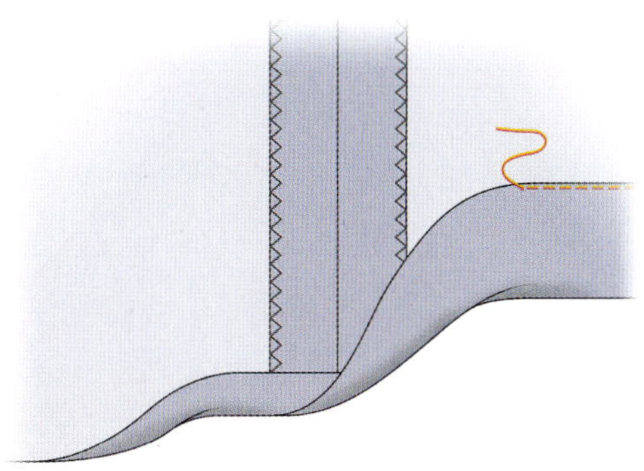

Fold the hem edge over to the wrong side by 3/8 in. (1 cm) and pin it in place. Press along the folded edge, taking care not to press on the pins and removing them as you go. Fold again, this time on the hemline. Pin, then baste (tack), the pressed edge in place. Press the hemline fold, then machine stitch the hem in place close to the first pressed edge. Unpick the basting stitches and give the hem a final press.

For Advanced hems, see page 88.

Envelope pillow

This is a great first sewing project, as the only thing you need to do be able to do is stitch in a straight line! You can leave the front plain, or make the back the front by adding a stunning button. Use a plain or small multi-directional printed cotton or closely woven linen soft-furnishing fabric, all of which look good and are easy to work with.

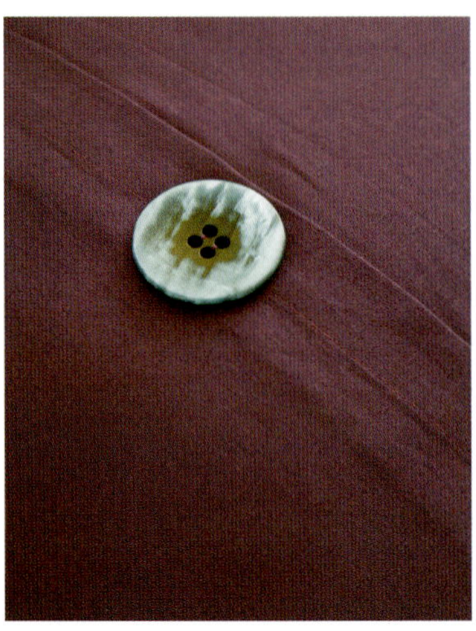

You will need

- ¾ yd (70 cm) of 54-in.- (137-cm-) wide fabric
- Matching thread
- 16 x 16-in. (41 x 41-cm) pillow form (cushion pad)
- One decorative two-hole button (optional)

Note

- ⅝-in. (1.5-cm) seam allowances are included unless otherwise stated.
- Stitch seams with right sides together.

1 Cut a 17¼-in. (44-cm) square for the front, with two edges on the straight grain parallel to the selvages. For the back, cut one 10¼ x 17¼-in. (26 x 44-cm) and one 13¼ x 17¼-in. (33 x 44-cm) piece of fabric, with the short edges on the straight grain.

2 Following the instructions on page 45, press and stitch a deep double-turned hem to the wrong side down one long edge of each back piece, with the first fold ⅜ in. (1 cm) from the raw edge and the second fold 1¼ in. (3 cm) from the first.

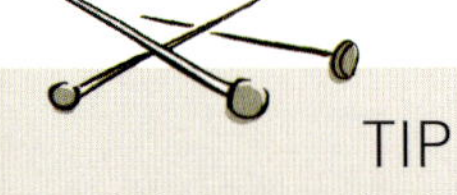

TIP

You may prefer to cut out the pieces in paper first, and then place them on the fabric and draw around them with tailor's chalk.

To add a braid trim as decoration (see page 80), make up the pillow following steps 1 and 2, then stitch the braid to the right side of the front or the small back piece. Continue from step 3.

3 Lay the front piece right side up on a flat surface, with the edges on the straight grain to each side. Place the small back piece right side down on the top of the front piece, with raw edges level. Place the remaining back piece right side down on the bottom of the front piece, keeping raw edges level and overlapping the hemmed edges. Pin and baste (tack) the pieces together around all raw edges. Machine stitch the pieces together, pivoting the fabric at the corners (see page 42). Neaten the seam allowances together (see page 44), remove the basting stitches, trim the corners (see page 43), and turn the cover through to the right side. Insert the pillow form (cushion pad) through the hemmed opening.

4 (Optional) If you want to add a button, mark the position and sew it in place in the center of the hem stitchline on the hemmed opening edge (see page 65).

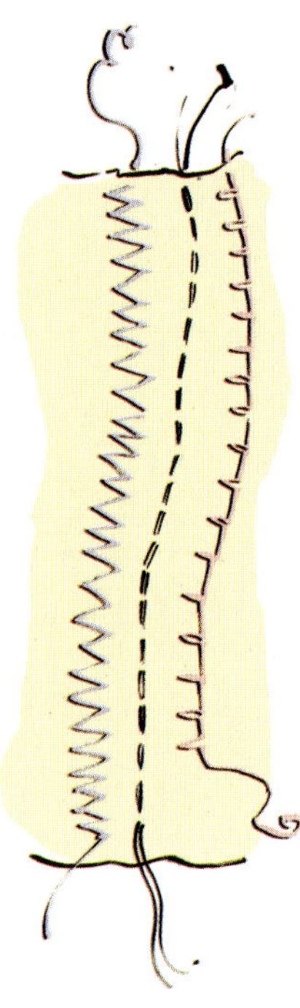

Simple stitches

In this workshop you will learn some really useful hand stitches and topstitching techniques, some of which you will use when you make your second project—an embellished scarf.

Some hand stitches are essential basics that every stitcher needs to know and, although most stitching is done by machine, many of these are used in conjunction with machine stitching to complete most sewing projects, and for lots of sewing repairs as well. Topstitching is generally used to highlight a feature such as a seamline, a collar, or a jacket edge, but it can also be used to great effect as a simple linear decoration on a plain fabric. Look at the gorgeous scarf on page 53 to see how topstitching and a bit of imagination can make something ordinary really exciting!

Basic hand stitches

These hand stitches are often employed in conjunction with machine stitching. They are not difficult to master—and once you know how to do them, you will use them again and again.

To insert a zipper, see page 78.

Running stitch

This is just like even basting stitch (see page 39), but the stitches are smaller. Running stitch is mainly used for hand gathering (see page 144), but it can also be used as a decorative stitch.

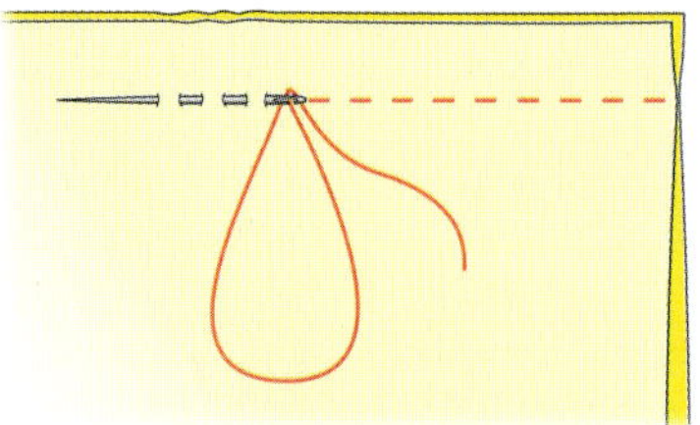

Thread your needle and secure the thread. Working from right to left (reverse this if you are left-handed), weave the needle in and out of the fabric, taking several stitches onto the needle before drawing the thread through.

Backstitch

This is a very strong stitch that looks like machine stitching on one side of the fabric and like overlapping stitches on the other. As well as securing hand stitching (see page 38), it is often used to repair seams.

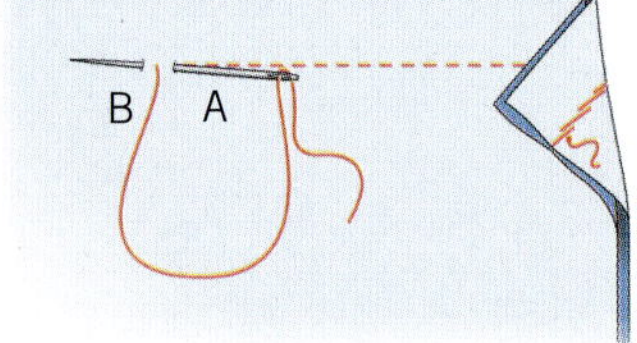

Thread your needle and secure the thread. Working from right to left (reverse this if you are left-handed), bring the needle and thread through to the front of the fabric. Insert the needle at A, 1/16–1/8 in. (2–3 mm) behind the point where it emerged, and bring it up at B, the same distance in front of that point. Draw the thread through and repeat.

Prick stitch

A variation on backstitch, the stitches on the top surface are shorter and more widely spaced. It is used to hand sew a zipper in place, especially in delicate fabrics, as the tiny stitch is barely visible.

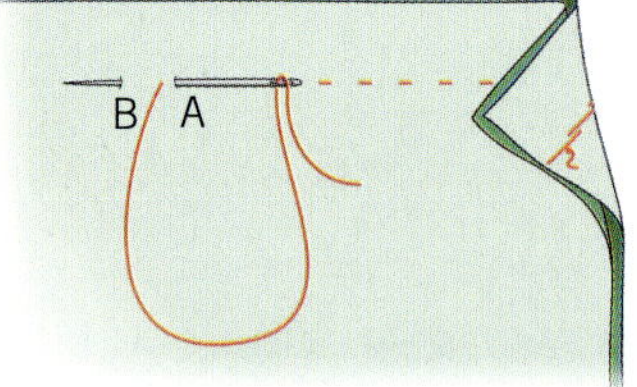

Thread your needle and secure the thread. Working from right to left (reverse this if you are left-handed), bring the needle and thread through to the front of the fabric. Insert the needle at A, one or two fabric threads behind the point at which it emerged, and bring it up at B, 1/8–1/4 in. (3–6 mm) in front. Draw the thread through and repeat.

Overhand stitch

This is used to hold two finished edges together.

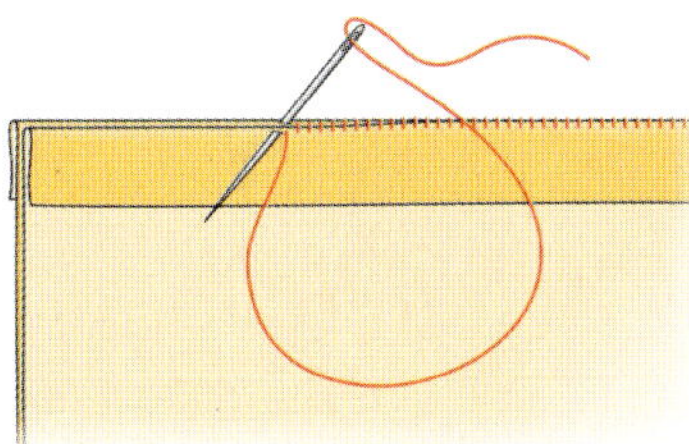

Thread your needle and secure the thread. Working from right to left (reverse this if you are left-handed), insert the needle diagonally through the edges, picking up one or two fabric threads from the back and then from the front edge. Draw the thread through. Insert the needle directly behind the thread from the previous stitch, and bring it out a little to the left, through the front edge. Continue in this way until the two edges are joined.

Slipstitch

This stitch is nearly invisible and is used to sew up a seam, or a gap in a seam, quickly and easily from the right side of the fabric.

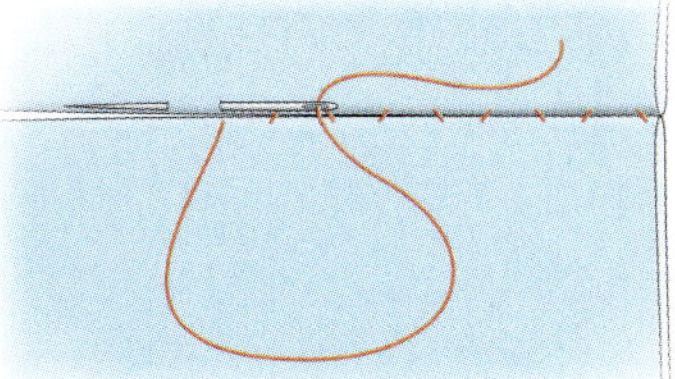

Thread the needle and secure the thread. Working from right to left (reverse this if you are left-handed), bring the needle through one folded edge, slip the needle through the fold of the opposite edge for about 1/4 in. (6 mm), and draw the needle and thread through. Continue in this way to join both edges.

Overcast stitch

This stitch is the most effective way of neatening an edge by hand, as the thread snakes smoothly along, enclosing the raw edges.

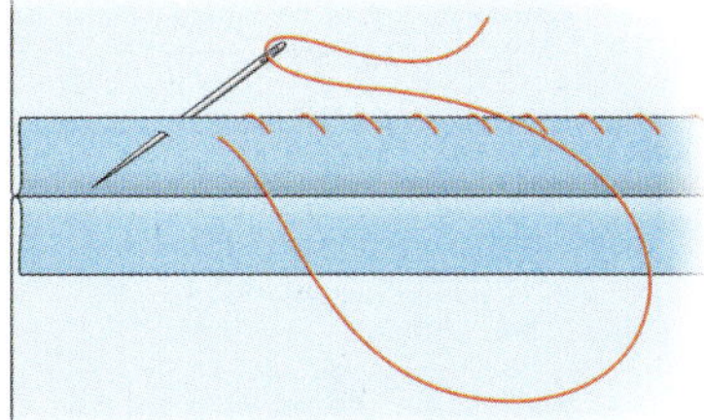

Thread your needle and secure the thread. Working from right to left (reverse this if you are left-handed), take tiny diagonal stitches over the edge of each seam allowance, about 1/8 in. (3 mm) deep and 1/4 in. (6 mm) apart.

Blanket stitch

This is a traditional embroidery stitch that is used to decorate fabric edges—originally the edges of blankets, hence the name. It can also be used to decorate the edges of appliquéd motifs (see page 83). You can choose the size and spacing of the stitches to suit your work; dainty ones look best on fine fabrics while larger, bolder stitches tend to suit heavier fabrics such as felt and fleece.

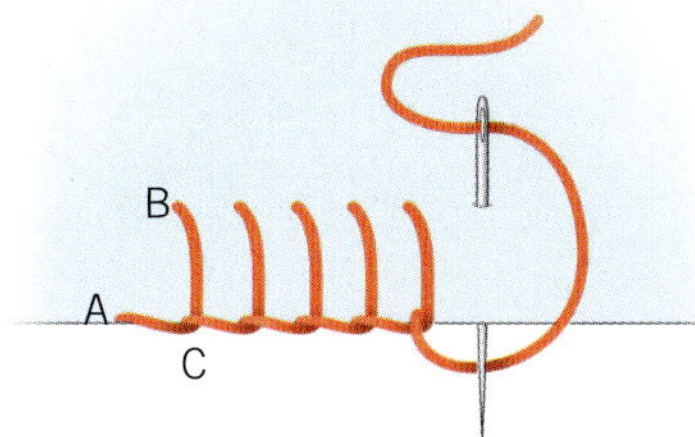

Thread your needle and knot the end of the thread. Work from left to right (reverse this if you are left-handed), with the fabric right side up and the working edge facing toward you. Tie a knot in the end of your thread and bring the needle out at the edge of the fabric at A. For the first stitch, insert the needle at B, to the right and above the edge then, bring it down to the working edge at C, keeping the working thread under the point of the needle. Draw the needle and thread through to form a looped stitch at the edge. Continue in the same way, spacing the stitches evenly.

Herringbone stitch

Herringbone is a strong, flat hemming stitch worked from left to right, with the needle pointing to the left. (Reverse this if you are left-handed.)

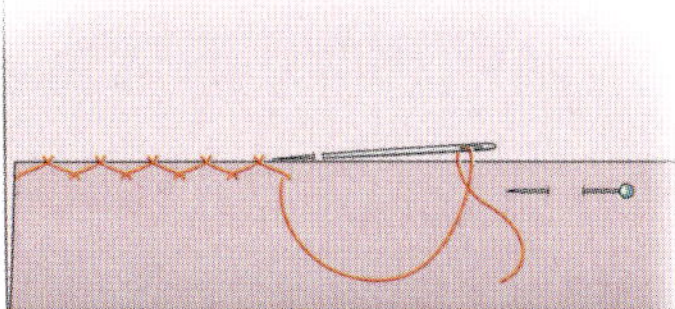

Fasten the thread from the wrong side of the hem and bring the needle out through the hem edge. Take a very small backward stitch into the garment directly above the hem edge, 1/4–3/8 in. (6–10 mm) to the right. Take the next stitch 1/4–3/8 in. (6–10 mm) to the right into the hem. As you stitch, you will see that the threads of the stitches cross over themselves.

Machine topstitching

Topstitched seams add a decorative finish that emphasizes the crisp, clean lines of smart tailored clothes, usually holding the seam allowances flat at the same time. Topstitching is worked on the right side of the fabric and can be functional as well as decorative—holding a hem or a pocket in place, for example. It is usually a simple straight stitch set at a longer length than normal for greater impact and to underline its decorative nature. A single or double row of topstitching are the most common, but you can use a lot more; in the 1930s, for example, collars were often completely topstitched with rows of stitching about 1/8 in. (3 mm) apart.

The thread can be a normal sewing thread, which is better for a fine fabric, or a heavier special topstitching thread, which is more suited to a thicker fabric. It is best to go for a shade darker than your fabric to emphasize the stitching but, depending on the effect you want to create, you could opt for a contrasting or lighter thread.

Topstitching a seam

The main consideration when topstitching along a seam is that the seam guidelines on your sewing machine may not be visible, so you need to use alternatives. The width of your presser foot or its distance from the seamline are good guides; alternatively, you can work a row of basting (tacking) stitches or place a strip of masking tape next to the topstitching line position, which you can follow.

Before you start topstitching, remember to check your thread color, stitch length, needle, and tension on a piece of spare fabric folded to the number of layers you will be stitching through, and adjust them if necessary.

Single topstitching a seam

Single topstitching is one row of stitching, usually worked parallel to a seam or along an edge.

Neaten the seam allowances on a plain stitched seam (see page 44), and press them both to the side that you are going to topstitch down. Working from the right side, stitch down the side of the seamline, using the presser foot, or its distance from the seamline, as a guide and sewing through both seam allowances at the same time.

Double topstitching a seam

Double topstitching is two rows of stitching, one on each side of a seamline, placed at equal distances from the seamline.

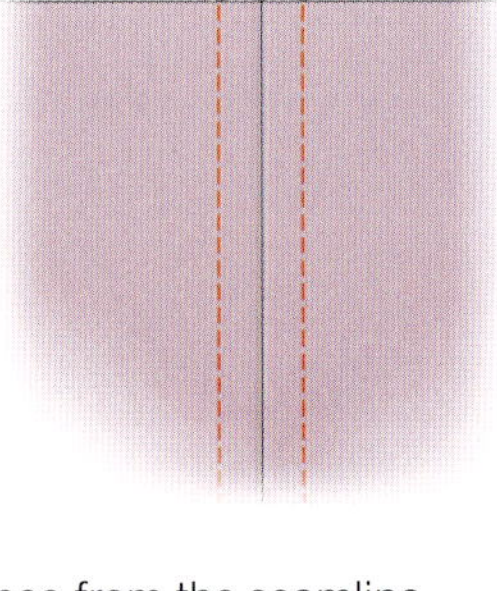

Neaten the seam allowances on a plain stitched seam (see page 44), and press them open. Working from the right side and using the width of your presser foot, or its distance from the seamline, as a guide to keep your stitching even, topstitch an equal distance from the seamline down both sides of the seam, always stitching in the same direction and stitching through the seam allowances at the same time.

Topstitching around a finished edge

Topstitching is often done around a finished edge, such as a collar, cuffs, or a pocket. Here the topstitching is worked parallel to the edge and has a double purpose; as well as being decorative, it prevents the underside of the edge from rolling to the outside.

Working from the right side, line up your finished seam edge on the chosen guideline and begin stitching at a raw edge. Turn any corners by lifting the presser foot and pivoting your fabric around the needle (see page 42), and trim the threads ends level with the raw edges.

Edge stitching

Edge stitching is similar to topstitching, but the row of machine stitches is worked very close to the edge or seamline (around 1/16 in./2 mm away). Edge stitching can be used along with topstitching as a decorative feature, to give a double-topstitching effect to finished edges. It can also be applied along the edges of pleats to help maintain the fold and to give a sharper crease (see page 146). If edge stitching finishes part way down a garment, as in pleats and not at a raw edge, then bring the thread ends through to the underside and knot (see page 40).

Understitching

Understitching, like topstitching, is worked on the right side of the fabric but it is purely functional. It is a row of stitching that holds a facing and the corresponding seam turnings together, so that they lie flat inside a garment.

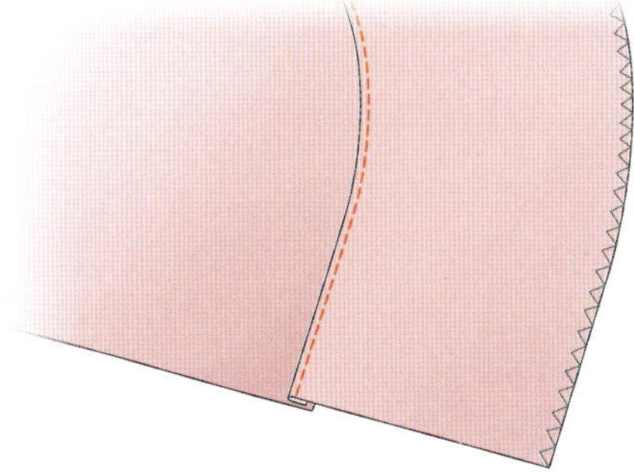

Layer the seam turnings (see page 43), with the narrowest seam next to the facing (see page 92). With the right side of the facing uppermost, topstitch close to the seamline, stitching through the facing and the seam turnings at the same time.

Bagging out and turning through

When two pieces of fabric are sewn together around all edges—as when making a scarf or sash belt, for example—the seam turnings are enclosed between the two layers. To achieve this, the item is "bagged out": the fabric pieces are placed right sides together, with the raw edges matching, and machined all around, leaving a gap in one seam—a bit like a bag. It is "turned through" to the right side by pushing the fabric through the gap in the seam. The edges are then pressed flat and the gap in the seam is slipstitched closed (see page 49).

Embellished scarf

This distinctive scarf cuts a dash in more ways than one—crisply cut-out leaves and simple topstitching turn a basic item into a striking fashion accessory. The topstitching also looks good on the reverse side, creating a subtle but effective texture.

Suggested fabrics

- For a crisp-looking scarf: felt, boiled wool, or fleece in two contrasting colors
- For a softer-looking scarf: a mix of fabrics such as boiled wool and silk—but remember, you cannot cut the leaf shapes from a fabric that frays

You will need

- $1^1/_2$ yd (1.3 m) of 36-in.- (90-cm-) wide fabric or $^1/_3$ yd (30 cm) of 60-in.- (150-cm-) wide fabric in two contrasting colors
- Leaf template traced off from pattern sheet at the back of this book
- Matching threads to both front and back of scarf
- Topstitching thread to match back of scarf
- Dressmaker's carbon paper —available from good notions (haberdashery) stores in white, red, blue, and yellow

Note

- $^3/_8$-in. (1-cm) seam allowances are included, unless otherwise stated.
- Stitch seams with right sides together.

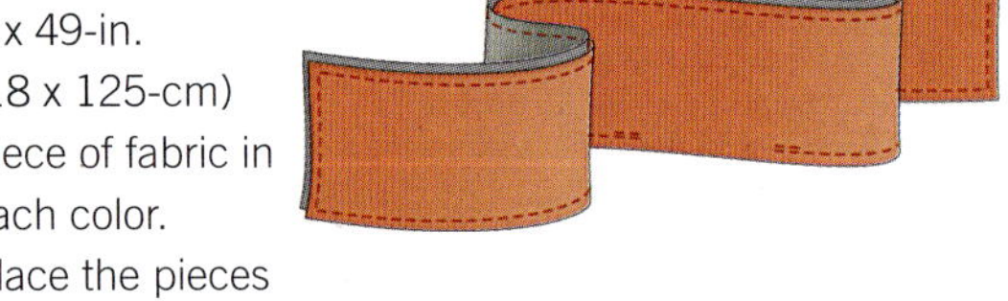

1 Cut one 7 x 49-in. (18 x 125-cm) piece of fabric in each color. Place the pieces right sides together, matching the raw edges. Pin, baste (tack), and machine stitch the two pieces together around the outer edges, leaving a 6-in. (15-cm) gap in the middle of one long side. Trim the seam allowances down to a generous $^1/_8$ in. (3 mm) and trim across the corners (see page 43). Turn the scarf through to the right side and slipstitch the gap closed (see page 49). With your iron on a medium dry setting and using a dry pressing cloth, carefully press the seamed edges flat.

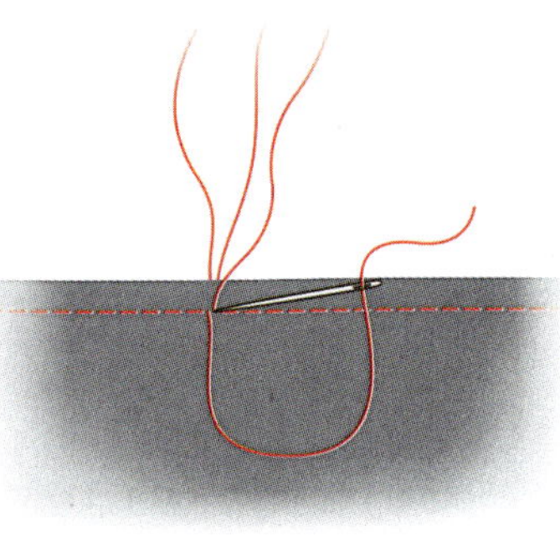

2 Wind your bobbin with thread to match the back of the scarf and thread the top of your machine with thread to match the front. Then, working with the front side of your scarf uppermost and leaving long thread ends, stitch around the outer edges of the scarf. Working with one thread end at a time, pass the end through the eye of a hand-sewing needle and invisibly work the end down in between the fabric layers.

3 Place the dressmaker's carbon paper, ink side down, on the right side of the scarf at one short end. Place the leaf tracing on top and draw over the design to transfer it to the fabric. Using a sharp pair of small pointed scissors (see page 22), carefully cut away the leaf shapes from the top fabric layer to reveal the color below. Transfer the design to the other end of the scarf and cut away the leaf shapes as before. Pin and baste (tack) around the leaf edges, stitching through both fabric layers.

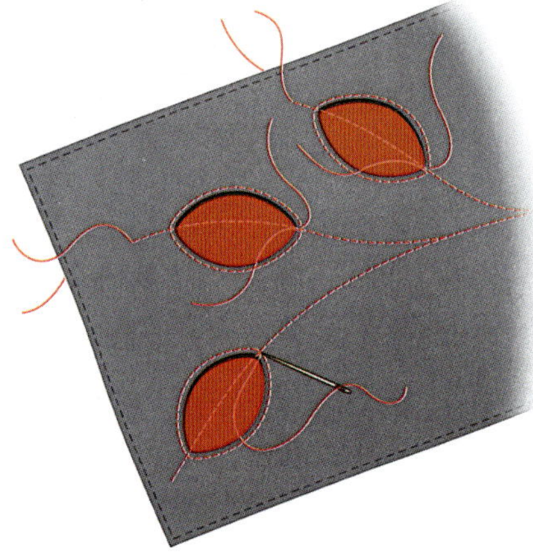

4 Re-thread the top of your machine with the topstitching thread, adjusting the tension if necessary for a well balanced stitch (see page 19). Leaving long thread ends, machine stitch along the lines of the stems, then stitch around the edge of each leaf shape, working about $^1/_8$ in. (3 mm) in from the cut edges and pivoting the fabric around the needle at the points (see page 42). Working with one thread end at a time, pass the end through the eye of a hand-sewing needle and invisibly work the end down in between the fabric layers. Remove the basting (tacking) stitches.

Bias binding & patch pockets

During this workshop you will learn how to make your own bias binding, which is used for all sorts of sewing applications, from finishing off edges on necklines and armholes to edging home-made quilts, tie-backs, and pillows (cushions). The other technique in this workshop is a simple patch pocket. Patch pockets are the simplest type of pocket, yet their shape, decorative trim, or position can transform them into an interesting fashion detail. At the end of this workshop you will be able to complete our third project, a gorgeous pinafore apron with bound edges and a large front pocket for all your bits and pieces. Let's get started!

Bias binding

Bias binding is a bias strip of fabric with folded edges, which is used to neaten a straight or curved edge in a practical or decorative way. It can be purchased ready-made from good notions (haberdashery) stores, normally made from cotton, poly-cotton, or satin acetate. However, the color choice can be quite limited and the widths are generally restricted to 1/2–5/8 in. (12–15 mm) and 3/4–1 in. (20–25 mm). It is more satisfactory to make your own binding, which will match your project exactly.

Making bias binding

Bias binding is made from strips of fabric cut diagonally across the fabric's width following the bias grain (see page 32).

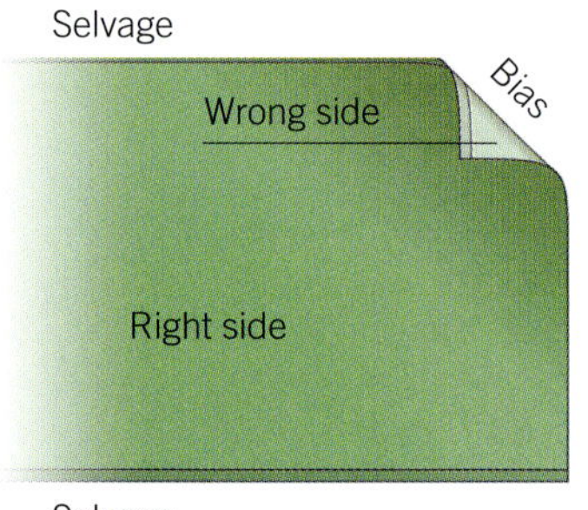

1 To find the bias of the fabric, fold the raw edge (running across the width of the fabric from selvage to selvage) over to form a triangle, so that it lies parallel to one of the selvages. Press and cut along the line.

2 Draw chalk pencil lines parallel to the bias, to your required width; this should be twice the finished flat width of the binding. Cut along these lines until you have enough strips to make the length you require to go all around the edges of your project.

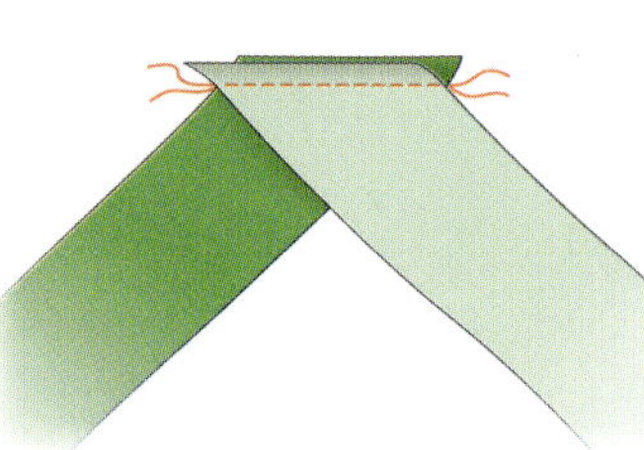

3 To join bias strips together, cut the two ends that are to be joined at a 45° angle. Place one strip on top of the other, right sides together, and stitch the pieces together diagonally —that is, on the straight grain (above). Trim the seam turnings and press the seam open (right).

4 With wrong sides facing, press the strip in half along its length. Open the strip out flat and press the long, raw edges over to the wrong side to meet at the central pressline.

Binding an edge

Any fabric edge can be finished with bias binding, in either self or contrasting fabric. There are two basic methods for applying it: machining and slip hemming. The machine method is used when both sides of the item will be seen. The slip hem method can be used when one side of the binding will not be visible—around the neckline of a garment, for example.

Machine method for a circular edge

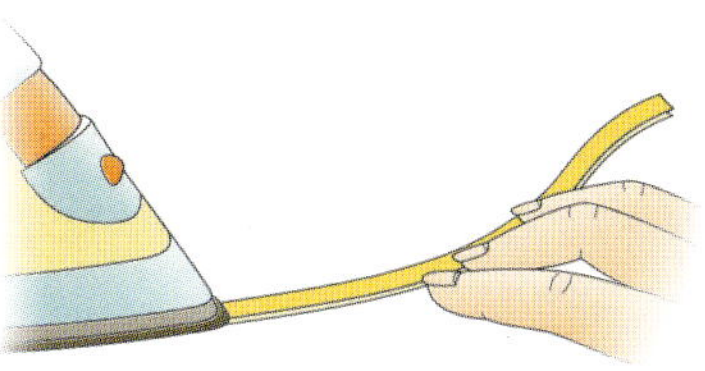

1 Turn back the starting end of the bias binding by 3/8 in. (1 cm) and press. Fold and press the bias binding in half along its length, with wrong sides together, making sure that one side is slightly wider than the other.

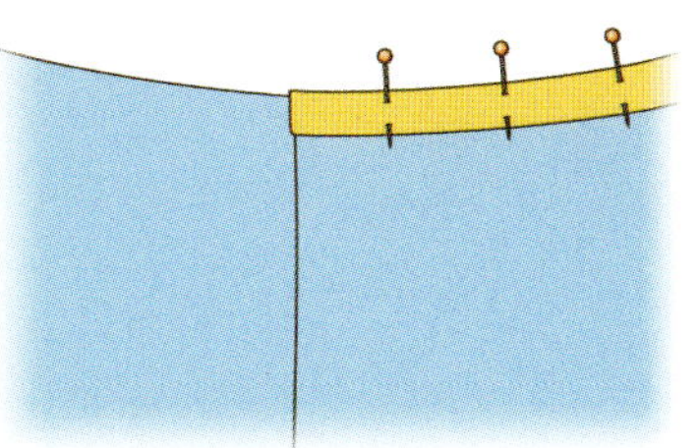

2 Align the short pressed end with a garment seam, if there is one, then sandwich the fabric edge between the binding layers, with the wider part underneath. Pin the binding in place all along the edge.

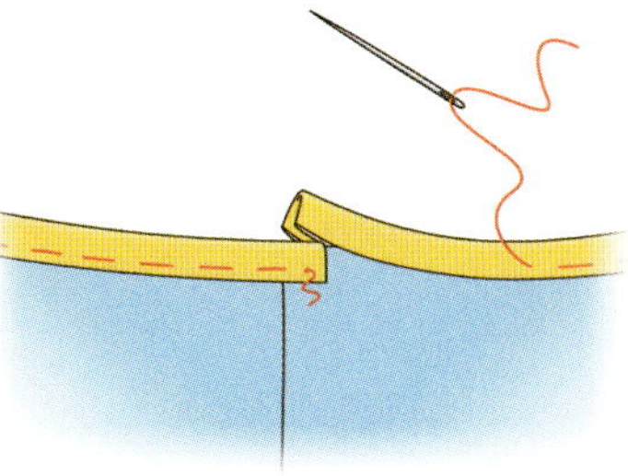

3 At the finished end, trim away the excess binding, allowing for 3/8 in. (1 cm) to underlap the folded starting end; baste (tack) the binding in place. Machine stitch the binding in place, working from the right side through all the layers of fabric and stitching close to the binding edge. Remove all the basting stitches.

TIP

Special tape-making gadgets of various sizes are available from good notions (haberdashery) departments. Simply thread your bias strip through the folder and press the folded tape as it is gently pulled out the other end.

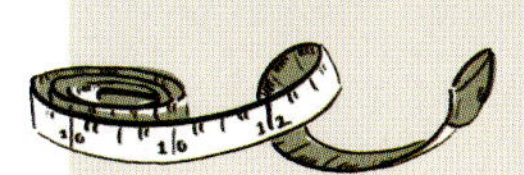

Slip hem method for a circular edge

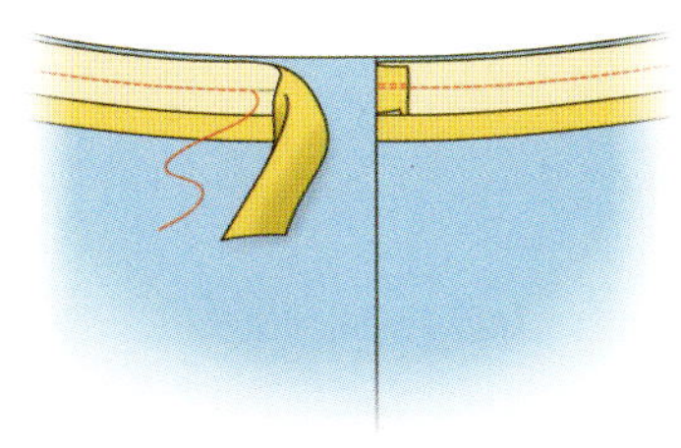

1 Open out one fold on the binding and pin to the garment edge, with the right sides facing and the raw edges level. Turn back the starting edge by 3/8 in. (1 cm) and align it with a garment seam, if there is one. Pin and baste (tack) the binding in place. Following the top foldline, machine stitch the binding in place, reverse stitching at the start and finishing the stitching about 2 in. (5 cm) from the starting point.

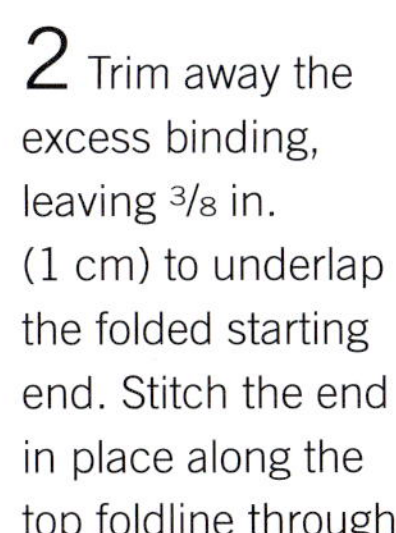

2 Trim away the excess binding, leaving 3/8 in. (1 cm) to underlap the folded starting end. Stitch the end in place along the top foldline through all the thicknesses of fabric. Press the seam allowances toward the binding. Bring the opposite folded edge of the binding over to meet the seamline, enclosing the raw edge. Pin in place. To finish the binding, slip hem (see page 91) the folded edge to the seamline.

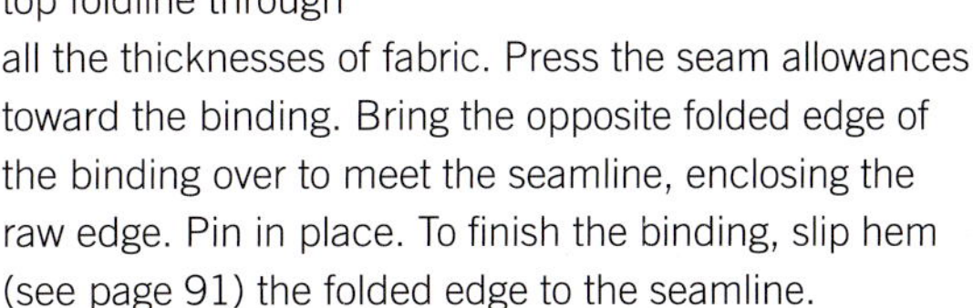

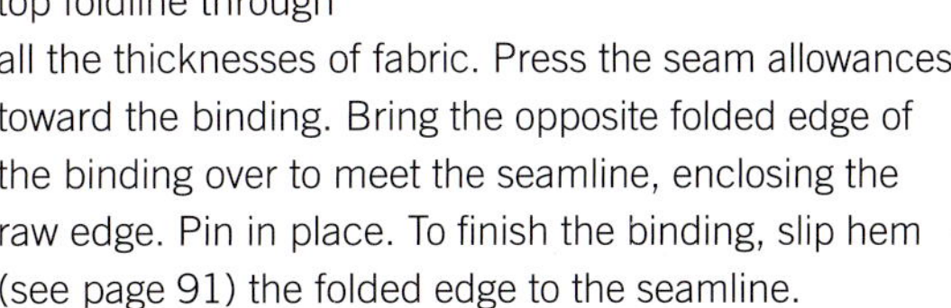

Binding a non-circular edge

If the edge to be bound is not circular, you do not need to press back the binding end at the beginning. Instead, prepare the binding as for a circular edge, then simply position the cut starting end of the binding in line with the cut edge of your project and pin it in place. Continue, either machining the binding in place (top) or slip hemming it by hand (bottom), and trim the finishing end of binding level with the opposite cut edge of your project.

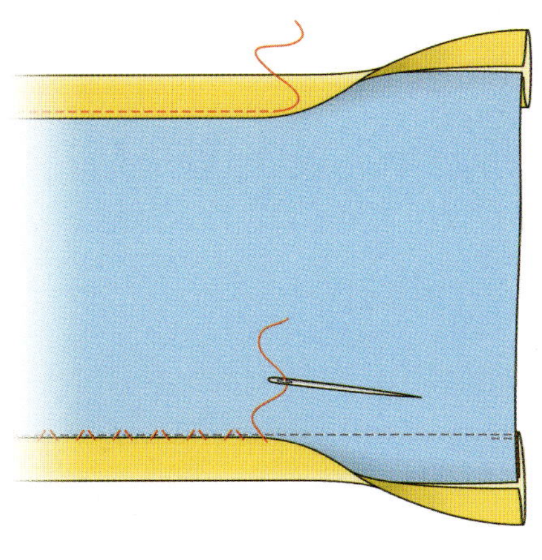

Patch pockets

Patch pockets are shaped pieces of fabric that are finished on all sides and then attached to the outside of a garment by machine or by hand. They may be square, rectangular, or curved, and are often decorated with topstitching (see page 50). They are one of the most visible signs of a garment's overall quality, so take your time when making them to ensure that they are positioned in the correct place and are level. If pockets are used in pairs, you must make sure that they are the same size and shape. You will find making a template out of thin cardboard cut to the exact finished size of your pocket is a helpful guide for pressing and stitching.

Patch pocket with square corners

A patch pocket is basically a piece of fabric with its top edge (the pocket facing) and seam allowances turned to the wrong side. To make it really neat and square, the lower corners also need to be mitered.

For more information on facings, see page 92.

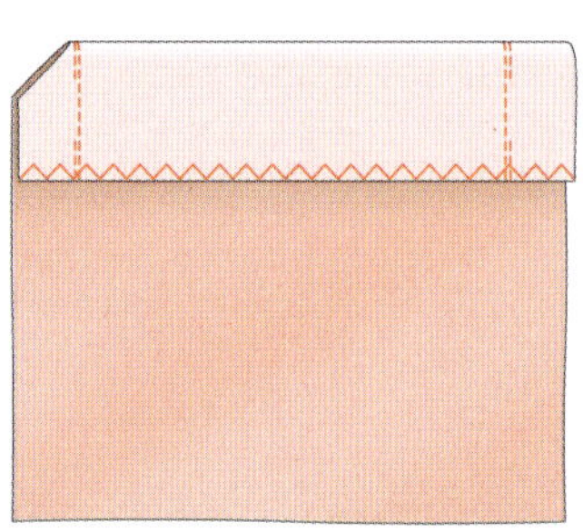

1 Neaten the top edge of the pocket facing (see page 44). Turn the pocket facing to the right side along the foldline. Pin, baste (tack), and machine stitch the top facing in place, working from the fold to the neatened edge on each side, along the seamline (usually 5/8 in./1.5 cm in from the raw edge), and reverse stitching at each end to secure (see page 40). Carefully trim across the top corners to reduce bulk (see page 43).

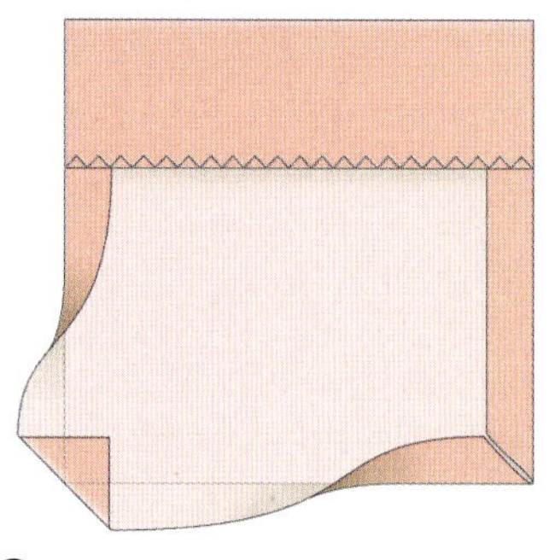

2 Turn the facing to the right side of the pocket, push out the corners with a small pair of scissors, and press flat. Press the seam allowances to the wrong side of the pocket down the sides and lower edge. Open out the seam allowances at the lower corners, then fold them diagonally across the corners, so the pressed foldlines match. Press the diagonal folds, then trim off the points, leaving a 1/4-in. (6-mm) seam allowance.

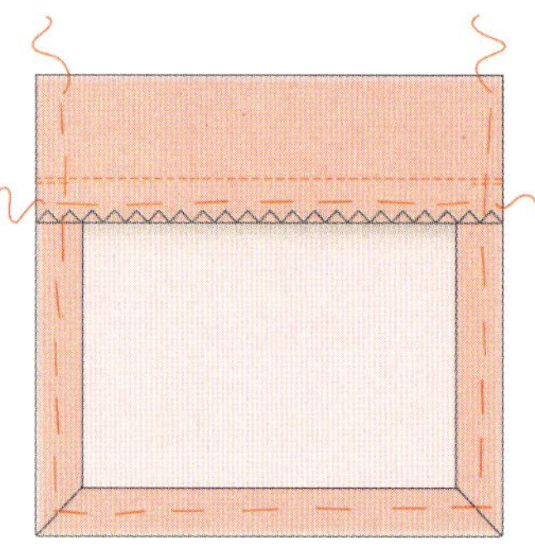

3 Baste (tack) the top facing and seam allowances in place. If desired, machine stitch the top facing in place, working about 3/8 in. (1 cm) above the neatened edge.

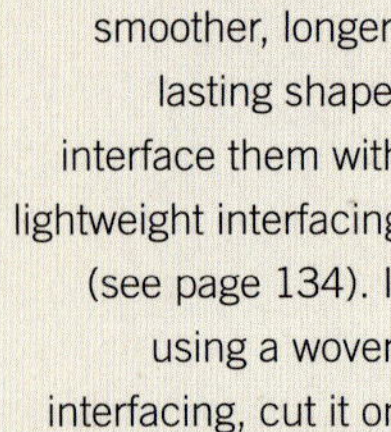

TIP

To give pockets a smoother, longer-lasting shape, interface them with lightweight interfacing (see page 134). If using a woven interfacing, cut it on the bias grain to avoid making the pocket look too stiff.

Applying patch pockets

Patch pockets can be applied by hand or machine, but machining a pocket in place is quicker, gives it more strength, and makes it secure. However, you must make sure that your stitching is as neat and precise as possible.

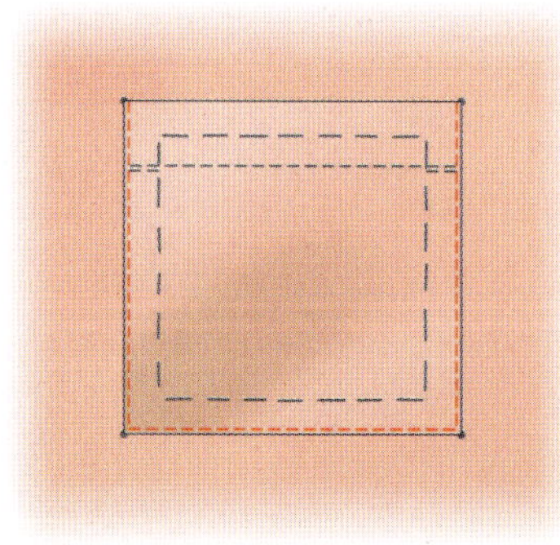

After transferring the pocket position onto the right side of your garment (see page 59), place your pocket on top; pin and baste (tack) it in place. Set your sewing machine to a medium-length stitch, and sew the pocket in place, stitching as close as possible to the pocket edge. Tie the thread ends to secure (see page 40). Remove all basting stitches.

Patch pocket with rounded corners

If the lower edges of a patch pocket are rounded, then you will find that there is extra fullness in the seam allowance when it is pressed to the wrong side. This fullness must be removed so that there is no overlapping of fabric, which would cause bulky lumps.

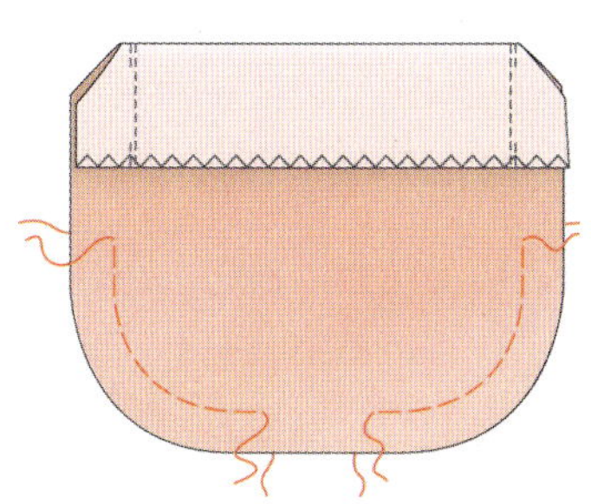

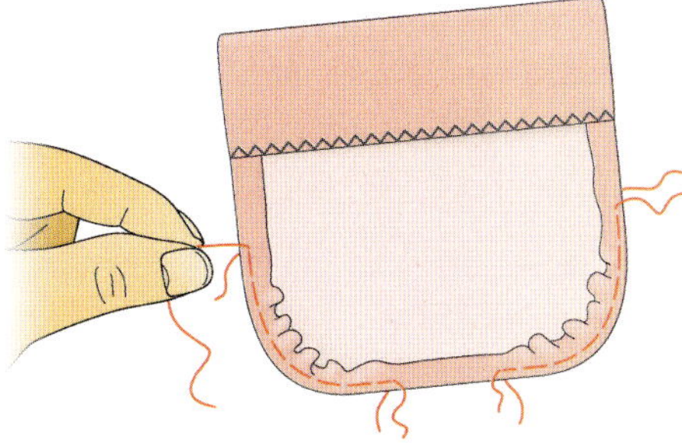

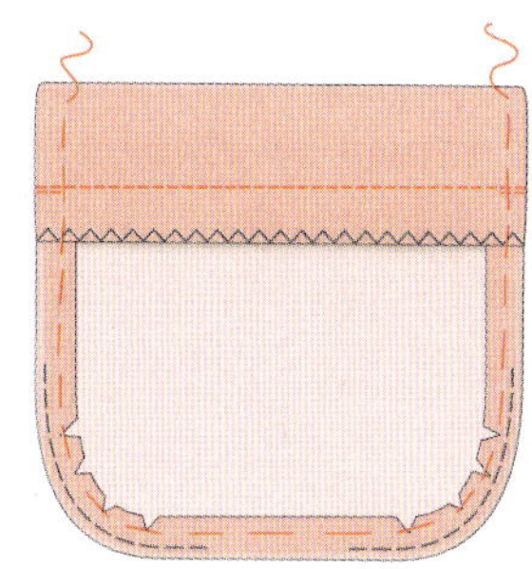

1 Follow step 1 of Patch pocket with square corners (opposite). On the right side of the fabric, make a row of ease stitching by setting your machine to the longest stitch length possible, and work around each lower corner, just inside the seam allowance. Trim the entire pocket seam allowances down to 3/8 in. (1 cm).

2 Turn the facing to the right side of the pocket, carefully push out the corners with the help of a small pair of scissors, and press flat. Gently pull on the bobbin thread of the ease stitching at each lower corner to gather it into a curved shape.

3 Press the pocket seam allowances to the wrong side by 3/8 in. (1 cm), snipping notches into the seam allowances around the curves to reduce bulk (see page 43), but taking care not to snip through the easing row of stitching. Baste (tack) the top facing and seam allowances in place. If desired, machine stitch the top facing in place, working about 3/8 in. (1 cm) above the neatened edge.

Reinforcing pocket corners

The stitching on pockets normally comes under a lot of strain as you push your hands in and out. It is therefore advisable to reinforce the corners to strengthen them and make them more secure.

Stitched triangles

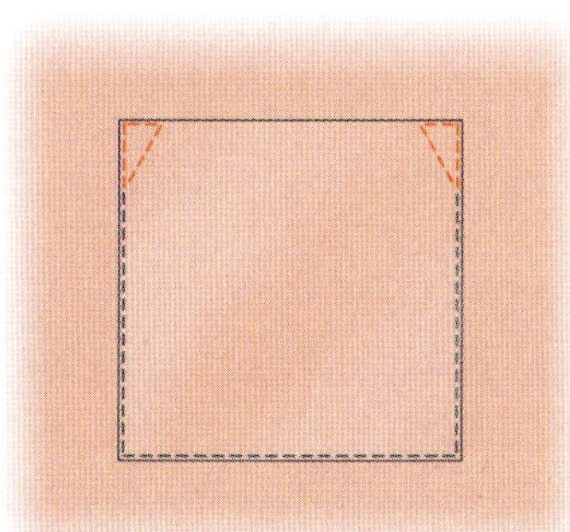

At each top corner, stitch a small triangle extending about 1/4 in. (6 mm) along the top edge of the pocket and then diagonally down to the side edge. You will often see this method used on shirts.

Zigzag stitching

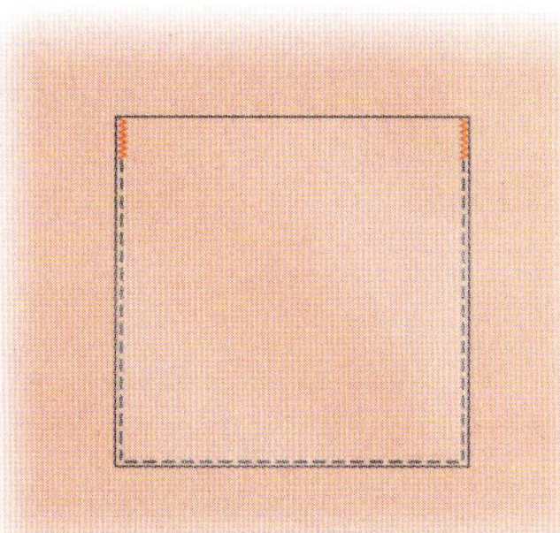

Using a closely spaced zigzag stitch 1/8 in. (3 mm) wide (see page 18), stitch down each side from the top edge of pocket for about 3/8 in. (1 cm), stitching over the straight stitches you used to apply the pocket. Tie the thread ends (see page 40).

Backstitch

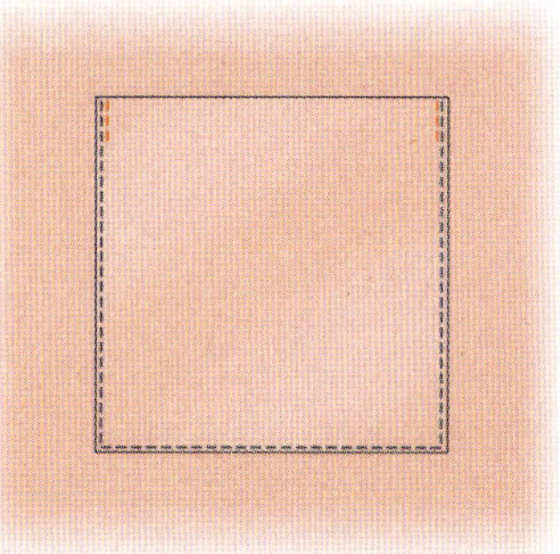

Backstitch or reverse stitch down each side from the top edge of the pocket for about 3/8 in. (1 cm), and tie the thread ends (see page 40). You will often see this method used on blouses.

Pocket flaps

Pockets can be decorated with various things from simple topstitching (see page 50), to pleats and tucks (pages 146 and 149). Another decorative effect is to add a pocket flap. These can have square or curved corners, or may even be more intricately shaped. They are normally located at the top of a patch pocket, but may be used for decoration on their own. There are two basic methods for making a pocket flap: one is a separate flap and the other is a turned-down flap.

Separate flap

A separate flap is attached to the garment above the opening for the pocket and then pressed down over the opening.

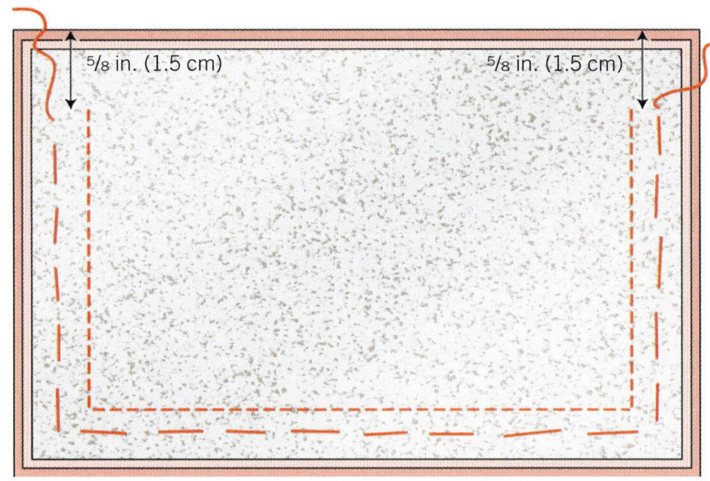

1 Cut a flap and facing from the same pattern piece and interface (see page 134) the wrong side of the flap. With right sides together, pin and baste (tack) the flap and facing pieces together down the sides and along the lower edge. Then stitch around the edges along the seamline, starting and finishing 5/8 in. (1.5 cm) down from the top of the flap. Remove the basting stitches, layer the seam allowances, trim the corners, and notch any curved seams to reduce bulk (see page 43).

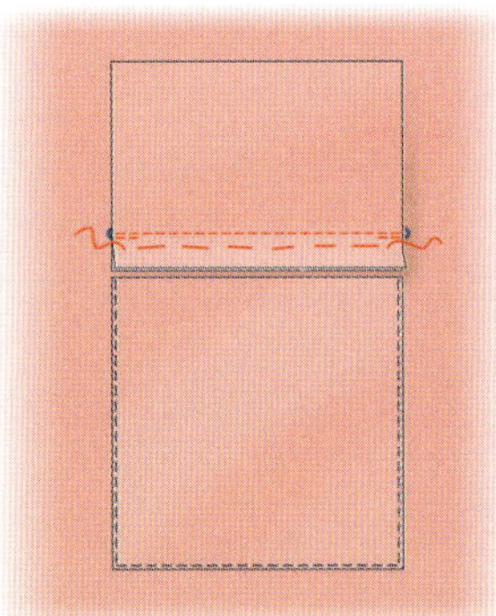

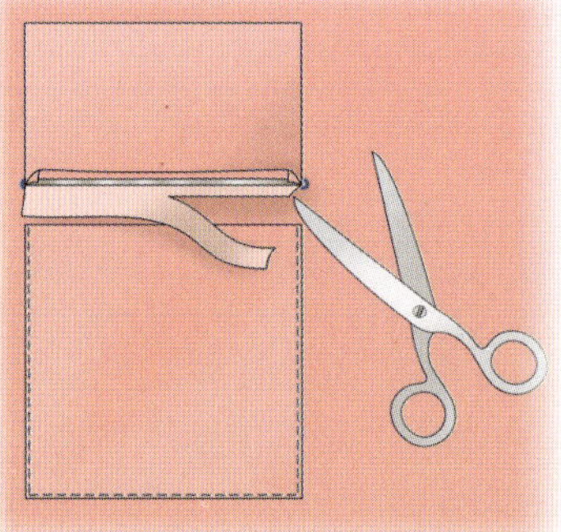

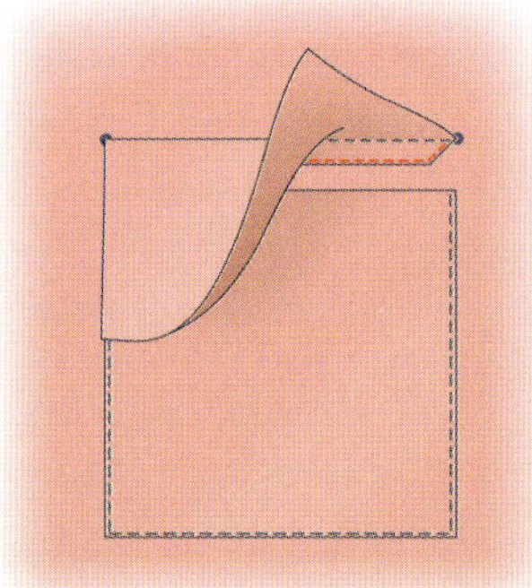

2 Turn the flap right side out and ease out the seams, making sure that the facing does not show on the right side. Carefully press the seamed edges flat. Mark the pocket flap positions (see page 59) above the patch pockets; pin and baste (tack) the flap to the garment with the right sides facing and the raw flap edges toward the pocket top. Machine stitch in place along the seamline, reverse stitching at each end to secure (see page 40).

3 To help eliminate all raw edges, hold the uppermost part of the seam allowance out of the way and carefully trim the lower seam allowance down close to the stitching. Press the upper seam allowance to the wrong side by 1/4 in. (6 mm) and fold the ends over.

4 Fold the upper seam allowance back down and machine stitch close to the edge, enclosing all raw edges. Tie the thread ends (see page 40) on the wrong side of the fabric. Fold the flap down over the pocket and press. The top edge of the flap may be topstitched (see page 50) to hold it in place.

Turned-down flap

With this type of flap, the pocket is cut extra deep, with the flap section extending up beyond the top of the pocket opening edge. It is then turned back on itself to the right side, creating a self-flap. The opening for the pocket in this instance is above the flap. This type of pocket is not really suitable for use with fabrics that have a nap or a one-way design.

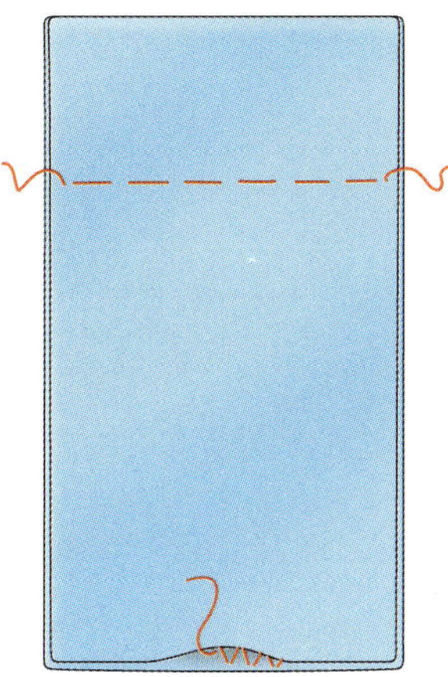

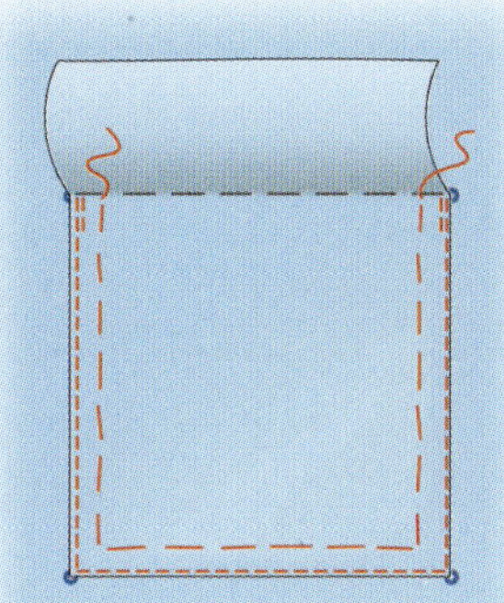

1 Cut out the pocket (and attached flap) double-sized, with a fold at the top edge. Fold the pocket in half, with right sides facing and raw edges level. Pin and baste (tack) the pocket edges together. Stitch on the seamline around all raw edges, leaving a small opening in the lower edge. Reverse stitch at each end of the seams to secure (see page 40). Layer the seam turnings and trim the corners to reduce bulk (see page 43).

2 Carefully turn the pocket and flap right side out through the opening, gently pushing out the corners with the help of a small pair of scissors. Press the pocket and flap flat and slipstitch (see page 49) the opening edges closed. Work a row of uneven basting (tacking) stitches (see page 39) across the pocket along the flap foldline.

3 After transferring the pocket position onto the right side of your garment (see below), pin and baste (tack) around the pocket, starting and finishing at the flap foldline. Machine stitch the pocket to the garment and reinforce the corners with one of the methods shown on page 57. Remove all basting stitches and fold the flap down over the pocket, leaving an opening above. Press in place.

Marking pocket positions

As already discussed, it is important to make sure that your pockets are correctly positioned and level. Pocket positions are normally printed on the pattern pieces.

For a patch pocket with square corners, simply mark the four corners and then line your pocket up with the marks. The quickest way to do this is to use a chalk pencil (see page 22) and to make a small dot on the right side of your fabric at each corner point.

For patch pockets with curved corners, mark the top corners as above, but then trace the lower curved edge onto the right side of your fabric, using a tracing wheel (see page 23) and dressmaker's carbon paper, both of which are readily available from good notions (haberdashery) stores and departments.

Bound-edged apron

Now we've reach the exciting bit, building on the skills that you have already learned. You are ready to make yourself a gorgeous pinafore apron—just the thing to make you feel more glamorous as you go about those messy household and garden chores!

You will need

- Apron pattern traced from the pattern sheet at the back of this book
- 1 2/3 yd (1.5 m) of 45-in.- (115-cm-) wide cotton print fabric
- 5 yd (4.5 m) of 1-in.- (25-mm-) wide bias binding, home-made (see page 54) or store-bought
- Matching threads

1 Overlap and stick together the shaded areas on apron pattern pieces 1A and 1B to make one complete piece. Fold the fabric in half, right sides together (see page 34). Placing the center front of the pattern pieces to the fold of the fabric, cut out one apron and one pocket. From the remaining fabric, cut out two 36 x 3-in. (91 x 8-cm) waist ties, making sure that the long edges run parallel to the selvages (see page 26).

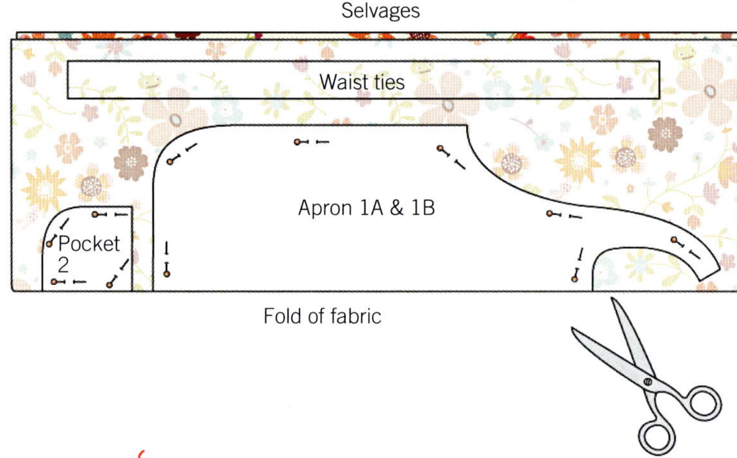

2 Bind the top straight edge of the pocket (see Binding a non-circular edge, page 55), and press under a 5/8-in. (1.5-cm) seam allowance around the lower edge (see Patch pocket with rounded corners, page 57).

3 Mark the position of the pocket on the front of the apron (see page 59) and apply the pocket (see page 56). Reinforce the top corners of the pocket with stitched triangles (see page 57).

BREA

4 Stitch the apron neck extensions together at the back neck seam, taking a 5/8-in. (1.5-cm) seam allowance. Neaten the seam allowances together (see page 44) and press to one side.

5 Starting at the back neck seam, bind the neckline (see Machine method for a circular edge, page 55). Next, bind the top edges of the apron, using the machine method (see Binding a non-circular edge, page 55).

6 Finally, bind the side and lower edges of the apron, as you did for the top edge, but leave 3/4 in. (2 cm) of binding extending at each end. Fold the binding extensions to the wrong side of the apron and baste (tack) in place.

7 With right sides together and the raw edges level, fold a waist tie in half lengthwise. Pin and baste (tack) the raw edges together, then, taking a 3/8-in. (1-cm) seam allowance, stitch down the long edges and across one short end. Reverse stitch at each end of the stitchline to secure.

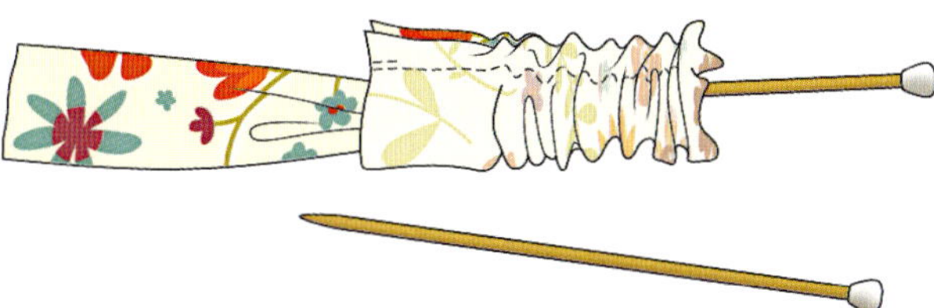

8 Trim the stitched corners to reduce bulk (see page 43), then carefully turn the tie right side out using a pointed object such as a knitting needle to help push out the corners. Fold the seam allowance in to the wrong side at the open end of the tie, and then press the tie flat, making sure the seam runs exactly along the edge. Slipstitch the open edges together (see page 49). Repeat steps 7 and 8 with the remaining tie.

Box stitching

This is used to attach straps and ties to garments and, as the name suggests, the stitching is in a square "box" shape, with a cross in the center, making it very strong. Box stitching is done in one operation, without removing the work to change direction.

1 Starting at one edge, machine stitch across the width of your strap or tie, then continue stitching around to form a square, finishing at the starting point with the needle down.

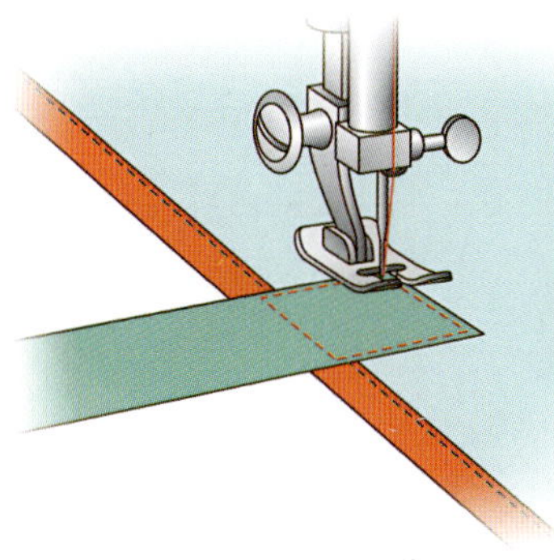

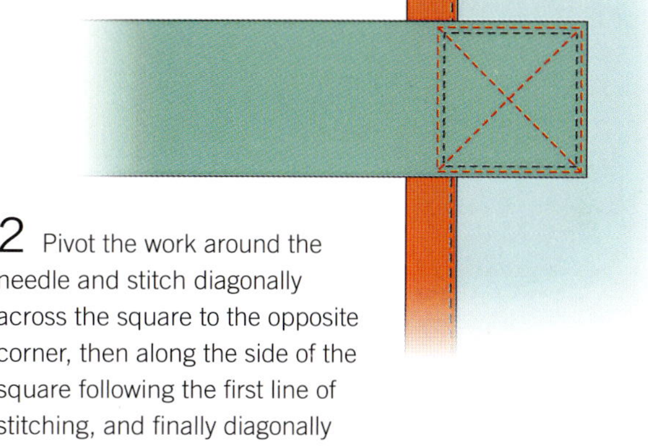

2 Pivot the work around the needle and stitch diagonally across the square to the opposite corner, then along the side of the square following the first line of stitching, and finally diagonally across the square to the opposite corner. To really reinforce the stitching, stitch around the square one more time. Remove the work from the machine and cut the threads.

9 To attach the waist ties, on the wrong side, overlap one end of each tie by about $1^{1}/_{4}$ in. (3 cm) at each side edge of the apron, covering the basted (tacked) binding extensions. Make sure that the long tie seams are parallel and facing the apron hem edge. Pin, baste, and machine stitch the tie ends in place with box stitching (see above). Remove all the basting stitches.

Fastenings

In this workshop, we introduce you to some of the most useful fastenings—buttons with buttonholes, and combination fasteners such as hooks and eyes. While some are purely functional and hidden from view, others are designed to provide an essential decorative element, like the stylish buttons on the bag on page 74. Each fastening has a purpose and we will tell you where and when to use them and how to attach them.

Buttons

The range of buttons is enormous, from tiny, delicate flower shapes to bright, bold, "gobstopper-" sized buttons, and jeans buttons that you can fix to your denim jacket using a special tool and a small hammer. You can even cover a button in fabric of your own choice.

Choosing a button needs careful consideration: will it suit the style of your project, your fabric type and weight, and the place where the button is to be positioned? Always stick to the size given on your commercial pattern, as the designer will have chosen a button size to suit the button spacing given. As a general rule, the weight of the fabric dictates the weight and size of the buttons you can use; in other words, smaller, more delicate buttons suit lightweight fabrics while large, chunkier buttons work best with thicker, heavier fabrics.

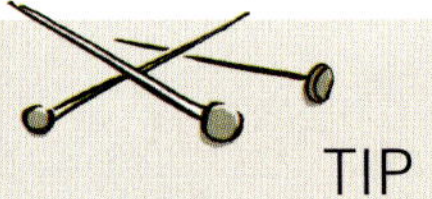

TIP

Start a button box. Carefully remove buttons from clothes you no longer wear and cannot recycle. You will be surprised how many you re-use and how much money you will save.

Button types

There are two types of button: shank buttons and sew-through buttons.

Shank buttons

These have a small "stub" or loop on the back of the button called a "shank," through which the button can be attached. The shank allows the decorative part of the button to sit on top of the buttonhole. Shank buttons are not the best choice for purely decorative buttons, as they will flop down without a buttonhole to keep them upright. They are best suited to medium- and heavyweight fabrics.

Sew-through buttons

These have either two or four central holes. If they are sewn on flat, they can be used as a decoration. For a closure, you will need to make a thread shank so that the button will lie flat on top of the buttonhole and not pull on the fabric below; the fabric thickness at the buttonhole indicates the length of shank you need. These buttons are best for lightweight fabrics and can be sewn on by hand, or by machine if your machine has a button foot and can do zigzag stitch (see page 18).

Jeans buttons

These buttons are really strong and are great for casual trousers and jackets. They are not sewn on to the fabric, but consist of two separate parts, a lower pin section and a button top, which are positioned on each side of the fabric and then hammered together. They come in packs complete with instructions and a special tool for attaching them; follow the manufacturer's instructions.

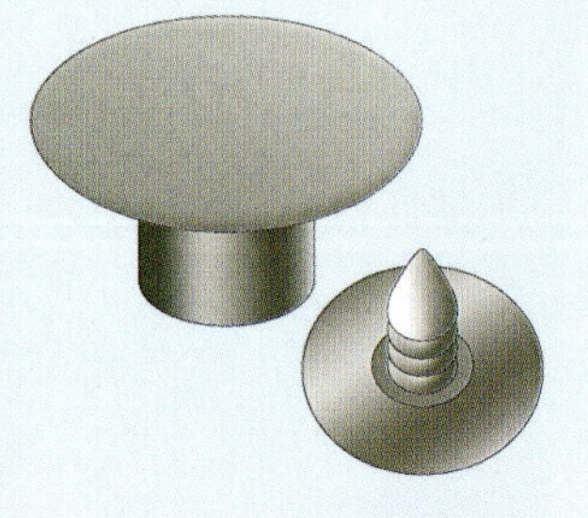

Attaching buttons

Buttons used for closures can pull at points of stress, such as the bust or waistline, and may even tear the fabric. It is therefore important to make sure that they are sewn through a minimum of two layers of fabric, or that the fabric is reinforced to take the strain. Use a strong topstitching thread, which is available from good notions (haberdashery) stores and is great for attaching buttons and stitching buttonholes on heavyweight fabrics.

Attaching a sew-through button by hand If the button is being used for a closure, you will need to add a shank. This is done by placing a matchstick across the top of the button and stitching over it. The same method is used for a two- or a four-holed button.

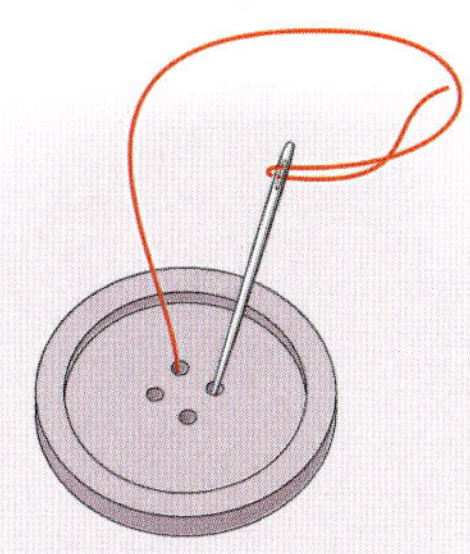

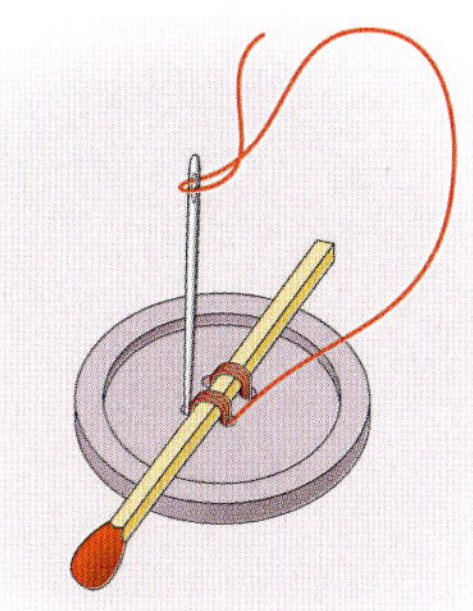

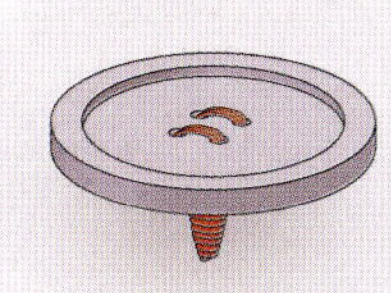

1 Mark the position of your button with a chalk pencil (see page 117) and secure your thread on the right side of the fabric at the button mark, with a backstitch (see page 38). Bring the needle and thread up through one hole in the button and start to pass it down through the second hole.

2 Lay a matchstick across the top of the button and pull the needle through to the wrong side so that the thread holds the matchstick in place. Pass the needle up through the third hole, over the matchstick, and down through the fourth hole. Take about six stitches through each pair of holes, then carefully slide out the matchstick.

3 Lift the button away from the fabric so that the stitches are taut, and pass the needle back down through the button only. Wind the thread tightly around the stitches to form a thread shank. Secure the thread on the underside with a couple of backstitches.

TIP

If the button is purely decorative, then no shank is required. Stitch the button on in the same way, omitting the matchstick and the shank.

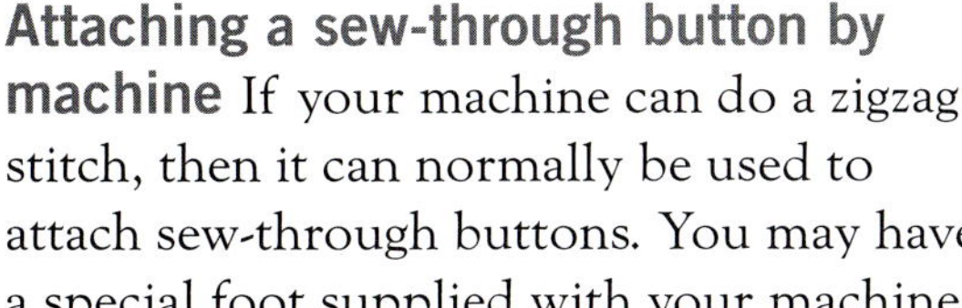

Attaching a sew-through button by machine If your machine can do a zigzag stitch, then it can normally be used to attach sew-through buttons. You may have a special foot supplied with your machine, which holds the button in place while you stitch (see page 21), but not all machines need them. Your machine manual will tell you which foot to use and exactly how to sew your button in place.

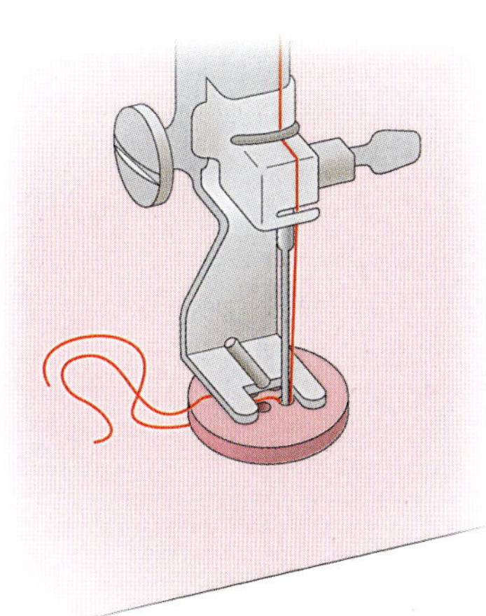

Sewing a button on flat

Refer to your manual to drop the feed dog (see page 11), attach the correct foot, and set your machine to a zigzag stitch. Mark the button position in chalk and place the button on top, positioning it under the machine foot with the holes in the button inside the slot in the foot. Lower the foot onto the button. Set the stitch width to the distance between the holes in your button. Slowly sew about ten stitches. Pull the fabric out toward the back of the machine. Cut the threads, pass the upper thread through a hand-sewing needle, and take it through to the underside of the fabric. Knot the ends and trim off any excess thread.

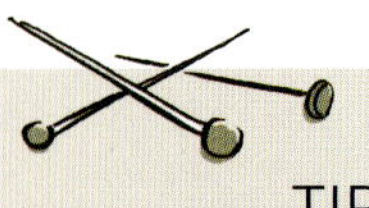

TIPS

- Practice first with a spare button and some scrap fabric.
- To double-check you have set the stitch width right, carefully turn the hand wheel (see page 11) toward you to make sure the needle enters both holes cleanly; re-adjust the stitch width if necessary.
- If you are not feeling confident, do not use the foot treadle; instead, simply turn the hand wheel manually several times until the button is stitched on.

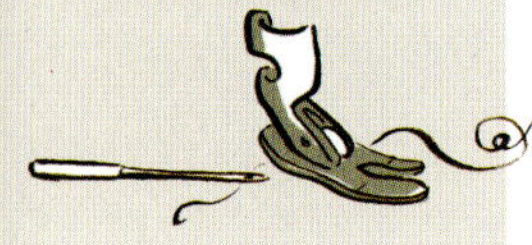

Creating a shank

Some machines have a button foot with an adjustable shank guide. However, if yours does not, you may be able to push a toothpick or machine needle into the groove on an ordinary button foot, so that the stitches will pass over it to form a thread shank. When you have stitched the button on, wind the upper thread around the shank several times, as shown for attaching a Sew-through button by hand (see page 65), before passing the upper thread through a hand-sewing needle to take it through to the underside of the fabric. Knot the ends together and trim off any excess thread.

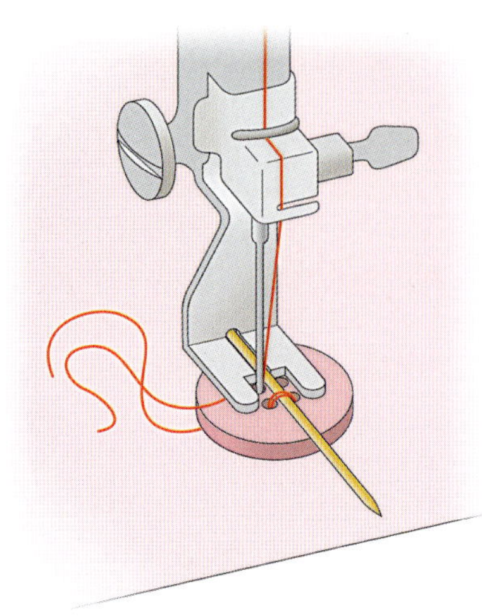

Attaching a shank button These buttons need be hand-sewn in place because the stitch hole is on the underside of the button, through the shank, which is inaccessible to the machine needle.

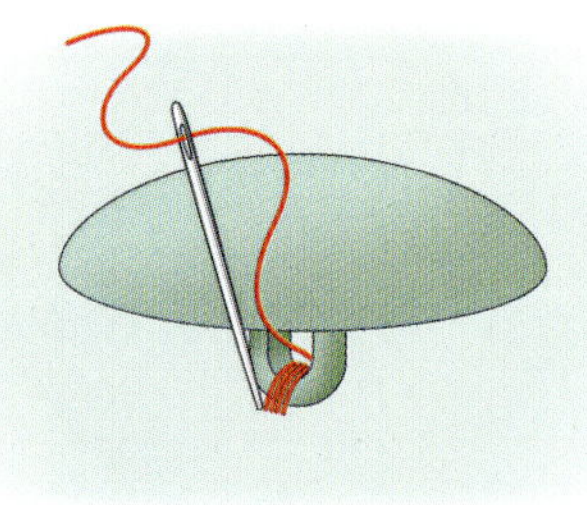

Mark the position of your button with a chalk pencil (see page 117) and secure your thread on the right side of the fabric at the mark, with a backstitch (see page 38). Position the button shank on the mark, with the shank hole parallel to the buttonhole. Bring the needle and thread through the shank hole, then take the needle down through the fabric layers and bring it up on the other side of the shank. Repeat, taking about six stitches through the shank, and secure the thread on the underside with a couple of backstitches.

Adding a thread shank to a shank button If your fabric is very bulky and thick, then you may need to add a thread shank below the button shank, too.

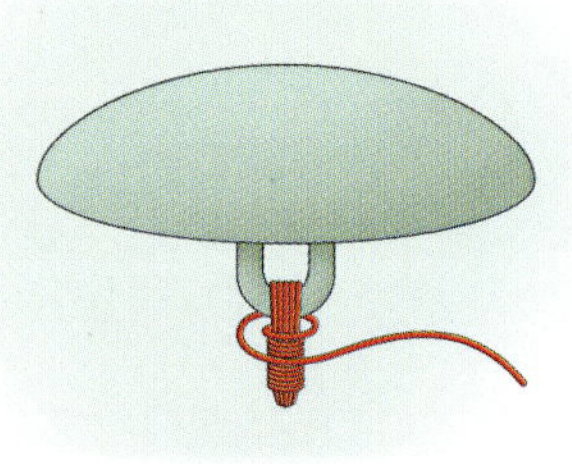

Attach the button as shown for a shank button (left), but insert a matchstick between the shank and the fabric and stitch over it. Remove the matchstick, lift the button away from the fabric so the stitches are taut, and wind the thread tightly around the stitches to form a thread shank. Secure the thread on the underside with a backstitch, as before.

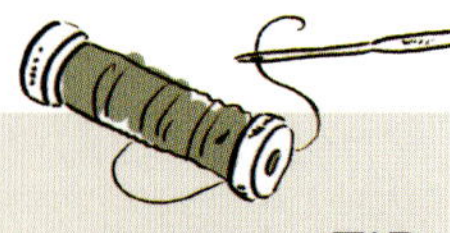

TIP

For delicate fabrics, substitute a small doubled square of fabric or seam binding for the reinforcement button.

Reinforcement buttons

Reinforcement buttons are useful at points of great strain and on garments made from heavy fabrics, such as coats. You can buy special clear plastic buttons for this purpose, but you can also use any small flat buttons, as long as they have the same number of holes as your main buttons. Reinforcement buttons are attached simultaneously on the inside of the garment, beneath your main buttons.

Follow the instructions for Attaching a sew-through button with a shank (above), but place a small flat button on the inside of your garment, directly under the main top button. Sew on as usual through all sets of holes and both buttons. On the last stitch, bring the needle and thread through the hole of the main top button only, remove the matchstick, and complete the shank.

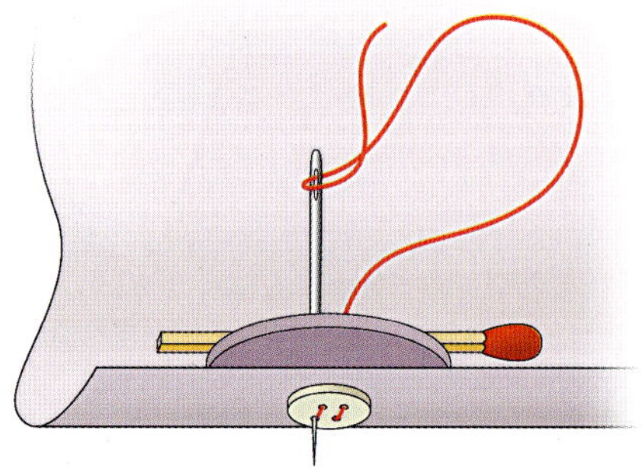

Fabric-covered buttons

If you cannot find a suitable ready-made button or you want a button covered in a matching fabric, then have a go at making them yourself. Self-cover buttons are available in white plastic or nickel finished brass. They consist of a top, which you cover, and a back-plate, which holds the raw edges of the fabric in place. The two button pieces clip together to form a whole. Plastic buttons are best for lighterweight fabrics and are available in sizes 1/2–1 1/8 in. (11–29 mm); metal buttons suit heavier weights and come in sizes 1/2–1 1/2 in. (11–38 mm) in diameter. Both are washable.

Covering a plastic button The fabric cover for the plastic top is gathered around the shank before the back-plate is clipped in place.

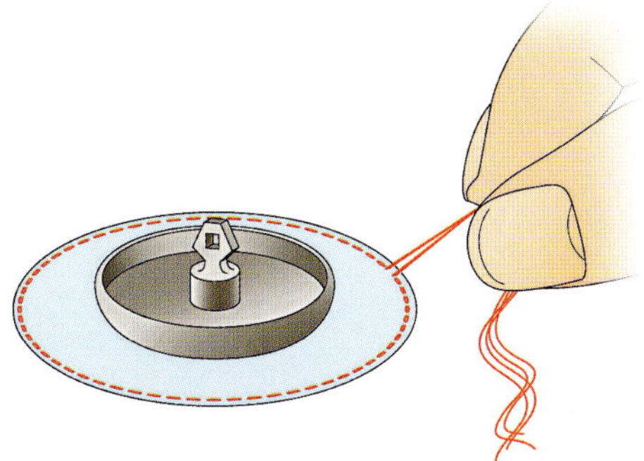

1 Cut the card circle from the back of the button pack to use as a template for the cover. Place it on the fabric, positioning any motifs centrally, then draw around it with a chalk pencil and cut out the fabric circle. Thread a needle so that the thread ends are equal (this is known as "double threading"). Leaving a length of thread at the start and finish, work a ring of tiny running stitches (see page 48) 1/8 in. (3 mm) in from the edge of the circle. Place the button top centrally on the wrong side of the fabric circle, then pull up the stitches evenly and tightly around the shank and secure the thread ends with a knot.

2 Push the back-plate onto the back of the button top, pronged side down, with the hole over the shank. Press firmly, until it clicks in place.

Covering a metal button The metal top takes no time at all to cover—it has teeth on the underside to grip the fabric in place.

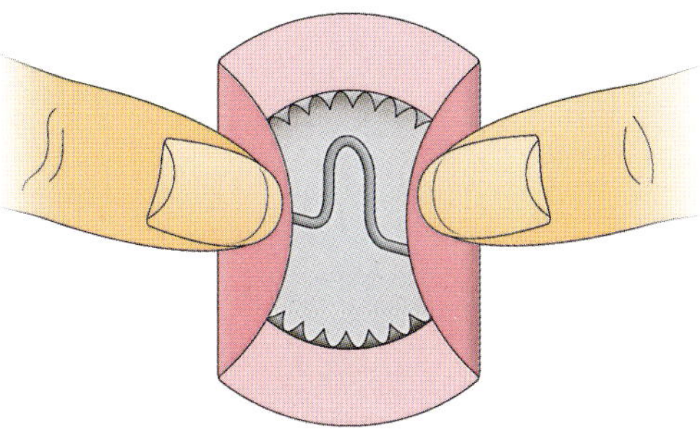

1 Cut out one fabric circle, as for Covering a plastic button (left). Place the button top centrally on the wrong side of the fabric circle and pull the fabric edges tightly around to catch on the teeth at opposite sides, working around the button top edge until the entire fabric edge is caught in place.

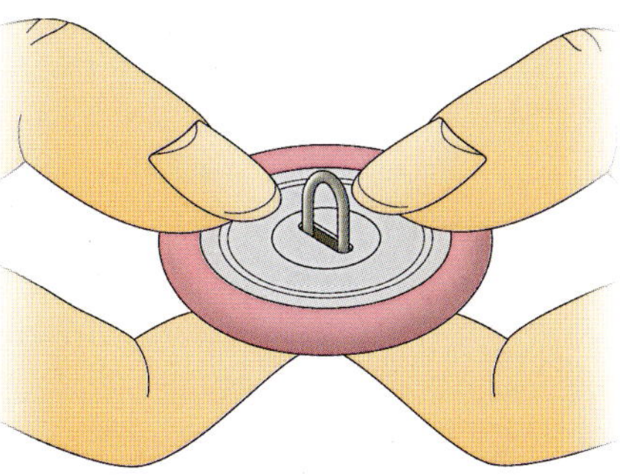

2 Making sure you have the back-plate right side up, slide the slit over the shank, and press firmly together at opposite sides to clip the pieces together.

TIP

If your fabric is sheer or loosely woven, use a circle of fabric together with a circle of lining to cover a button.

Buttonholes

There are two basic types of buttonholes. Worked buttonholes, which are the most popular, have stitched edges. Bound buttonholes, which are edged with narrow strips of fabric, are used on tailored clothes such as jackets and coats. We will be looking at machine-stitched worked buttonholes in this book, which are the easiest way to achieve a neat, professional finish.

The standard buttonhole shape is a square buttonhole, which is basically a slit through the fabric that is finished at the edges with machine zigzag stitch and a bar tack at each end (see page 69). It is stitched through all layers of the fabric at the same time—usually after the garment is complete—and cut after stitching. Most electronic and computerized machines offer several buttonhole variations, such as a rounded end, suitable for shirts and blouses in fine fabrics, and a keyhole buttonhole for jackets and coats. Check your manual to find out what your machine is capable of doing.

Calculating the length of a buttonhole

Working out the correct length for a buttonhole is crucial, as it must allow the button to pass through easily but hold the item securely fastened. Button positions and buttonholes are marked on sewing patterns, and slider or sensor buttonhole feet (see page 21) set the size of the buttonhole automatically when the button is placed in the rear of the foot—but it is still a good idea to know how to calculate a buttonhole length for yourself.

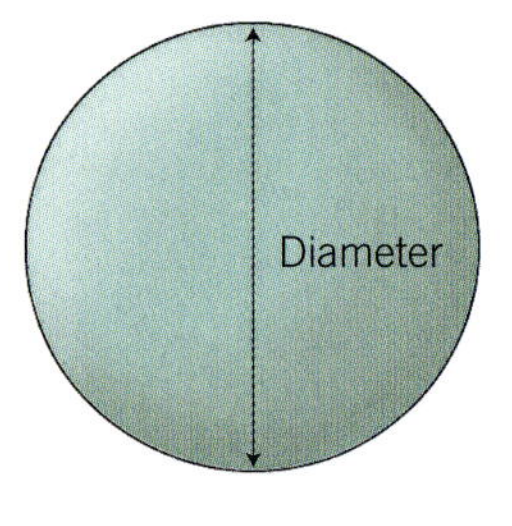

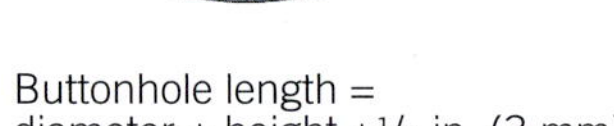

Buttonhole length = diameter + height +1/8 in. (3 mm)

The length of the buttonhole for a shank or sew-through button is determined by the diameter and height of the button. Add them together, then add an extra 1/8 in. (3 mm), which allows for the bar tacks at each end of the buttonhole.

Marking buttonholes

Vertical buttonholes normally sit along the center front line of a blouse or jacket, and are marked on commercial pattern pieces. When the garment edges are overlapped and fastened, the center lines should match. Buttons are positioned 1/8 in. (3 mm) down from the top of a vertical buttonhole. On horizontal buttonholes the button sits at the end of the buttonhole, so it must be positioned 1/8 in. (3mm) beyond the center front line, so that when the garment is fastened the buttons lie directly along the center.

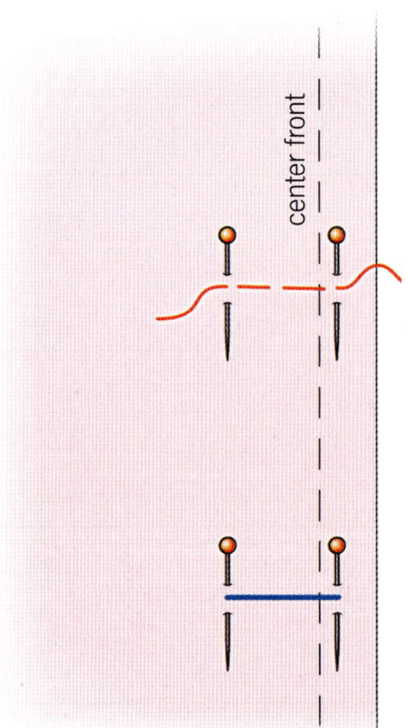

Place your pattern piece on top of your garment, matching the center front line. Mark the buttonhole positions at each end, with pins placed at 90° to the buttonhole. Remove the pattern piece, but leave the pins in position. Mark a line between the pins with either a chalk pencil or a line of basting (tacking) stitches.

TIP

Give yourself confidence by practicing making buttonholes on scrap fabric before doing it for real on your garment.

Stitching a buttonhole

Most electronic and computerized machines have built-in mechanisms that stitch buttonholes either semi-automatically or fully automatically, so there is no need to change the needle position or pivot the fabric. However, on older mechanical sewing machines you may have to work a hand-guided buttonhole. Please check your manual for the correct foot and settings for your machine.

Working a hand-guided buttonhole

This method involves setting your machine to a very close zigzag stitch. To work the bar tacks at each end, you will need the widest stitch setting; for the sides, you will need a stitch set at just less than half the width, to allow a gap between the two rows of stitching for making the slit.

1 Mark your buttonhole position and clip on the appropriate foot (usually a clear plastic one, so that you can see your stitching through it). Position the buttonhole marking centrally under the foot, lining up the needle with the end of the mark. Swing the needle to the left and make two full-width zigzag stitches across the end. Adjust the stitch width to just below half and carefully stitch down the left-hand side of the buttonhole, keeping parallel to the mark. Finish by swinging the needle to the right and down through the fabric. Raise the foot leaving the needle in the fabric.

2 Pivot the fabric through 180° and lower the foot. Make one stitch to the left and raise the needle. Adjust the stitch to full width and work four or five stitches to form a bar tack. Finish with the needle on the left.

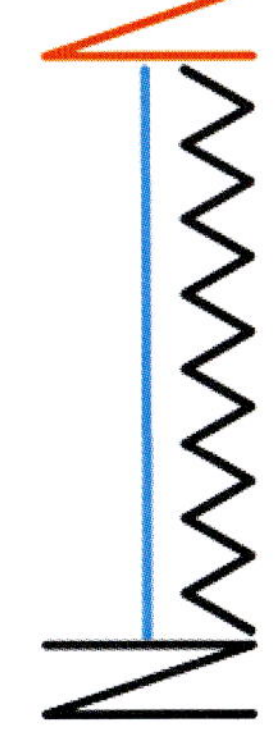

3 Raise the needle and reset the narrower stitch width, then stitch down the remaining side. Raise the needle, set the stitch back to full width again, and work three stitches to complete the final bar tack. Raise the presser foot and remove the work from the machine. Cut the thread ends, pull them through to the wrong side, and knot.

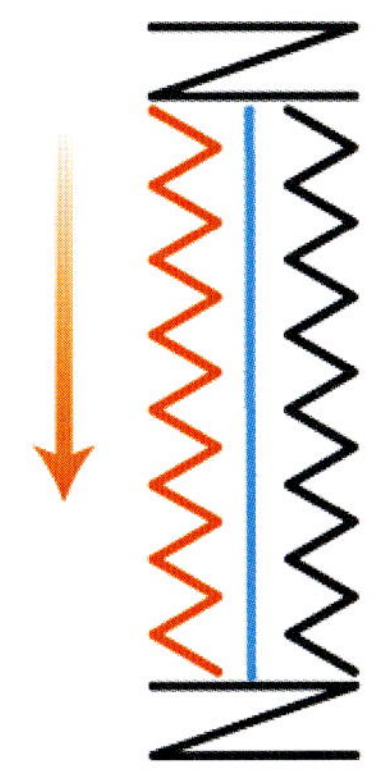

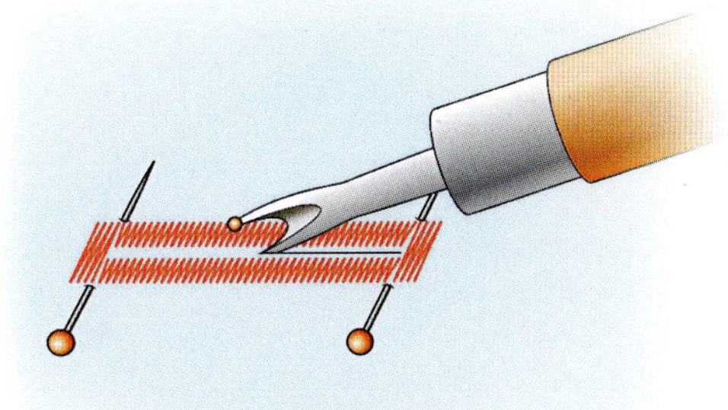

4 Place a pin at each end of buttonhole just before the bar tacks, to protect them. Using a stitch ripper (see page 23), carefully slit down the center of the buttonhole between the pins.

Working a semi-automatic buttonhole

A semi-automatic or sliding buttonhole foot has a gauge down the left-hand side to measure the buttonhole length. Before stitching you will need to mark your buttonhole position and move the slide so that the lower mark on the slider is level with the start of the buttonhole marking on your garment. Draw both threads to the left under the foot.

1 Set your machine to the first stage of the buttonhole; you may have to turn your stitch selector, or press a memory button on your machine to stitch each part of the buttonhole, so check your manual. Start the stitching: the machine will make the first bar tack. Then stitch backward up the left-hand side of the buttonhole. Stop at the top mark.

2 Press the memory button, or move your dial to stitch the next bar tack.

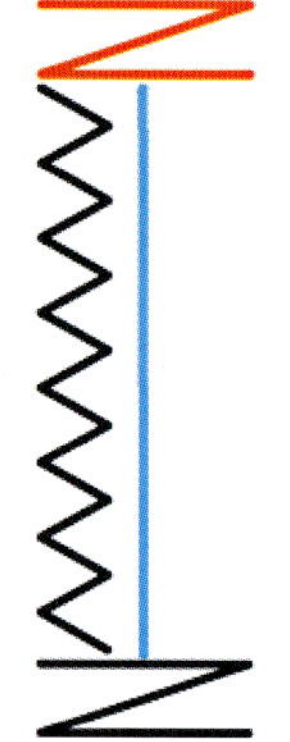

3 Finally, stitch down the remaining side of the buttonhole. Slit the center of the buttonhole as shown for a hand-guided buttonhole (see page 69).

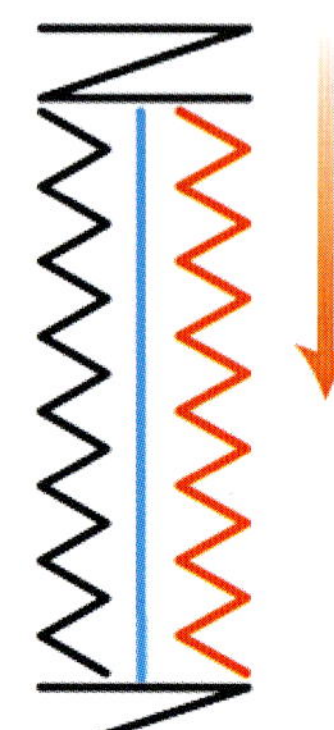

Working an automatic buttonhole

On a fully automatic buttonhole foot, you can set the buttonhole length by placing a button in the button holder. This cuts out the process of measuring beforehand. Double-check your instruction manual to find out the correct method for your particular machine.

TIP

If your stitching is not dense enough or if an extra-strong finish is required for a coat or jacket, stitch around the buttonhole a second time, over the first lot of stitching, to reinforce it.

Attach the buttonhole foot to your machine and set your machine to a square buttonhole. Put the button in the holder, pull the button holder to the back, and adjust it so that the button is held tightly in place. Pull the buttonhole lever down as far as it will go. Draw both threads to the left under the foot, then place the foot over the buttonhole position with the needle hole on the foot level with the front end of the buttonhole marking. The machine will complete the whole buttonhole to the correct length, usually all in one operation. Slit the center of the buttonhole, as shown for a hand-guided buttonhole (see page 69).

button holder

Combination fasteners

Combination fasteners are made up of two or more parts. They are mostly functional, but some can be decorative. This type of fastener includes snap fasteners, hooks and eyes, and tape fasteners.

Snap fasteners

There are two types of snap fastener: sew-on and non-sew. Both have the same method of closure—a ball and socket.

Sew-on snap fasteners, also called press studs, are purely functional and can be used where a lightweight fastening is required. They are also employed as an additional fastener and are frequently placed near the neckline edge of a garment that has a button closure. They are available in black and silver metal, or clear plastic.

Non-sew snap fasteners, sometimes called poppa snaps, are held in place by pronged rings. The holding power of these press fasteners is good, so they are suitable for heavy fabrics. They come in a variety of colors and types and in a number of weights and sizes, ideal for children's wear, casual wear, sportswear, and duvet covers.

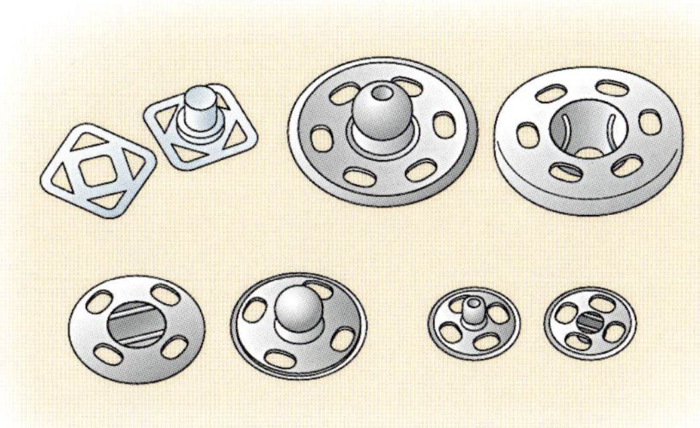

Sew-on snap fasteners

Metal sew-on snap fasteners are round and come in a range of sizes from 1/4–3/4 in. (6–20 mm) in diameter. Use them on medium- to heavyweight fabrics; the very large ones are sometimes used to close jackets. The plastic types are more delicate, and can be round or square. They are perfect for lightweight fabrics such as semi-sheers and lingerie, and are available in sizes 1/4–3/8 in. (6–10 mm).

Attaching a sew-on snap fastener

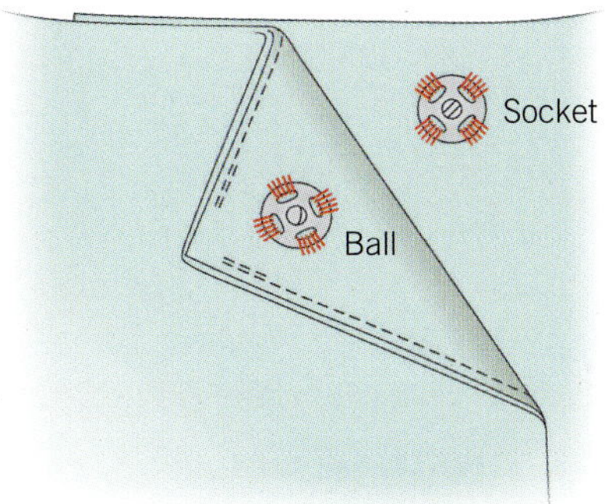

Position the ball half of the stud on the underside of the overlap, far enough in so that it will not show on the right side. Sew four hand stitches through each hole, without stitching through the right side of the garment; finish with backstitches at the stud edge. Position the socket half of the stud on the right side of the underlap to align with the ball. Stitch the socket firmly in place in the same way as the ball stud.

Non-sew snap fasteners

These fasteners consist of four parts: two caps, which form the top and base of the fastening, and a pronged ball and a pronged socket, which form the closure and anchor the caps to the fabric. There is also an open-ring version for knitted fabric that allows the fabric to show through. The position of the prongs can vary depending on the end use, but the application is pretty much the same. The fasteners come in packs complete with instructions and a special tool for attaching them; follow the manufacturer's instructions.

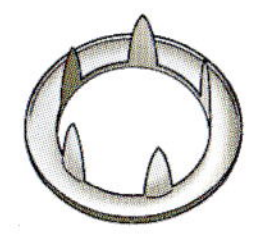
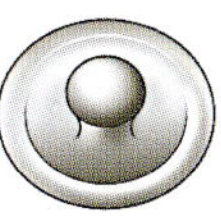

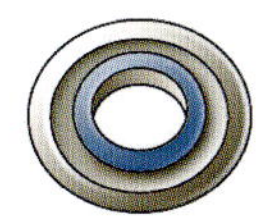

Hooks and eyes

Hooks and eyes are small, yet strong, metal fasteners. They are made in different sizes and strengths, and are frequently used on waistbands and at the top of zippers. When choosing a hook and eye, think about where it will be placed, the strain it needs to withstand, and the weight of the fabric: a small standard one is fine at a neckline, for example, but totally inadequate on a skirt waistband, where a special heavy-duty waistband hook and bar is required. Large covered hooks and eyes, with round loops, are also available for coats, jackets, and garments made from pile fabrics.

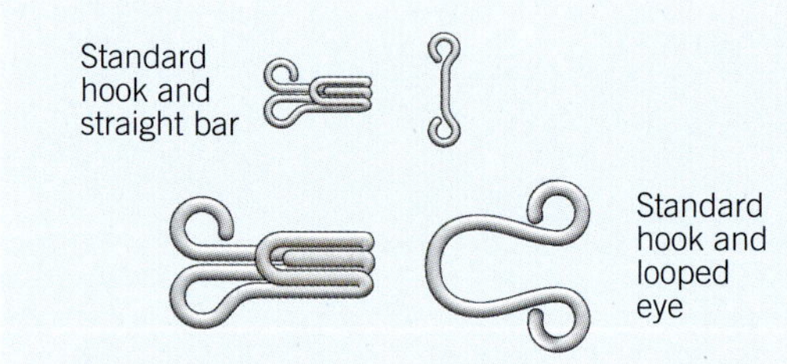

Standard hooks and eyes

These hooks and eyes come in a silver or black finish and range in size from 1 (the smallest) to 3 (the largest). The eyes may be straight or round; use a straight eye, often called a bar, when edges of your garment overlap and a round eye when edges meet.

Attaching standard hooks and eyes

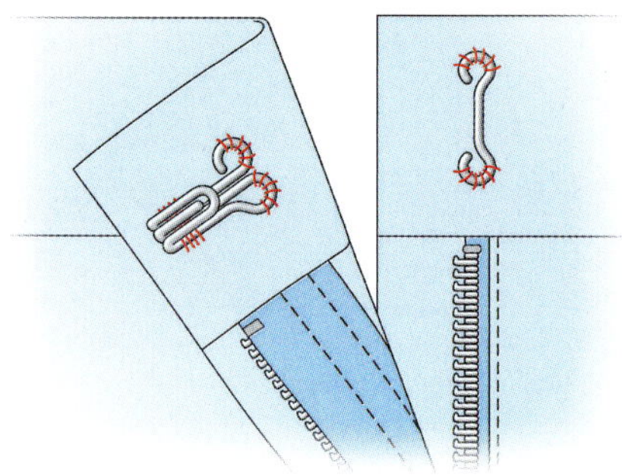

When edges overlap

Place the hook on the underside of the overlap about 1/8 in. (3 mm) in from the finished edge and mark the position with a chalk pencil. Secure the thread, then stitch around each hole without stitching through the right side of the fabric. Pass the needle between the fabric layers to the end of the hook and stitch around the neck to hold it flat to the fabric. Secure the thread with a couple of tiny stitches. Overlap the garment edges correctly, then mark the spot on the underlap where the hook end finishes. Stitch a straight eye in place at that position, stitching through each hole as before.

When garment edges butt together

Both the hook and eye are sewn on the inside. Place the hook 3/16 in. (2 mm) in from the inside edge, then mark the position with a chalk pencil and sew it in place, as shown left. Place a round eye on the other inside edge, aligned with the hook and with the loop extending slightly over the edge. Mark the position of the eye, secure the thread, and stitch in place through the holes, as for the hook. Pass the needle between the fabric layers and take three stitches around each side of the eye loop, near to the edge, to hold it flat to the fabric. Secure the thread with a couple of backstitches.

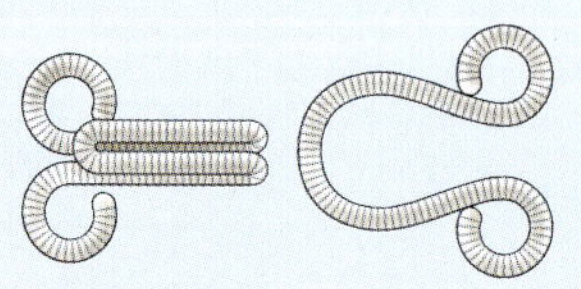

Covered hook and eye

Large, covered hooks and eyes are sometimes used as fasteners for coats and fur garments. On fabric coats they can be attached in the same way as standard hooks and eyes, but on fur coats they are often set into seams.

Waistband hook and bar

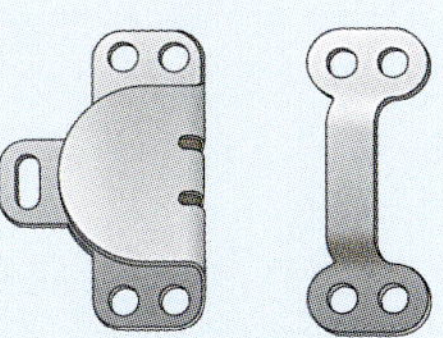

These special hooks and bars are made for use on skirt or pants waistbands. Flat and strong, they are designed to prevent the loop from sliding out of the bar easily. Use a strong topstitching thread to attach these fastenings, as they will be put under great stress.

Attaching a waistband hook and bar

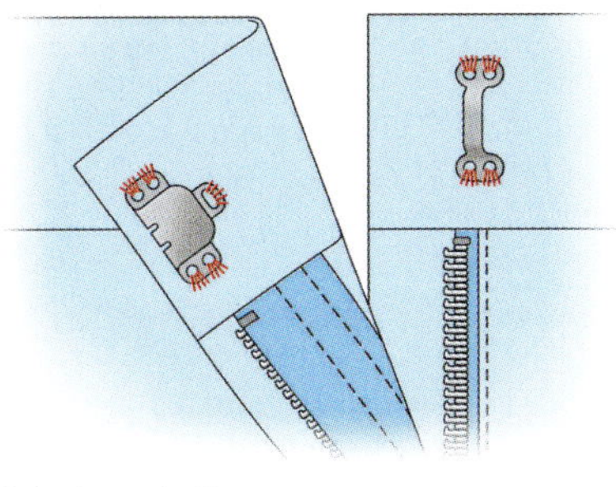

Place the hook centrally on the wrong side of the waistband overlap 1/8 in. (3 mm) from the fabric edge. Stitch in place; the front does not need to be secured. Close the opening, overlap the waistband, and place the bar on the right side of the waistband corresponding with the hook. Mark the bar position with pins, then stitch in place through each hole and all fabric layers. Secure the thread on the underside.

Tape fasteners

There are two main types of tape fasteners: hook-and-loop and snap fastener tape. Hook-and-loop fastener is made up of two tape strips—one with a looped pile, and the other with a hooked surface. When pressed together, the surfaces grip until pulled apart. Snap fastener tape has ball studs on one side and socket studs on the other, which pull apart to open.

Hook-and-loop fastener Hook-and-loop fastener comes in widths from 5/8–3/4 in. (16–20 mm) and is generally available in white, black, and beige. It may be entirely sew-on, stick-on, or sew-and-stick, where the backs of the tapes have a sticky-backed surface that is perfect for making Roman blinds (see page 106). The sew-on variety can be used on garments and on soft furnishings such as pillows (cushions) and loose covers.

Snap fastener tape Snap fastener tape, often called "poppa tape," is lighter than hook-and-loop fastener and is used on baby garments, children's wear, sportswear, and to fasten duvet covers. You will need to attach a zipper foot to your machine so that you can stitch past the snap fasteners. The short, cut tape ends of the tape are normally enclosed in a seam, so make sure that the snap fasteners are cut well clear of the seams.

TIP

To make sure the snap fasteners are aligned, cut your tape to the required length with the two halves fastened together.

Attaching hook-and-loop fastener

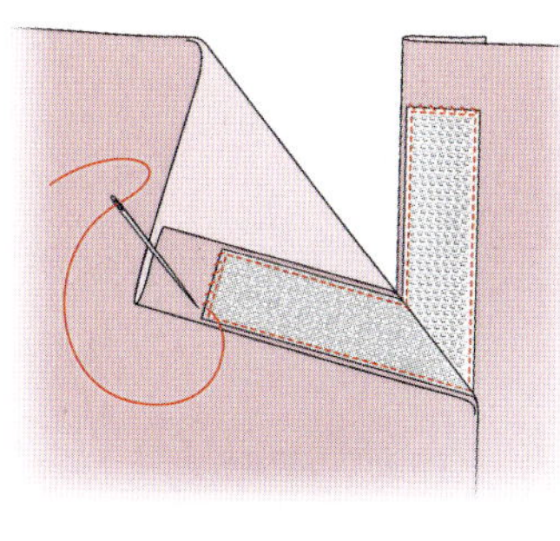

Cut the tape to length, then pin and baste (tack) the hook side to the right side of the opening underlap. The tape is tough, so use a thimble (see page 23). Machine stitch the tape in place along all edges, reverse stitching at each end to secure. Press the second side of the tape onto the first and fold over the other side of the opening. Pin in place, so that the tape is not visible from the right side. Separate the tapes, then baste and machine stitch in place, as before. Remove all basting stitches and overcast (see page 49) the cut ends, stitching through one layer of fabric only.

Attaching snap fastener tape

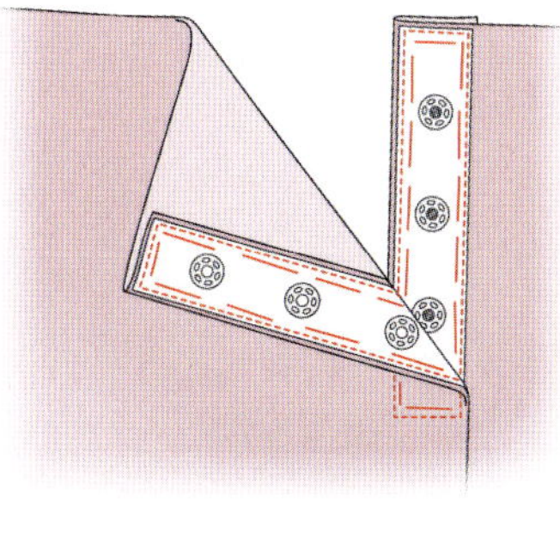

Cut tapes to length, then pin and baste (tack) the smooth side of the ball tape to the wrong side of the opening overlap, with the outer edge of the tape just inside the edge of the fabric. Using a zipper foot, stitch the tape in place, working close to the tape edges through all the layers of fabric and reverse stitching at the start and finish to secure. Position the smooth side of the socket tape on the right side of the underlap, with the sockets and balls aligned and the outer edge of the tape just inside the finished edge of the fabric. Pin, baste, and machine stitch the tape in place in the same way as the ball tape.

Lined tote bag

There's plenty of room in this versatile bag to stash all your kit. Made from stylish felt, the topstitching picks out the colors of the bright print lining and it fastens securely with a pair of matching buttons.

You will need

- Bag pattern pieces traced off from the pattern sheet at the back of this book (see page 114)
- 2/3 yd (60 cm) of 36-in.- (90-cm-) wide felt
- 2/3 yd (60 cm) of 44-in.- (112-cm-) wide coordinating cotton print fabric for the lining
- 1/4 yd (20 cm) of 36-in.- (90-cm-) wide lightweight iron-on interfacing (see page 134)
- Two 1-in. (25-mm) decorative buttons
- Two reinforcement buttons
- Matching threads
- Topstitching thread to match the lining
- Dressmaker's carbon paper—available from good notions (haberdashery) departments in white, red, blue, and yellow

Note

- 3/8-in. (1-cm) seam allowances are included unless otherwise stated.
- Stitch seams with right sides together, unless otherwise instructed.

1 From felt and lining fabrics, cut out two bag pieces, two straps, and one flap, keeping the grainlines parallel to the selvages and using the diagram as a guide. Using a chalk pencil, transfer the strap and flap positions to the wrong side of each felt bag piece. From the interfacing cut two straps and one flap, using the diagram as a guide. Staystitch the top edges of the felt bag and flap pieces and staystitch across the short ends of the strap (see page 141).

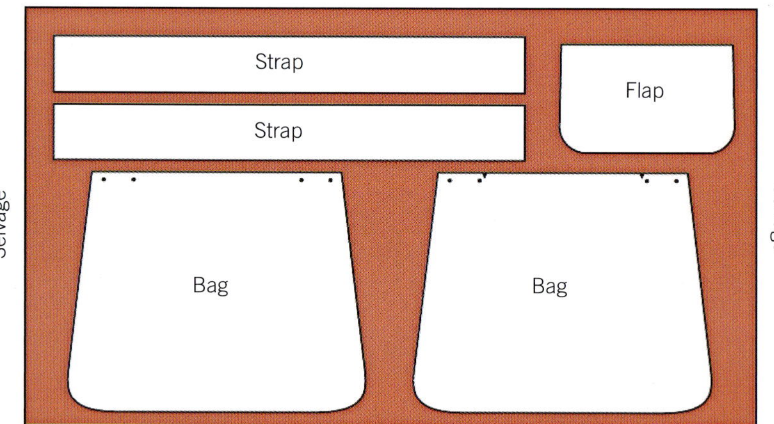

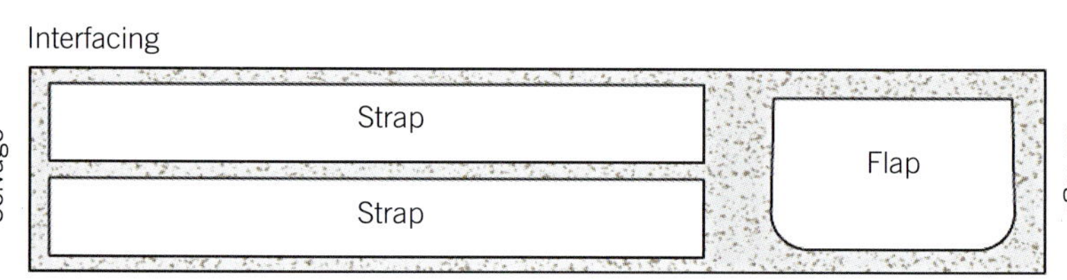

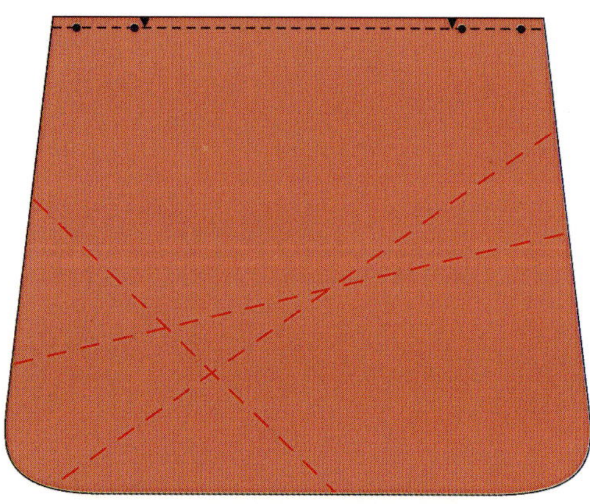

2 Trace the topstitching lines onto one felt bag piece. To do this, place the dressmaker's carbon paper ink side down, on the right side of the fabric. Lay the pattern piece back on top and trace over the design lines using a pencil. Remove the pattern and carbon paper to reveal the design. Thread the top of your sewing machine with the topstitching thread and set your machine to a medium-length stitch; topstitch along the three design lines.

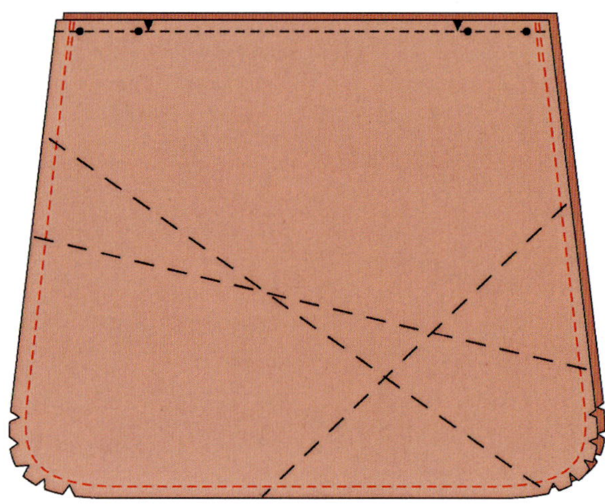

3 Re-thread your machine with standard sewing thread and change your stitch to a shorter length. With right sides together, pin and baste (tack) the topstitched front bag to the remaining felt bag piece around the side and lower edges. Machine stitch the pieces together, reverse stitching at each end to secure. For extra strength, work a second row of stitching over the first. Notch the seam allowances around the curves (see page 44) and turn the bag right side out. Press the seamed edges flat (see Tip, left).

4 Repeat step 3 with the two bag lining pieces, but leave a 5-in. (12.5-cm) opening centrally along the lower edge so that you can turn the lining right side out at a later stage.

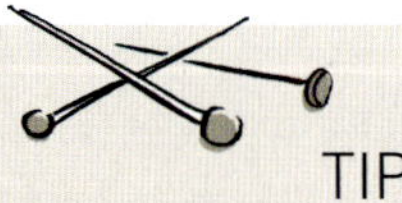

TIP

Press the felt with a medium dry iron. It is a good idea to use a dry pressing cloth between the iron and the felt fabric, as the felt may shine where seams and seamed edges are pressed.

5 Iron the interfacing to the wrong side of the lining flap (see page 134). With right sides together, pin and baste (tack) the felt flap to the lining flap around the lower edge. Machine stitch the pieces together, reverse stitching at each end to secure. Layer the seam allowances and notch the curves (see page 43).

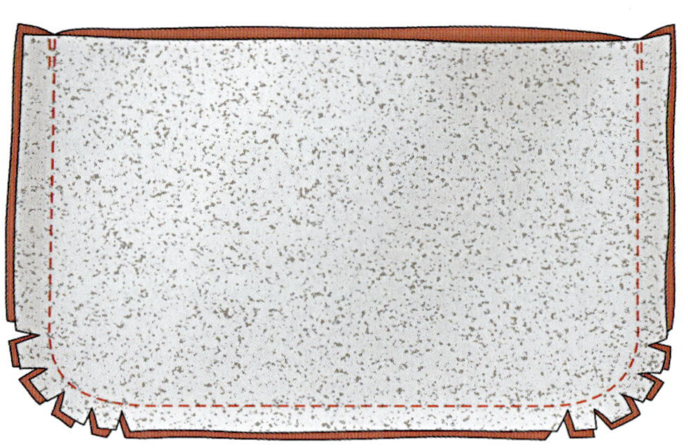

6 Turn the flap right side out. Working carefully from the lining side, press the seamed edges flat and then topstitch ¼ in. (6 mm) in from the seamed edge. Pin and baste (tack) the top raw edges together.

7 Iron the interfacing to the wrong side of each lining strap. With right sides together, pin and baste (tack) each felt strap to a lining strap down each long edge. Machine stitch the pieces together, reverse stitching at each end to secure. Remove the basting stitches and trim the seam allowances down to ¼ in. (6 mm).

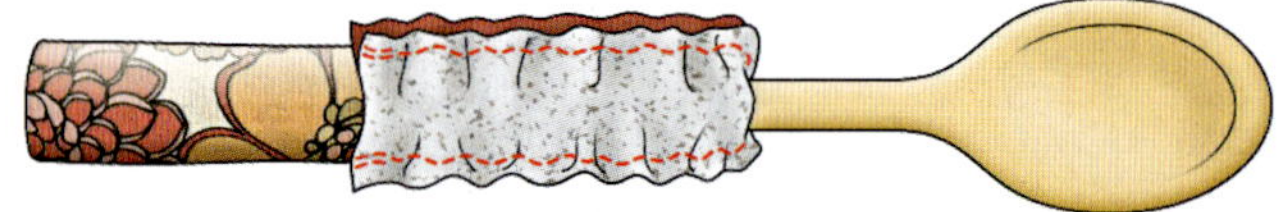

8 Machine stitch across one short end of each strap. To turn straps to the right side, push the handle of a wooden spoon or similar object into the stitched end and work it through the entire length. Unpick the short end and press the straps flat. Pin and baste (tack) across each short raw end and topstitch down each long edge.

9 With the right sides of the felt together, pin the basted (tacked) top edge of the flap centrally to the top edge of the back bag, between the marks; keeping the raw edges level, baste in place. With the right sides of the felt together, pin the short basted ends of one strap to the top edge of the back bag at the positions marked; keeping the raw edges level, baste in place. Repeat with the remaining strap and the front bag. Machine stitch both straps and the flap in place.

10 With right sides together, place the bag inside the lining. Keeping the raw edges level and matching the side seams, pin and baste (tack) around the top edge, sandwiching the flap and straps in between. Machine stitch the pieces together, then work a second row of stitching over the first to strengthen the flap and strap attachment. Trim and layer the seam allowances.

11 Turn the bag right side out through the opening in the lower edge of the lining. Slipstitch the opening edges together (see page 49). Push the lining inside the bag. Working from the lining side, press the seamed top edge flat.

12 Baste (tack) the bag and the lining together around the top edge, keeping the flap and straps clear. Topstitch ¼ in. (6 mm) in from this edge through all layers of fabric. Work two buttonholes at the positions marked on the flap pattern (see page 68) and stitch the buttons to the front bag to correspond, adding the reinforcement buttons at the same time (see page 66).

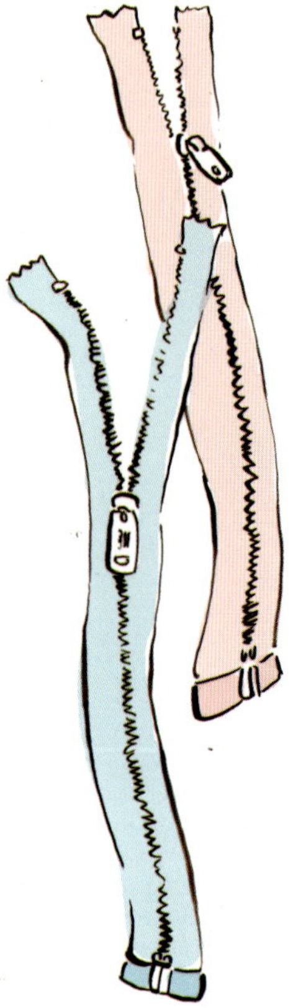

Zippers & decorative touches

This workshop cover the different types of zipper available and how to insert a conventional zipper. We will also be looking at decorative touches—ways to embellish your sewn items by adding a finishing flourish to an otherwise plain project. Once you have mastered these techniques, you will be able to go ahead and make the more advanced pillow (cushion) cover featured at the end of this workshop.

All zipped up

Elias Howe (who also invented the sewing machine) invented the zipper fastener in 1851. The "hookless fastener," as it was named, didn't become popular for clothing until the 1930s, but zippers are probably one of the most common types of fastening used today. Zippers are available in different types, weights, and lengths. There are three main types: conventional, concealed, and open-ended.

Conventional zippers

Plastic-toothed zipper

Top stops
Slider
Tab
Tape
Teeth
Bottom stop

Metal-toothed zipper

Top stops
Teeth
Slider
Tab
Tape
Bottom stop

These have either plastic or metal teeth attached to a woven tape. The zipper is permanently closed at the base with a "stopper" and locks at the top for firm fastening. Available in a wide range of colors, this type of zipper is sewn into an opening in a seam and is suitable for dresses, skirts, and tops. The plastic-toothed varieties are lighter and more pliable (ideal for lightweight cottons, viscose, silk, and polyester crepe de chine). Use metal zippers for thicker fabrics or where the opening requires a much stronger fastening, such as on jeans.

Concealed zippers

Concealed zippers have no teeth showing on the right side and are inserted with a special zipper foot attached to your machine. The zipper is stitched in place from the wrong side and for this reason it is harder to sew in place well. It is a good idea to master conventional zippers before attempting a concealed one.

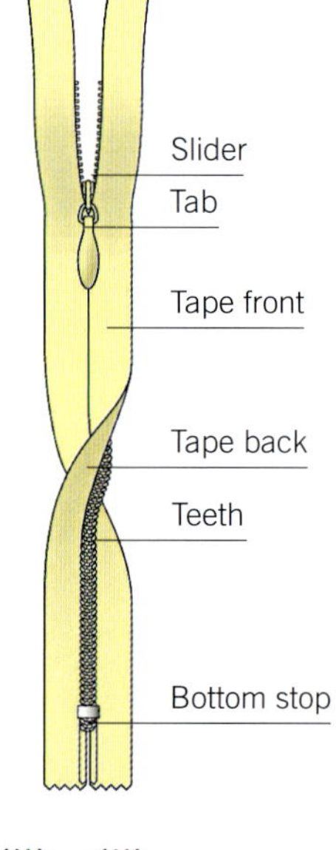

Open-ended zippers

These are open at both ends and are sewn into a seam that is required to open and close completely. They are available with both plastic and metal teeth, although color choice is usually more restricted than in the other two zipper types. Used in jackets and leisurewear, this type of zipper is inserted in much the same way as a conventional zipper, but it can also be sewn with the zipper teeth exposed, as a design feature.

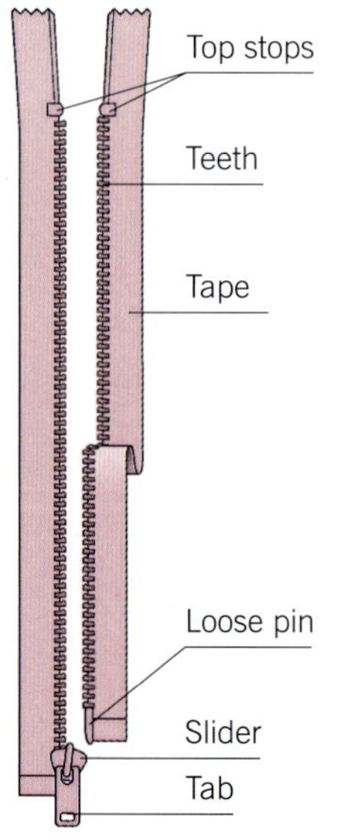

Inserting a conventional zipper

There are two ways of inserting a conventional zipper—the centered zipper method, where the zipper sits down the center of the opening with the stitching that holds the zipper in place machined at an equal distance from the seamline, and the lapped zipper method, in which one edge of the opening is stitched close to the zipper teeth and the open edge is lapped over the zipper teeth, covering the first row of stitching.

Centered zipper method

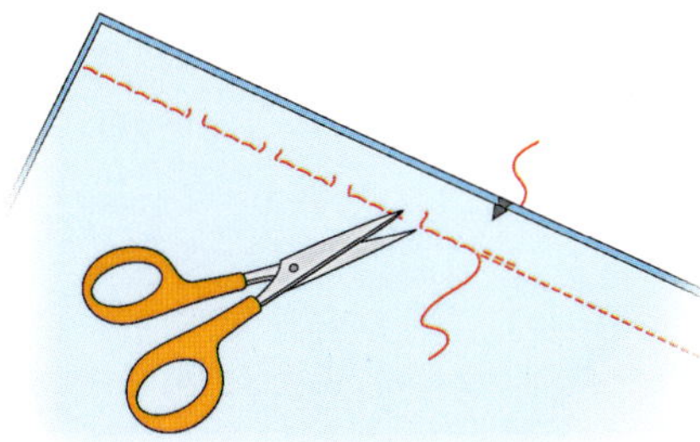

1 Stitch the garment seam up to the zipper notch; reverse stitch to secure. Adjust your machine stitch length to the largest size and machine baste (tack) the zipper opening edges together without reverse stitching at the ends. Using a sharp pair of small scissors, snip the stitches on the bobbin thread at 1/2-in. (12-mm) intervals along the zipper opening, to allow for easy removal later on. Neaten the seam turnings (see page 44) and press the seam open.

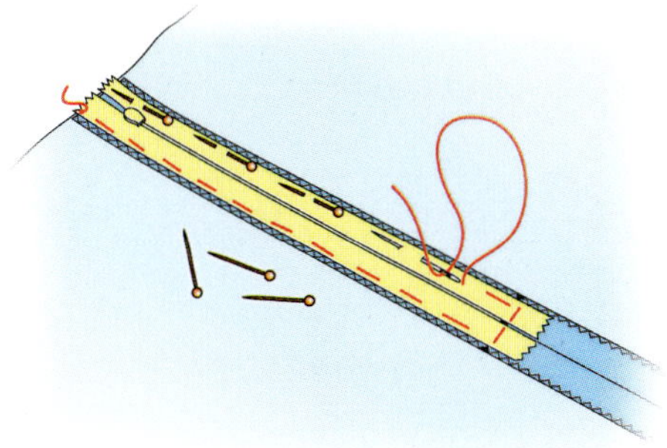

2 Place the zipper face down on the seam turnings, so that the zipper teeth run centrally down the seam and the bottom "stopper" is just below the notch. Pin and baste (tack) the zipper in place.

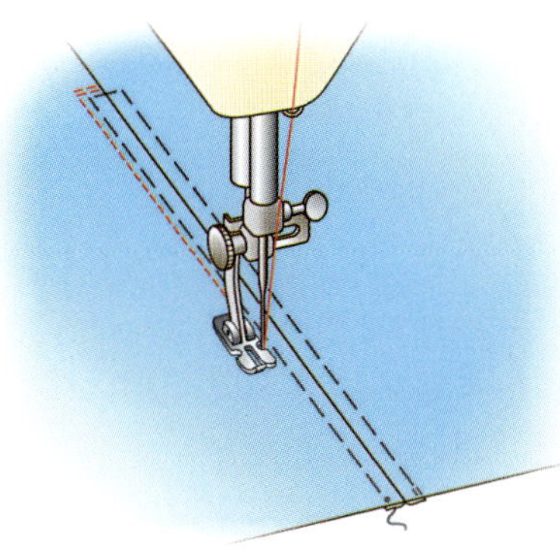

3 Working from the right side of the garment, with a regular stitch length on your machine, stitch the zipper in place. To do this, have your zipper foot to the left of the needle; starting just below the zipper stopper at the seamline, work three or four stitches across the bottom, pivot your work (see page 42), and stitch up to the top of the zipper, keeping your stitching parallel to the seamline. Reverse stitch at each end of the stitching to secure.

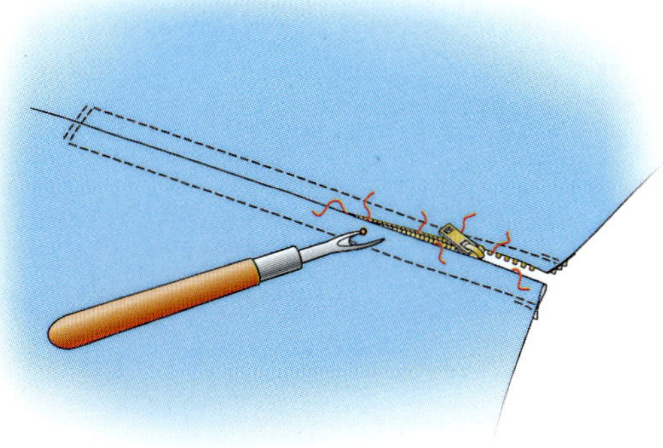

4 Re-position the zipper foot to the right of the needle; starting again at the base of the zipper, stitch the other side in place, as before. Remove the basting (tacking) stitches and unpick the seam covering the zipper teeth.

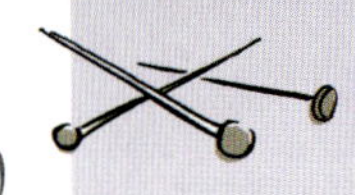

Lapped zipper method

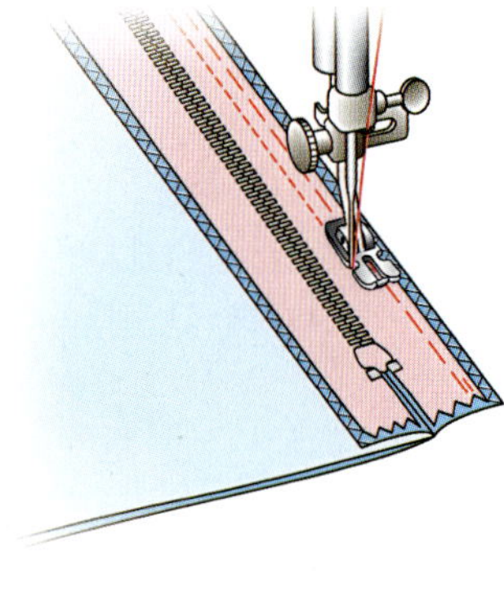

1 Follow step 1 of the centered zipper method. To position the zipper, open out the right-hand seam allowance and place the zipper face down on top, so that the zipper teeth run centrally down the seamline and the bottom "stopper" is just below the notch; pin and baste (tack) the zipper in place. Position your zipper foot to the right of the needle and machine stitch in place about 1/4 in. (6 mm) away from the teeth.

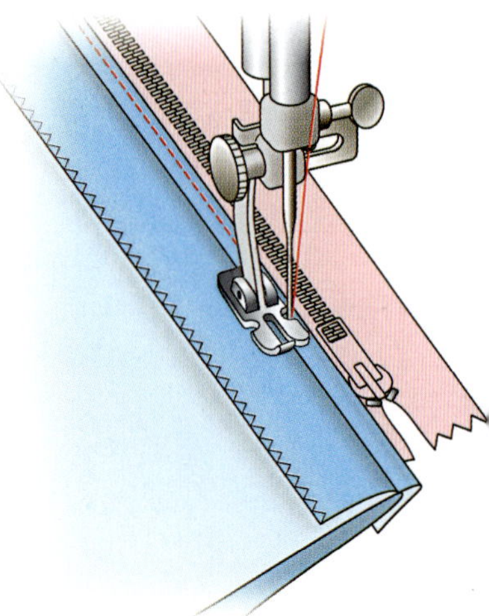

2 Turn the zipper face up, forming a fold in the seam allowance. Bring the fold close to the zipper teeth, but not over them, and pin in place. Re-position your zipper foot to the left of the needle and stitch along the edge of the fold through all thicknesses.

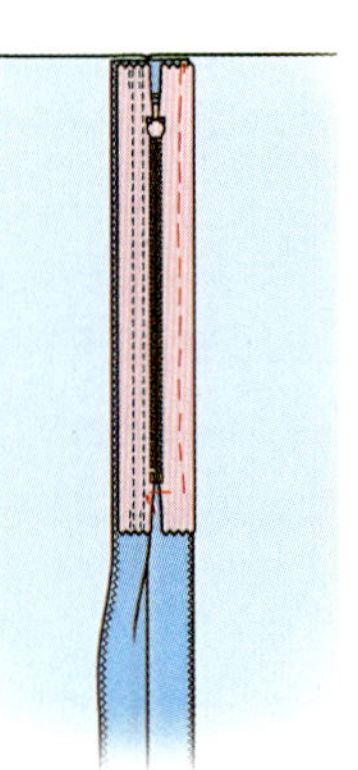

3 With wrong side uppermost, lay your garment out flat. Pin and baste (tack) the loose zipper tape in position, through all layers of fabric.

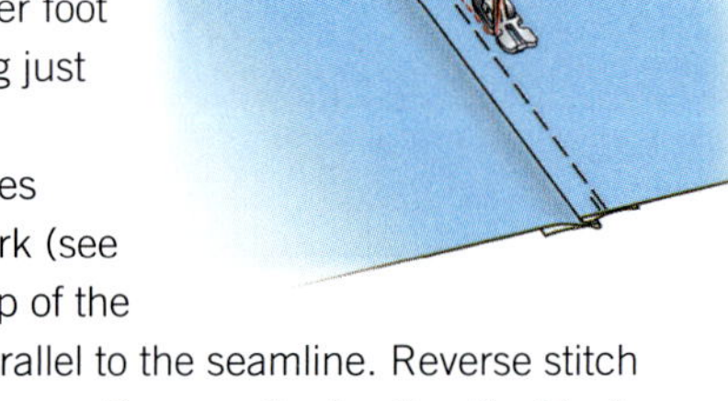

4 Working from the right side of the garment, with a regular stitch length on your machine, stitch the zipper in place. To do this, have your zipper foot to the right of the needle; starting just below the zipper stopper at the seamline, work four or five stitches across the bottom, pivot your work (see page 42), and stitch up to the top of the zipper, keeping your stitching parallel to the seamline. Reverse stitch at each end of the stitching to secure. Remove the basting (tacking) stitches and unpick the seam covering the zipper teeth.

TIPS

- If you cannot buy a zipper that is an exact color match, pick a shade that is darker, not lighter, than your fabric.
- Tweezers are helpful for removing any stubborn stitches, when unpicking the temporary stitches covering the zipper teeth.

Decorative edgings

There is an enormous variety of ready-made trimmings available from notions (haberdashery) stores. From lace and ribbons, to rickrack and Russia braid, fringing and tassels, each adds a finishing touch to an otherwise plain project—but sometimes it is preferable to make your own trimmings and decorations. The edging you choose should not be too heavy for the fabric to which you are attaching it. It can either match or contrast with it in both color and texture. If you want to use it to trim around a corner or curved edge, it is also important to check that the braid or edging is flexible.

A manufactured edging, whether it is beaded, fringed, corded, or bobbled, always has one decorative edge and a band or tape on the opposite side to stitch them on with. The band or tape can be set into a seam, or tucked under an edge and topstitched in place. These types of edgings are great for curtains and drapes, pillows (cushions), and tie-backs.

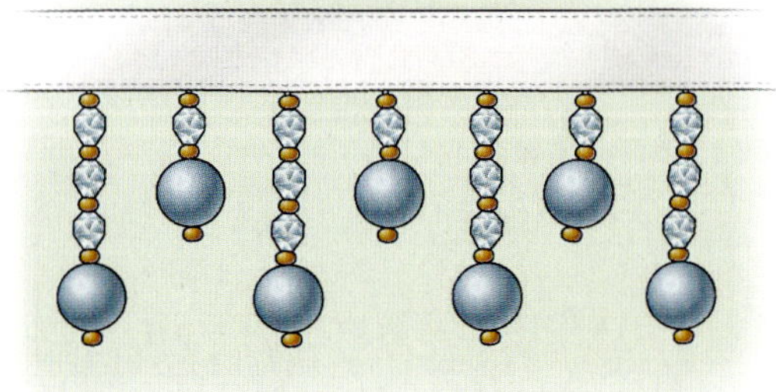

Flat trims

Flat trims such as ribbon can be topstitched to fabric. Crisp, mitered corners are essential.

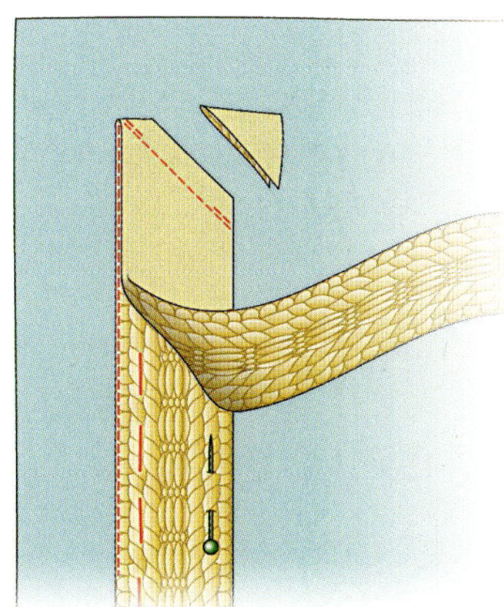

1 Pin and baste (tack) the trim right side up along the first edge, up to the corner. Machine stitch along the outer edge. At the corner, fold the trim straight back over the stitched length. Working from the corner point, machine stitch diagonally across the trim, reverse stitching at each end to secure. Cut off any excess trim close to the stitching to reduce bulk (see page 43).

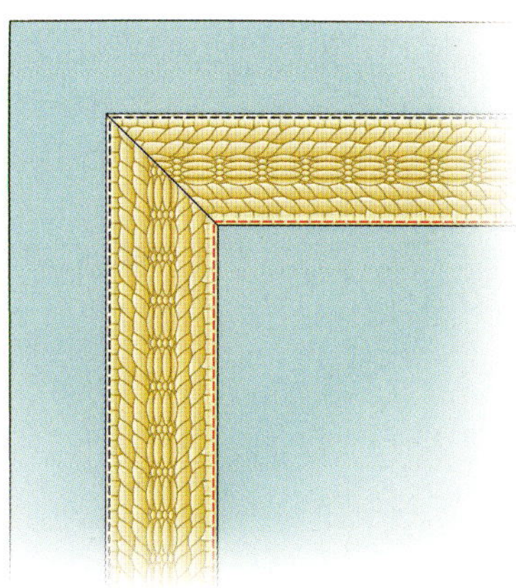

2 Fold back the trim along the next edge, and repeat step 1. Continue around your piece and then join the trim together to fit at the final corner. Stitch along the inner edge of the trim to anchor it firmly in place.

TIP

Cut strips of fabric along the selvage and pull away the threads to form a fringed trim. You can then set the selvage into a seam, such as around the edge of a collar or across a blouse yoke to form a fringed trim.

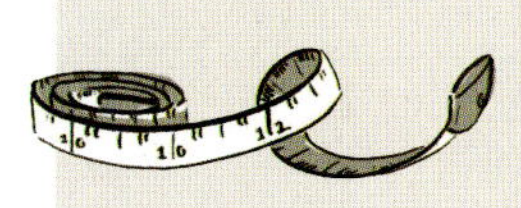

Fringing

Although there are plenty of ready-made fringes available, it is more creative and much more fun to make your own. Fringing is made by removing either the weft or warp threads (see page 26) at the edge of a piece of woven fabric. Not all fabrics are suitable: wool and linen fabrics with a plain weave (see page 26) are the best types to use. A fine wool scarf or linen napkins can be made quickly by this method.

1 Make sure that the edge of the fabric is cut absolutely straight. Decide how long the fringe should be and make a row of machine stitches along this line to prevent the fringe from growing deeper than you want it to be.

2 Using a pin, carefully remove the threads that lie parallel to the row of stitching, starting at the edge of the fabric and working inward until you have reached the stitching line. You will find it easier to pull out one or two threads at a time.

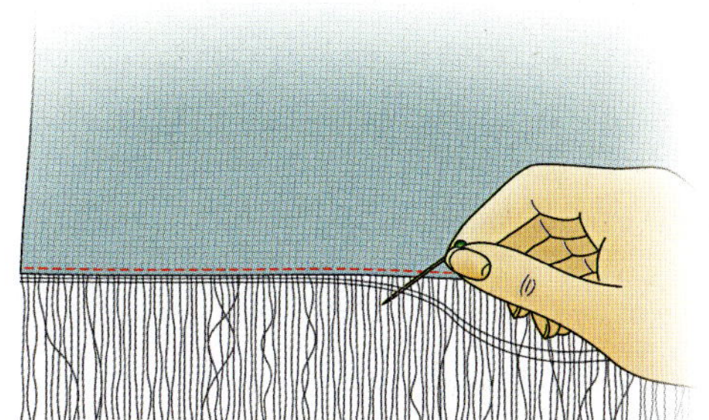

Piping

Piping is made from piping cord covered with a strip of bias-cut fabric or manufactured as a finished decorative cord attached to a tape with which to set it into a seam. Both types of cord are available from good notions (haberdashery) stores, but it is rare to come across ready-made piping in a good selection of colors; it is also often expensive, so it is better to make your own. Self-covering piping cord is normally white and comes in different sizes, with 00 being the finest and 6 the thickest.
Choose the size to suit the style of your project and fabric type.

TIP

If your finished article is to be washed, check that the piping cord is pre-shrunk.

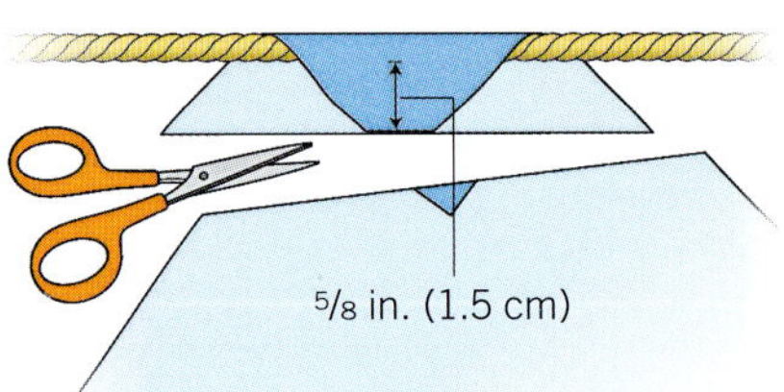

1 To gauge the width of your fabric strip, measure around the cord and allow an extra 1¼ in. (3 cm) for seam allowances. Alternatively, fold a corner of your fabric over the piping cord and pin, encasing the cord snugly, then measure ⅝ in. (1.5 cm) out from the pin and cut. Open out the fabric strip to find the correct width.

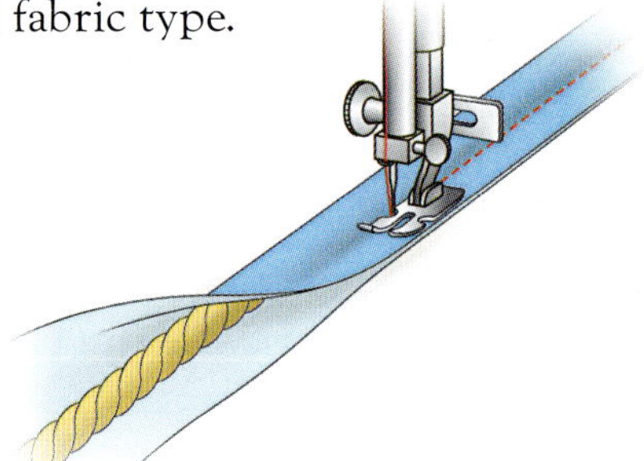

2 Cut out and make up the bias fabric strips following steps 1–3 of Making bias binding (page 54). To cover the cord, place the piping cord down the center of the bias strip on the wrong side. Bring the long edges of the bias strip together around the cord and stitch down the length close to the cord, using a zipper foot on your machine.

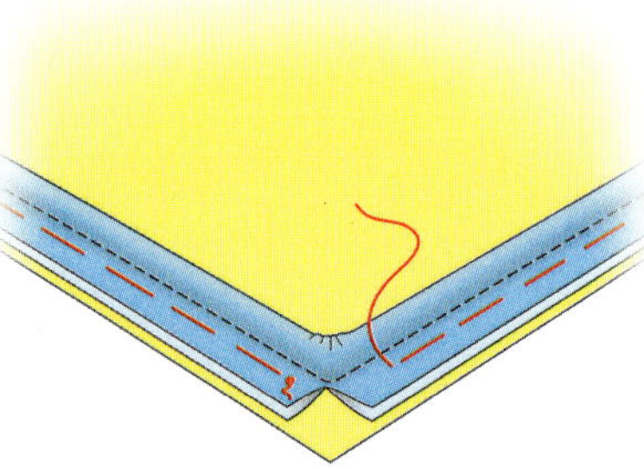

3 Baste (tack) the piping to the right side of one piece of fabric, with raw edges level and the cord facing inward. If the piping is going around a corner, snip into the piping seam allowances to help it bend. If the piping is going around a curved edge, clip into the piping seam allowances at regular intervals to allow it to curve smoothly (see page 43).

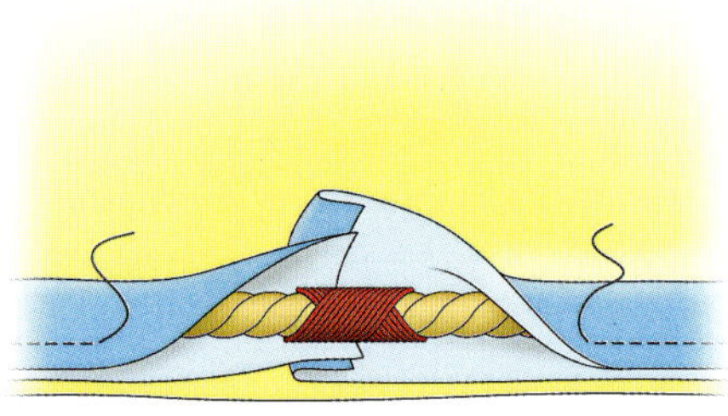

4 If the ends of the cord need to be joined, unpick the machine stitches on the piping for about 2 in. (5 cm) at each end and fold back the bias strip. Trim the cord ends so they butt together, then bind the ends together with thread. Turn under ¼ in. (6 mm) of fabric at one end of the bias strips to neaten, and slip this over the raw end. Baste (tack) the ends neatly in place.

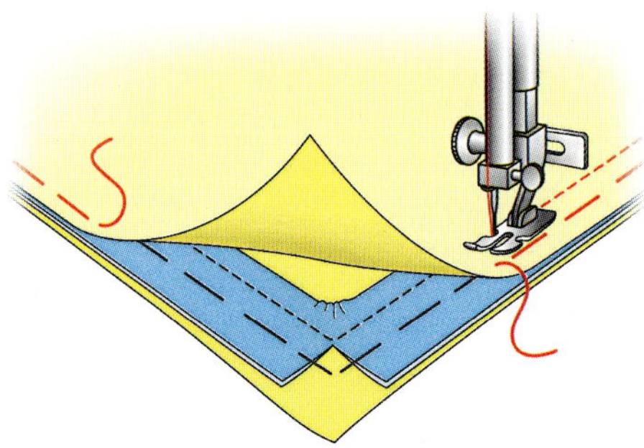

5 Lay the second fabric piece over the first, with right sides facing and raw edges level. Pin, baste (tack), and machine stitch the pieces together, close to the cord, using a zipper foot on your machine. Remove the basting stitches.

Appliqué

Appliqué is a very versatile method of applying small pieces of fabric to a background fabric to create decorative effects. Appliqué has been practiced all over the world for centuries, using many different styles and methods. In this book we will show you one of the simplest machine methods: satin-stitch appliqué, using paper-backed adhesive web. This paper-backed adhesive web is ironed on to your fabric, which melts the glue, allowing you to stick fabric pieces together.

TIP

You will find it easier to do appliqué before you start to construct your garment, so make sure that your motifs are correctly positioned.

1 Cut a piece of contrast fabric and paper-backed adhesive web (available from sewing stores) large enough to fit the motif that you want to appliqué. Using a hot iron and following the manufacturer's instructions, stick the adhesive web to the wrong side of your contrasting fabric.

2 Trace your motif onto the paper side of the adhesive web and cut out the shape. If you are using a motif on a printed fabric, there is no need to draw the shape on the paper, simply cut around the edges of the design.

3 Remove the paper backing from your motif and position it on your main fabric. Using a hot iron and following the manufacturer's instructions, stick the motif in place.

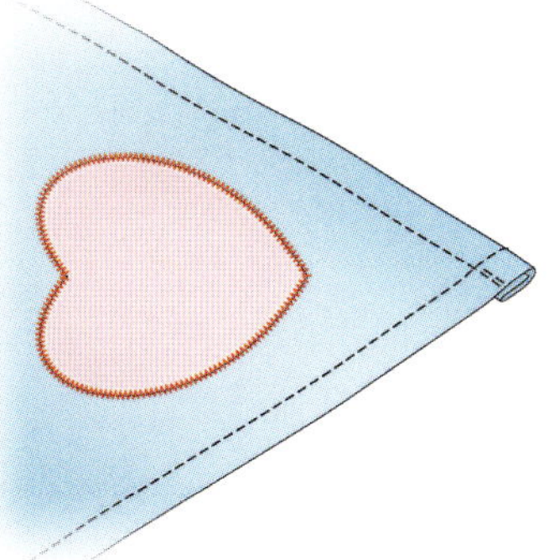

4 Set your sewing machine to a medium width, short length zigzag stitch and stitch around the edges of your motif, enclosing the raw edges. You can use either a matching or contrasting thread for your stitching.

Zippered & piped pillow

Once you have mastered edging techniques, there is no end to the different variations you can make. We used a contrast color of piping around the edges, but you could insert any type of edging—lace for a bedroom, bobble trim for a child's room, for example. Alternatively, you could use a plain fabric and decorate it with a braid or ribbon trim or appliqué a motif to the front. Let your imagination run wild! If you want to use a one-way printed fabric, see Allowing for pattern repeats on page 100 for details of how to work out how much fabric you will need.

You will need

- 2/3 yd (50 cm) 45-in.- (137-cm-) wide plain or small multi-directional fabric
- 3/4 yd (70 cm) 45-in.- (137-cm-) wide contrasting fabric for the piping
- 12-in. (30-cm) matching zipper
- 2 yd (1.8 m) No 5 piping cord
- Matching thread
- 16 x 16-in. (41 x 41-cm) pillow form (cushion pad)

Note

- 5/8-in. (1.5-cm) seam allowances are included unless otherwise stated.
- Stitch seams with right sides together, unless otherwise instructed.

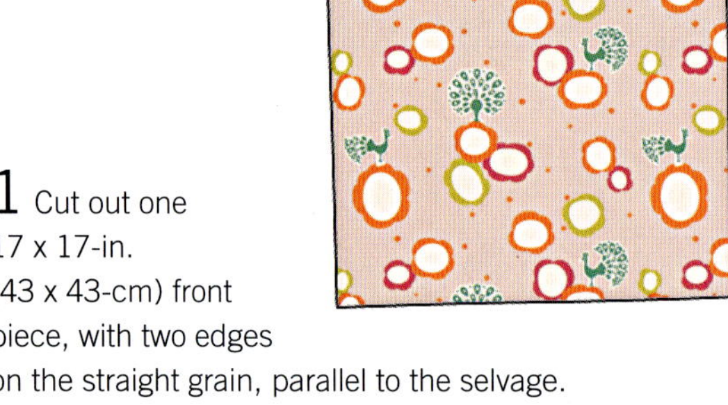

1 Cut out one 17 x 17-in. (43 x 43-cm) front piece, with two edges on the straight grain, parallel to the selvage. Cut out two 17 x 9-in. (43 x 23-cm) back pieces, with the long edges on the straight grain.

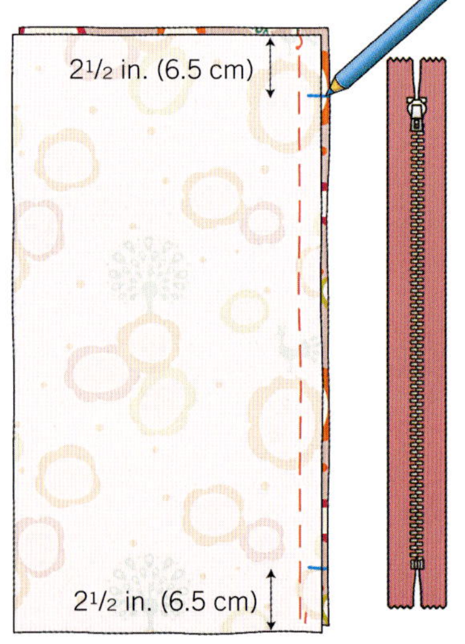

2 Place the two back pieces on top of each other, with the raw edges matching, and baste (tack) the center back edges together. Mark the zipper position with a piece of tailor's chalk or a chalk pencil along the center back seam allowances, 2 1/2 in. (6.5 cm) in from each short edge. Machine stitch the zipper in place, following instructions for the Centered zipper method on page 79; you will also need to work three or four stitches across the top of the zipper to the center seamline, pivoting your work as shown for the bottom of the zipper.

LOS ANGELES

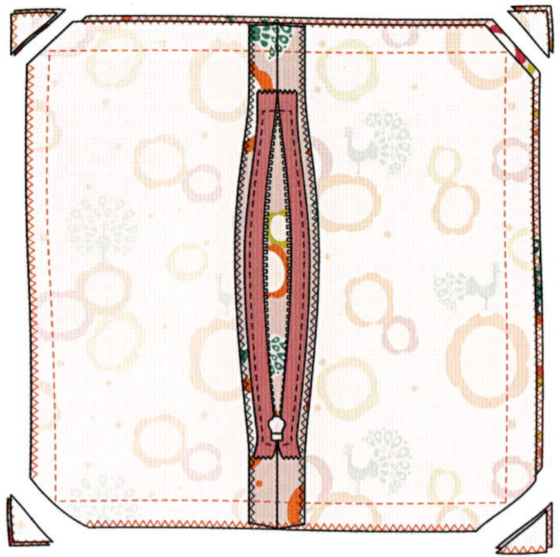

3 Make up and attach the piping cord to the right side of the front, following steps 1–4 on page 82, then open the zipper and attach the back following step 5. Neaten the seam allowances together (see page 44), remove the basting (tacking) stitches, trim the corners (see page 43), and turn the cover through to the right side. Insert the pillow form (cushion pad) through the zipper opening.

It's all in the detail

You could be forgiven for thinking that the back of a pillow is less important than the front, as it will not be on show, but taking care over the details will give your sewing projects that all-important professional-looking finish.

In the photo above left, you can see how carefully and accurately the fabric pattern has been matched across the center back seam on either side of the zipper. If you're planning to use a one-way printed fabric such as this, turn to page 100 for details of how to work out how much fabric you will need and how to match pattern repeats.

Now look at the photo above right and see how beautifully the piping matches a color in the fabric print. In both cases, the plain-colored piping picks out a color from a printed motif, rather than the background color, so it creates a distinctive edge. Always take your main fabric with you when shopping for piping fabric, so that you can be sure you've got a good match.

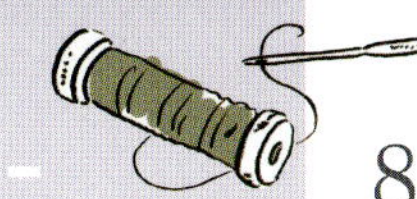

Pillow (cushion) types

Although pillows vary greatly in shape and size, there are basically only two types: knife-edged and box-edged.

A knife-edged pillow is one that is thickest at the center and then tapers off at the edges, so that there is no side depth. A box-edged pillow is the same thickness from the center to the edge, so the sides need to be covered with a separate boxing strip. A bolster is actually a type of box-edged pillow. Both types are used as scatter pillows, but the box-edged variety are also used for chair seat pads.

Knife-edged pillows are normally soft and filled with feathers or polyester fiber, whereas box-edged pillows are generally made from foam rubber wrapped with polyester batting (wadding) when used as seat pads. In this book, we only deal with knife-edged pillows and bolsters.

Making a pillow pattern

If you want to re-cover an existing pillow, or make a different size to the one that we have suggested, it is best to make yourself a paper pattern to work out how much fabric you will need to buy. To do this you will need to measure your pillow form (cushion pad).

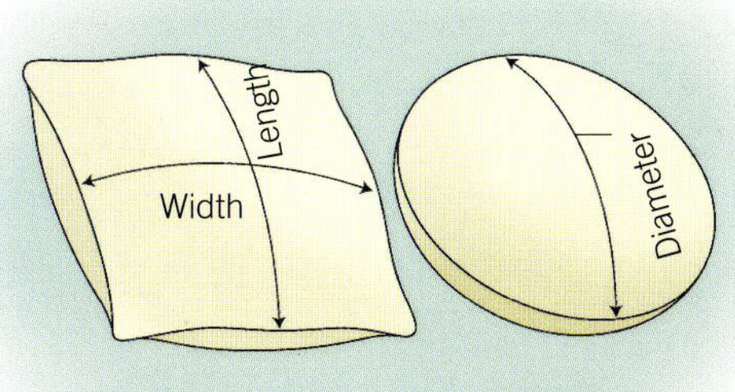

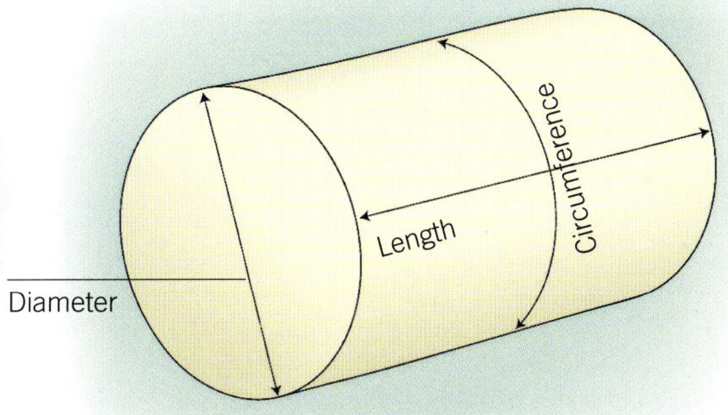

Knife-edged

If your form (pad) is square or rectangular, measure the length and width; if it is circular, measure the diameter. Draw up a pattern piece to these measurements for the front cover, adding a 5/8-in. (1.5-cm) seam allowance to all edges. For the back pattern piece, fold the front pattern in half and trace around the shape onto a second piece of paper, adding a further 5/8-in. (1.5-cm) seam allowance to what was the folded edge; this will become your center back seam. To calculate your zipper length, measure your pattern piece along the center back seam, and allow for a zipper approximately 5 in. (12.5 cm) shorter than this measurement.

Bolster

Measure the diameter of the ends, the length of the bolster, and the circumference. Draw up one pattern piece for the main part of the cushion, using the length and circumference measurements, and then one for the ends, using the diameter. (Remember to add a 5/8-in./1.5-cm seam allowance to all edges.) To calculate your zipper length, measure your main pattern piece along the length measurement, and allow for a zipper approximately 5 in. (12.5 cm) shorter than this measurement.

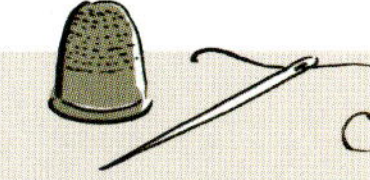

TIP

When estimating your fabric quantities and cutting out, always make sure that the edges of the pattern pieces where the zipper is to be sewn are placed along the straight grain, parallel to the selvages (see page 27).

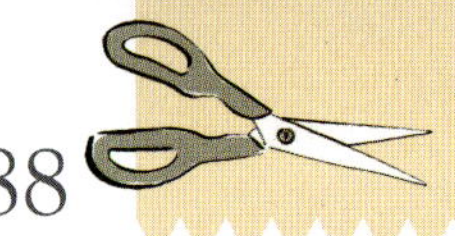

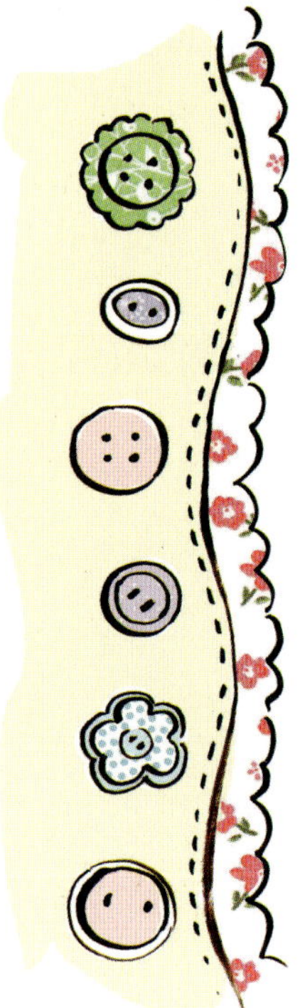

Advanced seams & hems

In Workshop 1 (page 38), we learned about simple seams and hems—but now that you are more experienced with your sewing, we can move on to more advanced methods.

Sheer fabrics such as delicate, spotted voile or the finest cotton lawn need extra care and attention. You will need to make your seams and hems neater and less conspicuous, as they are often visible from the right side, so self-enclosed ones, which look almost as good on the wrong side as they do on the right, are the perfect solution. When you have completed this workshop you will be able to dress your windows with the lovely sheer romantic voile curtains featured in Project 6, and to neaten the edges of more substantial curtains with discreet hems and mitered corners for a sleek, classic finish.

Self-enclosed seams

In self-enclosed, or self-neatening seams as they are often called, all the seam allowance is contained within the finished seam, so there are no edges to be neatened separately. They are very hard-wearing.

There are four basic types of self-enclosed seam—the French seam, the mock French seam, the flat-fell seam, and the self-bound seam. Neat and accurate stitching, trimming, and pressing are vital for all if you want to achieve a crisp, professional finish.The following instructions are given for 5/8-in. (1.5-cm) seam allowances. If your seam allowance is wider, it is best to trim it carefully and accurately to 5/8 in. (1.5 cm), unless you are using a pattern that indicates otherwise.

French seam

The French seam is only suitable for lightweight fabrics and for joining straight edges. It is stitched twice, once from the right side and then from the wrong side, and is often used on sheer or semi-sheer curtains, duvet covers, and pillowcases, and on some semi-sheer or unlined garments, providing the seams are not curved.

1 With the wrong sides of the fabric facing, pin and baste (tack) the two edges together. Machine stitch, working 1/4 in. (6 mm) in from the raw edges, reverse stitching at each end to secure.

2 Press the seam open, then refold the fabric, with the right sides together and the stitchline placed exactly on the folded edge. Press the folded edge flat, then pin and baste (tack) the pressed edge in place. Machine stitch once again, working 3/8 in. (1 cm) in from the seamed edge, enclosing the raw edges, and reverse stitching at each end to secure. Press the seam to one side.

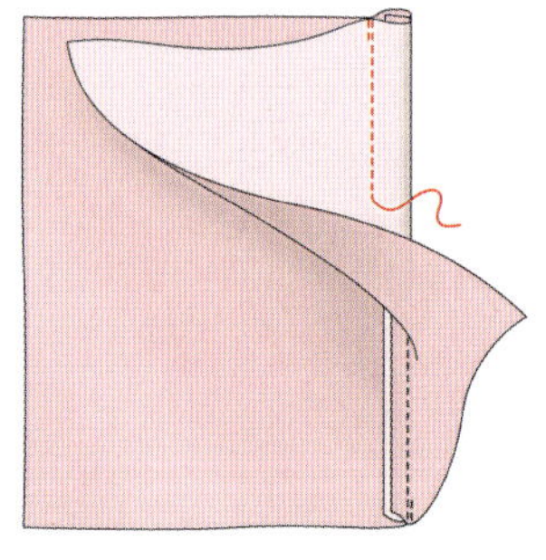

Flat-fell seam

This is a decorative, double-topstitched seam that is worked on the right side of the fabric, so care must be taken to keep the stitching and pressing even. Flat-fell seams are suitable for jeans, reversible clothes, sportswear, and menswear, or where added strength is needed, but do not use them on very thick fabrics, as they will be much too bulky.

1 With the wrong sides of fabric together, machine stitch a 5/8-in. (1.5-cm) plain straight seam (see page 40). Press the seam allowances open, then press them both to one side. Trim the lower seam allowance down to 1/4 in. (6 mm).

2 Carefully fold over the edge of the top seam allowance by 1/4 in. (6 mm), and press flat. Pin at right angles to the seam, enclosing all raw edges. Baste (tack) and machine stitch in place, working close to the pressed edge and stitching through all layers of fabric. Reverse stitch at each end to secure.

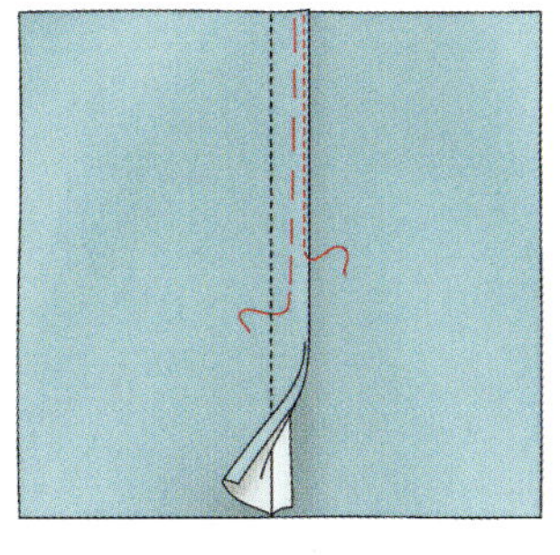

TIP

If you are using a flat-fell seam to join trouser legs or shoulders, make sure that you press both seams to lie in the same direction.

Self-bound seam

Although you may find it a little fiddly to do, the self-bound seam creates a neat, flat finish for visible seams. It works best with fine, lightweight fabrics that do not fray easily.

1 With right sides of the fabric together, machine stitch a 5/8-in. (1.5-cm) plain straight seam (see page 40). Do not press open, but carefully trim the upper seam allowance down to 1/8 in. (3 mm). Fold over the edge of the lower seam allowance to the right side by 1/8 in. (3 mm) and press flat.

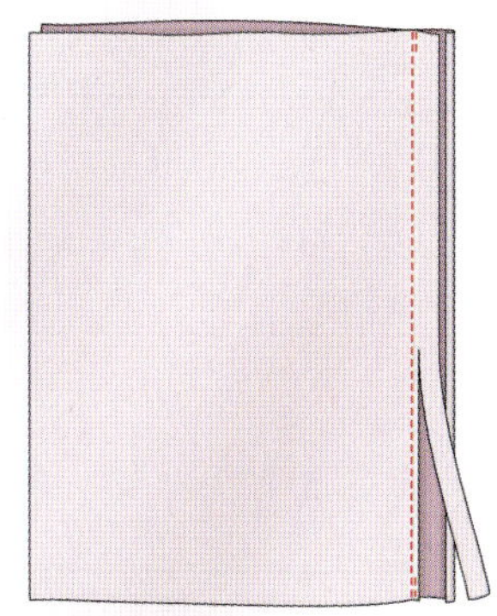

2 Fold the pressed edge over to meet the seamline, so that it just covers the stitching and encloses the raw seam allowances. Pin, baste (tack), and press it in place. Machine stitch in place, working close to the first pressed edge and stitching through all layers of fabric. Reverse stitch at each end to secure. Press the seam to one side.

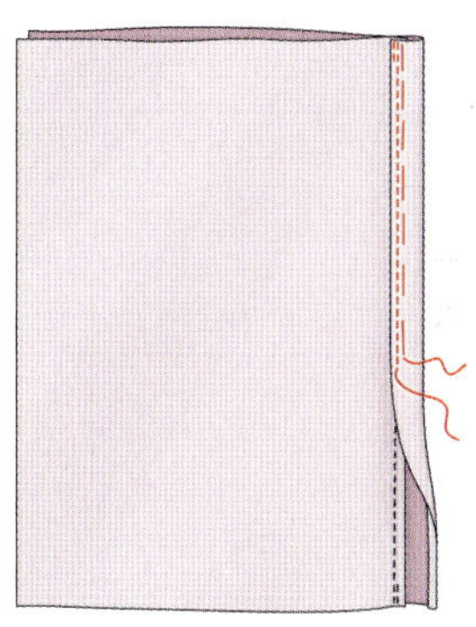

Mock French seam

This seam can be used instead of a French seam, especially on curves.

With right sides of fabric together, machine stitch a 5/8-in. (1.5-cm) plain straight seam (see page 40). Trim the seam allowances down to ½ in. (12 mm). Turn the seam allowance edges ¼ in. (6 mm) to the wrong side and press in place, matching the folded edges. Stitch the folded edges together and press the seam to one side.

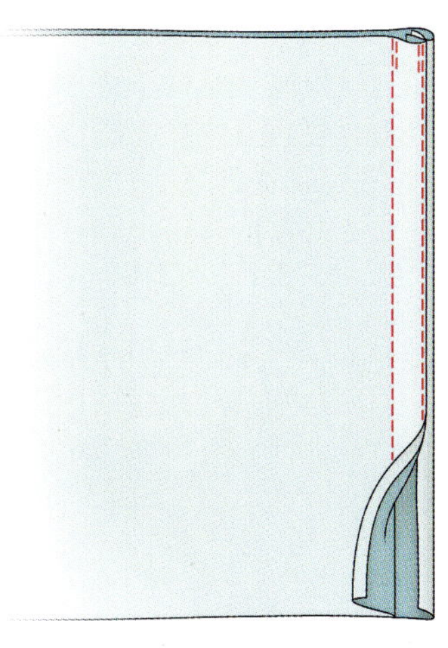

Inconspicuous hems

While topstitched hems look great on many items, a discreet finish is often preferable for others. There are many hemming techniques, but blind hemming by machine or by hand, slip-hemming by hand, and securing a hem with iron-on hemming tape are all methods that will be barely visible on the right side.

Blind hemming by machine

This type of hem is stitched using a blind hem foot (see page 21) and is a strong, fast way of achieving a fairly unnoticeable finish. It uses straight stitches on the hem allowance, with a zigzag stitch roughly every sixth stitch to catch in the main fabric layer. However, this method is a little trickier to master than it looks, so practice a few times on a scraps of your fabric before you attempt to stitch any real hems in place.

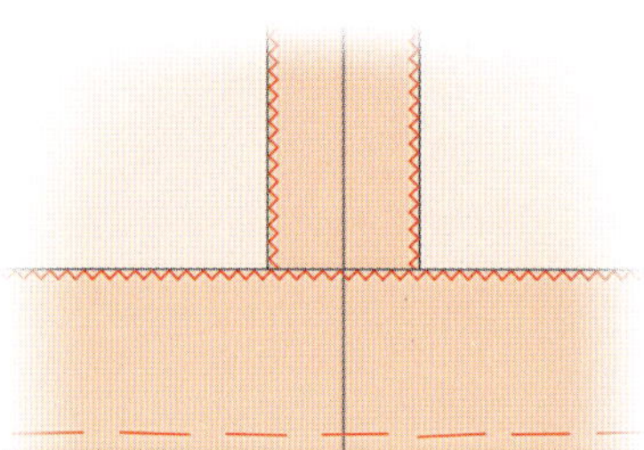

1 Neaten your hem edge (see page 44), and press the hem allowance to the inside, taking care not to stretch it. Pin and baste (tack) the hem in place close to the folded hem edge. Attach the blind hem foot to your machine and set your stitch selector to the blind hem setting (refer to your manual for the exact details).

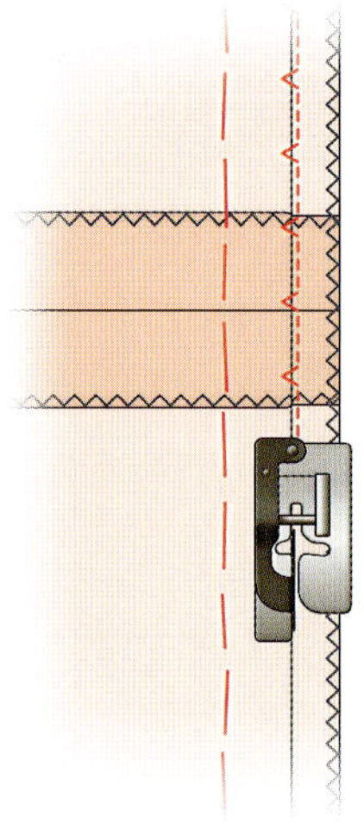

2 Lay the hem allowance face down and fold the garment back to reveal the neatened hem edge, so that it extends roughly 1/4 in. (6 mm) beyond the fold. Keeping the extension even, pin and baste (tack) it in place all round the hem. With the hem allowance still face down, position the fabric under the machine foot, with the folded edge up against the foot guide. Check the stitch width to make sure that the needle just pierces the fold when it swings over to the left side; if the needle moves over too far, the stitches will show on the right side of the fabric, so adjust the stitch width. When you are satisfied, stitch the hem in place, keeping the guide tightly up against the folded edge. Remove all basting stitches and smooth the hem back down.

Blind hemming by hand

These hand stitches are taken inside the hem—that is to say, between the hem and the actual garment. In the finished hem, no stitches should be visible. This is a quick and easy stitch that can be used on any flat, neatened hem. Do not pull the stitches too tight.

Neaten your hem edge (see page 44) and press the hem allowance to the inside, taking care not to stretch it. Pin and baste (tack) the hem in place close to the folded hem edge. With the hem allowance uppermost, work from right to left with the needle pointing to the right (reverse this if you are left-handed). Fold back the top edge of the hem allowance and fasten the thread just inside it. Approximately 1/4 in. (6 mm) to the left, take a very small stitch in the garment (no more than two or threads), then take the next stitch 1/4 in. (6 mm) to the left in the hem allowance. Continue in this manner, keeping the stitches even, until your hem is secured in place. Remove the basting stitches.

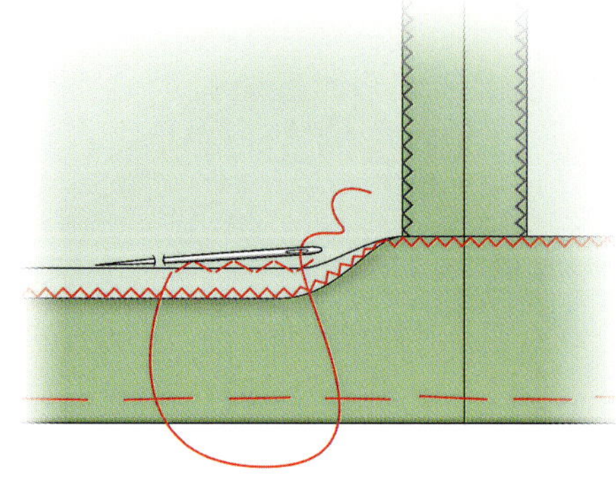

Slip hemming by hand

Slip hemming is used to secure a folded hem edge in place, and is commonly used for hemming curtains. This stitch is also known as uneven slipstitch and is almost invisible on the right side of your work.

Press the hem allowances to the wrong side, then pin and baste (tack) them place. Working from the right to the left (reverse this if you are left-handed), secure the thread on the inside of the hem fabric, then bring the needle out through the hem fold. Opposite in the garment, take a very small stitch (no more than two or three threads). Take the needle back into the folded edge and run the needle inside the fold for approximately 3/8 in. (1 cm). Bring the needle out and draw the thread through. Continue in this way, alternating the stitches between the fabric and the fold. Make sure the stitches are not pulled too tightly, otherwise the fabric will look puckered on the right side.

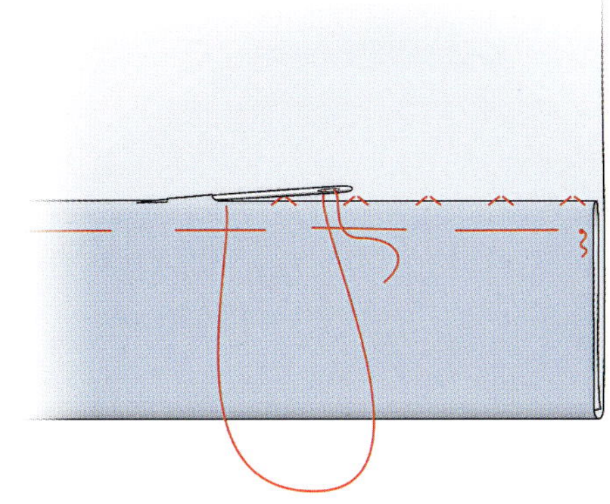

Iron-on hemming tape

Iron-on hemming tape is a strip of non-woven, web-like fabric that is inserted between the neatened hem allowance and the fabric; when the hem is steam ironed it "melts," bonding the two surfaces together. This is the quickest and easiest way to secure a hem, but you need to do it properly for a satisfactory result. Iron-on hemming tape can be used on any fabric that can be steam ironed, but ironing times vary depending on the fabric content and thickness. Iron-on hemming tape is available in 3/4-in. (2-cm) and 1 1/4-in. (3-cm) widths, but it can be applied to hems that are deeper than these measurements.

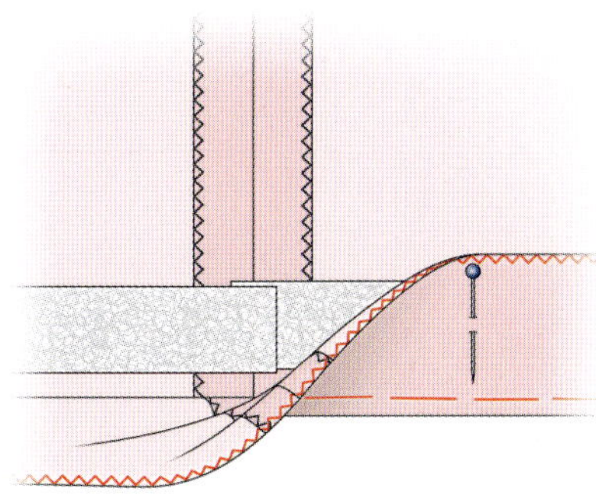
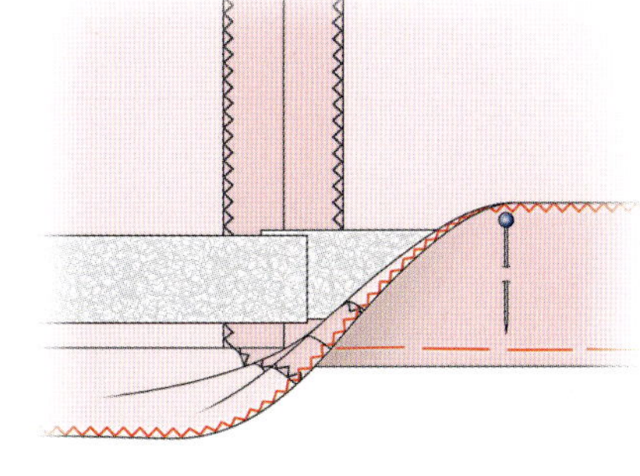

1 Neaten the hem edge (see page 44) and press the hem allowance to the wrong side; baste (tack) the hem in place close to the hem fold. Starting at a seam, slip the hemming tape between the hem allowance and the garment, with the top edge of the tape just below the neatened edge, pinning it in place as you work around the hem; overlap the tape ends by 3/8 in. (1 cm) to finish.

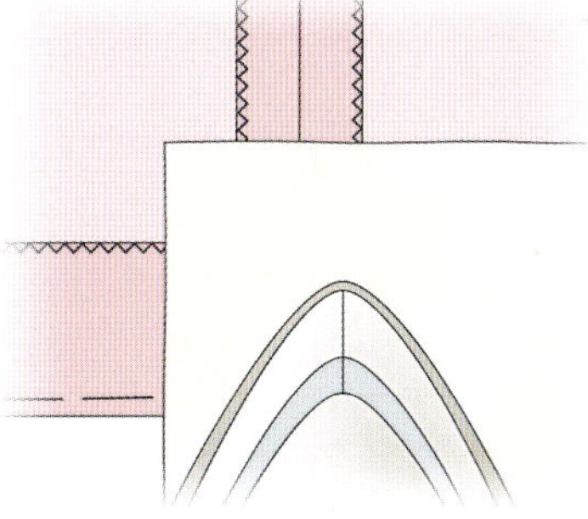

2 With your iron on the appropriate steam setting for your fabric, bond the hem lightly in place by pressing between the pins with the tip of the iron. Remove the pins. Finally, use a damp pressing cloth on top of the hem to press a section at a time, holding the iron on the cloth until it is dry. Continue all around the hem in this way, allowing the fabric to cool before handling it. Remove the basting (tacking) stitches.

Points to remember

- Do not stretch the tape during application or let the iron touch the tape—you will have a sticky iron that will be difficult to clean.
- Once applied, iron-on hemming tape is very difficult to remove, so make sure your hem is correct and level before you apply it.
- Do a pressing test on a scrap of your fabric, before you begin, to make sure the tape bonds securely and the hem looks good on the right side.
- On heavy fabrics, use the widest tape so that more of the hem is bonded to support the weight, and allow extra pressing time, particularly at the seams.

What is a facing?

A facing is the area of a garment or sewn item that turns to the inside, giving a finished appearance to what would otherwise be a raw edge of fabric. The facing can be a separate strip stitched to the edge of your item, or it can be an extension of the main piece itself, which is simply turned back to the inside. It is usually interfaced (see page 134) to add shape and support for the fastenings (see page 64) that close the opening.

Finishing hem corners

We have now discussed a few methods of securing hems in place, but what happens when your hem ends at a corner, such as on the front of a jacket or the side edge of a curtain? Here are three simple methods for finishing off corners: hemming a faced opening, mitering corners, and slipstitching corners.

Hemming a faced opening

You will come across faced openings when you make blouses, jackets, or coats. The method shown here is suitable for any fabric, but you will find that it is especially good for heavy fabrics, as the hem allowance is trimmed away at the corner in order to reduce bulk.

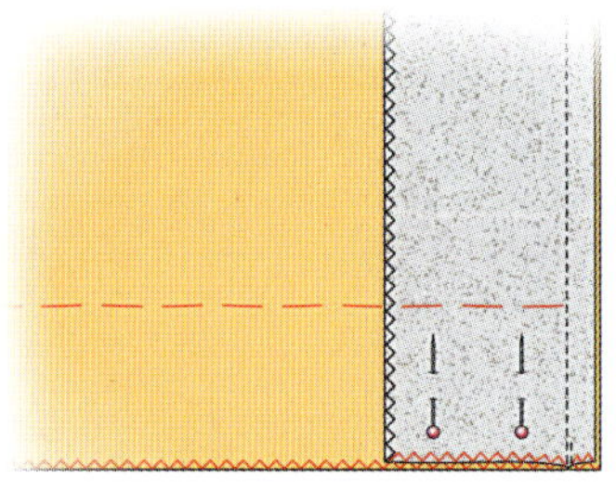

1 Neaten the hem edge (see page 44) and mark the hemline position with a row of uneven basting (tacking) stitches (see page 39). Fold the facing back onto the right side of the garment, keeping the hem edges level. Pin and baste in place.

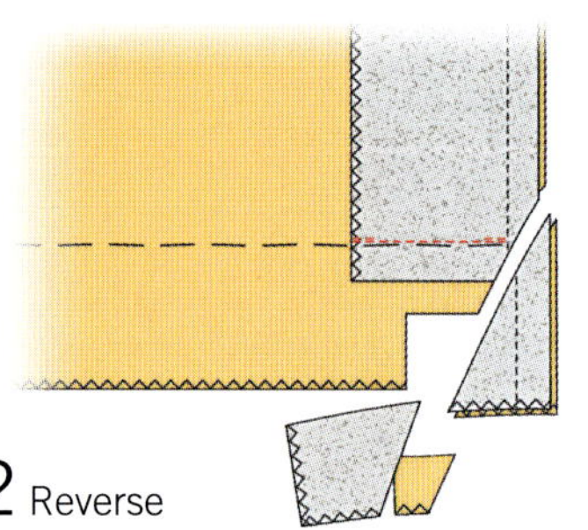

2 Reverse stitching at each end to secure, machine stitch the facing to the main garment along the basted (tacked) hem line, from the inner edge of the facing to the seam or fold at the garment edge. Layer the hem allowances as shown and clip the corners to reduce bulk (see page 43).

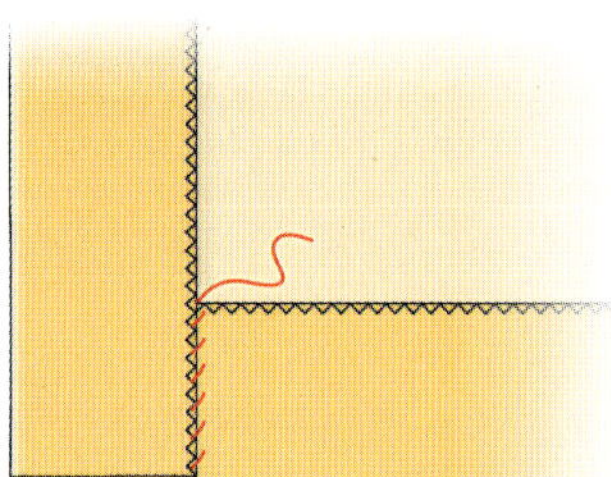

3 Turn the facing back to the inside of the garment and press the hem allowance to the wrong side along the basted (tacked) line. Secure the hem in place using your chosen method, then slipstitch (see page 49) the inner edge of the facing to the hem allowance.

Hem with slipstitched corners

If you are using a sheer fabric to make curtains, then the above methods are not suitable, as you will be able to see the seam allowances through the fabric. In this case you will need to allow extra-deep hem allowances so that you can double the hems entirely.

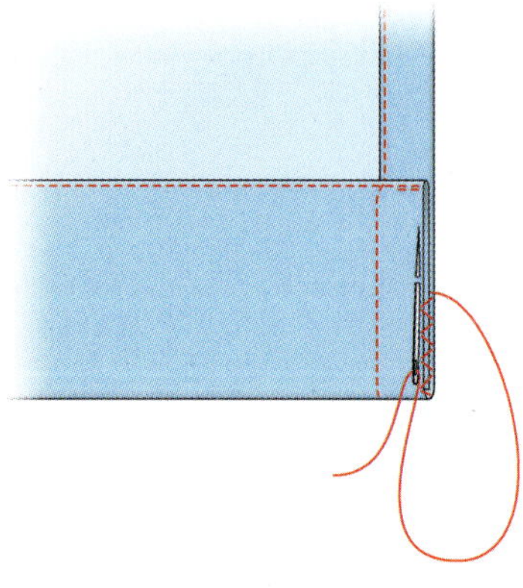

Work a narrow double-turned hem (see page 45) down the side edges of your project. At the base edge, fold over the required hem depth (normally 2 in./5 cm) to the wrong side. Pin in place along the entire length, including the side hems. Press along the folded edge, removing the pins as you go. Fold the hem up again so that the raw edge is enclosed and sits in the new fold line. Pin and baste (tack) the hem in place. Press the hemline fold, then stitch in place by machine or slip hem by hand (see page 91). To finish the hem corners, slipstitch (see page 49) the open edges of the base hem together.

Mitered corners

The need to miter a hem occurs most frequently in curtain making, but this method can also be used on garments. It is particularly useful for bulky fabrics. The definition of a miter is a joint in which each piece is cut at a 45° angle to its sides to form a neat, flat, right-angled corner. The hem edges should always be neatened appropriately before starting work; the miter can then be joined either by machine or hand stitching.

Hand-sewn miter This is the most popular way to secure a miter and gives a more "bespoke" finish.

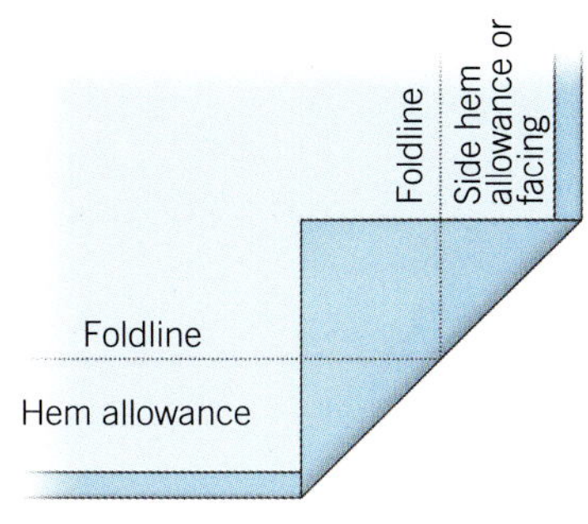

1 Pin and press the required lower hem allowances to the wrong side. Then pin and press the required side hem allowance (on a curtain), or neatened facing (on a garment) to the wrong side. Open out both hems (or hem and facing), then, using the corner point as a pivot and matching up the press lines, fold over a triangular corner. Press along the diagonal fold line.

2 Trim away the excess fabric from the folded corner to leave a 5/8-in. (1.5-cm) seam allowance.

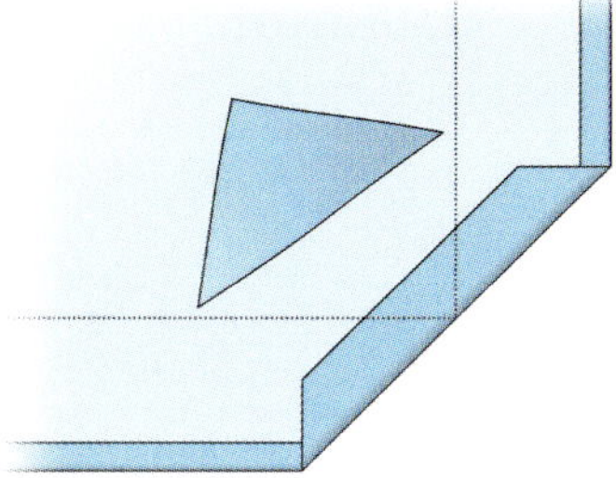

3 Refold the hems (or hem and facing) to form the miter and slipstitch (see page 49) the pressed diagonal edges together. You can now secure the remainder of your hem in place either by hand or machine (see page 90).

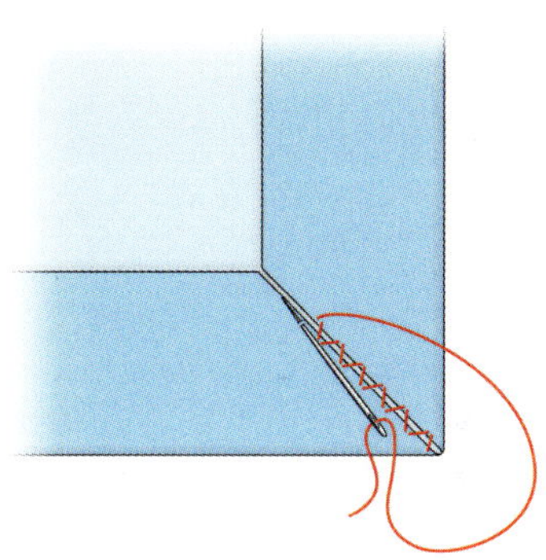

Machine-stitched miter In this method, the diagonal pressed edges are stitched together first and then trimmed to form the miter.

1 Follow step 1 of Hand-sewn miter (above). Open out the diagonal pressed corner. With right sides together, refold the corner diagonally in the opposite direction, so that the hem edges are level and the hem press lines lie on top of each other. Do not press, but pin the fabric layers together and stitch across the corner, following the first diagonal press line and reverse stitching at each end to secure.

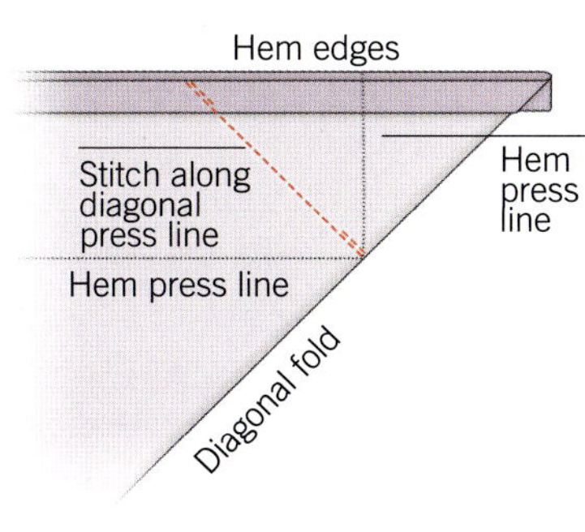

2 Trim away the excess fabric from the point to leave a ¼-in. (6-mm) seam allowance and trim the seam allowance at the corner to reduce bulk (see page 43). Press the seam allowances open, then turn the corner right side out, easing out the corner carefully with the help of a small pair of scissors. Press the corner flat and secure the remainder of your hem in place either by hand or machine (see page 90).

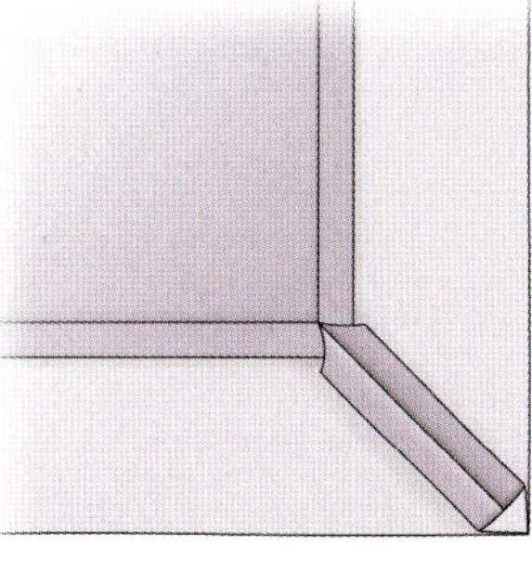

Sheer curtains

Gently gathered voile curtains, trimmed with a pretty contrasting rickrack braid, are the perfect way to add privacy to any room, diffusing the light and pooling on the floor for a romantic finish. Before you start this project, have your curtain track or pole fixed in position above the window.

You will need

- Sheer curtain fabric, such as muslin or voile (to work out the amount, see page 98)
- Standard gathered curtain heading tape, twice the length of your curtain track or pole, plus 1/4 yd/25 cm (see page 97)
- Contrast braid, twice the length of your curtain track or pole, plus 1/4 yd (25 cm)
- Matching threads
- Curtain hooks

Note

- 5/8-in. (1.5-cm) seam allowances are included unless otherwise stated

1 Cut out the required number of fabric widths to the length you have calculated, adding 5 in. (12.5 cm) for the heading allowance, 4 in. (10 cm) for a hem allowance, and 8 in. (20 cm) for "pooling" on the floor. If you want your curtains to finish directly at floor level or shorter, just below a windowsill, then do not add this last amount.

2 If an odd number of fabric widths is needed in total, cut the odd width in half lengthwise and join each half width to the outside, or back, edge of each curtain with French seams (see page 88). Always place a full width at the leading edge, the edge that you draw across the widow; with a pair of curtains, this will be at the center. Neaten the long side edges of each curtain with narrow double-turned hems (see page 45) and finish the base hem as shown for Hem with slipstitched corner (page 92).

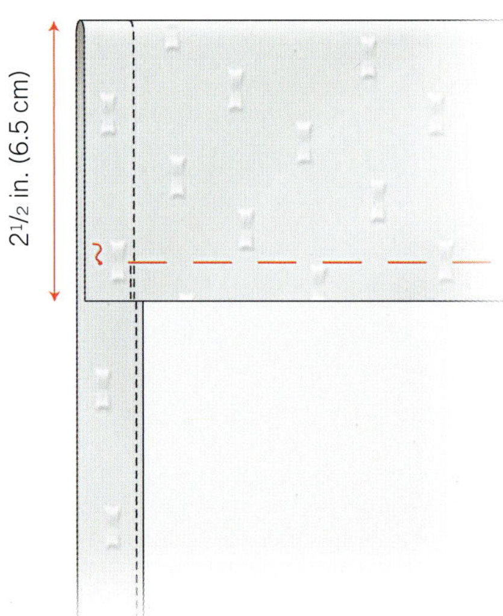

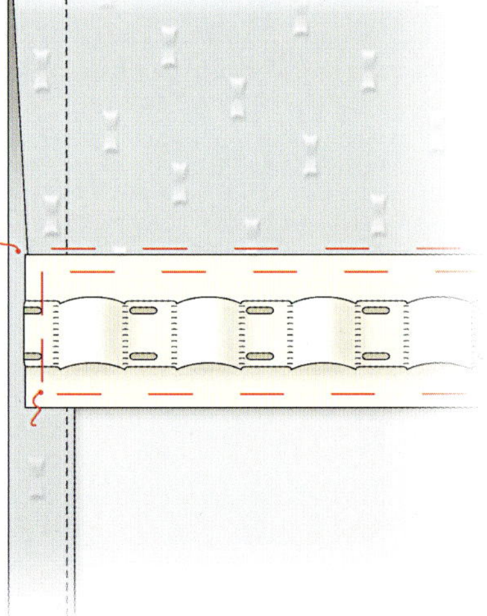

3 Working on one curtain at a time, lay the piece out flat wrong side up (the floor is often the best place for this, unless you have a very large table). At the top of the curtain, fold over half of the heading allowance (2 1/2 in./6.5 cm) to the wrong side; pin and baste (tack) in place 1/2 in. (1.2 cm) up from the raw edge.

4 Fold under about 5/8 in. (1.5 cm) of the heading tape at the leading edge end and pin it in place from the right side. Pull the tape draw cords through to the back of the tape and secure with a knot. Lay the heading tape right side up, with the upper edge against the basted (tacked) line, enclosing the raw edge; pin the tape in place. At the opposite edge of the curtain trim off the excess tape, allowing an extra 5/8 in. (1.5 cm) for folding over. Fold under the tape end and pin in place, leaving the cord ends free on the outside. Baste the tape in place around all the edges.

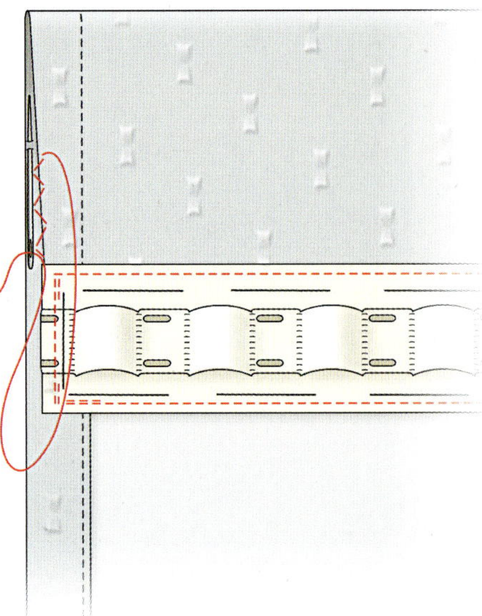

5 With the tape uppermost, machine stitch the long and short edges of the tape in place, working in the same direction for both long edges so as not to twist the seams; reverse stitch at each end of the stitchlines to secure. Remove the basting (tacking) stitches and slipstitch (see page 49) the open side edges of the heading together.

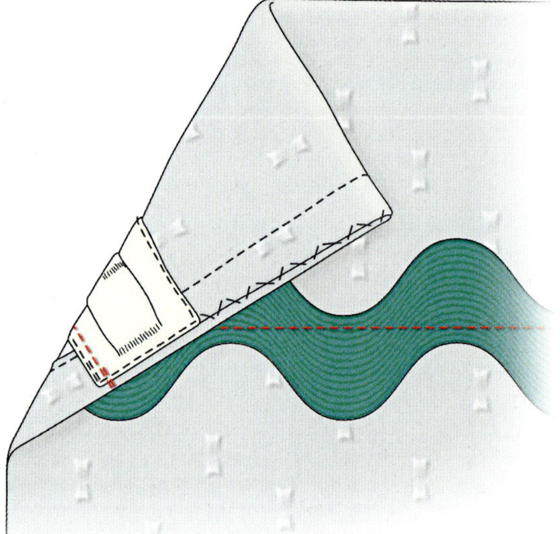

6 Lay the curtain out flat once more, with the right side uppermost. Fold under 1/2 in. (1.2 cm) at the end of the braid and, starting at the leading edge, position the braid on the curtain, placing it centrally over the lower line of tape stitching. Pin it smoothly in place across the curtain width and cut off the braid at the opposite side, allowing for the end to be folded under. Pin, baste (tack), and machine stitch it to the curtain, sewing along the center of the braid.

TIP

To tidy up the long loose cord ends on your heading tape, wind them up around your fingers and secure with an elastic band or a wire bag tie close to the top of your curtains.

7 Carefully pull up the tape draw cords to gather up the curtain to fit your curtain track and tie the cord ends together in a double bow at the back. Slot the correct number of curtain hooks into tape pockets to match your track runners or pole rings. Your curtain is now ready to hang.

Curtain headings

A curtain is attached to a track or pole by means of a heading, which is the decorative top of a curtain. Nowadays most people make curtain headings with the use of special heading tapes, which create different looks and styles, although there are some simple up-to-date methods that can be achieved without the use of tapes.

Heading tapes

Heading tapes are strips of fabric, bought by the yard (metre), that contain rows of pockets for inserting hooks and are used to suspend the curtain from a pole or track. Integral draw cords gather the fullness of the fabric in a decorative way. The most popular types are as follows:

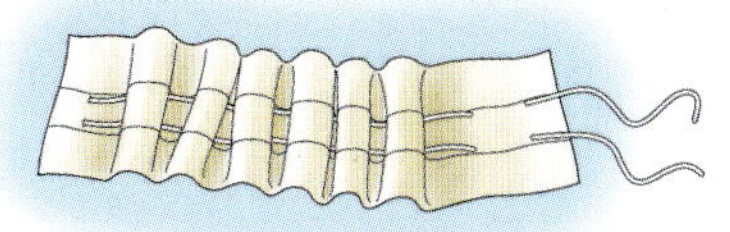

Standard gathering tape
This tape is roughly 1 in. (2.5 cm) deep. It gives a shallow random gathered heading suitable for more informal and unlined curtains. It has one row of pockets for hooks and is usually positioned at least 1½ in. (4 cm) below the top of the curtain, to conceal the track or rings on a pole. The fabric fullness for this tape should be 1½–2 times the length of your track or pole.

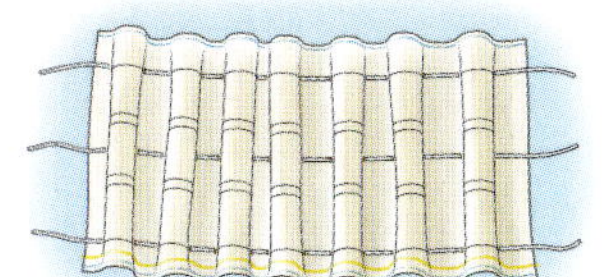

Pencil pleat tape
This tape is around 3 in. (7.5 cm) deep and creates close-packed pleats. It has two or three rows of pockets that allow you to adjust the height of the curtain; will hide your track, while hooks in the top row allow curtains to hang from rings and reveal the pole. This tape is attached close to the top edge of the curtain and needs a fabric fullness of 2½–3 times the length of your track or pole.

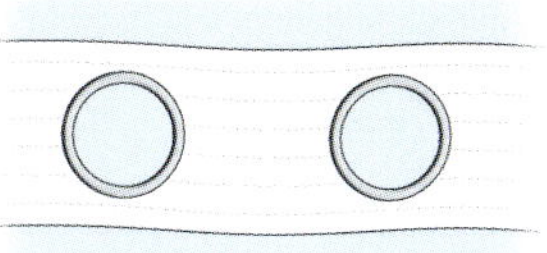

Grommet (eyelet) tape
This tape provides one of the simplest ways of creating an attractive heading without the need for traditional hooks and rings. This tape does not gather up, but contains grommets (eyelets), which are threaded straight onto a curtain pole. The tape is attached close to the top edge of the curtain and needs 1½ times the length of your track or pole; it is available in two ring sizes.

Non-tape headings

Other informal curtain headings can be achieved without the use of a tape, but you will need to finish off the top edge of your curtains with a facing (see page 92). These types of heading usually require 1½–2 times the length of your track or pole, depending on the weight of your fabric.

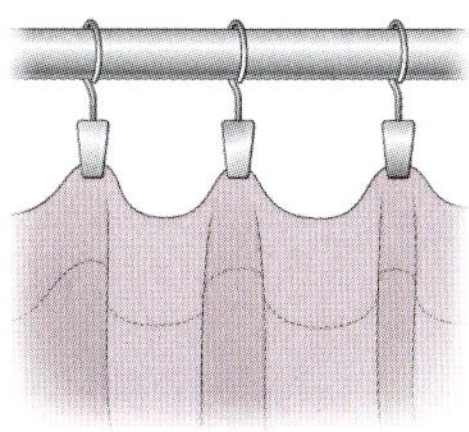

Curtain clips
These are small decorative pincer clips, which either thread onto a rod or clip over curtain rings. To use them, add a 1½-in. (4-cm) facing to the top of your curtain and simply clip the curtains in place.

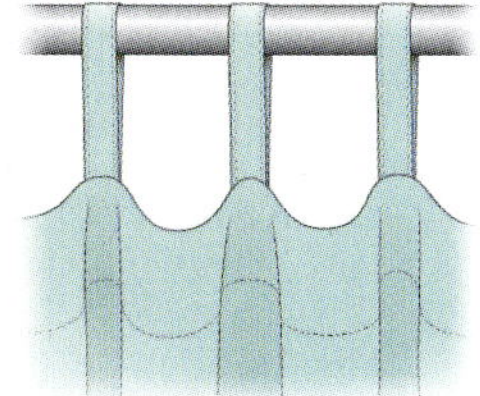

Ribbon ties and loops
These are an easy way to hang curtains and look attractive. For this heading, add a 2-in. (5-cm) facing to the top edge of your curtain, sandwiching the ribbons between the fabric layers. Either make loops to thread on a curtain pole, or add pairs of ribbons to tie around the rings; it is important to space them evenly.

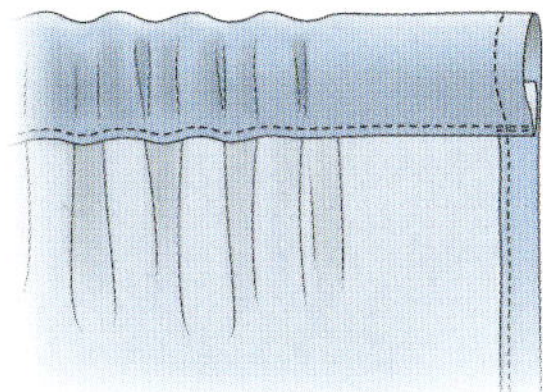

Casing
This type of heading is often used for sheer curtains; it is a hem that slips over a curtain rod or wire, forcing the fabric to gather into soft folds. This heading is best suited to fixed curtains, which do not have to be drawn. See Fold-down casings in Workshop 9, page 124.

Measuring & calculating for windows

In this workshop you will learn how to measure and calculate fabric quantities for window treatments. There is something intensely satisfying about making your own curtains and blinds—but while the idea may be great, the reality can be a little daunting. In this workshop we'll prove that measuring is not as complicated as it first seems and tell you how to avoid expensive mistakes. Once you've got the hang of it, you'll be able to make pretty unlined curtains for any room as well as the fabulous Roman blind featured on page 106.

Curtains

Unlined curtains are quick and easy to make, and probably the best ones to make for your first attempt. They are especially good for small windows or where something unobtrusive is required. However, they can also be used on larger windows, as dress curtains with blinds, as in the sheer curtain in Workshop 6.

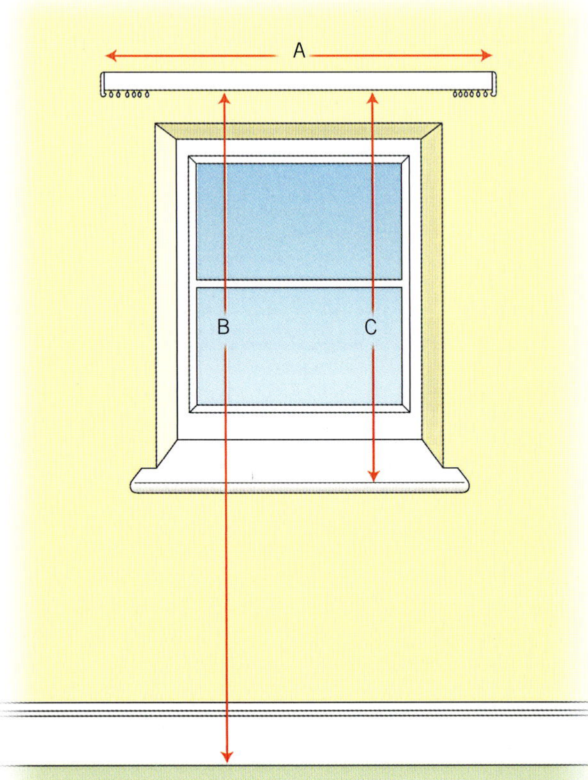

Measuring for curtains

Follow these simple steps and you're guaranteed to get it right; we've even included a chart for you to make a note of your calculations as you go along. Make sure that all your tracks and fittings are in place before you begin to measure, including carpets if you are making full-length curtains.

The two measurements that you require in order to work out how much fabric you will need are:

- The length of your curtain track or pole (measurement A), plus any overlaps at the center if your track has them (usually on corded tracks).
- The curtain length, from the track or pole to the floor (measurement B) or windowsill (measurement C).

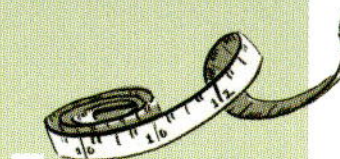

Working out the length

1 First, work out where you want the curtain heading to sit in relation to the curtain track or pole. To do this, hook a piece of the heading tape onto your track or pole. If you are using a pencil pleat heading (see page 97), measure downward starting from the top of the tape. If you are using a standard gathered heading, measure downward from about 1 1/2 in. (4 cm) above the top of the tape. For grommet (eyelet) tape, thread a length onto the pole and measure from the top of the tape.

2 Then work out where you want the curtain to end. For full-length curtains that just skim the floor, deduct 3/8 in. (1 cm) from measurement B so that the curtains will not drag on the floor; if you want curtains that "pool" or drape on the floor, add 4–8 in. (10–20 cm) to measurement B. For windows with a radiator below, make the curtains hang 2–4 in. (5–10 cm) below the windowsill. For sill-length curtains where the sill sticks out a long way, deduct 1/4 in. (6 mm) from measurement C to allow the curtains to sit just above the sill.

3 To work out the cut fabric length or drop, add on top and base hem allowances to the length you have just calculated.

Example
For a curtain that is 59 in. (150 cm) long, add 6 in. (15 cm) for a base hem, which will allow for a 3 in. (7.5 cm) double-turned hem, and 1 in. (2.5 cm) for a top hem. This gives a cut fabric length of 66 in. (167.5 cm).

Note: For a standard gathered heading, you will also need to add 2 in. (5 cm) so that the curtain sits above the pole or track.

Working out the width

1 The type of heading that you are going to use will determine the fabric fullness of your curtains (see page 97). Multiply your track or pole length by the fullness required for your heading.

Example
A pencil pleat heading needs a fabric fullness of 2 1/2–3 times the length of your track or pole, so a 47-in. (120-cm) track will need a total curtain width of 118 in. (300 cm) or 142 in. (360 cm), depending on the fullness you choose.

2 To calculate how many widths of fabric you will need to make your curtains, divide the total curtain width by the width of your fabric; this is normally either 48 in. (122 cm) or 54 in. (137 cm). If you are making a pair of curtains and an odd number of fabric widths are needed, cut the odd width in half lengthwise and join each width on to the outside, or back, edge of each curtain. Always place full widths at the center of your window.

Example
The required curtain width is 118 in. (300 cm). Divide this by the width of the fabric (48 in./122 cm) = 2 1/2 widths of fabric. So for a pair of curtains, you will need 1 1/4 widths of fabric in each curtain.

Note: Obviously you cannot buy half a width of fabric, so you will have to round up to the next full width—in this case three widths—and then trim away the excess fabric to your required width. You can use the fabric you have trimmed off to make matching pillows (cushions).

TIP
Never skimp on the fabric quantity: generous full curtains in a cheap fabric look far better than those made from half the amount of a more expensive fabric.

Working out fabric quantities

1 For plain fabrics or ones with a small printed design, simply multiply the cut length measurement by the number of fabric widths that you have just calculated.

2 If you have chosen a print fabric, see Allowing for pattern repeats, page 100.

Example
For a curtain with a cut length of 66 in. (167.5 cm) x 3 widths of fabric, you will need to buy 5 1/2 yd (5.1m) of 48-in.-(122-cm-) wide fabric.

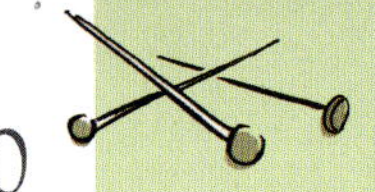

Allowing for pattern repeats

If you are using a patterned fabric, you will need to allow extra fabric to match the pattern.

Once you have calculated the cut length of your curtain, measure the depth of one complete pattern repeat (this is often noted on the fabric label). Divide the cut length by the pattern repeat and round it up to the next full repeat. This will give you the length you will need to allow for each cut drop or length of patterned fabric.

Example

For a pattern repeat of 10 in. (25.5 cm), divide your cut curtain length (say 66 in./167.5 cm) by 10 in. (25.5 cm) = 6.6 repeats. Round up to the next whole figure = 7. You will need to allow 7 x 10 in. (25.5 cm) = 70 in. (178.5 cm) for each cut curtain length to allow for accurate pattern matching.

Matching pattern repeats

On patterned fabrics, the patterns need to be matched first before you attempt to stitch the pieces together.

To match the patterns, fold and press 1 in. (2.5 cm) to the wrong side along one long edge of one fabric piece. Then, working from the right side, place the pressed edge on top of the second fabric piece, matching the design along the pressed fold. Pin and baste (tack) in place using slip basting (see page 39). Open out the pressed edge so that the fabrics are right sides together and machine stitch on the wrong side, along the foldline.

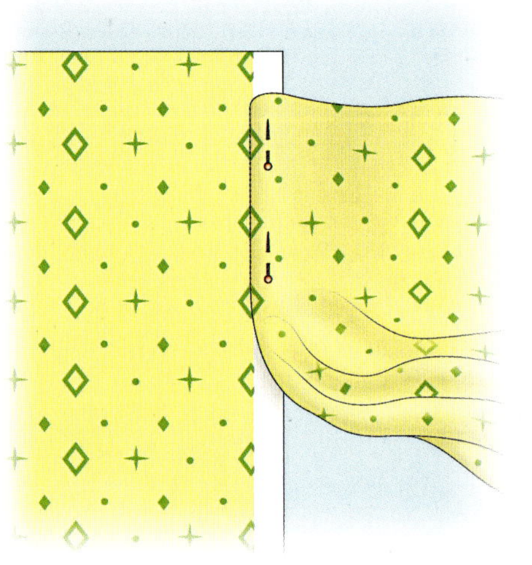

Choosing tracks and poles

We have already said that your track and pole should be in position before you start to measure up for your curtains, but how do you choose from the vast selection available? Here are a few pointers to help you decide what look is best for you.

Curtain poles

- Poles are generally designed to be visible above the top of the curtains; many decorative versions are available.
- You can now get poles that bend around corners for bay windows.
- The simplest poles rest on architrave brackets screwed to the wall.
- The curtain is supported by rings threaded onto the pole, or the pole is threaded directly through grommet (eyelet) heading tape.
- Place brackets about 1¼ in. (3 cm) in from the ends of the pole to allow for one curtain ring at each end.

Curtain tracks

- Tracks come in many lengths graded for light-, medium-, or heavyweight curtains.
- Metal tracks are more expensive, but they are stronger and last much longer than the plastic varieties.
- Metal tracks can be bent permanently around bays.
- Some tracks are ready corded, which is great for long curtains or ones that are light in color, as handling them can cause the "leading" edges to get grubby.
- Ideally, a track should have overlap arms to allow the curtain to overlap at the center when closed.

Fabric quantities for unlined curtains

To work out how much fabric you need, fill in your window measurements on this chart and add or subtract hem allowances and clearances as appropriate.

	Room 1	Room 2	Room 3	Room 4
1 Note length from track or pole to base of curtain				
Add 1 in. (2.5 cm) top hem allowance*				
Add 6 in. (15 cm) base hem allowance				
For full-length curtains: subtract 3/8 in. (1 cm) for clearance				
For curtains draping on floor: add 4–8 in. (10–20 cm)				
For sill-length curtains: subtract 1/4 in. (6 mm)				
For windows above radiators: add 2–4 in. (5–10 cm)				
Add all measurements together to obtain total cut length (**A**)**				
2 Note width of track or pole				
Multiply by 1 1/2–2 times for standard gathering tape				
Multiply by 2 1/2–3 times for pencil pleat tape				
Multiply by 1 1/2 times for grommet (eyelet) tape				
Add all measurements together to obtain total curtain width (**B**)				
3 Work out fabric quantity				
Note the width of your fabric (**C**)				
Divide B by C (round up to full widths) to work out how many fabric widths required (**D**)				
TOTAL FABRIC QUANTITY = A X D				

Notes:
*Add 2 in. (5 cm) for standard heading tape.
**For patterned fabrics, divide A by the depth of the pattern repeat to work out the cut length (see page 100).

TIP

If your curtains are going to be hung somewhere that they are likely to get dirty quickly, avoid dry-clean only fabrics and make them in something that is going to stand up to regular washing. Cotton is the best option.

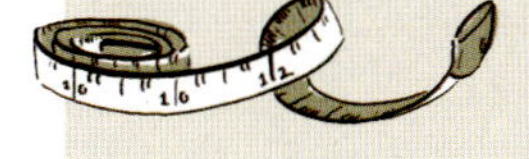

Blinds

Plain flat blinds, when lowered, cover the window with a neat rectangle of fabric, and have the advantage that they roll up or fold away into a relatively inconspicuous strip, letting in the maximum amount of light. Because of this, they are often the first choice for the modern home. However, to get a professional result you must pay attention to detail, especially when measuring up and making sure that the blind hangs square and true.

Blinds can be hung either inside (recess-fixed) or outside (face-fixed) your window by means of a blind support, which is made from a timber batten (see right).

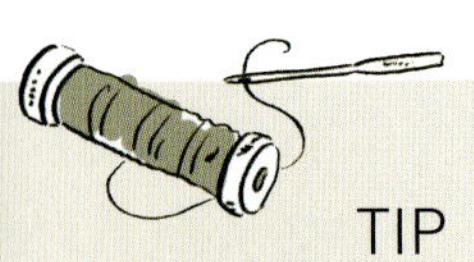

TIP

When measuring for blinds, fix your blind support in place before you begin. Use a steel measuring tape and take your time; measure twice to make sure you've got it right.

Positioning blind supports

A recess-fixed blind is held in place with a support that is screwed to the top of the window recess.

For a face-fixed blind, the support is screwed to the wall. The support is normally positioned 5 in. (12.5 cm) above the top of the window and extends beyond the sides by the same amount.

Measuring for blinds

The way you measure for blinds depends on whether the blind is to be recess- or face-fixed. The diagram below shows where to measure in order to work out how much fabric you will require for the different types of blind.

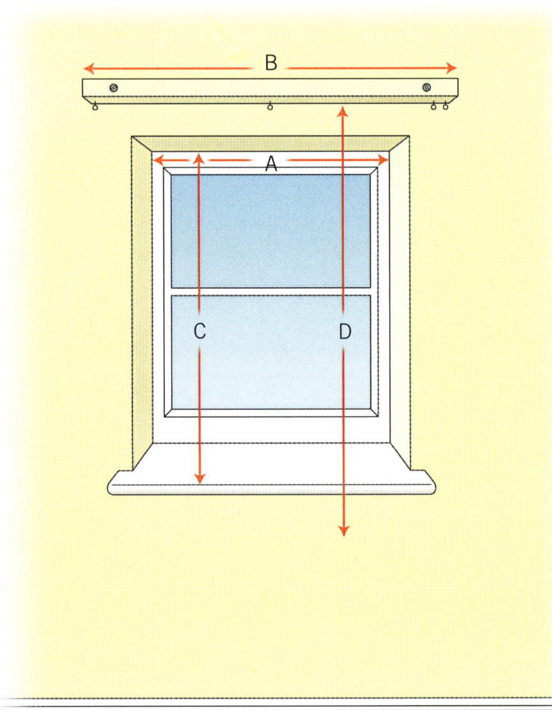

Measuring for a recess-fixed blind

1 To calculate the finished length of a recess-fixed blind, measure from the top of the timber support and subtract 3/8 in. (1 cm) for clearance, so that the blind will hang just short of the sill: measurement C.

2 To calculate the finished width, measure the width of the recess (measurement A) and subtract 3/4 in. (2 cm), so that the blind does not touch the sides of the window, which would restrict its operation.

Measuring for a face-fixed blind

1 To calculate the finished length of a face-fixed blind, measure from the wall across the top of the timber support and down to 2 in. (5 cm) below the window sill (measurement D).

2 To calculate the finished width, measure the length of the timber support (measurement B), and add 1/2 in. (12 mm).

How much fabric do I need?

Now that you have taken your measurements and made adjustments for clearance, you must add on the correct hem allowances before you can calculate your fabric quantities.

1 To work out the cut width of the blind, take the width measurement that you have just calculated and add on 4 in. (10 cm) for the two side hems.

Example:
For a 39-in.- (99-cm-) wide blind, add 4 in. (10 cm) for hems = 43 in. (109 cm) cut width.

2 To work out the cut length of the blind, add 1 in (2.5 cm) to measurement C or D for a top hem and 2³/₈ in. (6 cm) for a base hem; this will allow for a 1¹/₂-in. (4-cm) finished double-turned hem.

Example:
For a 55-in.- (140-cm-) long blind, add 3³/₈ in. (8.5 cm) in total for the hem allowances = 58¹/₂ in. (148.5 cm) cut length.

3 To calculate the total amount of fabric you will need to buy, divide your blind's cut width by your fabric width. On most occasions, you will need only one width of fabric. If two widths are required, cut the odd width in half lengthwise and join each width on to the outside edges of the blind, so that you have a full width at the center of your window.

4 Finally, multiply the cut length of your blind by the number of fabric widths. If you are using a patterned fabric, refer to Matching pattern repeats, page 100.

Making a blind support

If you are making a blind, you will need to make a timber support from which to suspend your blind. To achieve the perfect-looking finish, paint it to match your décor.

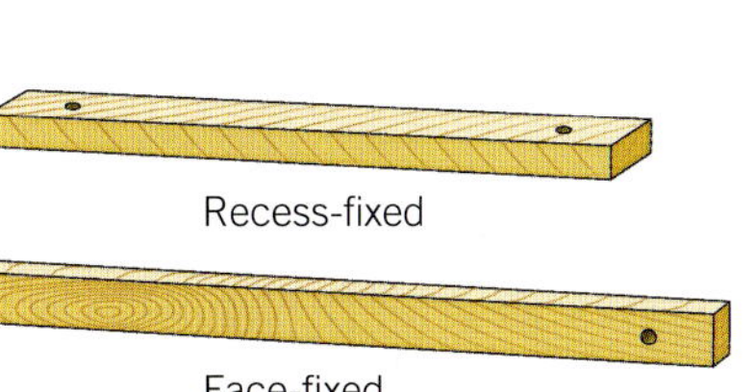

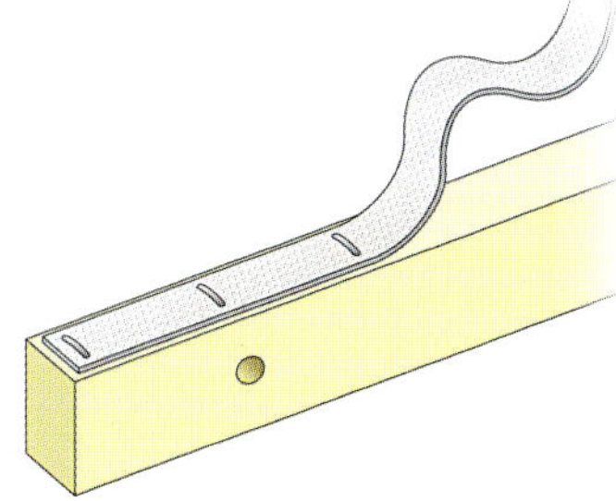

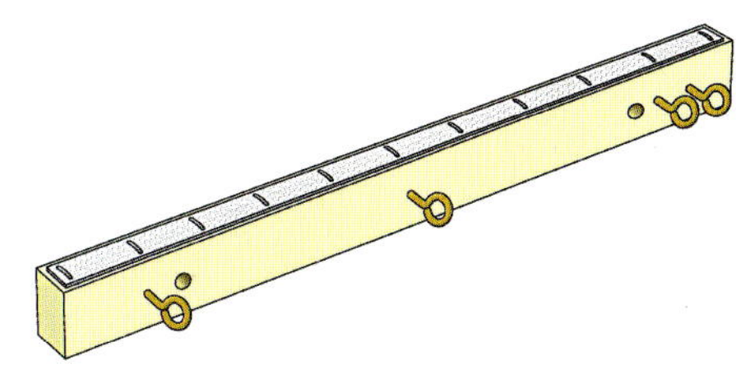

1 For either a recess-fixed or a face-fixed blind, cut a piece of 1 x 2-in. (2.5 x 5-cm) timber to the finished width of your blind (see left). For a recess-fixed blind, drill a hole in the wider *underside* of the timber, 3 in. (8 cm) in from each end. For a face-fixed blind, drill a hole in the wider *face* side of the timber support, 3 in. (8 cm) in from each end. Paint the timber with two or three coats of paint, leaving it to dry between coats.

2 Using a staple gun, staple the hook side of a length of hook-and-loop fastener tape (see page 73) to the support. For a face-fixed blind, staple the hook side of the tape to the *top* narrow edge of the support; for a recess-fixed blind, staple the hook side of the tape to the narrow *front* edge of the support.

3 If you are making a simple hand-rolled and ribbon-tied blind, then screw your blind support in place. For a Roman blind, which operates by use of cords, you will need to add some screw eyes. Using a bradawl, mark the positions of the screw eyes on the *underside* of the support; place one at the center and one 2 in. (5 cm) in from each end. Add a fourth screw eye 1 in. (2.5 cm) in from the cord-operating side. Screw your support in place.

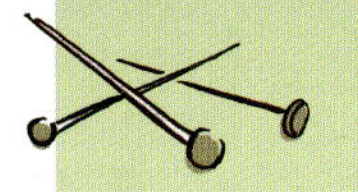

Fabric quantities for blinds

To work out how much fabric you need, fill in your window measurements on this chart and add or subtract hem allowances and clearances as appropriate.

	Room 1	Room 2	Room 3	Room 4
1 Note length from support to base of blind				
Add 1 in. (2.5 cm) top hem allowance				
Add 2 3/8 in. (6 cm) base hem allowance				
Subtract 3/8 in. (1 cm) clearance for a recess-fixed blind				
Add all measurements together to obtain total cut length (**A**)				
2 Measure width of support				
Add 4 in. (10 cm) for side hems				
Subtract 3/4 in. (2 cm) clearance for a recess-fixed blind				
Add 1/2 in. (12 mm) for a face-fixed blind				
Add all measurements together to obtain total cut blind width (**B**)				
3 Work out fabric quantity				
Note the width of your fabric (**C**)				
Divide B by C to work out how many fabric widths required (**D**)				
TOTAL FABRIC QUANTITY = A X D				

Points to remember

- Very few windows and walls are perfectly straight or "true." If your walls are seriously out of alignment, a recess-fixed blind will not hang well. Opt for a face-fixed blind, or curtains, instead.
- Do not choose checked fabrics, especially if your windows are not perfectly straight —they will emphasize the problem.
- For a very wide window, make several blinds instead of just one; it is hard to get one large blind sitting straight when pulled up.
- When working out the spacing of Roman blind tapes (opposite), mark your calculations on paper so that you can check that they fit accurately into the finished length of your blind.

Jargon buster

Dazed and confused by all those technical terms? Then check out our handy guide to help cut through all that technical stuff.

Bradawl: A pointed tool for making holes for screw eyes in a timber support.
Cleat: A double-pronged hook around which the operating cords of a blind are secured.
Cord pulls: These can be made of lightweight wood, or weighted metal, with a rubber band around the widest part to be gentle on your walls.
Lath: A flat, thin piece of timber that slots into the base of a blind so that the fabric hangs straight.
Rings: These small rings can be made of plastic or metal and are sewn onto blinds to hold and guide the cords.
Roman blind cord: A fine cord used to operate the blind to move up and down.
Roman blind tape: Is manufactured with a special channel through which to insert Roman blind rods or dowels.
Screw eyes: Sometimes known as "vine eyes," these are rings with a screw thread attached. They are fastened into the support to guide the cords across the top of the blind to the operating side.
Support: A device such as a wooden batten from which a blind can be hung. This can be attached to the outside or inside of a window.

Positioning Roman blind tapes

A Roman blind is operated by cords, which pull up the blind in a series of neat folds. To ensure that it folds up easily and gives support to the blind, wooden dowels are inserted into slotted tapes stitched across the blind. It is essential that you space these tapes correctly.

1 Decide on the number of folds you require—normally four for a standard-sized blind, but you may need less for a short one or more for a longer one.

2 From your blind length, subtract 4 in. (10 cm) from the top for clearance. This will prevent the Roman blind tapes and rings catching on the supporting screw eyes, and will also allow the folds to lie evenly.

3 Divide the remaining depth of the blind by twice the number of folds (f) plus 1 (for the distance between the base of the blind and the first tape position.) In most cases, this will be 2 x 4 = 8 + 1.

For example: For a blind 48 in. (122 cm) long, subtract 4 in. (10 cm) at the top = 44 in. (112 cm). Divide the remaining length by twice the number of folds + 1 (so if there are four folds this will be 9). Therefore the fold spacing will be 44 in. (112 cm) ÷ 9 = 4⁷/₈ in. (12.4 cm).

4 Using a tape measure, mark the spacing positions for four rows of tape (to form the four folds), with pins along each side hem, then lightly draw lines across the blind, joining the pins, using tailor's chalk (see page 22) and a ruler. You are now ready to attach the tapes.

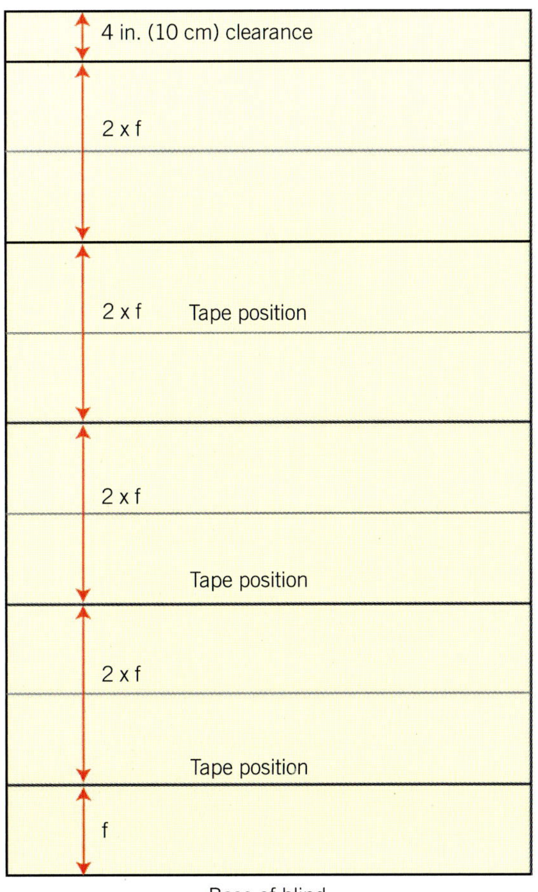

Unlined Roman blind

This blind is stunning and so easy to make, so grab your sewing machine and have a go! Here's all you'll need to know...

You will need

For the blind

- Cotton or linen plains and prints; to calculate fabric quantity, see page 100
- Matching thread
- Sew-and-stick hook-and-loop tape fastener cut to finished width of blind
- 1/4 in. (6mm) wooden dowels cut to finished width of blind minus 4 1/4 in. (11 cm); allow one per fold of blind (see page 105)
- Roman blind tape; for quantity, muliply width of blind by number of folds (see page 105)
- Fine Roman blind cord; for quantity, multiply length of blind by seven
- 15 small plastic rings
- Thin 1-in.- (2.5-cm-) wide wooden lath cut to width of blind minus 5/8 in. (1.5 cm)
- Cord pull

For the blind support and fixing (see Making a blind support, page 103)

- 1 x 2-in. (2.5 x 5-cm) timber batten, cut to width of finished blind
- Medium brass screw eyes
- Cleat to secure cords
- Screws
- Staple gun

1 Measure your window and calculate your cut blind size, then cut out your fabric. If you need to join fabric widths, use French seams, or Mock French seams if you need to match any pattern repeats (see page 100). Press a 1-in. (2.5-cm) double-turned hem (see page 45) down each side of the blind. Pin, baste (tack), and machine stitch in place.

2 Press over 3/4 in. (2 cm) to the wrong side along the base edge, then press over a further 1 1/2 in. (4 cm) to form a double-turned hem. Pin, baste (tack), and machine stitch in place.

3 Press over 1 in. (2.5 cm) to the wrong side along the top edge of the blind. Trim the hem allowance down to 5/8 in. (1.5 cm) and baste (tack) in place. Attach the fluffy side of the hook-and-loop tape to the wrong side of the blind at the top edge, enclosing the raw edge as shown on page 73.

4 To calculate and mark the spacing for the Roman blind tapes, see page 105. Cut lengths of tape to fit the width of your blind. Place the tapes on the blind, positioning the top edge of each piece along the chalked lines. Pin, baste (tack), and machine stitch the tapes in place along the top edge only, starting and finishing 3/4 in. (2 cm) in from each end of the tape and reverse stitching to secure.

5 Insert the wooden lath through the base hem channel and slipstitch (see page 49) the open ends closed. Insert the dowels through the casings in the tapes. To neaten the raw ends, fold over a double-turned hem at each end and slip hem to secure (see page 49).

6 Lay the blind wrong side up on a flat surface. Sew a plastic ring to the loose edge of each Roman blind tape, placing them 2 in. (5 cm) in from the side edges of the blind. Sew a third ring to each tape at the center point. Knot a length of cord to each of the bottom rings and thread the cords vertically up through the rest of the rings.

7 Using the hook-and-loop tape, attach your blind to the blind support. Working from the wrong side of the blind, thread the cords up through the screw eyes directly above, then pass them across to the operating end, making sure that all cords go through the fourth screw eye.

8 Attach the cord pull to the loose ends of your cords and screw the cleat to the side of the window frame. To raise your blind, pull on the cord pull and secure the cords around the cleat in a figure of eight.

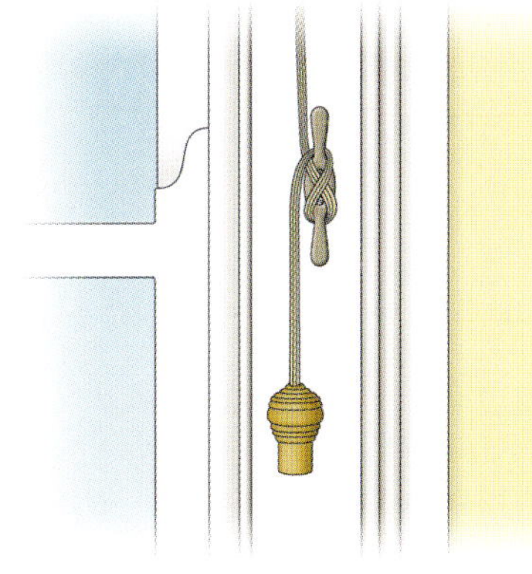

Understanding dress patterns

After working through the projects so far, you should now have the confidence to tackle a simple garment. In this workshop we'll show you how to take body measurements accurately, choose the right pattern size, use a pattern, and make simple alterations. Then, with all this information under your belt, you can have a go at the gorgeous pinafore dress on page 118; trimmed with funky appliquéd flowers, it's the perfect dress for every little girl aged 2 to 5 and will be a firm favorite in her wardrobe.

Taking body measurements

Whether you are planning to make clothes for yourself or your children, you need to determine which size pattern to buy. Do not use your dress size as a guide: sizing varies from brand to brand and you cannot rely on it. You must measure yourself accurately.

Measuring yourself

Trying to measure yourself can be quite tricky, so it is best to ask a friend to help. Do not take measurements over clothing; for the most accurate results, strip down to your usual underwear and take off your shoes. Tie a piece of string around your waist as a helpful guide for taking vertical measurements. Keep a note of your measurements on the chart opposite: you will need to take them with you when you go to choose a pattern and also refer to them later when you come to make any alterations.

Basic measurements

1 Bust
Measure around the fullest part of the bust; do not allow the tape measure to slip down at the back.

2 Waist
No breathing in! Take this measurement firmly around the waist, but make sure it is comfortable.

3 Waist to hips
The distance from your waist to the widest part of your hips, approximately 7–8 in. (18–21 cm) from your waistline.

4 Hips
Take the tape measure around the widest part of the hips.

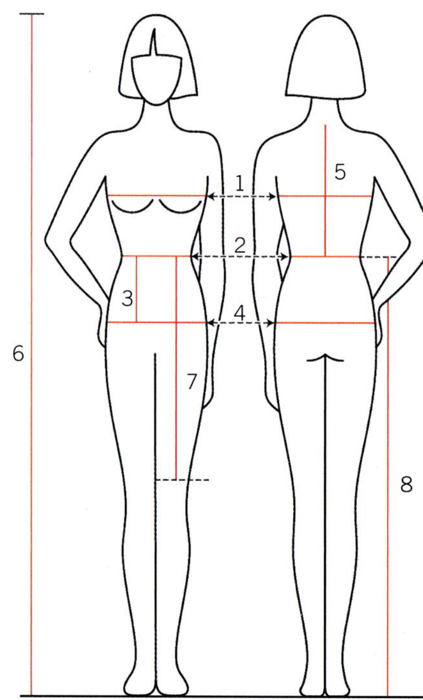

5 Back neck (nape) to waist
Measure from the neckbone at the center back down to the string tied around your waist.

6 Height
Remove your shoes and stand with your back against a wall. Place a ruler on top of your head, mark the wall lightly with a pencil, and measure from the mark to the floor.

7 Finished length (skirt)
Put on your shoes and measure from the string at your waist down to the required hem depth.

8 Finished length (pants)
Put on your shoes and measure from the waist to the floor at the side of the body.

Measuring children

Children can be difficult to measure, as they never stay still for long. If you have trouble, take measurements from garments that fit them well and compare them to the garment measurements chart on the pattern envelope. Age is indicated on children's and toddlers' charts, but as children's physical development can vary wildly within an age group, it is best to compare body measurements if possible.

For infants' patterns (babies who are not yet walking), you only need the weight and height—the length of the baby, but measured with the foot at a right angle to the leg, as if the baby is standing.

Basic measurement chart

Keep a record of your basic measurements in the chart below, using a pencil. It is best to re-measure yourself every six months to make sure that you have not changed in size. Note your measurements in the first column, the pattern body measurements in the second, and the difference between the two in the third. A difference of 1/4 in. (6 mm) in length and 3/8 in. (1 cm) in width means that you will have to adjust the pattern slightly; see page 115.

	Your measurement	Pattern measurement	Difference
BUST			
WAIST			
HIPS			
BACK NECK TO WAIST			
WAIST TO HIP			
HEIGHT			
PATTERN SIZE			

Types of pattern and what they tell you

In addition to commercial dressmaking patterns, there are free sources such as sewing magazines and books. Generally, all patterns work in a similar way, but there are a few differences in how they look.

Complimentary patterns

Patterns provided by magazines, or in books like this, are a great way to introduce yourself to dressmaking, as you do not have to spend a fortune on the pattern to start with. The fact that they are free does not mean they are no good— some fit a lot better than commercial patterns. Generally with these patterns you will find:

- **Photographs** illustrating the garment and its variations, printed along with the step-by-step sewing instructions in the main book or magazine.
- **The pattern sheet** is normally inserted separately, at either the center or the back of the publication. You will need to trace out the pattern pieces before you start, as they often have a multitude of different patterns and sizes printed on both sides of a sheet (see page 114).
- **The size chart and fabric quantities chart** is normally printed with the pattern sheet, although it may be with the step-by-step instructions instead. You will need to compare your measurements to work out the correct size to trace and how much fabric to buy.
- The recommended **fabrics, trimmings, and outline drawings** will also be supplied, but these too may be printed either with the step-by-step instructions or on the separate pattern sheet.

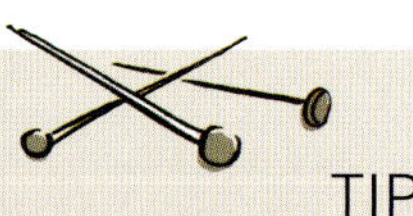

TIP

If the width of your chosen fabric is not included, ask the sales person help you work out how much you will need—but bear in mind that the pattern will contain no cutting layouts for that width (see page 116).

Commercial patterns

These patterns are made from three main parts: the envelope, the instruction sheet, and the pattern tissue.

Commercial pattern envelopes contain a wealth of information. The front gives you the style number, pattern size, and illustrations of each garment and its variations, usually called views, which are included in the pattern. The back of the envelope is printed with all the information you need to prepare for your project and makes an excellent buying guide, so read it carefully.

Envelope information will include:

- An **image of the finished garment**, plus the different versions called views. It will also show the ease of the pattern's construction; always choose an "easy"-rated style for your first attempt.
- **Notions or requirements:** these are the trimmings, fastenings, and any other items that you will need in order to complete your garment.
- **Suggested fabrics**, as recommended by the pattern's designer to suit the style best. To ensure that you select a suitable fabric, advice on the use of diagonals, plaids, stripes, and napped fabrics is also given.
- The **fabric quantities chart** tells you exactly how much fabric you need to buy for each size and view, in several fabric widths. Interfacing and lining (see page 134) quantities will also be given if required. A "star" guide is used on commercial patterns to indicate whether the amounts given in the fabric quantities charts are for one-way fabrics, for example, fabrics with or without a nap (pile), or both.
- **Finished garment measurements**—usually the length and the width at the hemline, but sometimes more—are a guide for any adjustment you might wish to make.

Inside the pattern envelope, you will also find an instruction sheet that provides the following information:

- Outline illustrations of all views
- A pattern piece diagram
- Cutting layouts
- Step-by-step sewing instructions for the pattern you are going to make, plus important details on how to use your pattern.

Finally, of course, the pattern envelope also contains the pattern tissue. Each pattern piece is printed separately on the tissue, so they do not need to be traced out.

The main difference between commercial and complimentary patterns is that commercial patterns are sized not only for different body measurements, but also different figure types. Women's figures vary greatly in shape from one person to another, so this is an attempt by the pattern companies to cut out as many fitting issues for you as possible.

Recognizing your figure type

Once you have taken your measurements, you need to assess what figure type you most closely resemble. These figure types are normally printed in the back of each pattern book. Overall height is one indicator, but more important are the back neck-to-waist and waist-to-hip measurements. Although figure types are not supposed to signify age groups, an age level may be suggested by the styles and designs in that group. It is best to stay in your figure type if you can, as these will tend to fit you better.

Misses, Misses Petite, and Misses Plus

"Misses" is considered to be the average figure type—height 5ft 5 in.–5ft 6 in. (165–167.5 cm) without shoes, with a well developed and proportioned body. The hips are measured at 8 in. (20 cm) below the waist and the back neck to waist is longer than the other figure types. "Misses Petite" figure is 1 in. (2.5 cm) shorter overall than "Misses," with the hip measured at 7 in. (18 cm) below the waist, but the proportions are similar. "Misses Plus" is for the well proportioned and developed figure.

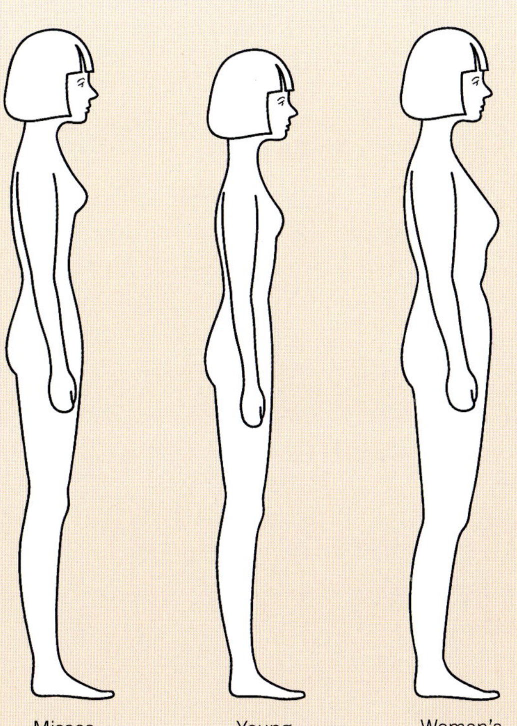

Young junior/teen

This group is for the young developing miss—about 5ft 2 in.–5ft 5 in. (157–165 cm) without shoes—with a small bust, waist larger in proportion to hips, and hips measured at 7 in. (18 cm) below the waist.

Women's

For the larger, more fully mature figure—average height 5ft 5 in.–5ft 6 in. (165–167 cm)—with the hip measured at 8 in. (20 cm) below the waist.

Buying the right pattern size

Compare your measurements to the measurement charts to decide which figure type is most like your own (commercial patterns only). Your pattern size is determined by your circumference measurements, so refer to the appropriate category again to find the bust, waist, and hip measurements that correspond most closely to yours. Very few of us have a standard figure, so there are often discrepancies between our measurements and those on the chart; depending on the pattern you choose, select a size that corresponds to the most important area of fit.

- For a dress, blouse, or jacket, buy a pattern nearest to your bust size and adjust the other measurements to fit.
- For skirts and trousers, buy a pattern nearest to your hip size and adjust the waistline to fit.
- If you choose a multi-pattern that includes several different garments—blouse, skirt, and pants, for example—select the size that corresponds to your bust size and adjust the other areas if necessary. Many styles come with a multiple of sizes in one pattern envelope, which can be a great help if your bust is one size and your hips are another. If there is a large difference, or you are worried about adjusting the fit, it can be a good idea to buy two sizes of the same pattern and use the appropriate pattern pieces from each.
- Be guided by the description of the garment on the pattern. A blouse may be described as "fitted," "loose fitting," or "very loose-fitting." If you don't want a loose fit, for example, choose a smaller size or another style.

Selecting the right pattern pieces

The pattern piece diagram enables you to easily identify the pattern pieces you will need to use. If your pattern doesn't have one of these, then it will usually have a list of the pieces. As a last resort, look at the cutting layouts (see page 116), which can help you to identify them.

Seven pieces given
This diagram shows an illustration of all the pattern pieces included in the pattern, and identifies the pieces needed for each view. It also shows whether any pieces need to be extended. The pattern pieces are clearly labeled by name, number, and view, and are listed accordingly. There is often a key that tells you which piece to use for which view.

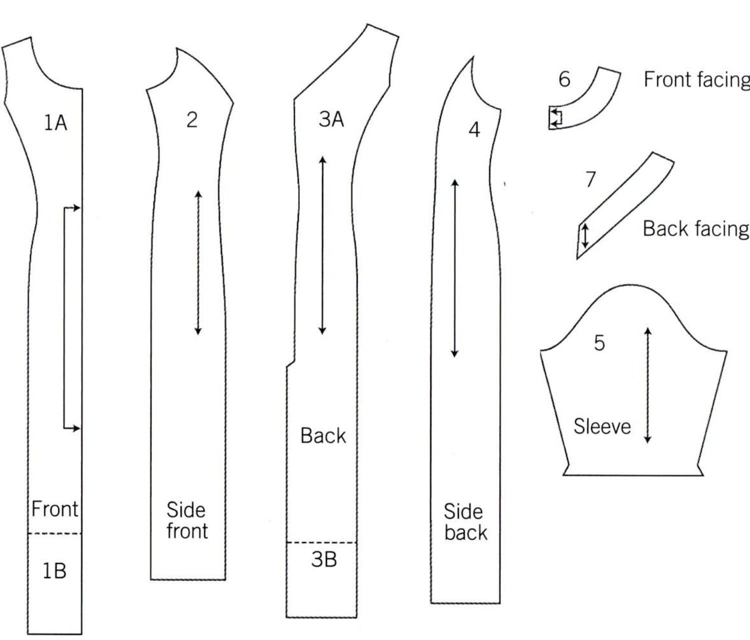

Understanding pattern markings

All pattern pieces have pattern markings or symbols, which provide information essential for every step of the making-up process, from identifying pattern pieces and cutting out to constructing the garment. They are fairly standard on all patterns, but it helps to understand the functions they perform. They can be split into two groups: preparation and cutting-out markings and construction markings. Here are the most common:

Preparation and cutting-out markings

These markings help you to cut out the pattern pieces, alter the pattern to obain a better fit (see page 115), and lay your pattern pieces out correctly and in the most economical way on your fabric.

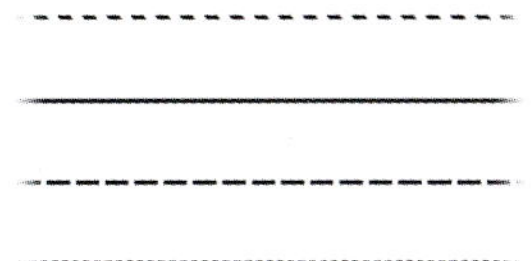

Cutting lines

Multi-sized patterns have different cutting lines for each size. See the key for the correct line for your size and follow it around each pattern piece carefully.

Alteration lines

Double parallel lines show you where to lengthen or shorten a pattern piece.

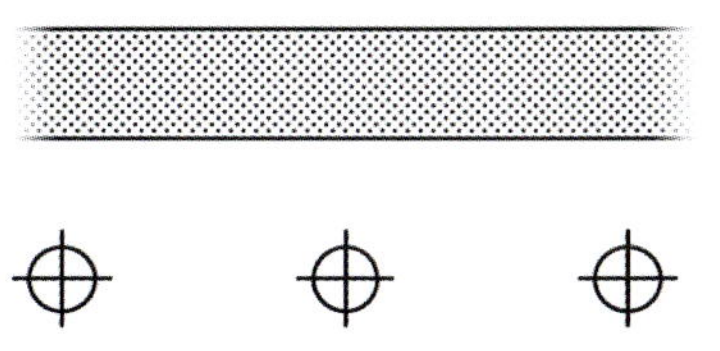

Extension marks

These are used when two pieces of a pattern have to be joined together to make one complete pattern piece. The symbols may vary depending on the pattern brand and may be a shaded area (top), or a row of crossed circles (bottom), at the edges to be joined. Overlap the matched symbols to join the pieces together and form a whole.

Straight grain or grainline

A straight line with arrowheads means place on the straight grain of the fabric, an even distance from the selvage.

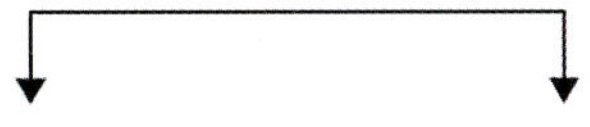

Fold

This mark tells you to place your pattern piece exactly on the folded edge of the fabric. Make sure that it is carefully lined up with the fold, as it is easy to increase or decrease the size of your garment piece.

Construction markings

Other marks are used to help you match pieces of fabric together correctly and to show where zippers, buttons, and other garment features such as pockets are to be positioned.

Notches

These are marked as triangles or diamonds and are used for matching pattern pieces when sewing. You will find notches are placed in groups of one or more notches, but they will correspond with adjoining pieces. Small circles or squares are sometimes also used as extra matching aids for joining pieces, such as a sleeve to an armhole.

Dots

Dots show the position of pockets, buttons, zippers, and eyelets, for instance. They are also used as positions to sew up to or cut in to.

Button and buttonholes

The line shows the position and length of the buttonhole; the button position may be marked with a broken line or a dot.

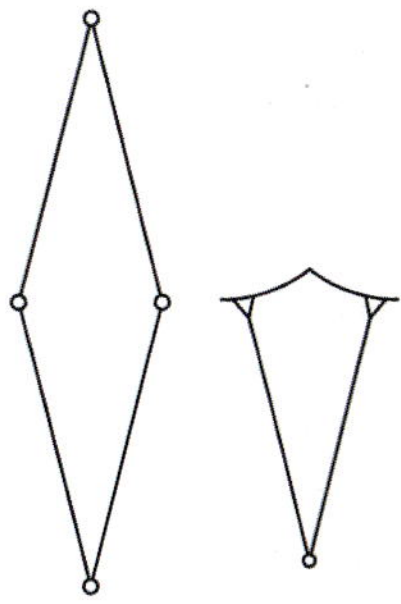

Darts

On a dart, notches or dots should be brought together (see page 132). The solid or broken lines shown are stitching lines that meet at a point.

Tracing a complimentary pattern

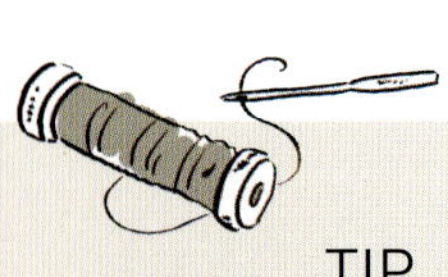

TIP
If you are going to be tracing a lot of patterns, invest in a roll of tracing paper from a graphic design shop. Alternatively, you can also use greaseproof paper from supermarkets, or use a tracing wheel (see page 23) to trace the pieces onto brown paper or left-over wallpaper.

Patterns like the ones at the back of this book generally have a multitude of different patterns and sizes printed on both sides of a pattern sheet, so you will need to trace off the pattern pieces before you start. Follow our four easy steps to getting this right:

1 Make a note of the pattern pieces you require and check the key to find out which line you need to follow for your size.

2 Carefully trace around the appropriate lines onto paper (see Tip, left) and cut out each pattern piece following the lines you have traced.

3 Lay the cut-out pattern pieces back on the pattern sheet to double-check that you have traced along the correct lines, then transfer all information, including the words and pattern markings, onto each pattern piece.

4 Make sure that you add extra length to pieces if required; join relevant pattern pieces if requested and place pieces to fold of paper where stated.

Handling tissue-paper patterns

Do not be in too much of a rush, as tissue patterns can tear easily; it pays to take your time to prepare the pieces properly. Here are four simple steps:

1 Open out your pattern tissues and, using the pattern piece diagram, identify the pieces you need for the view and size that you are making. Put any remaining pieces back in the pattern envelope to avoid any confusion.

2 Smooth out the pieces and press out the creases with a warm, dry iron if necessary, then cut the pieces you need apart from the rest, cutting well away from the actual cutting lines; the excess tissue is useful if you have to make pattern alterations.

3 If your measurements do not match those of the chart size exactly, you may need to adjust the fit and/or length. Make any necessary pattern alterations before you trim the pattern to your size (see page 112 and opposite).

4 When you are satisfied that the fit and length are correct, trim the pattern pieces along the cutting lines for your measurements.

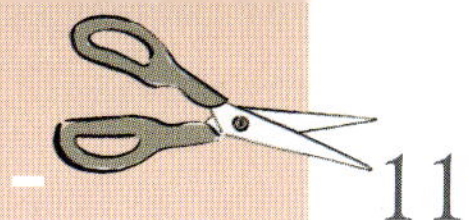

Altering your pattern

Once you have written down your body measurements (see page 109) and compared them with those of your chosen pattern, you can decide where you need to make any adjustments. The most common adjustments are to the length. It is best to do these first, and then make any waist adjustments.

Lengthening and shortening

Some patterns indicate the best place to do this alteration, but if this is not the case then you must draw your own straight line at right angles to the straight grain (see page 113) marked on the pattern piece. It is important to keep the alteration exactly at right angles to the grainline, center front or center back, when placed to a fold (see page 113), to ensure that the pattern is kept true to the straight grain of the fabric.

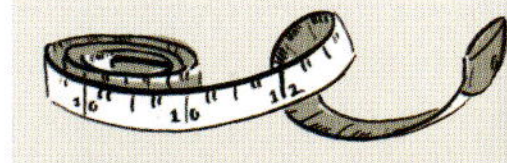

TIP

To lengthen or shorten tapered or flared pants and skirts by a large amount, draw an alteration line across the pattern piece at right angles to the grainline and either cut and spread the pattern or make an even pleat, as shown in the illustrations for the bodice, left.

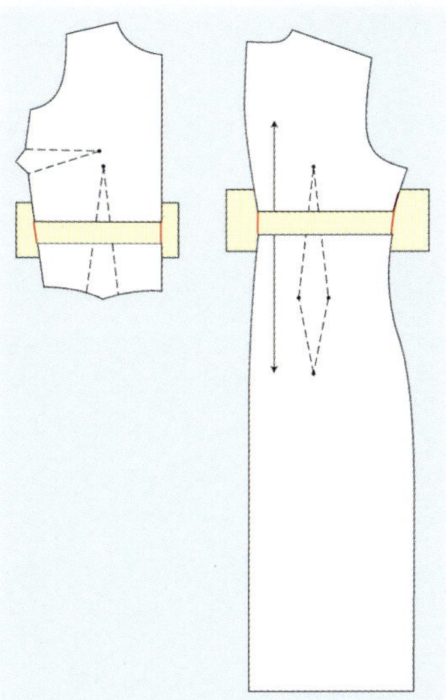

To lengthen a bodice
Cut along the alteration line and place a separate piece of paper underneath the cut. Carefully spread out the pattern pieces to your required length, measuring along the line to ensure that the gap is even, and then stick the extra paper in place using sticky tape. Do not forget to alter all the corresponding pattern pieces, where appropriate, by the same amount. Once the alteration has been made, redraw the side seams to keep the line as close as possible to the original shape.

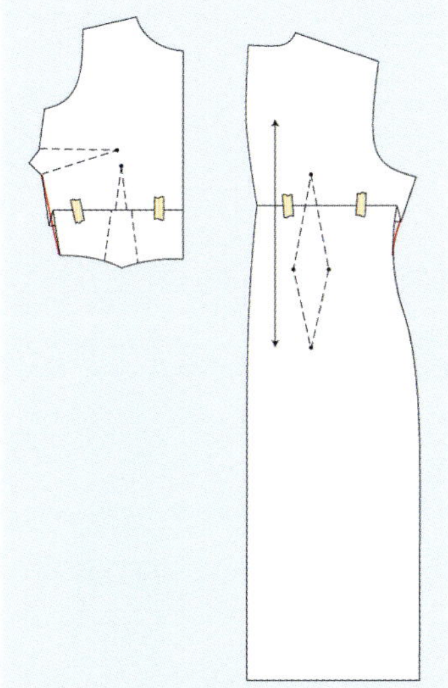

To shorten a bodice
Make a pleat along your alteration line, measuring half the depth of the required amount and keeping it even all along the fold. Tape it in place. To ensure that the original shape is retained, redraw a new side seam on the pattern, tapering it smoothly and gradually into the original line. Do not forget to alter any corresponding pattern pieces to match.

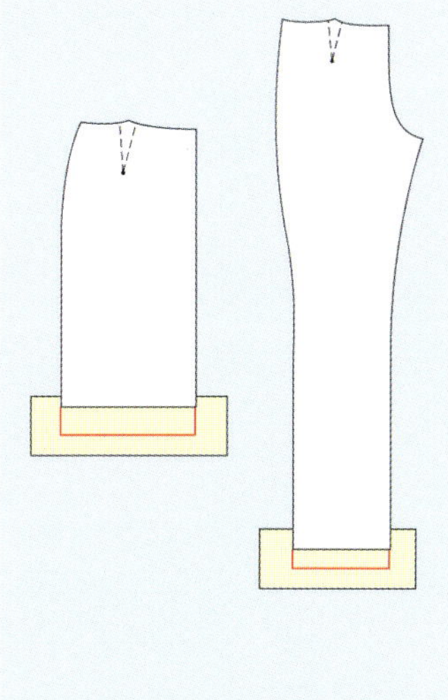

To lengthen pants and slim skirts
Stick a spare piece of paper under the hemline and add an equal amount to the hem edge. Alter corresponding pattern pieces to match. To shorten, trim an equal amount away from the hem edge.

Altering waists

You can make quick adjustments to increase or decrease the waist on skirts or trousers by altering the side seams. But if you are decreasing, do not reduce by more than 1 in. (2.5 cm) in total using this method, or you may affect the style of the garment.

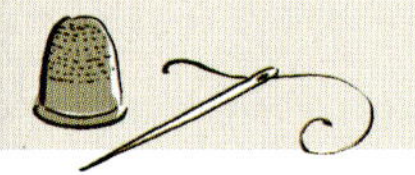

TIP

Use Scotch® Magic™ tape for your pattern alterations; this non-yellowing tape does not dry out and peel off with time, and it can also be written on, which is perfect for your alterations.

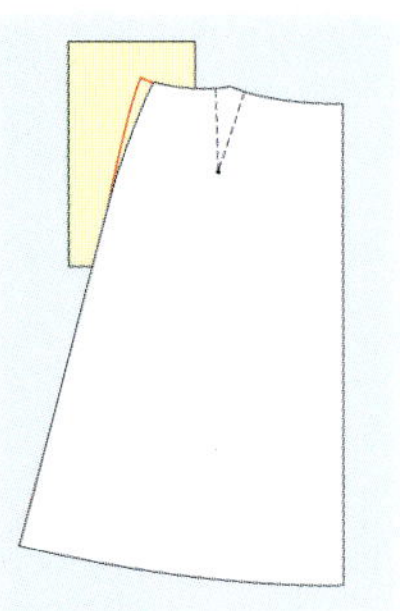

To increase the waist measurement

Add a quarter of the total amount to the waist at each side seam, front and back, tapering the new line to the original hipline.

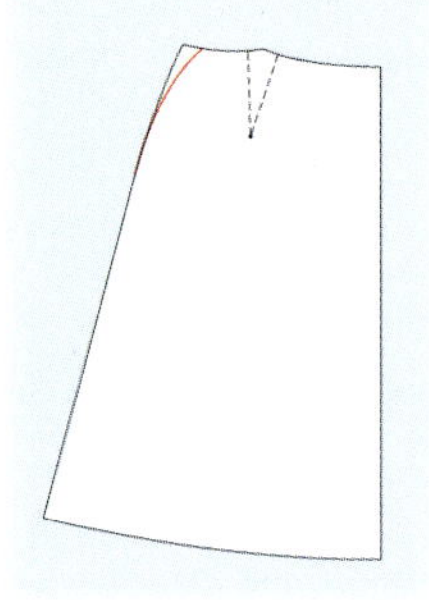

To decrease the waist measurement

Deduct a quarter of the total amount from the waist at each side seam, front and back, tapering the new line back to the original hipline.

To enlarge or reduce a waistband to correspond

Add or subtract the same amount at the side seam positions. Either cut and spread the pattern out evenly by the amounts needed and tape a piece of paper underneath, or deduct the same amount by pleating out the required amount. Tape in place.

Using cutting layouts

Now that your pattern pieces are ready, it is time to study the cutting layouts. We looked at cutting out on page 32, so you know how to prepare and fold your fabric and how to use your shears. Cutting layouts show how your fabric should be laid, and where the various pattern pieces should be placed to achieve the economical fabric usage given in the fabric quantities chart. Always read the key for the cutting layouts: it provides the information you need to cut out your pieces successfully.

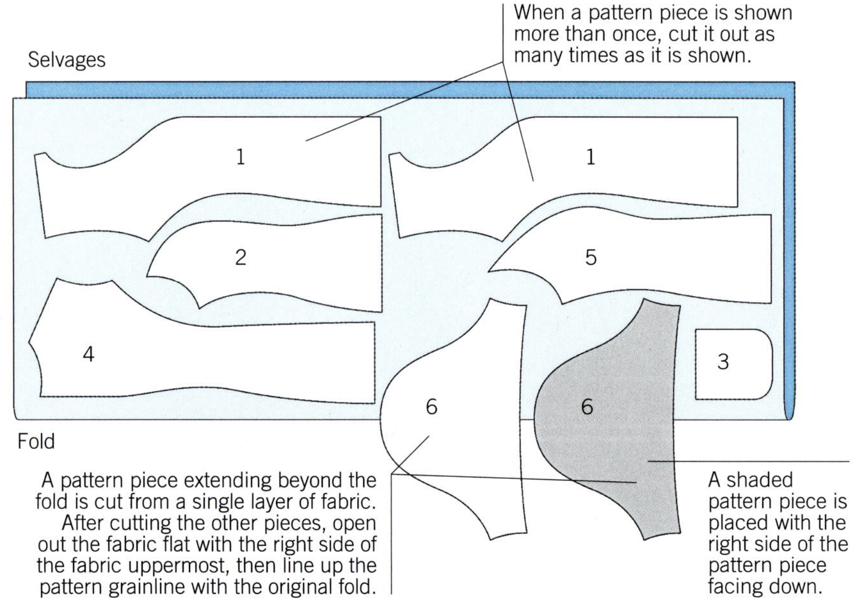

Understanding cutting layouts

Each layout gives the numbers of the pattern pieces required for that view, so you can check that you have not missed any out. It also shows whether any pattern pieces have to be extended or lengthened and whether they need to be cut from lining and/or interfacing (see page 134) as well as from fabric. Find the layout(s) for your view, size, and fabric width. Place all the pattern pieces on the fabric as shown in the diagram, bearing in mind that you may be able to fit pattern pieces more closely together for smaller sizes.

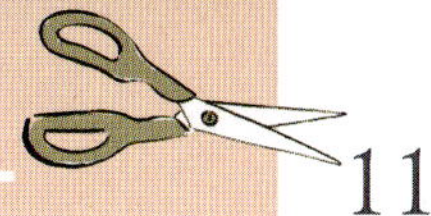

Cutting out your fabric pieces

With the pattern pieces in position, it is time to think about cutting out. Accuracy is vital: not only will the fit be better, but cutting too far inside or outside the cutting lines can make a difference to the size. This guide is pretty much a guarantee against making mistakes, so use it as a checklist:

- If you are using a tissue pattern, pin the pattern pieces to the fabric, spacing the pins about 8 in. (20 cm) apart and pinning through both fabric layers on a double thickness, or weight them down with something heavy.
- If you are using a traced pattern on thicker paper, weight down your pattern pieces and mark carefully round each piece with tailor's chalk (see page 22), then remove the weights and pattern pieces. Carefully pin inside each cutting line, pinning through both fabric layers on a double thickness.
- Make sure that the grainlines on pattern pieces run absolutely parallel to the selvage by measuring from each end of the grainline arrow to the selvage and adjusting the position of the pattern pieces until the distances are equal.
- Check that foldlines on pattern pieces are placed exactly on the fold of the fabric.
- Before you start to cut out the fabric, double-check the pattern pieces against the cutting layout to make sure that they are correct.
- If you pinned your pattern pieces onto the fabric, carefully cut around the edges. Do not trim the pattern or cut too far away from the edges. If you have chalked around your pieces, cut along the lines.
- Do not cut through any fold lines.

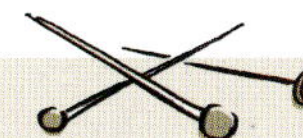

TIP
Prolong the life of your favorite tissue patterns by tracing around them onto a roll of old wallpaper and transferring all the markings before they become unusable.

Transferring pattern markings

After cutting out the fabric pieces, transfer all your construction pattern markings from the tissue pattern to the fabric before you unpin it—or, if you are using a traced pattern, carefully place the pattern pieces back on top of the corresponding cut pieces ready to transfer the pattern markings.

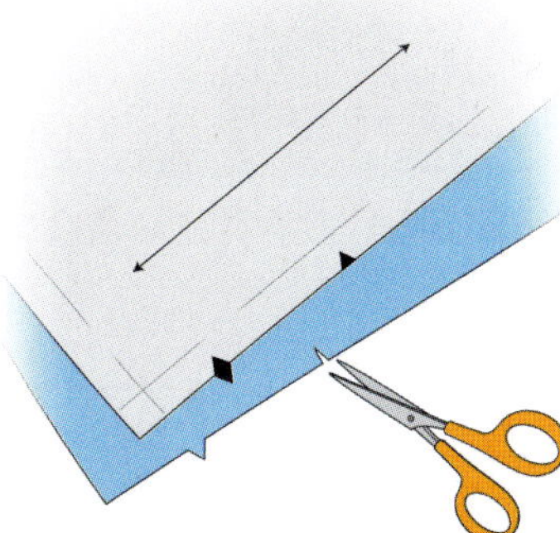

Marking notches
Notches can be marked by cutting around the extending outer edges of the diamonds or by making a small snip about 1/8 in. (2–3 mm) deep into the seam allowances at the triangles.

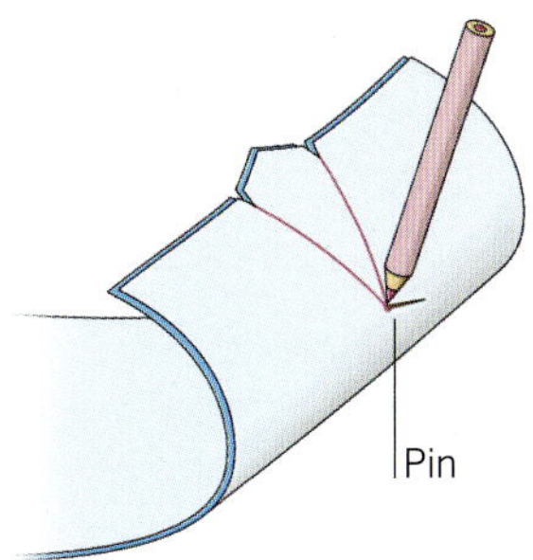

Marking dots, circles, and darts
Make a small hole in the pattern and mark the position with a chalk pencil on the top layer of fabric. At the dot position, push a pin straight down through the fabric layers and mark the dot on the other layer of fabric with a chalk pencil. If you wish, you can also draw in the dart lines with a chalk pencil and ruler to help you with your stitching (see page 132).

Girl's pinafore dress

This pretty pinafore has real flower power: a jazzy print lines the bodice and provides the flowers appliquéd onto the skirt. It's finished with neat little ribbon waist ties and fastens at the shoulders with matching buttons.

Fabric suggestions

For the dress
Needlecord, corduroy, lightweight denim, cotton drill. This style is not suitable for large checks, stripes, and diagonals.

For the lining and appliqué
Coordinating printed cotton, poly-cotton, or linen, with a simple design that can easily be cut out for appliqué.

You will also need

- Pinafore dress pattern pieces traced off from the pattern sheet at the back of this book (see page 114)
- Pack of paper-backed adhesive web
- Two 3/4-in. (2-cm) diameter buttons
- 1 2/3 yd (1.50 m) of 3/8-in. (10-mm) ribbon in two matching colors for the tie belt
- Lightweight iron-on interfacing (see page 134)

Age	2–3	4–5
Height	36¼–38 1/2 in. (92–98 cm)	41–43¼ in. (104–110 cm)
Chest	21–21 5/8 in. (53–55 cm)	22½–23¼ in. (57–59 cm)
Waist	20 1/2–20 7/8 in. (52–53 cm)	21¼–21 5/8 in. (54–55 cm)
Finished length (back neck to hem)	21 in. (53 cm)	23½ in. (60 cm)

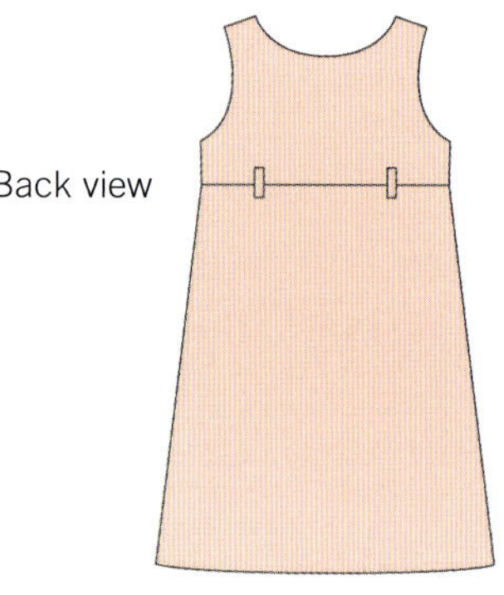

Fabric quantities

45-in- (112-cm-) wide fabric		
Fabric Lining	1 yd (0.90 m) ½ yd (0.50 m)	1 yd (0.90 m) ½ yd (0.50 m)
60-in- (150-cm-) wide fabric		
Fabric Lining	2/3 yd (0.60 m) ½ yd (0.50 m)	2/3 yd (0.60 m) ½ yd (0.50 m)
36-in.- (90-cm-) wide iron-on interfacing		
	¼ yd (0.20 m)	¼ yd (0.20 m)

Dress—all sizes 45-in.- (112-cm-) wide fabric

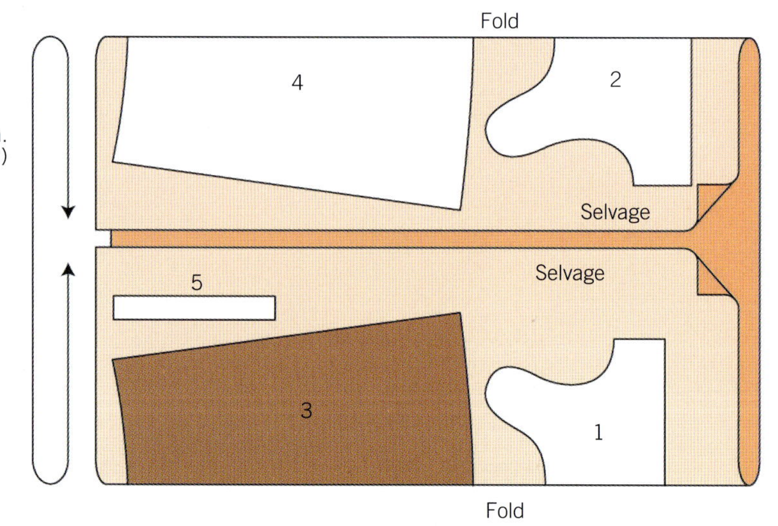

Dress lining—all sizes 45–60-in.- (112–150-cm-) wide fabric

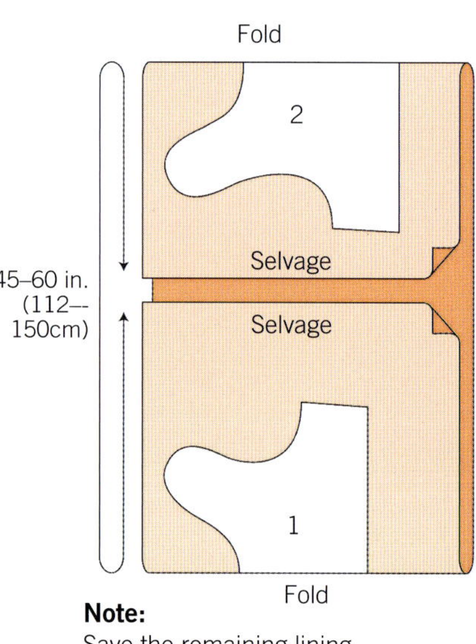

Note:
Save the remaining lining fabric for appliqué flowers

Cutting out your fabric

Use pattern pieces 1, 2, 3, 4, 5, 6, and 7.

Note:
Fabric quantities and cutting layouts are given for one-way fabrics only. If using fabric with a two-way design, you may be able to lay the pattern pieces into a smaller amount of fabric, but remember, grainlines must still run parallel to the selvage.

Dress—all sizes

60-in.- (150-cm-) wide fabric

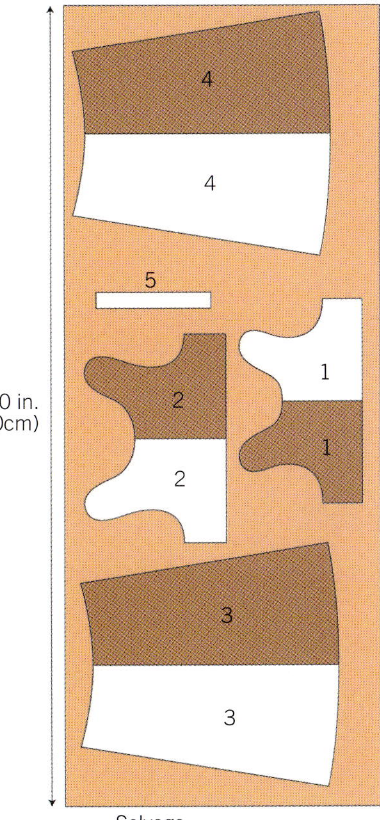

Interfacing—all sizes

36-in.- (90-cm-) wide

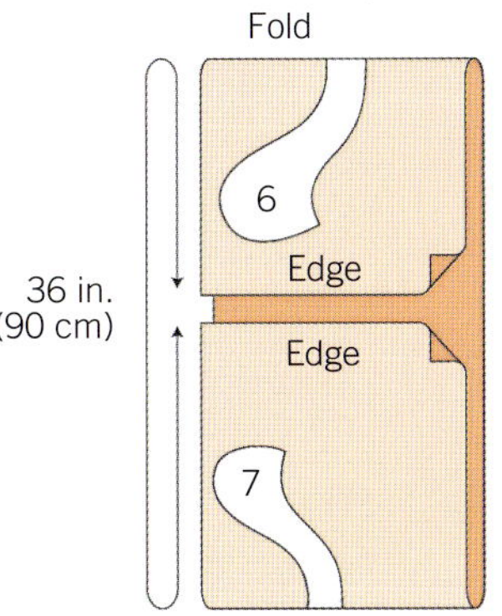

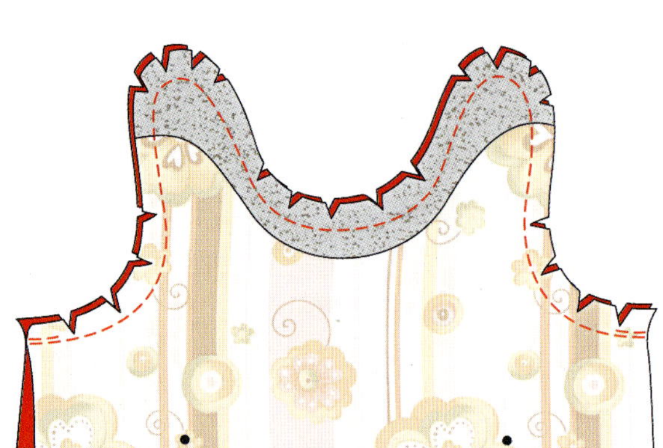

Note:

- 3/8-in. (1-cm) seam allowances are included unless otherwise stated.
- Stitch seams with right sides together and notches matching.

1 Following the appropriate cutting layout, cut out all your fabric pieces. Using an iron, press the interfacing to the wrong side of the bodice lining neckline and armhole edges. With right sides together, pin, baste (tack), and machine stitch the front bodice to the front bodice lining around the armhole and neckline edges, starting at one side seam edge and finishing at the other. Trim and layer the seam allowances and notch the curves (see page 43).

2 Turn the front bodice to the right side. Press the seamed edges flat, making sure the seamlines are placed exactly on the edge. Repeat steps 1 and 2 with the back bodice and back bodice lining.

3 With right sides together, pin and baste (tack) the front bodice and lining to the back bodice and lining at the corresponding side seam edges, matching the raw edges and armhole seams. Stitch the bodice and lining side seams in one continuous line of stitching. Press the seams open.

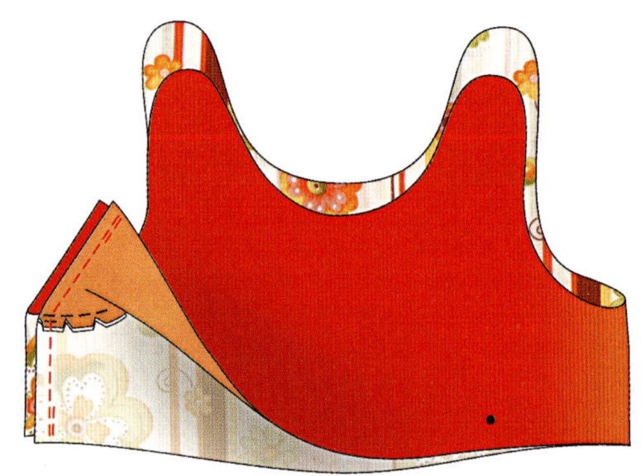

4 Pin and baste (tack) the bodice and lining waist edges together, matching the side seams. Then edge stitch the bodice neckline and armhole edges (see page 51).

5 Work a buttonhole on each back bodice shoulder extension at the positions marked on the pattern (see page 68).

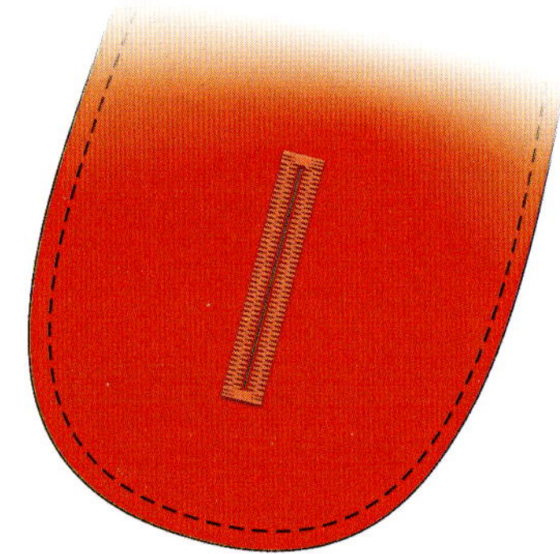

6 Cut out designs from your remaining lining fabric and, using the photograph on page 119 as a guide, appliqué them to the right side of the front and back skirt pieces (see page 83).

7 With right sides together, pin, baste (tack), and machine stitch the front skirt to the back skirt at the side seams. Neaten the seam allowances together (see page 44) and press toward the back skirt. Matching the side seams, pin and baste the bodice to the skirt at the waist edges, then machine stitch them together. Neaten the turnings together and press them toward the bodice. Working from the right side, topstitch around the skirt waist, 1/16 in. (2 mm) up from the seamline (see page 50).

8 Neaten one long edge of the belt loop strip. Fold the raw edge over to the wrong side of the strip by 3/8 in. (1 cm) and press. Press the neatened edge over the raw edge, enclosing it, so that the strip measures 3/8 in. (1 cm) wide. Topstitch 1/16 in. (2 mm) in from each pressed edge (see page 50). Cut the belt loop strip into four equal lengths.

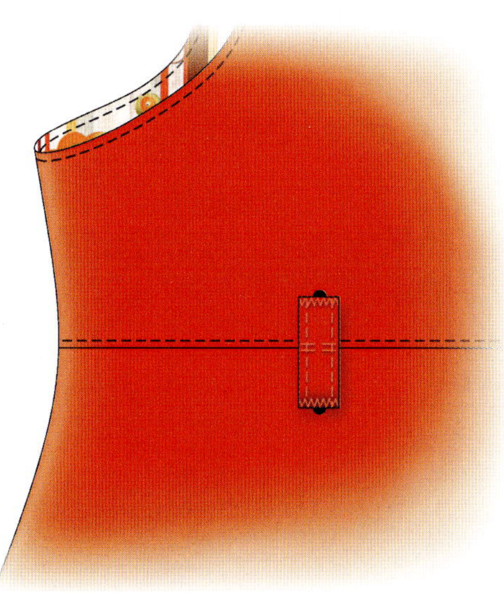

9 Press the short ends of the belt loops to the wrong side so that each one measures 1 3/8 in. (3.5 cm) long. Pin and baste (tack) the loops to the dress with the pressed ends to the dots on the bodice and skirt. Set your machine to a close narrow zigzag, and stitch the loops in place. Then machine stitch a single row of straight stitches across the center of each loop, reverse stitching at each end to secure, to create two channels for the ribbon ties.

10 Neaten the hem edge. Pin, baste (tack), and press it to the wrong side by 3/4 in. (2 cm). Topstitch in place with two rows of stitching 1/4 in. (6 mm) apart. Sew buttons to the front bodice at the positions marked on the pattern (see page 65). Thread the ribbon lengths through the belt loops; the dress is now ready to wear.

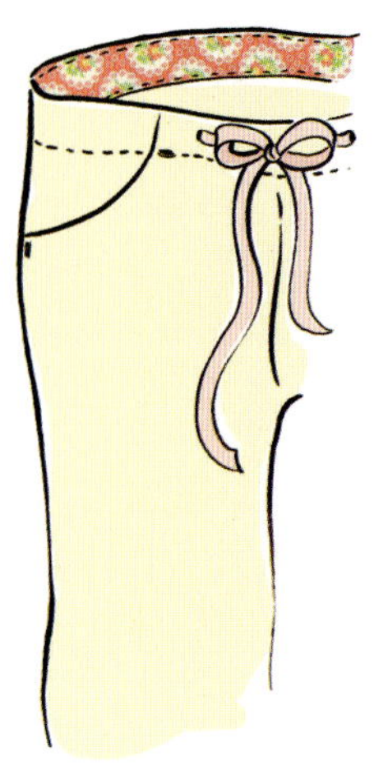

Inside pockets & casings

Now we are going to look at inside pockets—the ones that are hidden in side seams or positioned as stylish hip pockets, as in jeans. We shall also be covering casings—a kind of fabric "tunnel" made to enclose an elastic, cord, or curtain rod, over which the fabric is gathered up. Once you've accomplished these techniques, you'll be able to make the gorgeous linen drawstring pants on page 128, which combine hip pockets with a waist casing for comfort and style.

Inside pockets

Inside pockets are functional pockets, where the pocket pieces are hidden inside the garment. They may be in-seam pockets, where the pocket pieces are placed in the seams, or hip pockets that are anchored to the garment at the waist and side seam edges. Unlike patch pockets, however, which can be placed more freely to flatter the wearer, their placement for easy access is important.

In-seam pockets

In-seam pockets are concealed in side seams or front panel seams. They can be constructed in two main ways: as "grown-on" sections to the main garment piece, where the two are cut as one, with no seam at the pocket opening, or as an "extension," which is made up of a separate pocket piece stitched to a small projection on the garment piece. This is designed to extend into the pocket opening, so that you cannot see the seam. The second method is most often used, as it requires less fabric.

"Grown-on" pocket Here the pocket is part of the garment and appears as a projection on the corresponding garment pieces. It is stitched as one with the garment seam. No stitching is visible from the right side.

1 With right sides together and the raw edges matching, pin, baste (tack), and machine stitch the corresponding garment pieces together in one continuous row of stitching, pivoting your work at the pocket corners (see page 42), matching any dots or notches, and reverse stitching at the start and finish to secure. Reinforce the pocket area by working a second row of stitching on top of the first, starting and finishing before and after the corners.

2 Snip into the seam allowance of the back garment at the pocket corners. Neaten the garment seam allowances separately and the pocket seam allowances together (see page 44), neatening the front and pocket edges in one continuous row of stitching. Press the garment seams open and the whole pocket toward the center front.

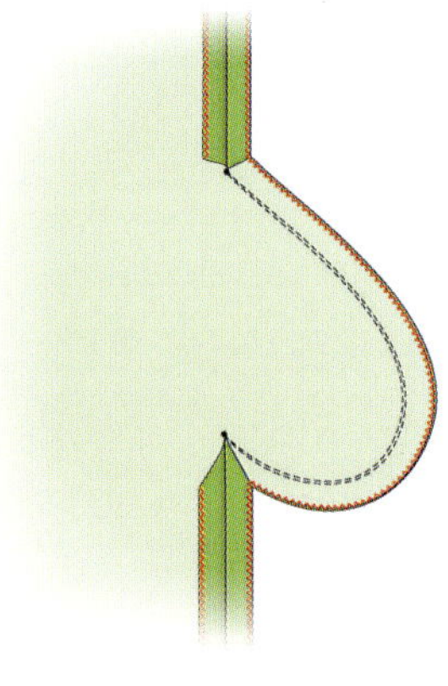

Extension pocket With this method the garment has small projections that extend partway into the pocket, where they are stitched onto the pocket pieces. The pocket pieces can be cut from lining, which reduces the bulk on thicker fabrics, and also uses less fabric.

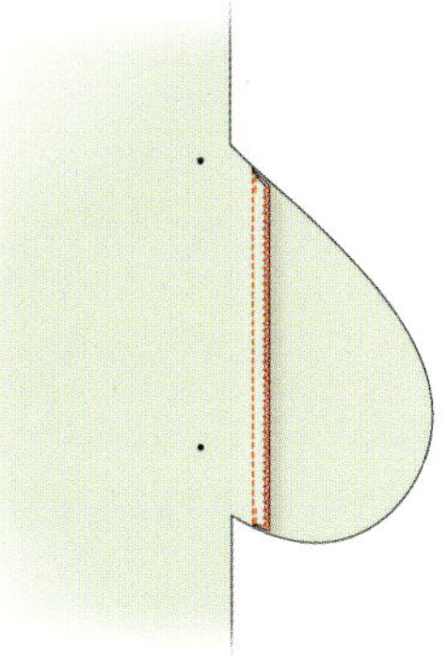

Pin, baste (tack), and machine stitch each pocket piece to the corresponding seam extension, matching any notches. Trim the seam allowances to 3/8 in. (1 cm), neaten them together, and press them toward the pocket piece. Refer to the "Grown-on" pocket, steps 1 and 2, to stitch the corresponding garment and pocket pieces together.

Hip pockets

Front hip pockets feature predominantly in pants and skirts. The shape of the opening edge may be curved, straight, or angled and is usually topstitched for decoration. All hip pockets consist of a pocket back, which forms part of the garment, and a pocket facing. The pocket back is cut from fabric, and the pocket facing is usually cut from lining; however, if your fabric is light- to medium-weight, it may also be cut from fabric. The pocket opening edge is usually interfaced (see page 134) to prevent it from stretching.

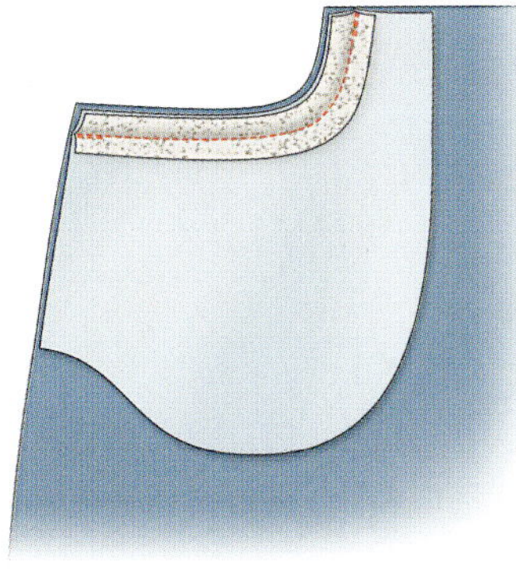

1 Cut a strip of iron-on interfacing 1 in. (2.5 cm) wide, shaped to fit the pocket facing opening edge; press the interfacing to the wrong side of the pocket facings using an iron (see page 134). With right sides together, pin and baste (tack) the pocket facings to the corresponding garment fronts at the opening edges, matching the waist and side seam edges. Machine stitch them together, reverse stitching at the start and finish to secure.

2 Trim and layer the seam allowances, notching them at any curves (see page 43), then press the seam allowances toward the facings. Understitch (see page 51) the seam allowances to the facings and press the facings to the wrong side of the front. Topstitch along the pocket opening edges if desired (see page 50).

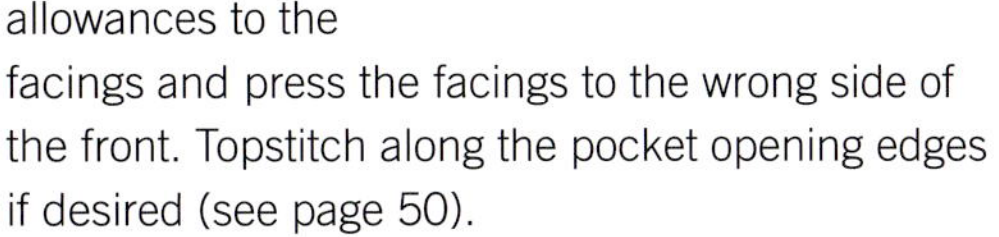

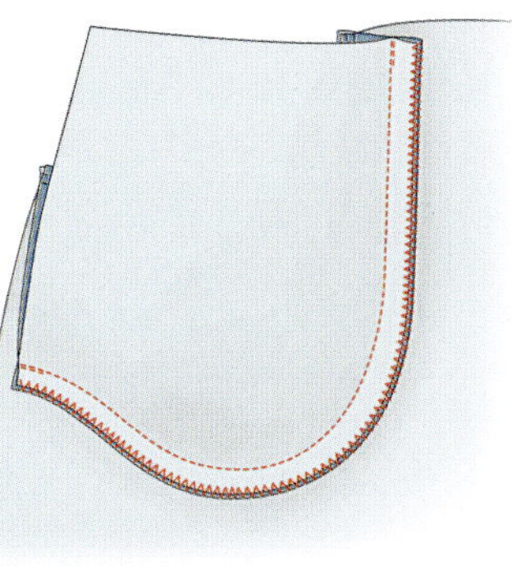

3 With right sides together, pin and baste (tack) the pocket backs to the corresponding pocket facings around the long curved edges. Stitch them together, reverse stitching at the start and finish to secure. Neaten the seam allowances together.

4 Baste (tack) the pockets to the garment fronts at the waist and side seam edges. Reinforce each end of the pocket opening with a short row of close zigzag stitches (see page 44), placed parallel to and just outside the waist and side seam stitchlines.

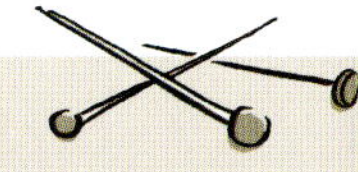

TIP

If you need to alter a pattern at the waist, remember that the pocket pieces must be amended to match.

Casings

Casings often go unnoticed, but they are a very significant and effective way of gathering up fabric with either elastic or a drawstring or onto a curtain wire or pole. A casing is simply a "tunnel" formed out of fabric. There are two main types of casing: "fold-down" and "applied." Both can be worked either on the flat, with the ends of the casing open (as, for example, on a curtain heading or bag), or circular, as around cuffs and waists. A casing needs to be 1/4 in. (6 mm) wider than whatever is being threaded through it.

Fold-down casings

A fold-down casing is formed by turning down an extension on the garment or item to the inside (forming a hem), which is stitched in place. It works best on straight edges and makes an excellent waist finish for pull-on garments and curtain headings. It can be a simple plain fold-down casing, or one with an added heading, which extends beyond the casing to create a frill when the fabric is gathered up. This looks particularly attractive on sheer curtains and little girl's skirt and pants waists.

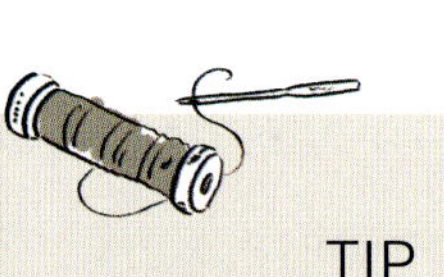

TIP

Remember to allow extra depth for screw eyes and fixed finials if you are intending to thread your casing onto a curtain wire or rod.

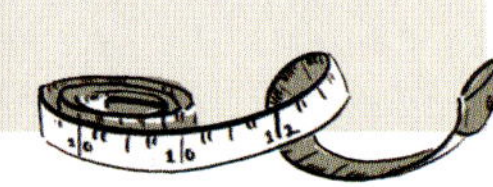

Flat fold-down casing This is the most basic type of casing; as the ends are left open, it is easy to thread a drawstring through the "tunnel" or to pass a curtain wire along its length. It is usually made on a straight edge, and you will need to have hemmed the side edges of your project before forming the casing.

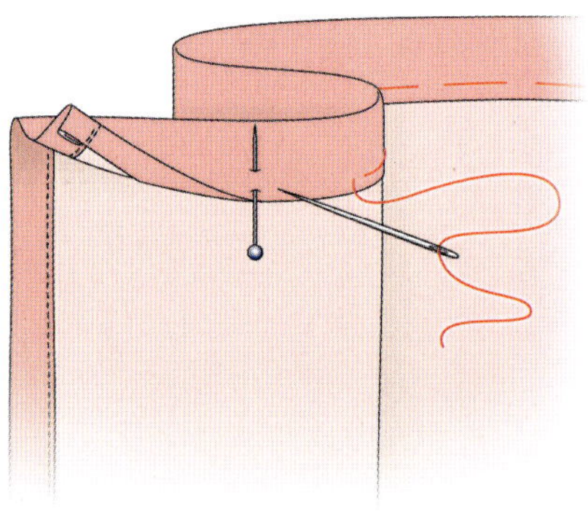

1 Fold and press your hem allowance to the wrong side along the top edge of your item, then trim away any excess hem allowance to measure 1/4 in. (6 mm). Fold over the casing depth to the wrong side, then pin and baste (tack) it in place.

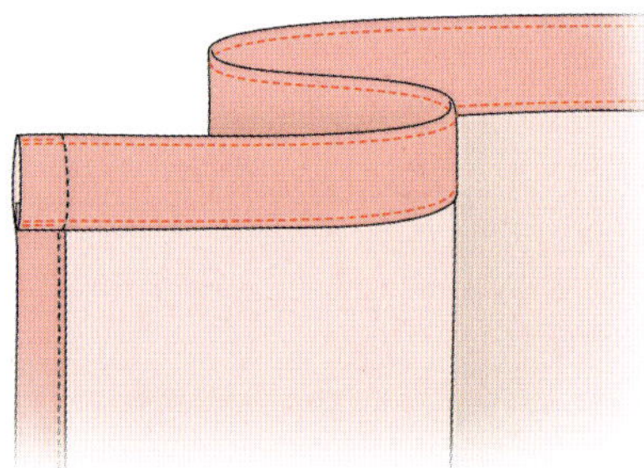

2 Machine stitch the lower edge of the casing in place, reverse stitching at each end to secure. Work a second row of stitching close to the top folded edge, reverse stitching to secure.

Circular fold-down casing On a circular casing, you need to leave a gap in your stitching so that you can insert elastic, or to work buttonholes (see page 68) if you plan to use a drawstring, so that the cord can be passed through to the right side for tying before the casing is stitched in place.

Casing for a drawstring

Work two buttonholes at the positions marked on your pattern and follow step 1 of the Flat fold-down casing. Then machine stitch the lower edge of the casing in place, overlapping the ends of the stitching to secure. Work a second row of stitching close to the top folded edge, overlapping the ends of the stitching to secure. See page 127 for inserting the drawstring.

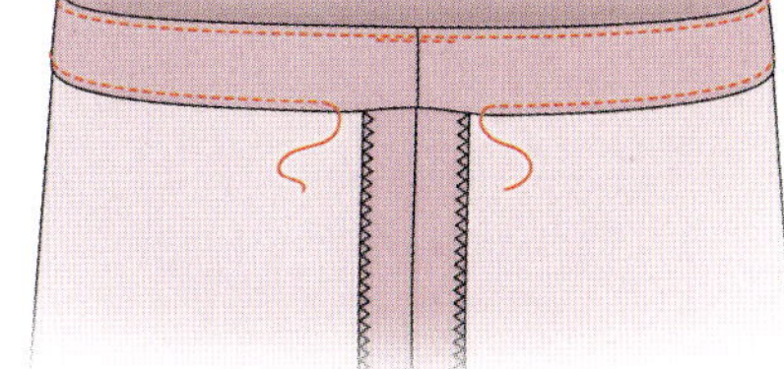

Casing to insert elastic

Follow step 1 of the Flat fold-down casing, then machine stitch around the lower edge of the casing, leaving a gap through which elastic can be threaded. Work a second row of stitching close to the top folded edge, overlapping the ends of the stitching to secure. See page 127 for inserting the elastic.

Headed fold-down casing A headed casing is made in very much the same way as the flat and circular fold-down headings, but it has extra fabric allowed for a heading. If you want to turn a plain fold-down casing into a headed one, decide on a heading depth and add twice this amount to whatever you allowed for your casing depth.

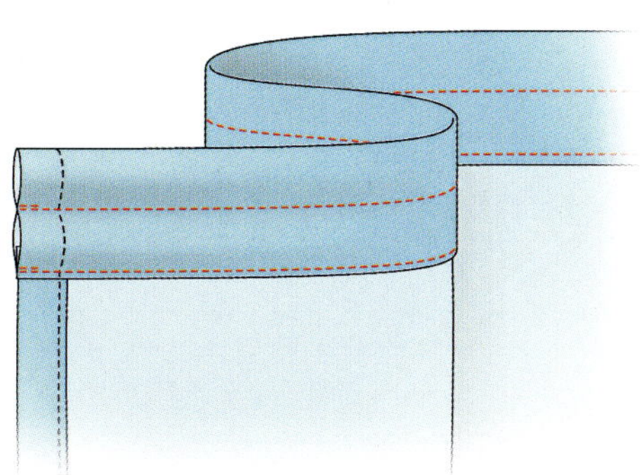

Follow the instructions for the flat or circular fold-down casing, omitting the second row of stitching. Instead, measure up from the lower stitching line to the depth of your casing and work a parallel row of basting (tacking) stitches around the casing at this position. Machine stitch a second row of stitching (no opening needed) following the basted line, reverse stitching or overlapping the stitching ends to secure. Remove the basting stitches.

Applied casings

A fold-down casing is not always suitable for a project, particularly if you have hip pockets that come right up to the waist edge. Here, an applied casing—a separate strip of fabric cut on the straight or bias grain (see page 132)—is required. It is ideal for shaped waist edges and where a blouson effect is required around a waistline.

How to work out the size of your casing
Your casing should be at least 1/4 in. (6 mm) wider than whatever you are threading through the "tunnel," plus 3/4 in. (2 cm) for seam allowances. The length is determined by the circumference of the garment at the place where it is going to be stitched, plus 3/4 in. (2 cm) for hems at each end.

Applied casing around a waistline

These casings are normally applied in a circle; you do not need to leave a gap in the stitching for inserting elastic, as the ends of the strip will meet at a seam, leaving you with an opening. If you are using a drawstring, you will still need to work your buttonholes first, as marked on your pattern. This type of casing can be applied to either the outside or the inside of a garment waistline, but in this book we will only be stitching them to the inside.

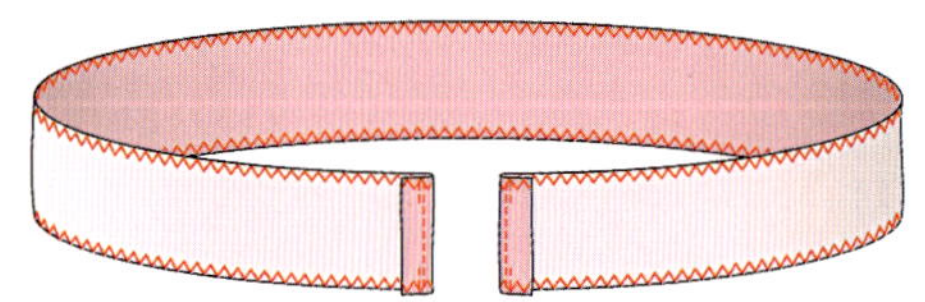

1 Refer to How to work out the size of your casing, above left, then cut a strip of fabric on the straight grain if your casing is straight, or on the bias grain if it needs to curve. Neaten both long edges of the strip (see page 44) and then press the short ends to the wrong side by 3/8 in. (1 cm) and machine stitch in place.

2 Starting and finishing at one side seam, place the strip right side up on the wrong side of the garment at the position marked on your pattern. Pin, baste (tack), and machine stitch the casing in place, working 3/8 in. (1 cm) in from each long neatened edge and overlapping the stitching ends to secure. See opposite for inserting a drawstring or elastic.

Applied casing at a waist edge Applied casings at waist edges are normally worked on the circle for a totally pull-on waist finish. Occasionally, they may be applied on the flat, when a zipper fastening is involved, but as this method is quite advanced, we will not be dealing with it in this book.

TIP

Use pre-packed bias binding for a quick applied casing, rather than cutting out your own strip from fabric.

1 Follow step 1 of the Applied casing around a waistline, but only neaten the lower long edge of the strip. Trim the top seam allowance to 3/8 in. (1 cm). Starting and finishing at one side seam and with right sides facing, pin, baste (tack), and machine stitch the casing to the top edge of your item, taking a 3/8-in. (1-cm) seam allowance and overlapping the stitching ends to secure. Trim the seam allowance down to 1/4 in. (6 mm) and press the seam open.

2 Fold over and press the casing to the wrong side of the garment. Pin, baste (tack), and machine stitch the lower edge of the strip in place, working 3/8 in. (1 cm) in from the long neatened edge. Work a second row of topstitching just below the top edge of the casing, overlapping the ends to secure. See opposite for inserting a drawstring or elastic.

Threading a casing

Casings are usually threaded with elastic, drawstrings, or plastic covered wires and rods for curtains. The elastic must be firm, flat, preferably non-roll, and cut slightly shorter than the measurement of the area it is going to fit. Drawstrings can be a length of ribbon, leather, or cord, or even made from fabric. The length depends on how you want to tie it at the waist; it is often best to thread your drawstring first and try it out, before you cut it to the finished length.

Drawstrings

To insert a drawstring, attach a safety pin to one end of the cord, insert it through one of the buttonholes, and work it around the garment until it emerges back out through the other buttonhole.

Curtain wires and rods

Insert screw eyes into each end of the curtain wire, and push one end through the casing, gathering the fabric up until it emerges out the other end of the casing. Alternatively, insert your rod through the casing channel and gather the fabric up along its length.

Elastic

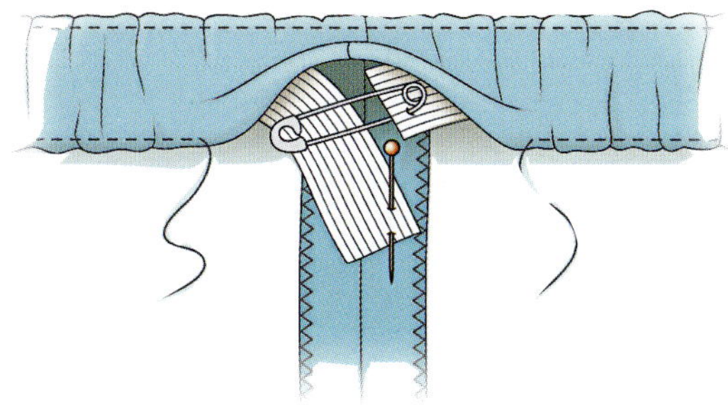

On both fold-down and applied casings

1 Attach a safety pin to one end of the elastic and pin the other end to the garment to stop it from disappearing into the casing. Thread the elastic through the casing, making sure it does not twist as you work it around. Adjust the elastic to fit, overlap the ends, and box-stitch them together (see page 63); trim off any surplus elastic.

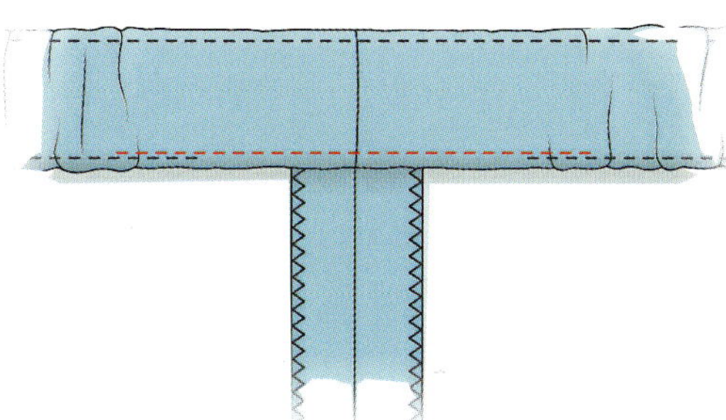

On a fold-down casing

2 Stretch the elastic slightly to keep your work flat, and then machine stitch along the lower edge, overlapping the stitching at each end and taking care not to catch the elastic as you sew.

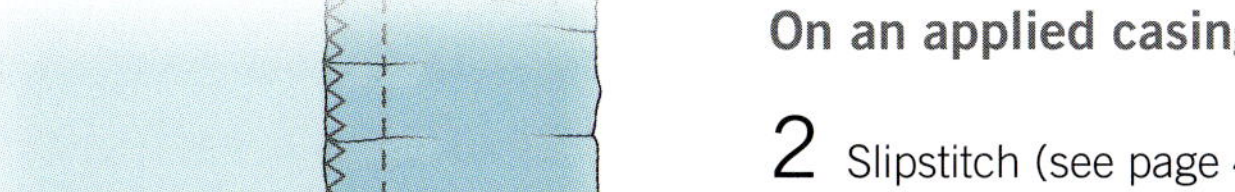

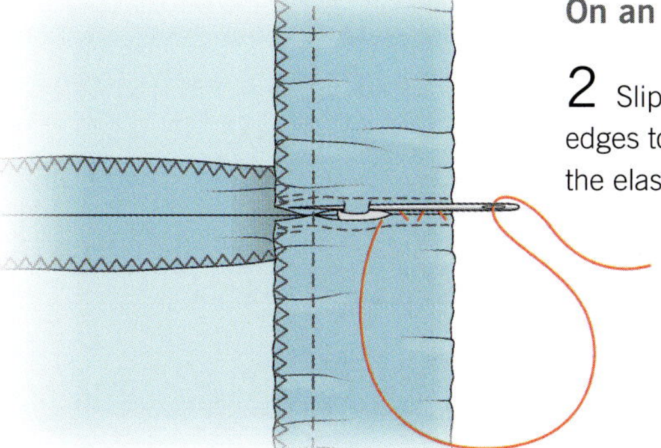

On an applied casing

2 Slipstitch (see page 49) the opening edges together, taking care not to catch the elastic as you sew.

Drawstring pants

Made in a fresh-soft linen fabric, with neat topstitched hip pockets and a drawstring waist; these pants are just perfect for vacations or for simply lounging around at the weekend.

Fabric suggestions

- Main pants: Soft linens and cottons, viscose, sand-washed silk. Avoid checks and large patterns.
- Contrast waist casing and tie belt: Fine cotton prints and plains.

You will also need

- Pants pattern pieces traced off from the pattern sheet at the back of this book (see page 114)
- Lightweight iron-on interfacing (see page 134)
- Matching thread

Size chart

Size	US 6 (UK 8)	US 8 (UK 10)	US 10 (UK 12)	US 12 (UK 14)	US 14 (UK 16)	US 16 (UK 18)
Waist	24 in. (61 cm)	25 in. (64 cm)	26½ in. (67 cm)	28 in. (71 cm)	30 in. (76 cm)	32 in. (81 cm)
Hips	33½ in. (85 cm)	34½ in. (88 cm)	36 in. (92 cm)	38 in. (97 cm)	40 in. (102 cm)	42 in. (107 cm)
Finished length (waist to hem*)	41¼ in. (105 cm)	41½ in. (105.5 cm)	41¾ in. (106 cm)	42 in. (106.5 cm)	42¼ in. (107 cm)	42½ in. (107.5 cm)

* Please note: The waist on these pants is dropped by 1½ in. (4 cm) below the natural waistline.

Fabric quantities

45-in.- (112-cm-) wide fabric						
Main	2¾ yd (2.40 m)	2¾ yd (2.40 m)	2¾ yd (2.40 m)	2¾ yd (2.50 m)	2¾ yd (2.50 m)	2¾ yd (2.50 m)
Contrast	¾ yd (0.70 m)	1 yd (0.80 m)	1 yd (0.80 m)	1 yd (0.90 m)	1 yd (0.90 m)	1 yd (0.90 m)
60-in.- (150-cm-) wide fabric						
Main	1¾ yd (1.60 m)	1¾ yd (1.60 m)	1¾ yd (1.60 m)	2¼ yd (2.10 m)	2⅓ yd (2.20 m)	2⅓ yd (2.20 m)
Contrast	¾ yd (0.70 m)	1 yd (0.80 m)	1 yd (0.80 m)	1 yd (0.90 m)	1 yd (0.90 m)	1 yd (0.90 m)
36-in.- (90-cm-) wide iron-on interfacing						
	¼ yd (0.20 m)	¼ yd (0.20 m)	¼ yd (0.20 m)	¼ yd (0.20 m)	¼ yd (0.20 m)	¼ yd (0.20 m)

Front view

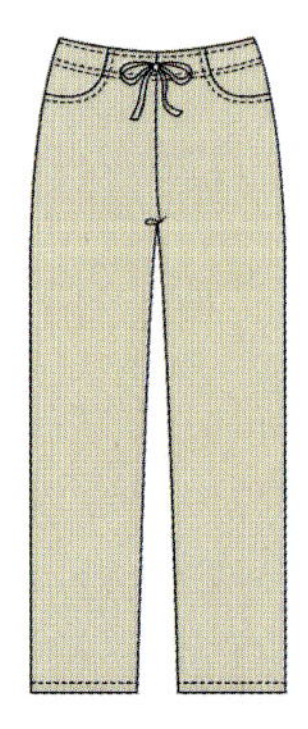

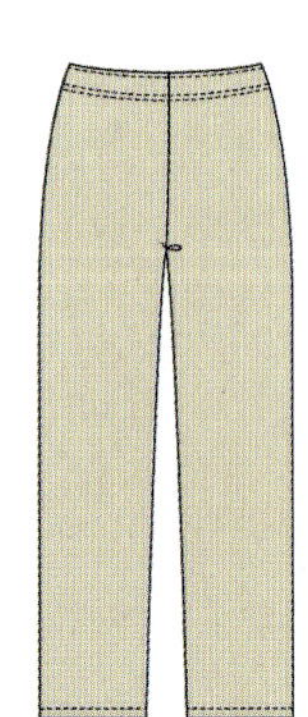

Back view

Cutting out your fabric

Use pattern pieces 1A and 1B, 2A and 2B, 3, 4, 5A and 5B, 6, and 7.

Pants—all sizes

45-in.- (112-cm-) wide fabric

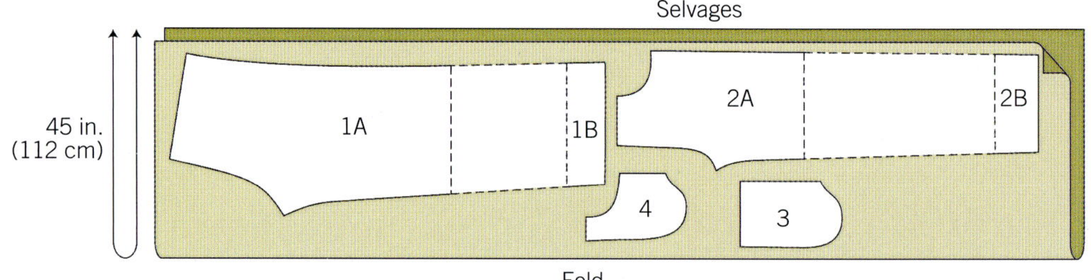

Key for cutting layouts

- Right side of fabric
- Wrong side of fabric
- Reverse side of pattern
- Extended section of pattern

Pants—sizes US 6, 8, 10 (UK 8, 10, 12)

60-in.- (150-cm-) wide fabric

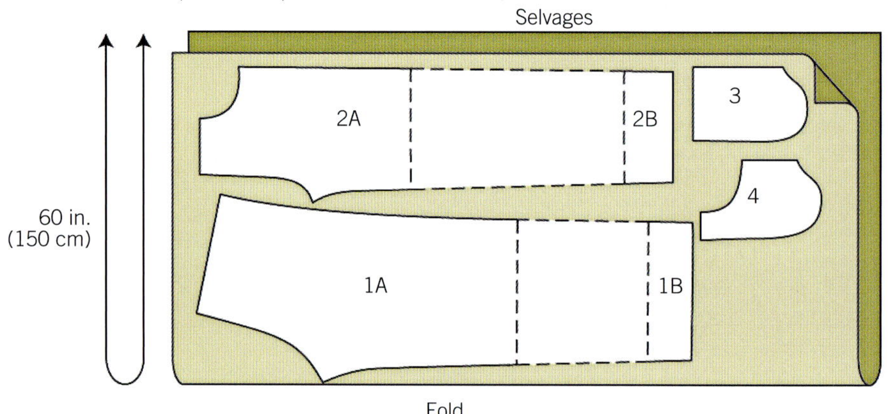

Interfacing—all sizes

36-in.- (90-cm-) wide

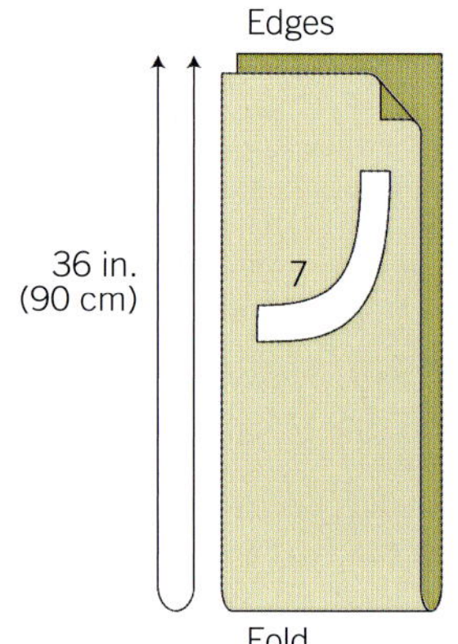

Pants—sizes US 12, 14, 16 (UK 14, 16, 18)

60-in.- (150-cm-) wide fabric

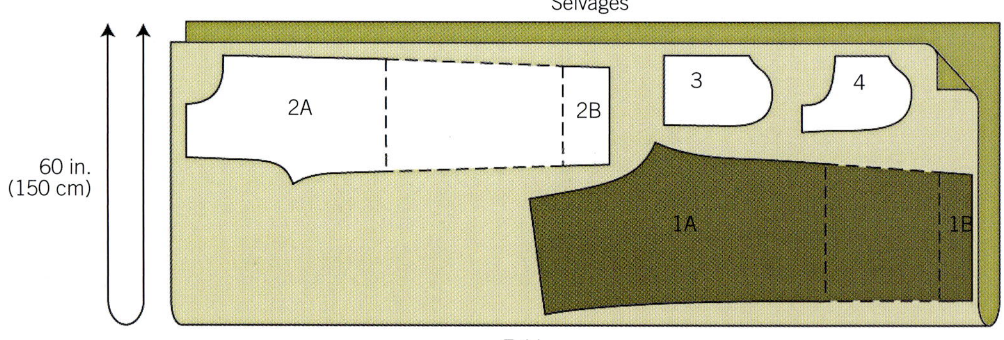

Note:

- 5/8-in. (1.5-cm) seam allowances are included unless otherwise stated.
- Stitch seams with right sides together and notches matching, unless otherwise stated.

Note:
Fabric quantities and cutting layouts are given for one-way fabrics only. If you choose a fabric with a two-way design, you may be able to lay your pattern pieces into a smaller amount of fabric—but remember, grainlines must still run parallel to the selvage.

Contrast casing and tie—all sizes

45–60-in.- (112–150-cm-) wide fabric

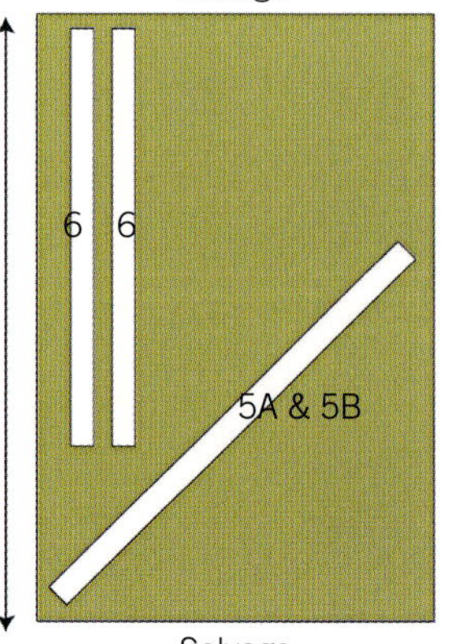

1 Following the appropriate cutting layout, cut out all your main and contrast fabric and interfacing pieces (see page 117). Cut two 1¼-in. (3-cm) squares of iron-on interfacing. Following the manufacturer's instructions, iron them to the wrong side of the front trousers at the buttonhole positions marked on the pattern (see page 134). Work and slit the buttonholes (see page 68).

2 Make up the front hip pockets following steps 1, 2, and 3 of the instructions on page 123, then edge stitch the pocket opening edges close to the edge (see page 51). Baste (tack) the pockets to the garment fronts at the waist and side seam edges.

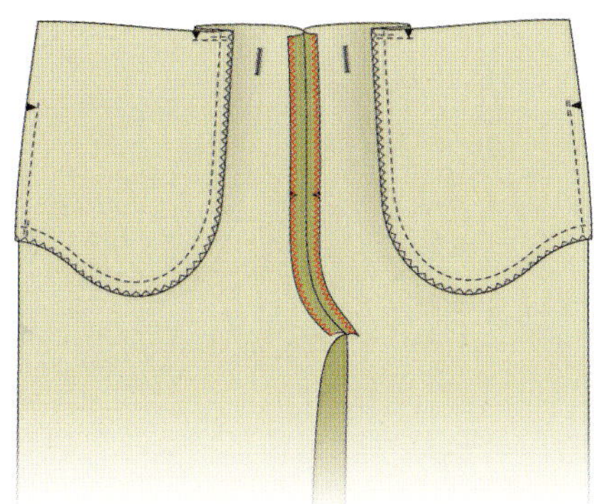

3 With notches matching (see page 113), pin, baste (tack), and machine stitch the front legs together at the center front crotch seam and the back legs together at the center back crotch seam, reverse stitching at each end of the stitchlines to secure. Press the seams open, and neaten the seam allowances separately (see page 44).

4 With notches matching and the right sides of the fabric together, pin, baste (tack), and machine stitch the front and back legs together at the side seams, reverse stitching at the start and finish to secure. Press the seam allowances toward the back legs and neaten the edges together. With right sides of fabric facing, pin, baste (tack), and machine stitch the inside leg seams in one continuous line of stitching, matching the center front and center back seams. Press the seams open and neaten the edges separately.

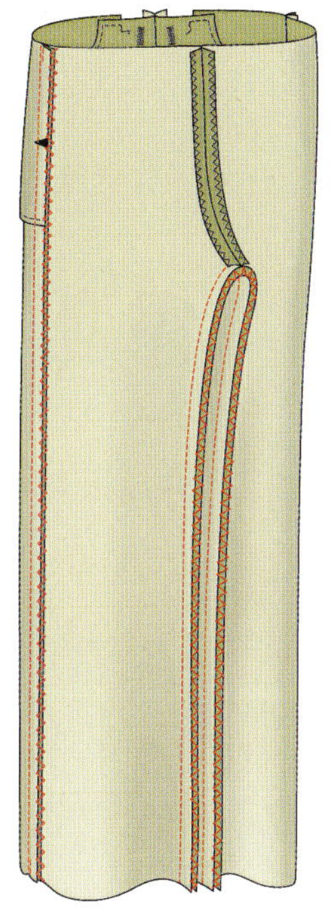

TIP
As a shortcut, instead of making a fabric drawstring tie for the waist, use a ½-in.- (12-mm-) wide braid or cord to match the color of your casing fabric.

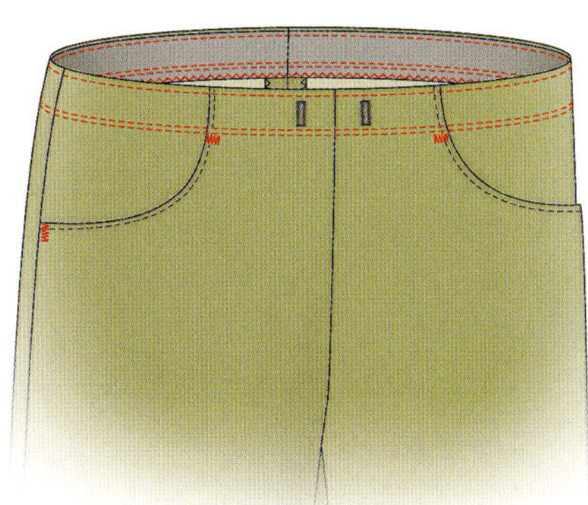

5 Attach the casing to the waist edge following the instructions for Applied casing at a waist edge (see page 126). Slipstitch the open edges of the casing together (see page 49), then work a third row of topstitching around the lower edge of the casing a foot's width above the first. Reinforce the pocket openings with a short row of close zigzag stitches (see page 18), at both the side seams and just below the waist casing.

6 With right sides facing, stitch the two tie sections together at one short end to make one continuous strip. Press the seam allowances open. Fold and press the short raw ends of the tie to the wrong side by ⅜ in. (1 cm), then make up the tie following step 4 of Making bias binding on page 54. Fold the strip in half along its length, with wrong sides together. Machine stitch the pressed edges together and insert the tie through the casing (see page 127).

7 Neaten the hem edges and fold them over to the wrong side by 1¼ in. (3 cm). Pin, baste (tack), and machine stitch in place, working close to the neatened edge. Press the pants; they are now ready to wear.

Darts & underlying fabrics

We have mentioned interfacing on several occasions in this book—but what is it? In this workshop we will explain exactly what it is, as well as the differences between lining, underlining, interlining, and interfacing, and when to use them.

We will also be looking at darts. These, too, were mentioned in Workshop 9; here you will find out why we need darts and the best way to stitch them. Finally, for our project we have a gorgeous flattering A-line skirt, which incorporates both darts and interfacing.

Darts

A dart is a fold in a piece of fabric that is stitched to give a garment shape, so that it fits around the body. Darts are generally used on women's garments to shape the fabric out at the bust and hips and in at the waist. On very tailored garments, they may also be used to shape the back shoulder and elbows.

There are two main types of darts: plain and contour. You may also come across French darts, which are constructed in a special way, but in this book we will be dealing with only the first two types.

Plain darts

Plain darts are folds in the fabric stitched with a tapering seam to form a point. A plain dart is shown on your pattern piece as a triangle with two stitchlines and sometimes a central foldline; there may also be two notches at the edge and a dot at the point (see page 113).

Stitching a plain dart The stitchlines need to be matched, and then stitched together to form the dart. Always make sure that the darts on the right and left sides of a garment mirror each other in length and placement.

1 Transfer the dart markings to the wrong side of your fabric; see Transferring pattern markings, page 117. Working from the wrong side, fold the dart in half through the center, matching the stitchlines and other markings. Pin and baste (tack) the dart in place.

2 Starting from the wide end of the dart, stitch toward the point, reverse stitching at the start to secure. To finish, take the last couple of stitches a thread's width from the fold. Cut the thread ends, leaving at least 4 in. (10 cm). Knot the ends together (see page 40), but do not pull too tightly. Trim the thread ends to 3/8 in. (1 cm).

3 To press, lay the dart flat on an ironing board with the fold of the dart to one side and iron toward the point—but no further, otherwise you will crease the rest of the garment.

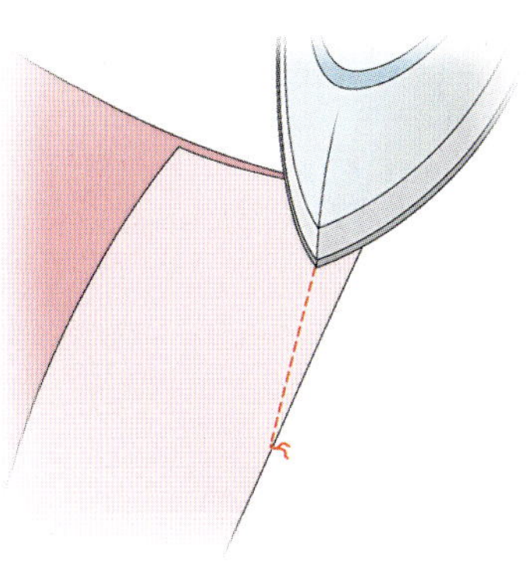

4 Open out the fabric and press the dart in the direction instructed; this is usually toward the center for waist darts and toward the waist on bust darts.

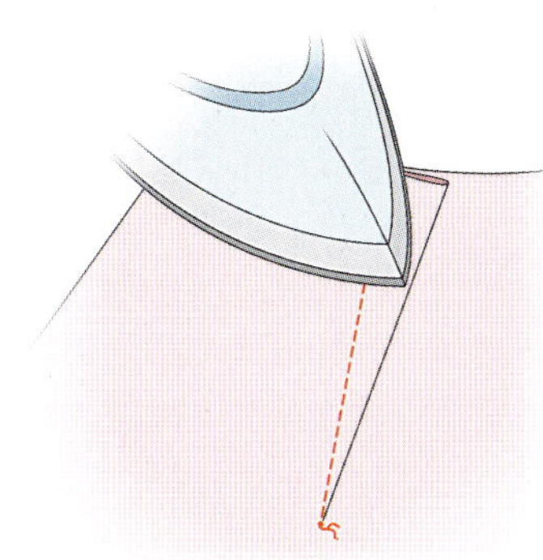

Contour darts

These long darts, which have a point at each end, are used on fitted and semi-fitted dresses. The widest part of the dart fits into the waistline and then tapers off to fit the bust and the hip, or the back and the hip. They are usually shown on patterns as a long thin diamond, with stitchlines and a series of dots to be matched.

Stitching a contour dart

1 Transfer the dart markings to the wrong side of your fabric; see Transferring pattern markings, page 117. With the right sides of the fabric together, fold along the center of the dart. Match and pin the dots and stitchlines at the waist first, then at the points, and then at any marks in between. Baste (tack) the dart in place just inside the stitching lines and remove the pins.

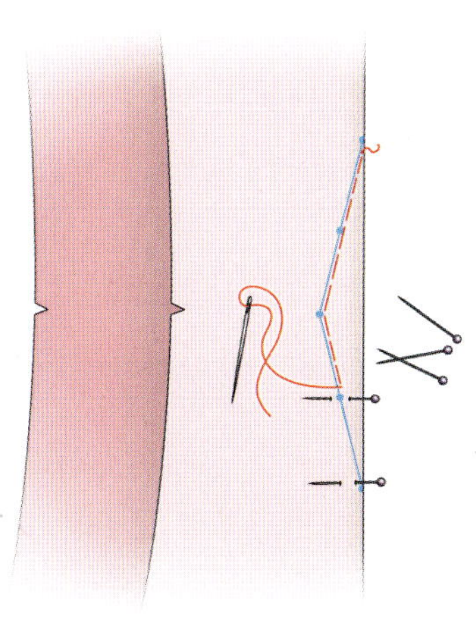

2 A contour dart is stitched in two halves, always starting at the middle (waistline) and stitching toward the point. Instead of reverse stitching to start, overlap the stitching at the waist and tie the ends of the thread at both points, as shown in step 2 of Stitching a plain dart, page 132.

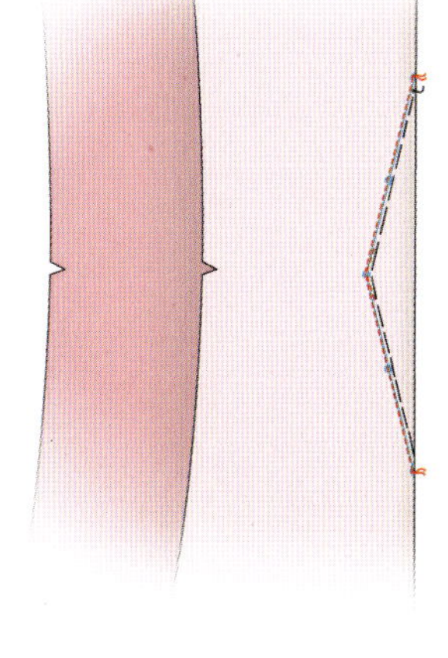

3 Remove the basting (tacking) stitches and clip into the dart at the waistline to within 1/8 in. (3 mm) of the stitchline; this will allow for the dart to curve smoothly at the waist. Press the dart flat as it was stitched, then press it toward the center of the garment.

TIP

Practice stitching darts on scrap fabric before you attempt your garment, as it is important to make your stitching straight and pairs of darts the same length.

Underlying fabrics

Underlying fabrics are the hidden parts of a garment that help it retain its shape and wear longer. There are four main types of underlying fabrics: interfacing, underlining, lining, and interlining. Each has a specific function that influences the garment's appearance. Of the four types, the most commonly used are interfacing and lining; underlining and interlining are mainly found in tailored garments, so we will not be going into detail about these. However, if all four were being used, the order of application would be underlining first, interfacing second, then interlining, and finally lining.

The chart on the opposite page sets out what each type of underlying fabric is used for and where in a garment it is normally found; it also specifies what kinds of fabric are suitable in each case, and gives some useful tips on things to look out for—although your pattern envelope should normally provide you with the basic information on what to buy.

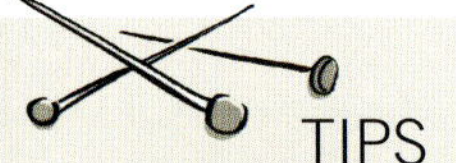

TIPS

- Always try the interfacing on a scrap of fabric before you begin to check how much heat and pressure is needed to set the adhesive firmly in place. Once it has cooled down completely, you should not be able to peel it off easily.
- If you wish, use a pressing cloth to protect the sole plate of your iron.

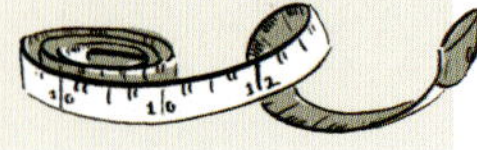

Interfacing

Interfacing is a special type of fabric applied to the inside of a garment to strengthen and stiffen specific parts, such as collars, facings, and buttonholes. Interfacings come in several weights and degrees of crispness and can be woven or non-woven, sew-in or iron-on. With such a wide range available, it is possible to find an interfacing suitable for every type of fabric. If you are unsure which is best for your fabric, ask the salesperson for a recommendation.

Applying iron-on interfacing Iron-on interfacings are the easiest to use and are the ones that we recommend for the novice stitcher. They have heat-sensitive glue on one side; the manufacturer normally provides instructions for your iron heat setting on the ends of the interfacing rolls, but this information may also be printed down the edges of the interfacing itself.

Lay the cut interfacing pieces adhesive side down on the wrong side of the garment pieces. To fix the interfacing in position, set your iron to a steam setting following the manufacturer's instructions, then place the iron firmly on it for a few seconds at a time. Lift the iron and reposition it; do not slide the iron across, as this could move the interfacing and cause creases. Allow the interfacing to cool. Check that it is fused all over and re-press any loose areas. Continue stitching your garment together as normal.

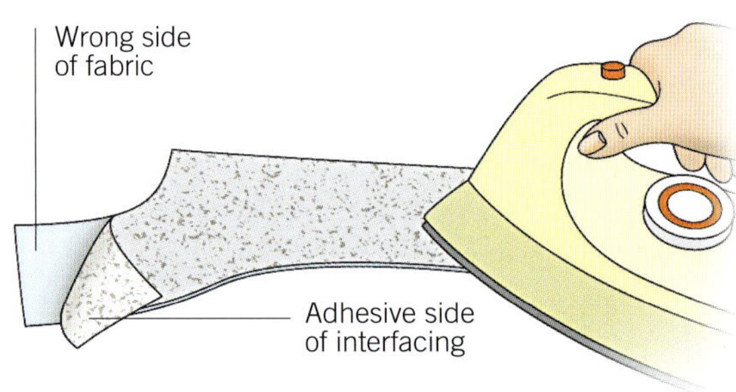

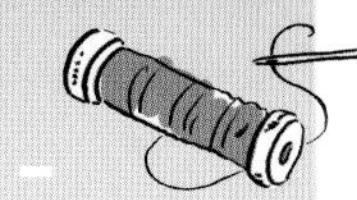

Underlying fabric types and selection

	Purpose	Where used	Types	Points for buying
Underlining	To support and reinforce delicate fabrics such as lace. To reinforce seams and other construction details on delicate fabrics. To give opaqueness to sheer fabrics and hide their inner construction from the outside. To prevent stretching in areas of stress. To act as a layer on which to attach hems, facings, and interfacings. Always stitched as one layer with the main fabric.	Whole garments or sections of garments.	Batiste and Habutai silk make perfect underlinings for lightweight fabrics. Taffeta, muslin (cheesecloth), and organdie are suitable for medium-weight fabrics. Crepe-de-chine and satin are ideal for lace. Special underlining fabrics are also available in a wide range of weights and colors.	Should be relatively stable and lightweight. Color and care should compliment the garment. The finish—for example, soft or crisp—should be appropriate for the style of the garment. Generally, the underlining should not hinder the natural drape of the garment.
Interfacing	Provides strength and stability to edges and garment details. Reinforces and prevents stretching.	Entire garment pieces such as collars, cuffs, flaps, and belts. Garment areas such as opening edges, buttonholes, hemlines, neck edges, and armholes.	Woven or non-woven, sew-in or iron-on; can be light-, medium-, or heavyweight. Comes in neutral colors such as white, cream, gray, and black. Woven canvas interfacings are also available for tailoring.	Interfacing should be lighter in general than the fabric. It should give support and body without overpowering the main fabric. Care should be compatible with the garment. For general use, non-woven iron-on interfacings are ideal. Sew-in types are best on sheer or fine fabrics where the iron-on adhesive may show through.
Interlining	Used to make a garment thicker and warmer.	Bodies of jackets and coats; sometime sleeves.	Lightweight, fluffy fabrics, such as brushed cotton, flannelette, and felt, which trap the air and increase insulation. Special insulating fabrics are also available, such as polyester batting (wadding) and domette.	Needs to be lightweight. It should not be too bulky. It should provide warmth. Care properties should match the rest of the garment.
Lining	Gives garment a luxurious finish. Covers up internal construction details. Allows garment to slide on and off easily. Supports loosely woven fabrics and prevents them from stretching around the seat of pants and skirts.	In entire jackets, coats, waistcoats, dresses, skirts, and pants, or just in parts.	For everyday garments, acetate, polyester taffeta, and blouse fabrics are most suitable. Use silk for luxury and woolen garments only.	Color is important, especially if the garment opens to reveal it. Weight and care should be compatible with the garment. Should be smooth, opaque, and durable. An anti-static finish is desirable.

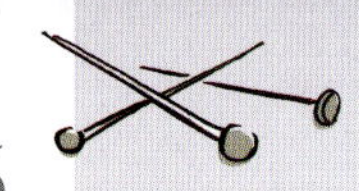

Applying light- to medium-weight sew-in interfacing Sometimes it may be necessary to use a sew-in interfacing, especially on a sheer or fine fabric such as voile or organza, where an iron-on adhesive might show through.

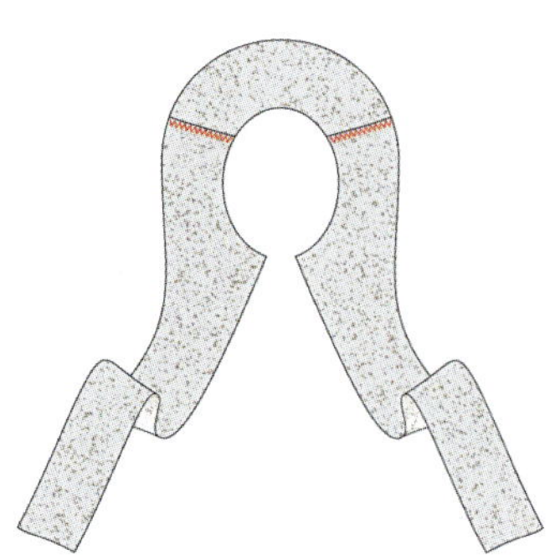

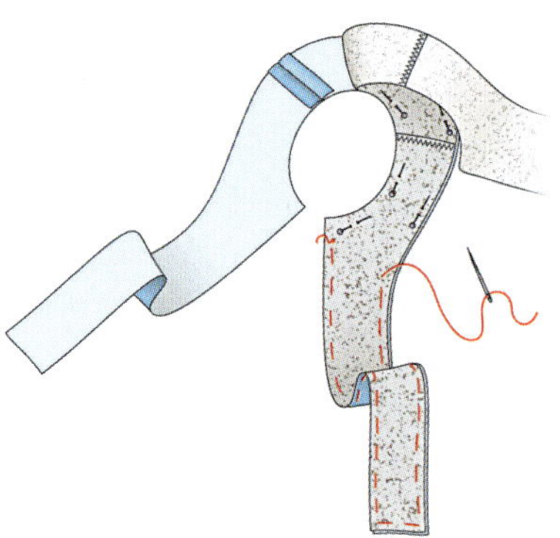

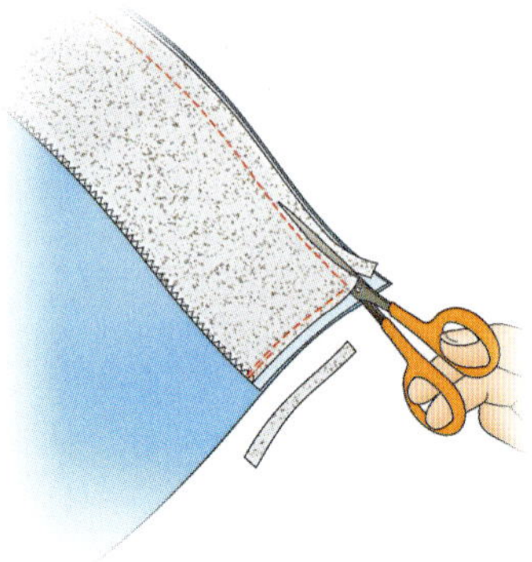

1 Using your pattern, cut out the appropriate pieces from interfacing. If the pieces are for a facing, join any shoulder seams first with a lapped seam (see opposite), to form a whole unit. Remember to join the shoulder seams on your garment facings, too, with plain seams (see page 40).

2 Lay the interfacing pieces on the wrong side of your garment pieces; pin and baste (tack) in place around all edges. Then neaten together any edges that will not be stitched into a seam (see page 44).

3 Machine stitch the interfaced pieces to your garment. Remove the basting (tacking) stitches and trim away the interfacing on the seam allowances as close to the stitching as possible. Layer and trim the main seam allowances as required (see page 43).

Applying interfacing to a foldline Sometimes one edge of an interfaced section falls at a foldline, rather than at a seamline. Securing an iron-on interfacing in this situation is easy, as it is ironed in place at once, but the sew-in type of interfacing requires a little more care and attention.

Interfacing adjacent to a foldline
The edge of the interfacing may be positioned right next to the foldline, as it would be on an integrated front facing (see page 92). Pin and baste (tack) the interfacing around all edges, then hem the edge that is against the foldline in place by working a herringbone stitch over the foldline (see page 49); this stitching will remain in place.

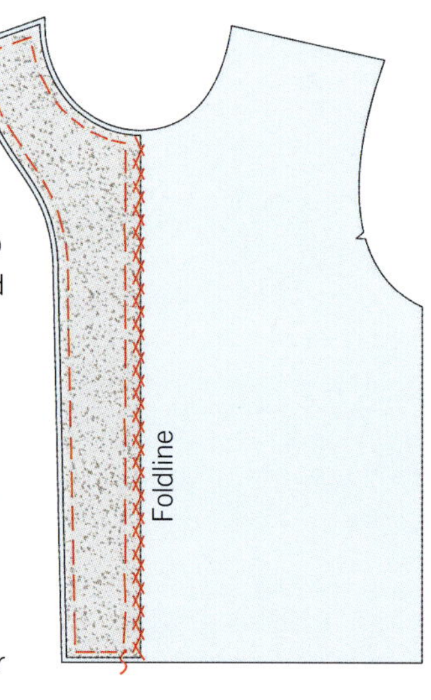

Interfacing beyond a foldline
Sometimes the interfacing may extend beyond the foldline by 3/8 in. (1 cm), as on a one-piece collar. Here, the finished edge will be rounder than when it stops directly at the foldline. Once again, pin and baste (tack) the interfacing in place, then prick stitch (see page 48) the interfacing in place along the foldline. This stitching will also remain in place.

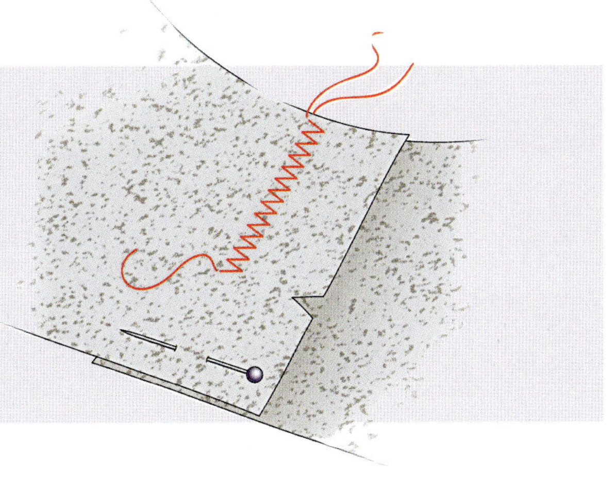

How to work a lapped seam

Lap the fabric edges as shown, lining up the seamlines; pin and baste (tack) in place. Stitch over the seamline with a wide zigzag stitch. Trim away the seam allowances close to the stitching.

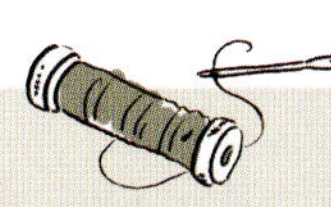

TIP

To avoid "seating" on pants and skirts, add a half-lining, which finishes halfway down the top leg. This can be made up in the same way as a free-hanging lining (see left).

Lining

Lining gives your garment a smooth, luxurious feeling for added comfort as well as a quality finish. It can be cut from the same pattern as your garment, or it may have separate pattern pieces. A lining may be fully stitched in, as in the yoke of the girl's pinafore dress on page 118, or it may be free-hanging.

Applying a free-hanging lining This method can be used to attach a lining to a skirt, dress, or pants that will be finished at the top edge with either a waistband or facing (see page 142). Before you attach a lining, your garment shell must be almost complete, including the stitching of main seams, darts, zippers, and sleeves.

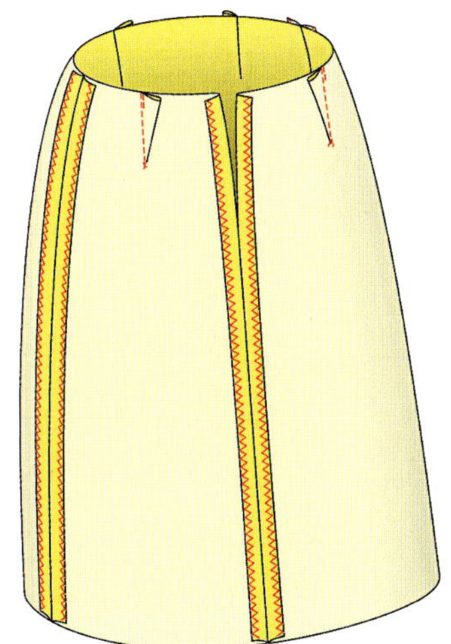

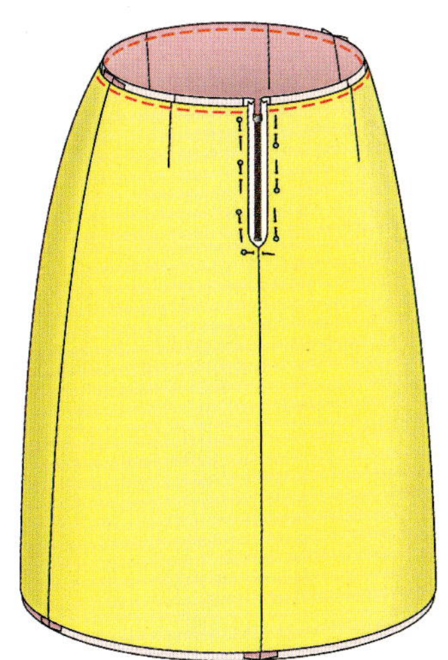

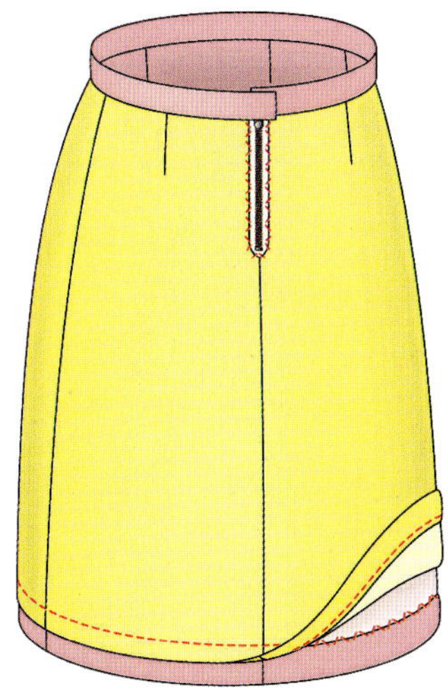

1 Cut out and make up all sections of the lining, keeping any zipper opening edges open. Neaten the seam allowances (see page 44) separately and press them open. If the lining is to end at the armholes, neaten the edges with bias binding (see page 55).

2 With wrong sides together, match and pin the lining to the garment around the waist or neck edge. Turn under and pin the lining to the zipper tapes. Baste (tack) the lining in place at the pinned garment edges and around the zipper, plus any armholes if they are being faced.

3 Slip hem the lining to the zipper tapes (see page 91). Apply the waistband or top facing. Hem the garment and lining separately, making the lining 3/4 in. (2 cm) shorter than the garment.

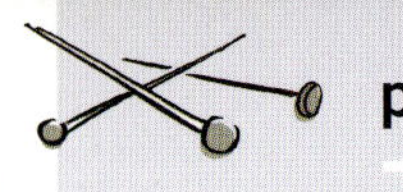

A-line skirt

The universally flattering A-line skirt in a pretty print fabric is an essential item in any wardrobe. This skirt is not lined, but it would be very easy to add a lining following the instructions for Applying a free-hanging lining on page 137.

Fabric suggestions

Lightweight cottons, chambray, soft linens, viscose.

You will also need

- Skirt pattern pieces traced off from the pattern sheet at the back of this book (see page 114)
- Medium-weight iron-on interfacing (see page 134)
- Matching threads
- 8-in. (20-cm) zipper
- Hook and eye

Note

- 5/8-in. (1.5-cm) seam allowances are included unless otherwise stated.
- Stitch seams with right sides together and notches matching, unless otherwise stated.

Size

Size	US 6 (UK 8)	US 8 (UK 10)	US 10 (UK 12)	US 12 (UK 14)	US 14 (UK 16)	US 16 (UK 18)
Waist	24 in. (61 cm)	25 in. (64 cm)	26 1/2 in. (67 cm)	28 in. (71 cm)	30 in. (76 cm)	32 in. (81 cm)
Hips	33 1/2 in. (85 cm)	34 1/2 in. (88 cm)	36 in. (92 cm)	38 in. (97 cm)	40 in. (102 cm)	42 in. (107 cm)
Finished length (waist to hem)	21 in. (53.5 cm)	21 in. (53.5 cm)	21 in. (53.5 cm)	21 in. (53.5 cm)	21 in. (53.5 cm)	21 in. (53.5 cm)

Fabric quantities

45-in.- (112-cm-) wide fabric						
Main	1 1/8 yd (1.00 m)	1 1/8 yd (1.10 m)	1 1/4 yd (1.20 m)	1 1/4 yd (1.20 m)	1 1/4 yd (1.20 m)	1 1/4 yd (1.20 m)
Contrast	1/2 yd (0.50 m)	2/3 yd (0.60 m)	2/3 yd (0.60 m)	2/3 yd (0.60 m)	3/4 yd (0.70 m)	3/4 yd (0.70 m)
60-in.- (150-cm-) wide fabric						
Main	2/3 yd (0.60 m)	2/3 yd (0.60 m)	2/3 yd (0.60 m)	2/3 yd (0.60 m)	2/3 yd (0.60 m)	2/3 yd (0.60 m)
Contrast	1/2 yd (0.50 m)	2/3 yd (0.60 m)	2/3 yd (0.60 m)	2/3 yd (0.60 m)	3/4 yd (0.70 m)	3/4 yd (0.70 m)
36-in.- (90-cm-) wide iron-on interfacing						
	¼ yd (0.10 m)	¼ yd (0.10 m)	1/4 yd (0.10 m)	1/4 yd (0.10 m)	1/4 yd (0.10 m)	1 1/4 yd (1.00 m)

Front view

Back view

Cutting out your fabric

Use pattern pieces 1, 2A and 2B, and 3.

Note:
Fabric quantities and cutting layouts are given for one-way fabrics only. If you choose a fabric with a two-way design, you may be able to lay your pattern pieces into a smaller amount of fabric—but remember, grainlines must still run parallel to the selvage.

Print fabric—all sizes

45-in.- (112-cm-) wide fabric

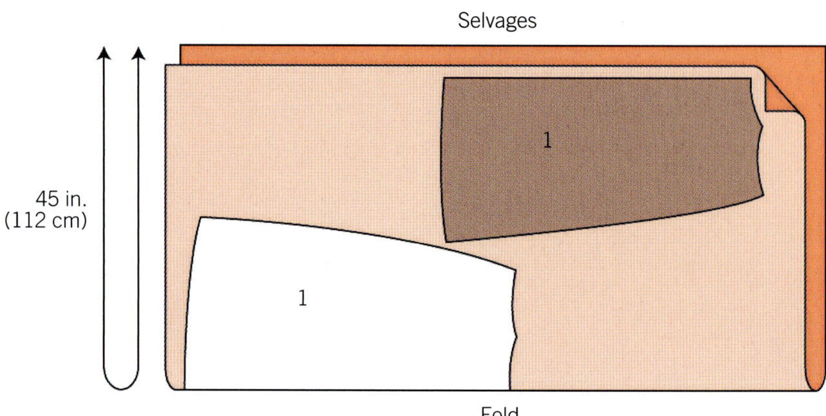

Print fabric—all sizes

60-in.- (150-cm-) wide fabric

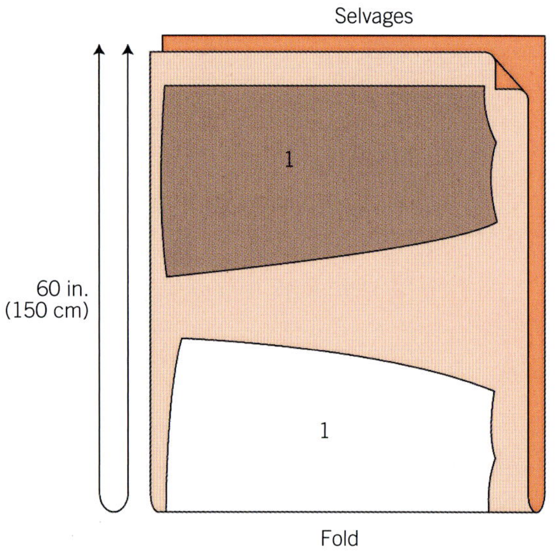

Contrast fabric—all sizes

45-in.- (112-cm-) and 60-in.- (150-cm-) wide fabric

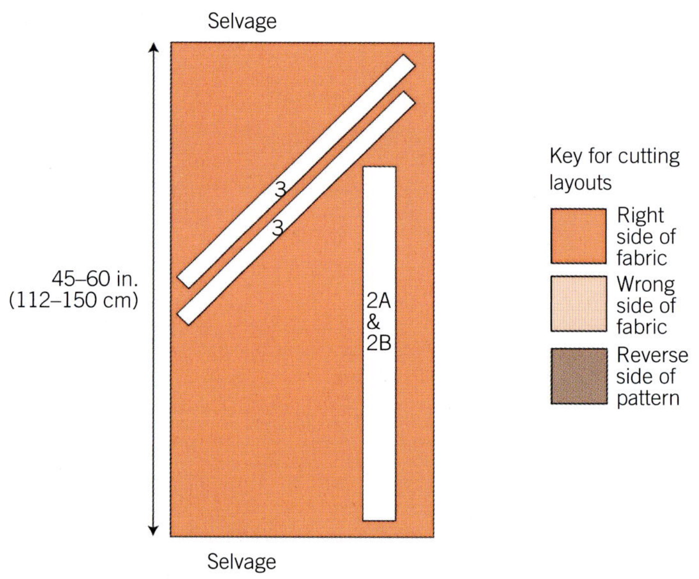

Interfacing—sizes US 6, 8, 10, 12, 14 (UK 8, 10, 12, 14, 16)

36-in.- (90-cm-) wide

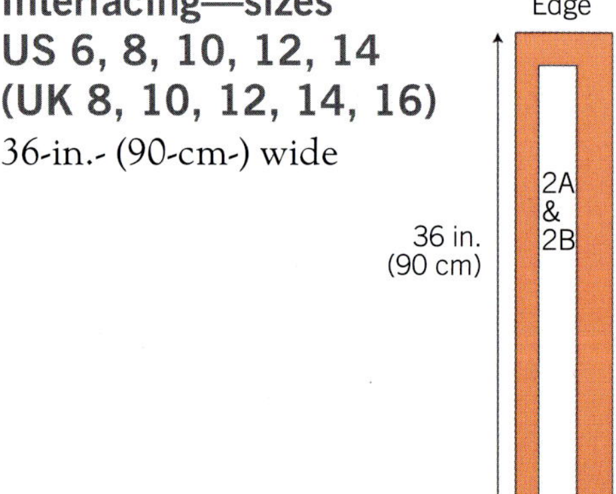

Interfacing—size US 16 (UK 18)

36-in.- (90-cm-) wide

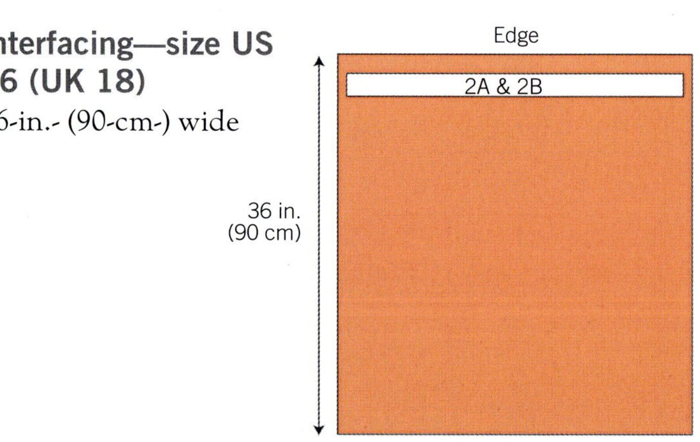

1 Following the appropriate cutting layout, cut out all your fabric and interfacing pieces (see page 117). Staystitch the waist and hem edges of all skirt pieces (see below). Stitch the darts on the front and back skirts (see page 132) and press toward the center front and center back.

2 With right sides facing, pin and baste (tack) the back skirts together at the center back seam. Machine stitch the center back seam from hem edge to zipper notch, reverse stitching at each end to secure. Press the seams open and then neaten the seam allowances, including the zipper opening edges, separately. Insert a zipper, following the lapped zipper method on page 80.

3 With right sides facing, pin, baste (tack), and machine stitch the back skirt to the front skirt at the side seams, reverse stitching at each end to secure. Neaten the seam allowances separately and press the seams flat. Attach the waistband, following the straight waistband method shown on page 142.

4 With right sides facing, join the contrast hem strips together at the short ends to form a ring. Neaten the seam turnings together and press to one side. With right sides together, pin, baste (tack), and machine stitch the contrast strip to the skirt hem edge, matching the side seams and raw edges and taking a $^{3}/_{8}$-in. (1-cm) seam allowance. Neaten the seam turnings together and press toward the skirt. Run your thumbnail over the lower raw edge of the strip to fray the edge slightly and make it go wavy.

Staystitching

Staystitching is a row of machine stitching that is worked on the cut garment pieces before you start to sew them together. It is used on curved and bias seams such as necklines and waist edges, to stop them from stretching while you are making the garment up.

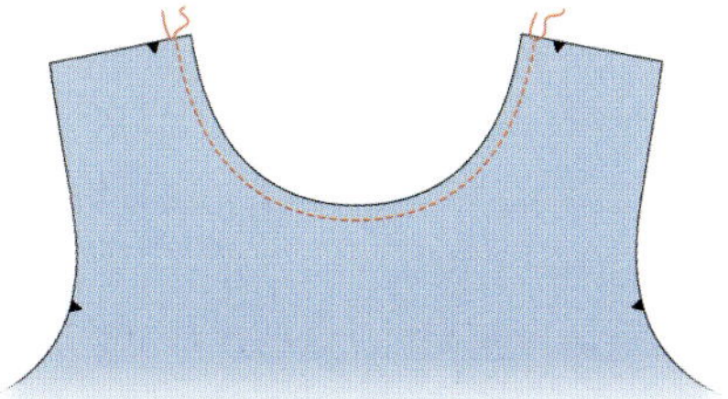

Work a row of medium-length straight stitches just inside the seam allowance of your cut piece. Lay the cut piece back on your pattern to double-check it is still the same size and shape. Continue making up the garment as normal.

Waist finishes

The waistline finish acts as an anchor to hold the garment in the correct position on your body. There are two ways to finish a waistline edge: fixed methods such as a waistband, or flexible methods like an elasticated or drawstring casing, which is covered in Workshop 9 (see page 124).

Straight waistband

Waistbands give a neat finish to a garment. They can be of varying depths, but generally they are made to fit the waist edge, with a small extension at one end to allow for the ends to overlap and for you to work a buttonhole and attach a button or hooks and eyes for fastening.

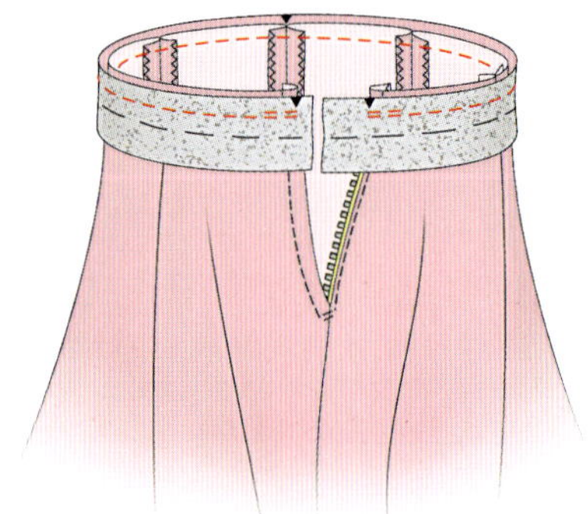

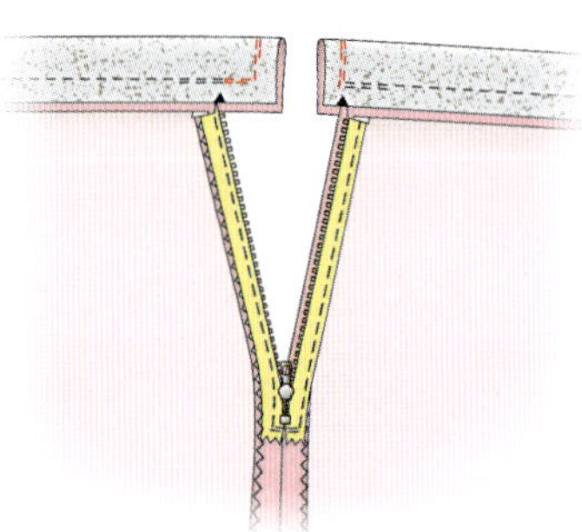

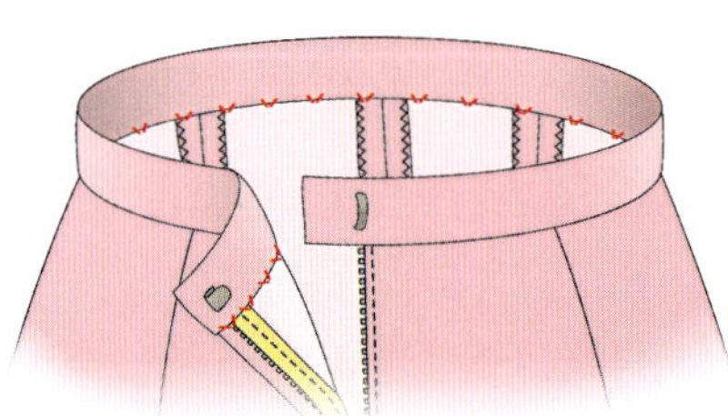

1 Apply interfacing to the wrong side of the skirt waistband (see page 134). Press the waistband in half lengthwise, with wrong sides together. Open the waistband out flat again and then, with right sides together, pin, baste (tack), and machine stitch the long notched edge of the waistband to the skirt waist edge, matching the notches at each end of the waistband to the zipper opening edges and the remaining notches to the side seams.

2 Fold the waistband in half against the pressline, with right sides together. Pin, baste (tack), and machine stitch across the short end of the waistband at the left-hand zipper opening, from the folded edge to the waistband stitchline. At the other end, pin, baste, and machine stitch around the waistband extension from the folded edge to meet the waistband stitchline.

3 Snip the corners of the waistband seam turnings to reduce bulk (see page 43), then turn the waistband right side out. Press the loose waistband edge to the wrong side and slip hem (see page 90) the pressed edge along the machine stitches, enclosing the raw edges. Attach fastenings to close the waist (see pages 64 and 73).

Waistline with shaped facings

Waist facings provide a clean smooth finish that does not extend above the waistline edge.

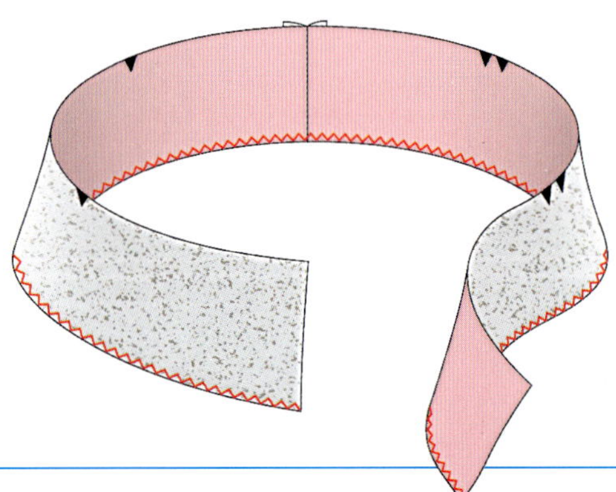

1 Cut the facing from fabric and interfacing and apply the interfacing (see page 134). Stitch the side seams together with plain seams (see page 40) and press open. Neaten the lower edge with the appropriate finish (see page 44).

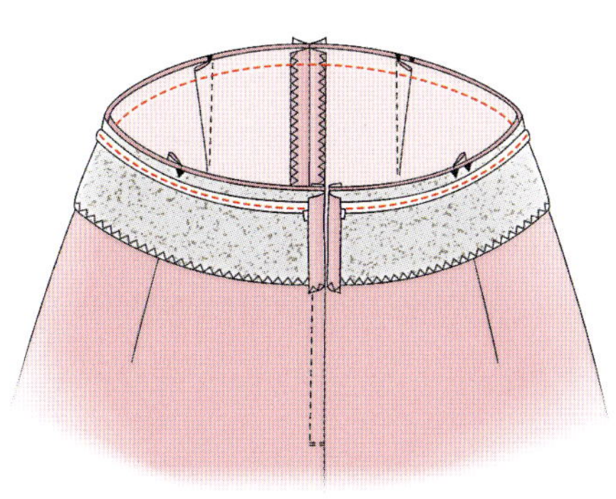

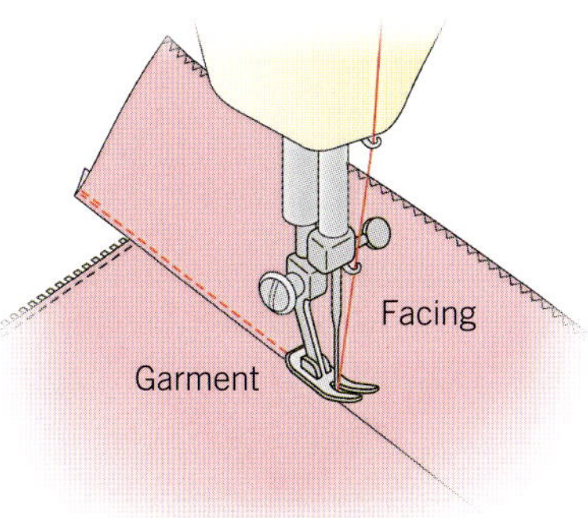

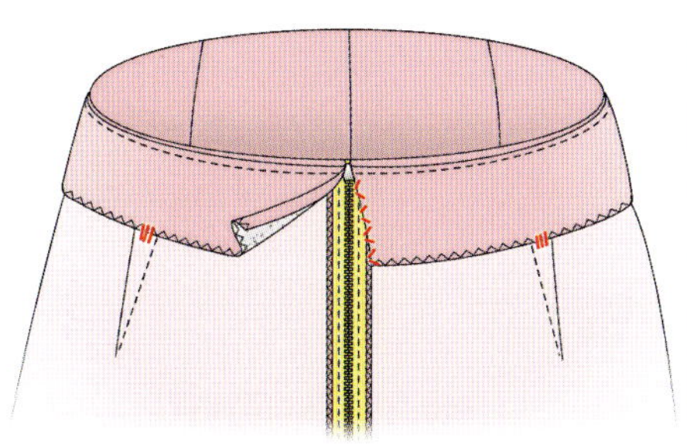

2 Pin the facing to the garment, right sides together, matching all seams and notches. Pin a 1/4-in. (6-mm) cotton tape over the waist seamline and baste (tack) in place through all thicknesses. Stitch the seam and then layer the seam allowances, clipping into the curves (see page 43).

3 Press the facing and the seam allowances away from the garment. Working from the right side, understitch the seam allowances to the facing (see page 51); this will stop the facing from rolling to the outside of the garment during wear.

4 Turn the facing to the inside of the garment and press along the waist edge. Hand stitch the lower edge of the facing to the garment side seams and darts. Turn under the seam allowances at the facing ends and pin in place, making sure that they do not catch in the zipper, then slip hem the facing ends to the zipper tape (see page 90). Attach fasteners to close the waist (see page 72).

Grosgrain (Petersham) ribbon finish

Curved grosgrain (Petersham) ribbon about 1 in. (2.5 cm) deep is available from notions (haberdashery) stores by the yard (metre) or in pre-packed quantities. It gives a similar appearance to a shaped faced waist edge, but is quicker to do.

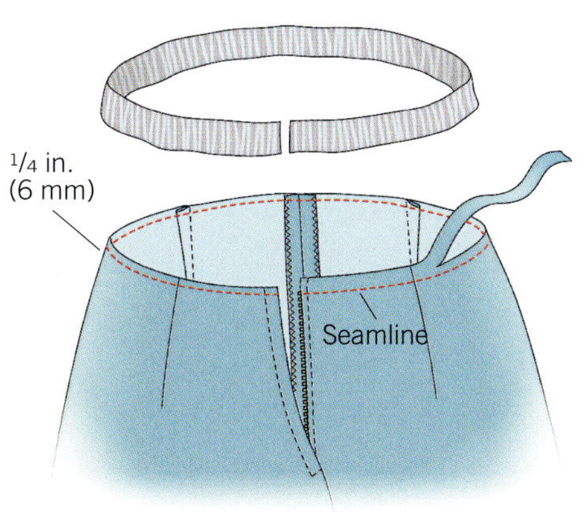

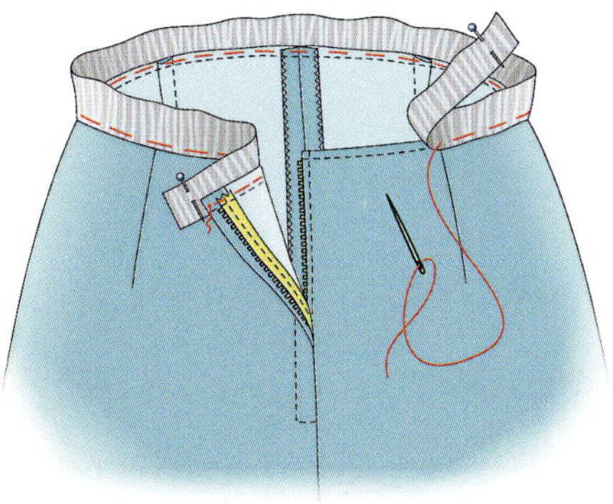

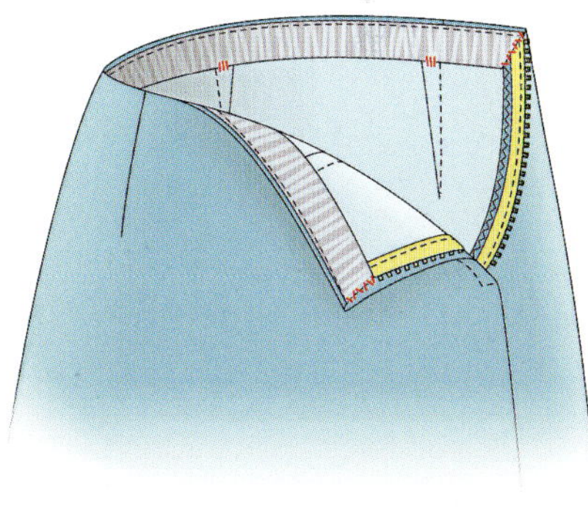

1 Staystitch the garment waist along the seamline (see page 141), then measure the waist along this line and cut a length of ribbon equal to this length, plus 1 1/4 in. (3 cm) for hems. Trim the garment waist seam allowance down to 1/4 in. (6 mm).

2 Lap the wrong side of the ribbon over the right side of the garment waistline so that the edge of the "inside" curve on the ribbon is just over the staystitched line and the cut ends extend 5/8 in. (1.5 cm) beyond the zipper opening edges. Pin, baste (tack), and machine stitch the ribbon in place, stitching close to the edge of the ribbon.

3 Turn the ribbon to the inside of the garment and press along the waist edge. Fold under the ribbon ends and pin in place; double-check that they do not catch the zipper, then slip hem the ends to the zipper tape (see page 90). Baste (tack) the lower edges of the ribbon to the side seams and darts. Attach fasteners to close the waist (see page 72).

Gathers, pleats & tucks

Soft gathers, neat pleats, and crisp tucks are decorative ways of drawing fabric in for fit. This final workshop introduces you to these techniques, which have a wide variety of applications and give you lots of scope to add interesting details to your projects.

The project at the end of this workshop is a fresh white linen blouse. With tucks at the front and back, this soft, long-length blouse has a neat little rounded collar and long sleeves—it's a wardrobe staple that you'll want to wear for ever.

Gathers

Gathers are tiny, soft folds that are formed by drawing up a calculated amount of fabric into a smaller area. They add fullness to a wide range of garments, but the most popular use is in frills—an exuberant trimming that looks good on both garments and home furnishings. There is also a purely functional variation of gathering, called ease stitching, which is essential in areas of garment construction, such as the top of a sleeve.

Calculating the amount of fabric for gathering

If you are using a pattern, this is all done for you, but if you are adding a frill or making a gathered skirt, the width of fabric you need for gathering depends on the fullness you require and the type of fabric you are using: thicker, heavier fabrics require less fullness than soft, lightweight fabrics. As a general rule, you will need three times the finished gathered width for very full gathers, twice the width for medium gathers, and one and a half times the width for minimal gathers. Widths of fabric are stitched together to obtain the correct measurement. Try a test piece—gather up a measured width of fabric to the fullness you require to find the ratio you need.

Machine gathering

Machine gathering is worked by stitching two rows of long machine stitches across the edge to be gathered, within the seam allowances. The fabric is then gathered up by pulling on the bobbin threads.

Gathering tips

Follow these easy steps to organize your work and prepare your machine for gathering.

- Join all the fabric pieces to be gathered to the required width, then stitch, press, and neaten the seams (see page 44); for frills, hem the free edge as well (see page 45).
- Loosen the upper tension slightly so that the fabric will slide along the bobbin thread more easily. (Refer to your instruction manual.)
- Set your machine to a longer stitch—1/16 in. (2 mm) for lightweight fabrics to 1/8 in. (3 mm) for heavier fabrics. Test your tension and stitch length on a scrap of your fabric first.
- Work on the right side of the fabric, as this will give you easy access to the bobbin threads. (These are the threads that are pulled to form the gathers.)
- Leaving long thread ends, stitch between any seams, keeping the seam allowances out of the way, because gathering does not work well through two layers of fabric.

Gathering the fabric

Before you attempt to gather your fabric, refer to the Gathering tips, opposite.

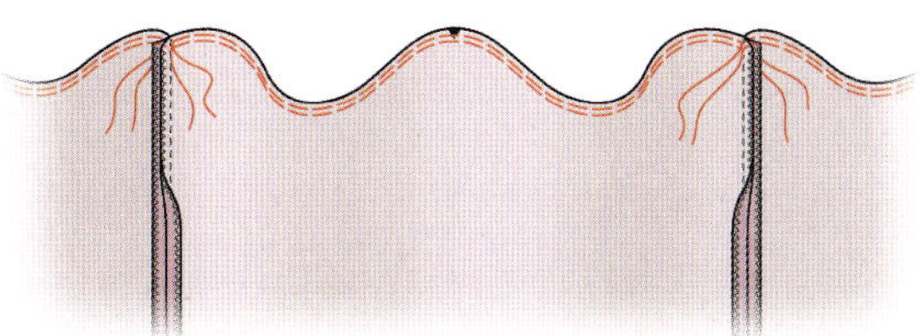

1 Leaving long thread ends, work two parallel rows of gathering stitches ¼ in. (6 mm) apart within the seam allowance along your fabric edge, with the outer row of stitching a thread's width from the seamline and stitching between any seams where necessary.

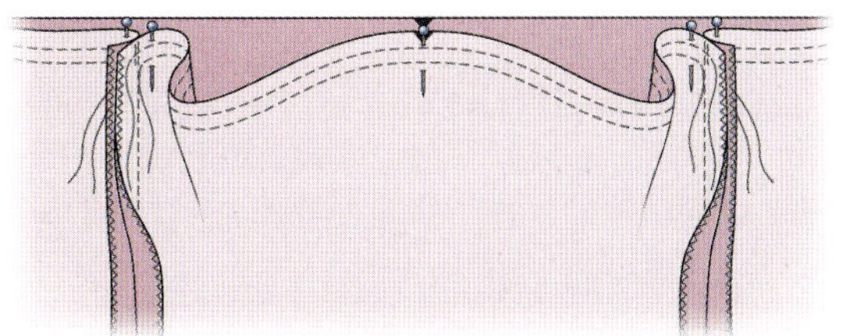

2 Divide the stitched edge and the edge to which it will be attached into four or more equal sections and mark them with a pin. With the right sides together, pin the stitched edge to the corresponding edge, matching marker pins. If you are using a dress pattern, pin the stitched edge to the corresponding edge, with the right sides together, matching corresponding pattern markings and seams.

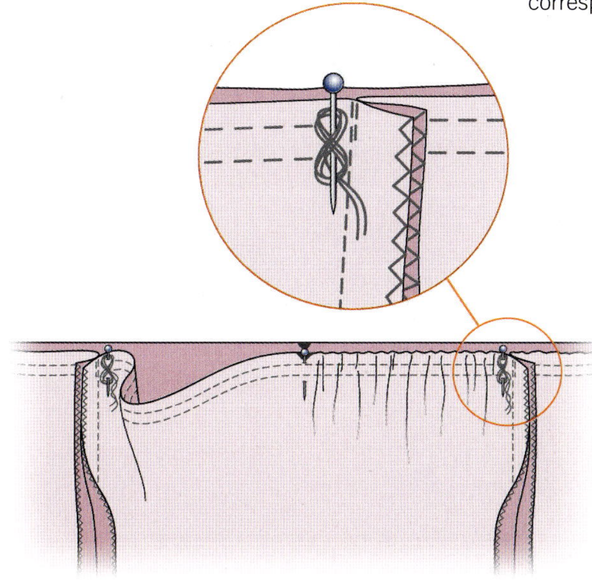

3 At one end, secure the bobbin threads by twisting them around a pin in a figure eight. At the other end, pull both gathering threads together and gently ease the gathers along the threads. When the gathered edge fits the piece to which it is going to be stitched, secure the thread ends around another pin, as before. On long edges, gather the fabric from each end toward the center, rather than trying to gather across the entire piece in one go.

4 Unwind the thread ends around each end pin and knot each set together to secure them; trim ends to about 1 in. (2.5 cm). With the gathered side up, baste (tack) the two layers together between the two rows of stitching, using short stitches. Remove the pins.

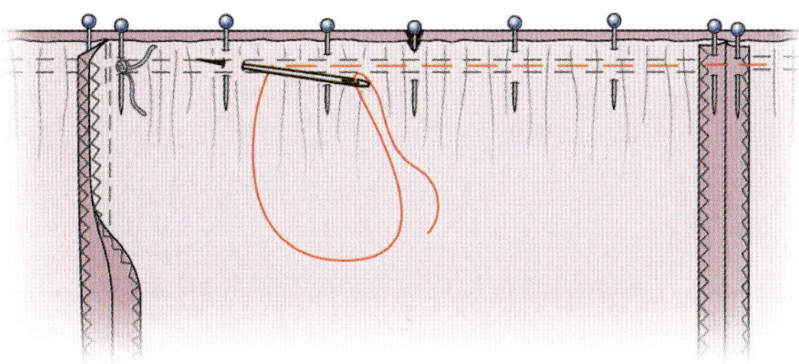

Automatic gathering Some machines provide an automatic gathering foot, which gathers up the fabric as it stitches; some gathering feet gather one layer of fabric while stitching it to another flat piece of fabric. Thread tension and stitch length are adjusted to increase or decrease the amount of fullness, so a gathering foot is difficult to use in conjunction with a dress pattern or where you want to achieve a specific fullness. Always refer to your instruction manual when using a gathering foot.

5 Return your machine stitch length and tension to the appropriate setting. With the gathered side on top and reverse stitching to start and finish, machine stitch the gathered edge to the corresponding edge, holding the fabric on either side of the machine foot as you sew to prevent the gathers from being pushed and stitched into pleats. Remove the basting (tacking) stitches.

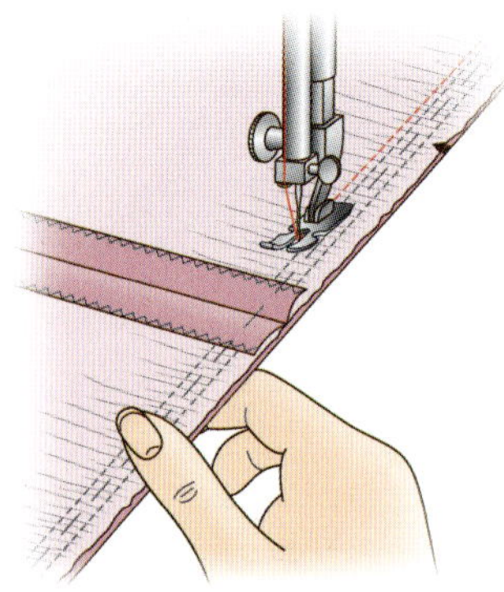

6 Diagonally trim matched seam allowances to reduce bulk (see page 43). Using the tip of the iron, press the seam allowances flat as they were stitched—but do not press the gathers. Neaten the seam allowances together. Open the sections out and press the seam toward the flat section. Press the gathers by sliding the point of the iron into the gathers toward the seam.

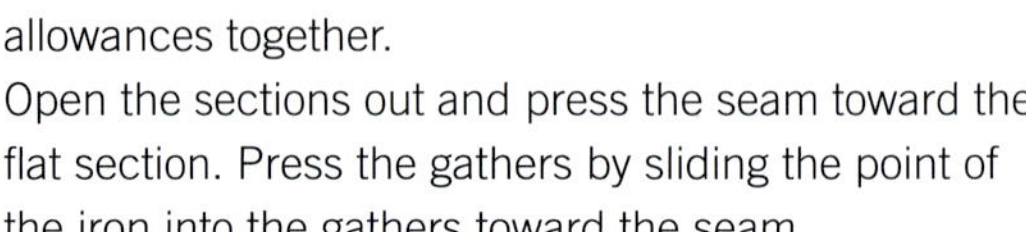

Ease stitching

On some garments you maybe required to do ease stitching, which provides a bare amount of fullness, called ease, at a place where it is needed. It is worked in the same way as gathering, but the stitches are about 1/8 in. (3mm) long and drawn up just enough to pull in the fibers of the fabric to fit a smaller area, without forming any puckers or gathers. It creates a rounded curve in an area such as the top of a sleeve (the "cap" or "head") so that it can accommodate the curve at the top of the arm, or at the elbow to allow for the arm to be bent.

Pleats

Pleats are vertical folds that are usually formed by doubling fabric back on itself and securing it in place. They hang best on the straight grain (see page 32) and can appear as a single pleat, a group of pleats, or an entirely pleated section, which may be pressed into sharp creases or left un-pressed to fall in soft folds. Pleats can be folded in several ways to give a variety of styles, but the most useful and easiest pleats to use are inverted pleats and box pleats.

Choosing fabrics for pleating

Not every fabric will hold a pressed pleat: smooth, crisp, light- to medium-weight, firmly woven fabrics, such as linen and gabardine, pleat the best—but for soft, un-pressed folds you can choose a fluid fabric that does not crease easily, such crepe de chine. It is easier to maintain sharp pleats if you use a fabric that can be dry-cleaned, because the pleats are pressed as part of the process. If you have to wash the fabric yourself, you may need to re-form and press the pleats, though you can edge stitch the folds (see page 51) to make life easier. Avoid checked and striped fabrics, as they require exact folding and matching.

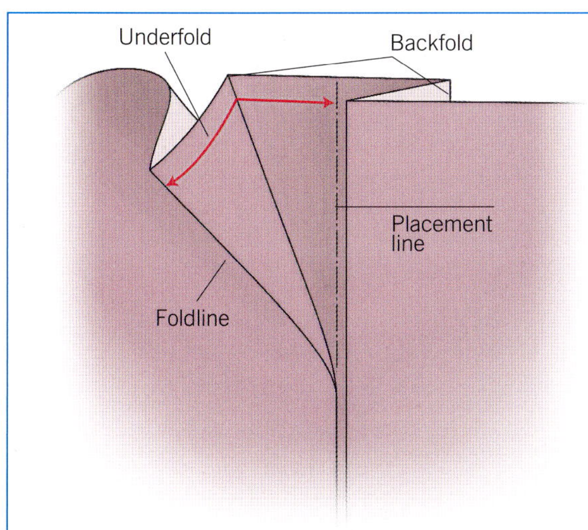

Understanding pleats

Each pleat has a foldline and a placement line, which are shown on the pattern and should be transferred to the fabric. Arrows are usually printed on the pattern to show the direction of the fold.

To form the pleat, the foldline is brought to the placement line. The area between the two is called the underfold and its creaseline is called the backfold.

TIP

If you are not following a pattern and want to form an inverted or box pleat, fold your fabric on the straight grain, as illustrated in the diagrams on the left, then pin in place and check the effect. As a rough guide, allow 3–4 in. (7.5–10 cm) for each underfold to allow the pleats to hang well.

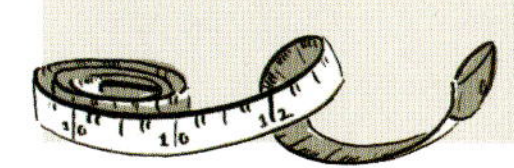

Inverted pleats and box pleats

These pleats probably have the widest use, as they are popular for both clothes and home furnishings.

Inverted pleats have two foldlines that meet at a common placement line; the backfolds face away from each other. There is also a version that has a separate back to the pleat, which allows for more economical use of your fabric. Box pleats have two foldlines and two placement lines. The folds face away from each other and the backfolds face toward each other.

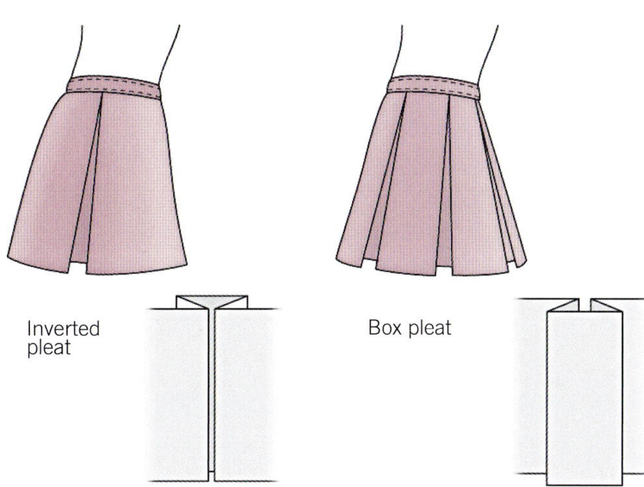

Forming inverted and box pleats

Both inverted and box pleats are formed on the right side of the fabric using exactly the same process; the only difference between them is in the direction of the foldlines to the placement line. The diagrams below illustrate how to form a single inverted pleat.

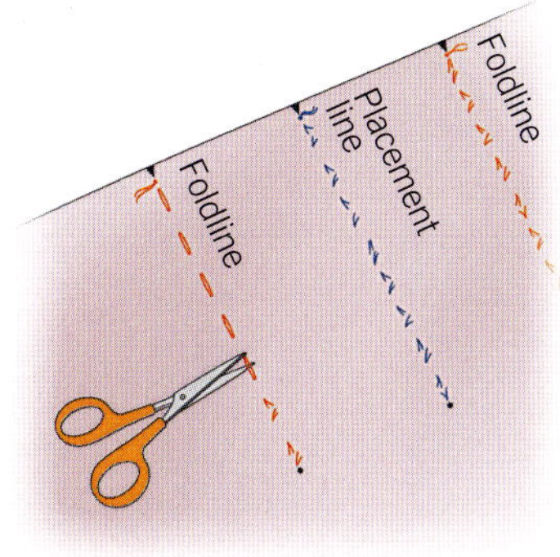

1 To transfer the pleat markings onto the right side of the fabric, using double thread, work a row of large uneven basting (tacking) stitches through the pattern and the fabric (see page 38). Cut the thread at the center of each long stitch and carefully remove the pattern, avoiding pulling out the threads.

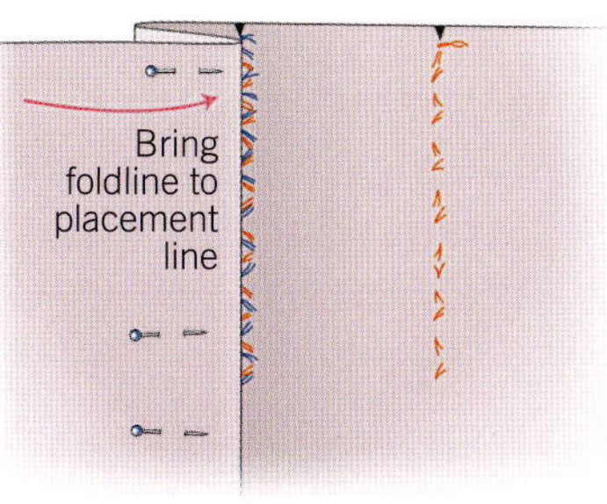

2 Working from the right side, fold the fabric along a foldline, then bring the fold to its placement line. Pin the pleat in place through all the layers. Repeat with the second foldline, bringing it over to meet at the placement line, and remove all the thread markings as you pin. Baste (tack) the pleat in position close to each foldline, stitching through all the layers of fabric and removing the pins as you go.

3 You can leave the pleats soft, or press them with sharp creases. To do this, work with the right side up and press the pleat in place, using a damp pressing cloth between the fabric and the iron. Let the pleat dry before moving it off your ironing board and removing the pressing cloth. With the wrong side up, press the pleats again, using a pressing cloth as before.

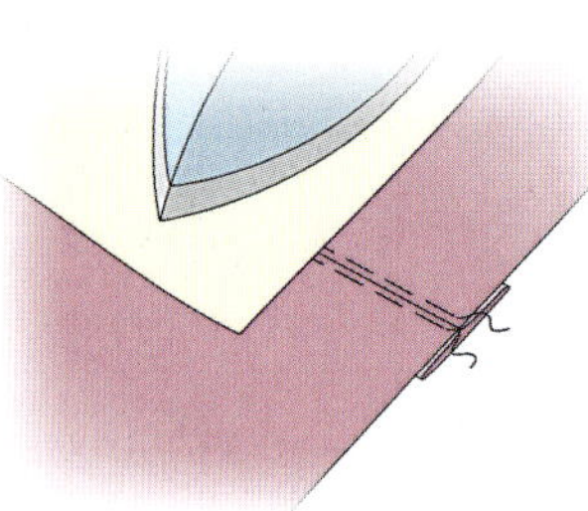

4 If the backfolds have left an impression on the right side of your garment, with the right side up, slide strips of thick paper under the fold of each pleat and press again. Leave the basting (tacking) stitches in place for as long as possible during the construction of your item.

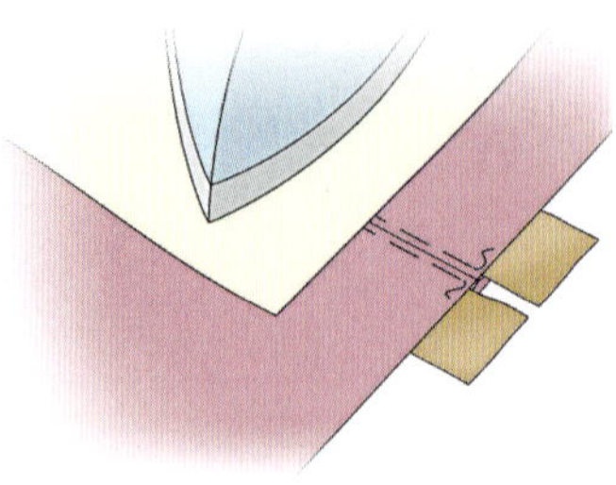

TIPS

- Use one thread color for the foldlines and another for the placement lines. Spun polyester thread is good for this, as it leaves fewer indentations in the fabric after pressing.
- If you have decided on the finished length of your item, for pressed-in pleats, it is best to neaten and turn up the hem edge before you form the pleats.

Inverted pleat with separate underlay

This type of inverted pleat provides a more economical use of fabric; it has a separate underlay that forms the underside, or back, of the pleat and is joined at the backfold positions with a seam. The underlay can be the same fabric as the rest of the garment, or a contrasting fabric.

1 Transfer the foldlines to the wrong side of your fabric, as in step 1 of Forming inverted and box pleats. With the right sides facing, bring together and match the foldlines. Baste (tack) them together along the foldline positions. Open out the pleat extensions and press flat.

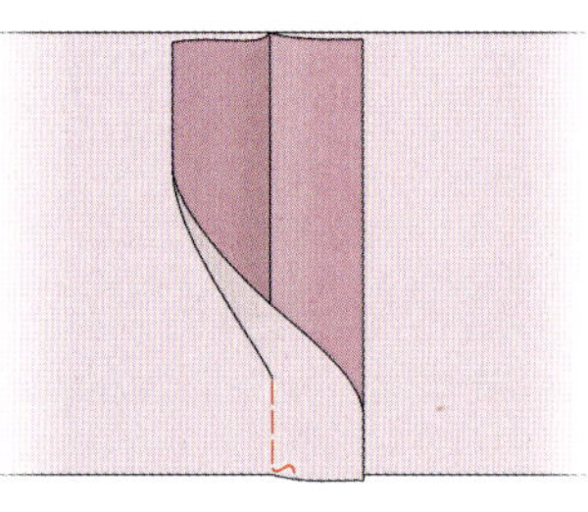

2 With the right sides together, place the pleat underlay on top of the pleat extensions, matching any pattern markings, and pin them together at the raw edges; baste (tack) the pleat edges together. Stitch the pleat edges together, starting just over twice the hem depth up from the hem edge, working to the top, and reverse stitching only to finish. Remove the basting stitches and press the seams flat.

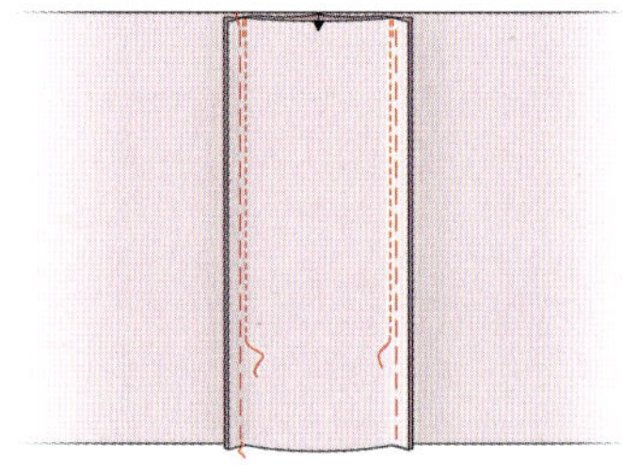

3 Carefully unpick the foldline basting (tacking) stitches. Neaten the hem edge of both your item and the underlay, then fold up the hems to the wrong side and stitch in place (see pages 45 and 90). Pin and re-baste the unstitched edges of the pleat extensions and underlay together, then machine stitch each side from the matched hem edges to the previous stitching, reverse stitching to begin and overlapping the stitching to finish.

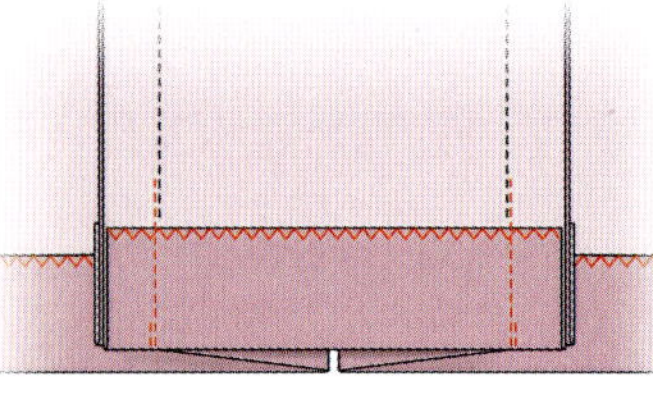

4 Press the seams flat as sewn, then diagonally trim across the corners of the seam allowances at the hem edges. Neaten the main seam allowances together, then neaten the base corners and hem edges with closely spaced overcast stitch (see page 49).

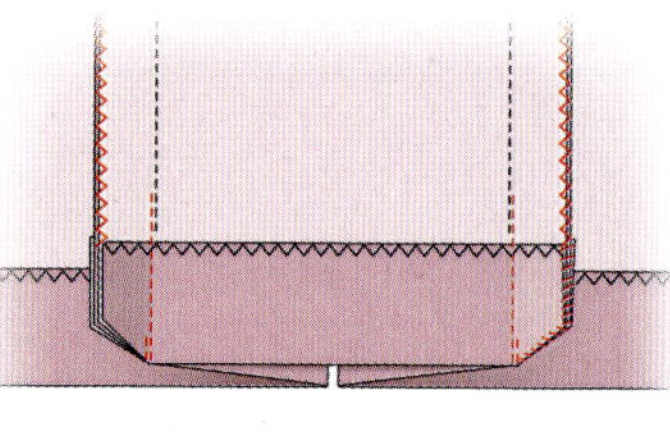

Tucks

Tucks are stitched folds of fabric that are usually folded on the straight grain. Each tuck has two stitching lines that are brought together and stitched to create a fold. The width of a tuck and the spacing between them depends on the fabric thickness and the effect you want to achieve. Most tucks are purely decorative and add delicate feminine details to blouses, children's clothes, and pillows (cushions).

Tucks with a space between them are called **spaced tucks**; those that meet, or overlap, are called **blind tucks**; and tucks stitched to a certain point, then released, are called **release tucks**. Release tucks can be used to control fullness over the bust and hips. There are also very narrow tucks, called **pin tucks**, but these are best left to experienced stitchers.

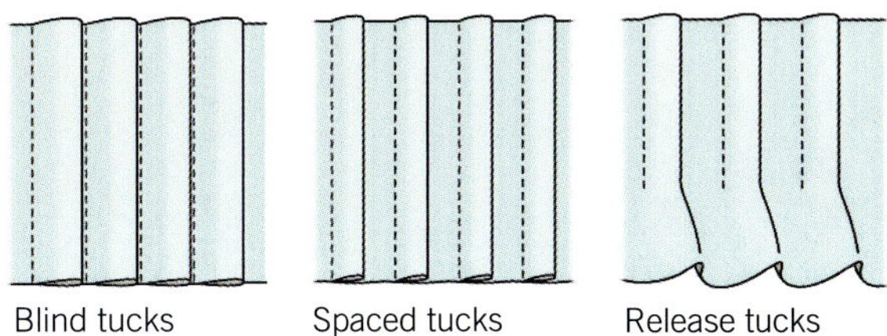

Blind tucks Spaced tucks Release tucks

Stitching tucks

There is no need to transfer all the stitching lines from the pattern: mark the lines for one tuck at the edge of a group, then use a simple card gauge to baste (tack) the remaining tucks in place.

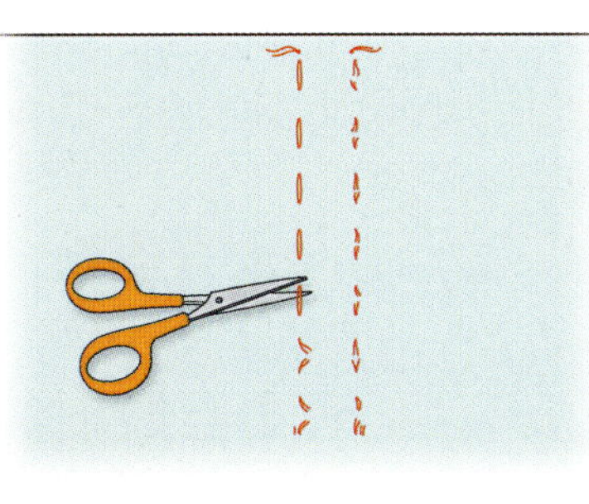

1 To mark the stitching lines of the first tuck, use double thread and work a row of large uneven basting (tacking) stitches through the pattern and the fabric (see page 39), then cut the thread at the center of each long stitch. Remove the pattern carefully to avoid pulling out the threads.

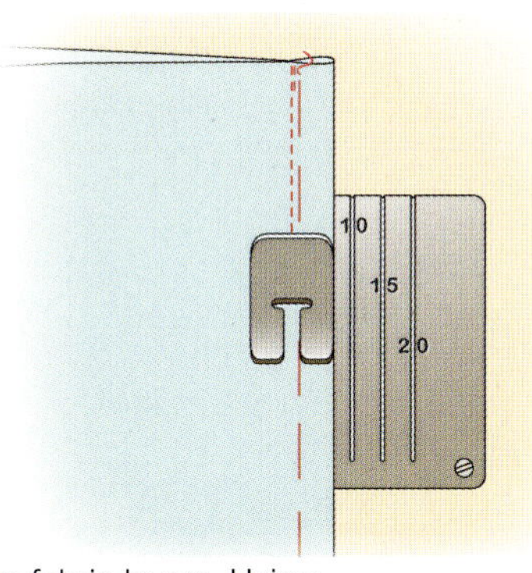

2 With wrong sides together, fold the tuck along the center to bring the stitching lines together. Pin in place outside the stitching line. Remove the marker threads, then press in the fold. Baste (tack) and machine stitch the tuck in place, using your machine foot or seam guide as an aid to keeping your stitching even and straight. Remove the basting stitches, then open out the fabric layers. Using a pressing cloth between the fabric and the iron, press the tuck flat in the required direction.

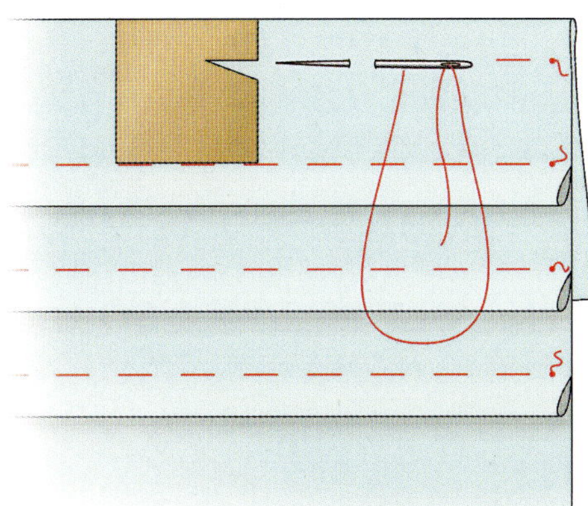

3 To mark and stitch your remaining tucks, make a cardboard gauge. First, determine the width of your tuck and the space between the stitching lines on successive tucks. Cut a piece of card as long as the sum of these two widths; from one end, mark off the tuck width and make a notch. Place the lower edge along the stitching line of the previous tuck and the upper edge along the fold. Work from right to left, creating one tuck at a time. Staystitch across the ends of the finished tucks within the seam allowance to keep them in place (see page 141).

Soft long-length blouse

Fresh and cool, this versatile long-line blouse in soft white linen has pretty tucks at the front and back and a neat little rounded collar. It can be layered over a short-sleeved T-shirt or vest and looks great partnered with jeans, leggings, and cropped pants, or belted as a dress when summer comes.

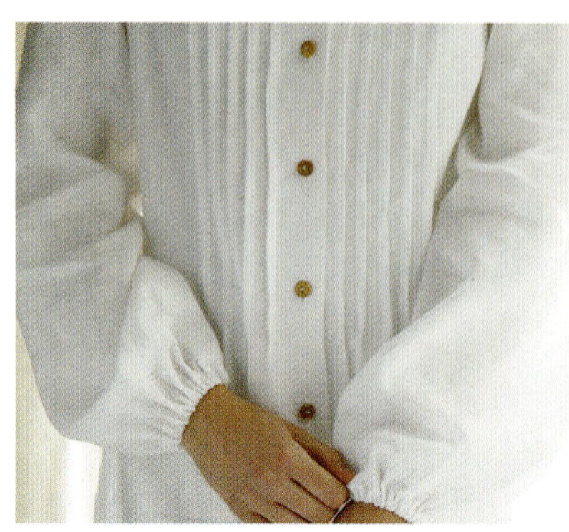

Fabric suggestions

Soft linens and cottons, cheesecloth, and viscose. Avoid checks, stripes, and large prints.

You will also need

- Blouse pattern pieces traced off the pattern sheet at the back of this book (see page 114)
- Lightweight iron-on interfacing (see page 134)
- Matching thread
- ½ yd (0.50m) of ¼-in.- (6-mm-) wide elastic
- Six buttons ½ in. (12 mm) in diameter
- One sew-on snap fastener

Size

Size	US 6 (UK 8)	US 8 (UK 10)	US 10 (UK 12)	US 12 (UK 14)	US 14 (UK 16)	US 16 (UK 18)
Bust	31½ in. (80 cm)	32½ in. (83 cm)	34 in. (87 cm)	36 in. (92 cm)	38 in. (97 cm)	40 in. (102 cm)
Waist	24 in. (61 cm)	25 in. (64 cm)	26½ in. (67 cm)	28 in. (71 cm)	30 in. (76 cm)	32 in. (81 cm)
Hips	33½ in. (85 cm)	34½ in. (88 cm)	36 in. (92 cm)	38 in. (97 cm)	40 in. (102 cm)	42 in. (107 cm)
Length (back neck to hem)	30¾ in. (78 cm)	30¾ in. (78 cm)	30¾ in. (78 cm)	30¾ in. (78 cm)	30¾ in. (78 cm)	30¾ in. (78 cm)

Fabric quantities

45-in.- (112-cm-) wide fabric						
	2⅛ yd (2 m)	2¼ yd (2 m)	2⅓ yd (2.1 m)	2½ yd (2.2 m)	2½ yd (2.3 m)	2½ yd (2.3 m)
60-in.- (150-cm-) wide fabric						
	3⅛ yd (2.8 m)	3⅛ yd (2.8 m)	3⅛ yd (2.8 m)	3¼ yd (2.9 m)	3¼ yd (2.9 m)	3¼ yd (2.9 m)
36-in.- (90-cm-) wide iron-on interfacing						
	⅔ yd (0.5 m)	⅔ yd (0.5 m)	⅔ yd (0.5 m)	⅔ yd (0.5 m)	⅔ yd (0.5 m)	⅔ yd (0.5 m)

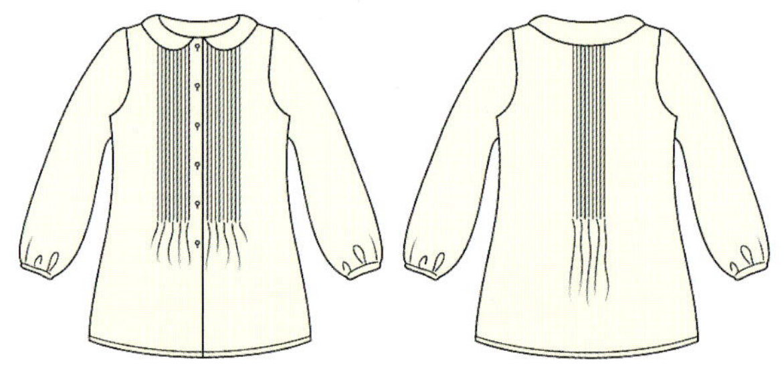

Front view Back view

Cutting out your fabric

Use pattern pieces 1A and 1B, 2A and 2B, 3, 4, 5A and 5B, and 6.

Please note
Fabric quantities and cutting layouts are given for one-way fabrics only. If using a fabric with a two-way design, you may be able to lay pattern pieces into a smaller amount of fabric, but remember, grainlines must still run parallel to the selvage.

Blouse—all sizes
45-in.- (112-cm-) wide fabric

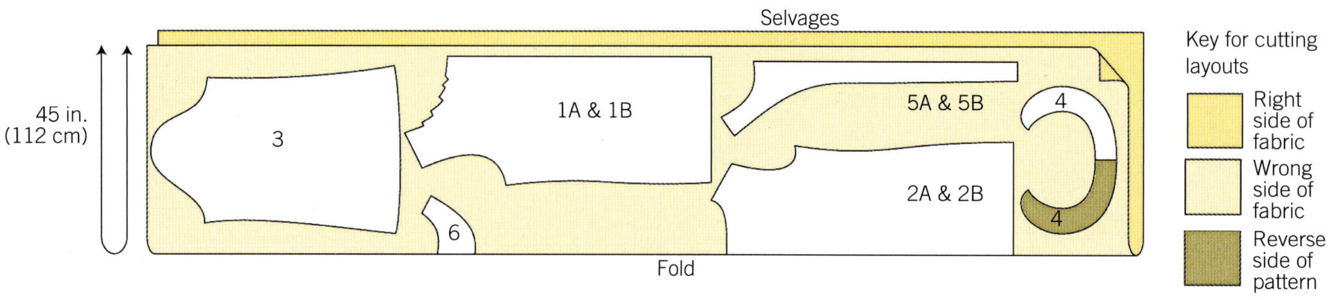

Blouse—all sizes
60-in.- (150-cm-) wide fabric

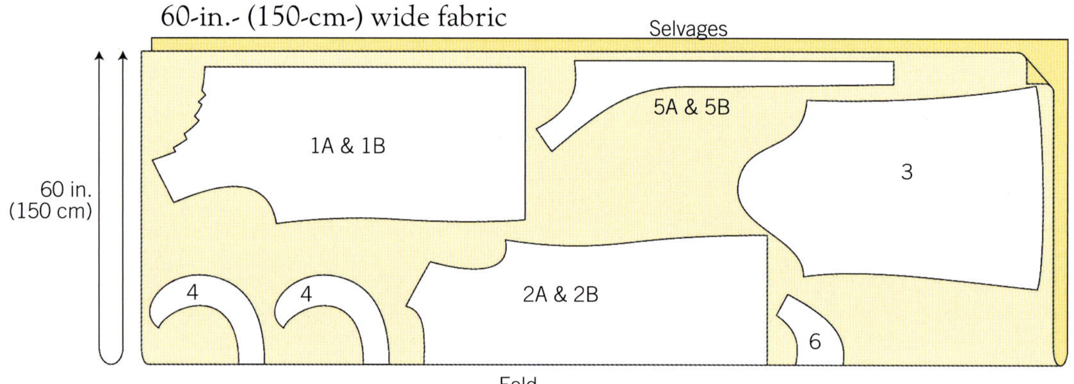

Interfacing—all sizes
36-in.- (90-cm-) wide interfacing

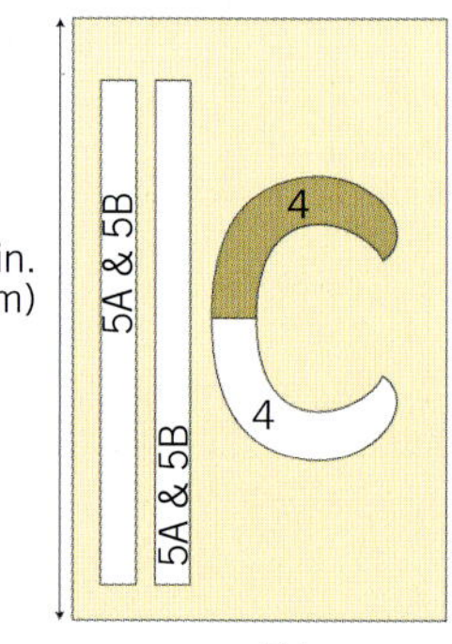

Note:
- 5/8-in. (1.5-cm) seam allowances are included unless otherwise stated.
- Stitch seams with right sides together and notches matching, unless otherwise stated.

1 Following the appropriate cutting layout (see above), cut out all your fabric and interfacing pieces.

2 Working from the neck edges and stitching 1/4 in. (6 mm) from the folded edge, stitch the tucks on the right side of the blouse fronts and back (see page 149). Press the front tucks toward the side seam edges and the back tucks to the right, then staystitch the neck edges, stitching the tucks in place at the same time (see page 141).

Pin, baste (tack), and machine stitch the fronts to the back at the shoulder seams, reverse stitching at each end to secure. Press the seams open and neaten the seam allowances separately.

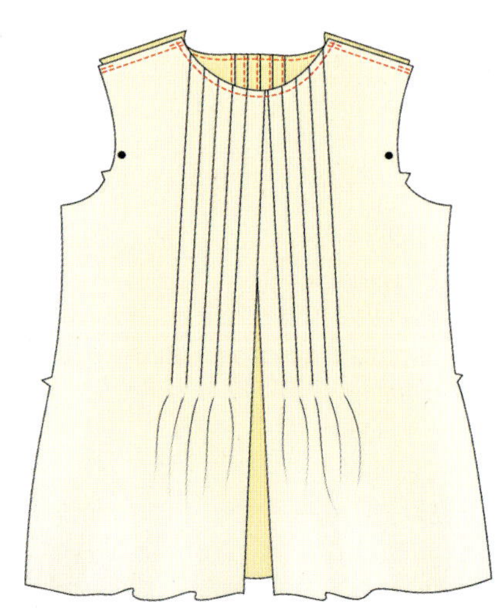

3 Taking a 3/8-in. (1-cm) seam allowance, make up and attach the collar and facings to the blouse front and neck edges, following steps 1–5 of Attaching a flat collar, page 154. Catch the edges of the facings to the shoulder seams and one center back tuck with a couple of herringbone stitches (see page 49). With right sides together, pin, baste (tack), and machine stitch the blouse fronts to the back at the side seams, matching notches and reverse stitching at each end to secure. Press the seams open and neaten the seam allowances separately.

4 With the right side up, work two parallel rows of ease stitching around the top of each sleeve head, between the outer dots (see page 146). With right sides together, pin, baste (tack), and machine stitch the sleeve underarm seam. Press the seam open and neaten the seam allowances separately. Turn the sleeve right side out.

5 With the right sides together, matching dots and notches, pin the sleeve to the corresponding armhole, with the top dot to the shoulder seam and the underarm seam to the side seam. Gently pull up the ease stitching so that the sleeve fits the armhole and pin it in place at 3/8-in. (1-cm) intervals.

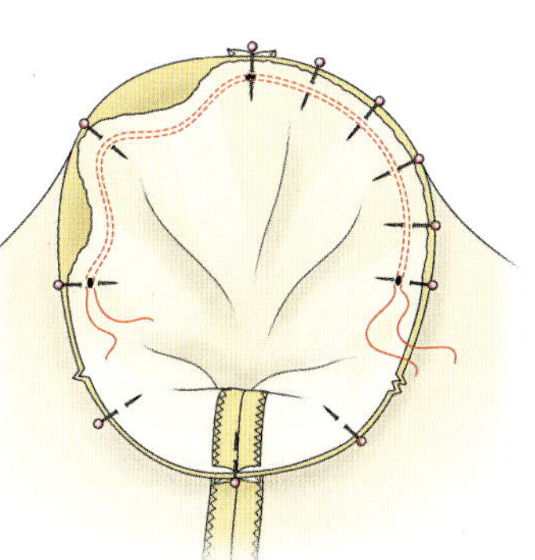

6 Check that there are no puckers and that the sleeve fits the armhole well, then remove the pins and the sleeve. With the sleeve right side out, steam press around the wrong side of the sleeve head to shrink out any "dimpling" in the easing area, as shown.

7 With the right sides together, re-pin the sleeve to the armhole as before, then baste (tack) it in place using small basting stitches. With the wrong side of the sleeve uppermost and starting at the underarm seam, stitch the sleeve to the armhole along the seamline, using your fingers to control the easing and overlapping the stitching to secure at the end. Remove the basting stitches.

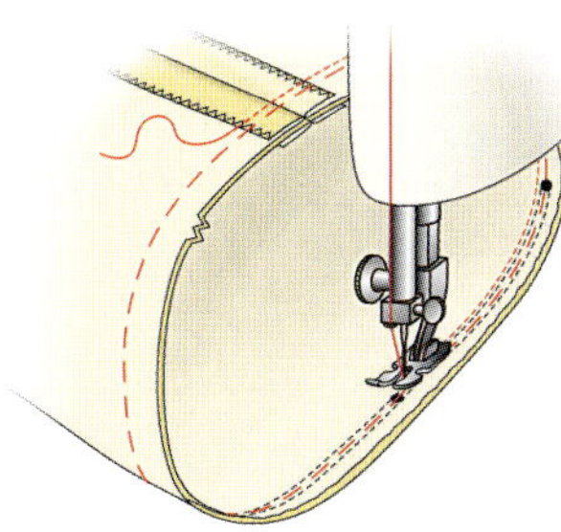

8 Neaten the armhole seam allowances, following the method for Zigzag neatening without an overcasting foot, page 44. Then, to form the wrist casings, see Circular fold-down casing on page 125, insert the elastic as shown on page 127.

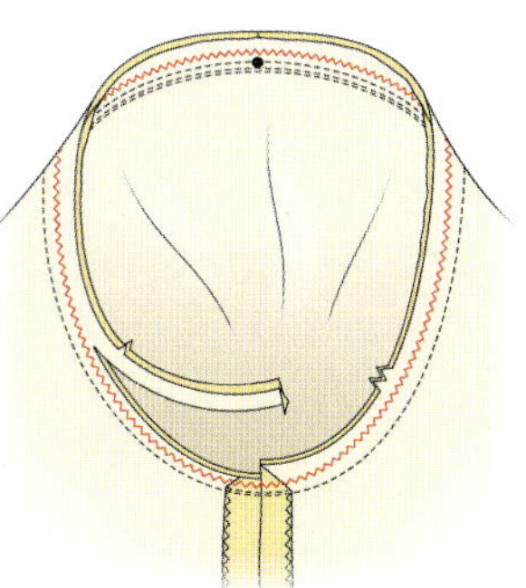

9 Neaten the hem edge, then pin, baste (tack), and machine stitch the lower edge of each facing to the blouse fronts, working 5/8 in. (1.5 cm) up from the neatened edge. Clip the corners and turn right side out. Press the seamed edges flat and press the hem to the wrong side by 5/8 in. (1.5 cm); pin, baste, and machine stitch in place close to the neatened edge.

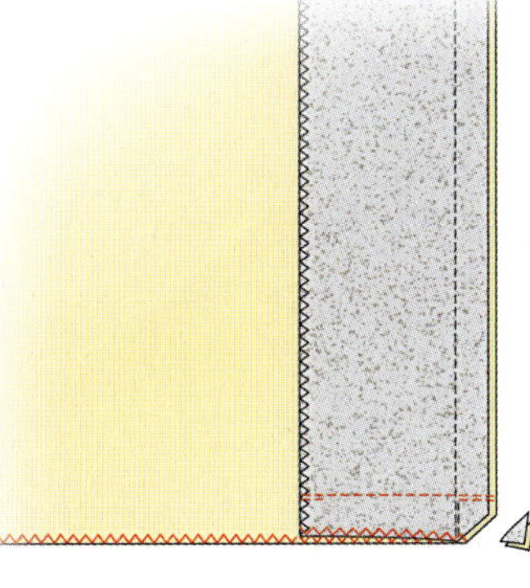

10 Work the buttonholes and attach the buttons at the positions marked on the pattern (see pages 68 and 65). Finally, stitch the snap fastener to the top of the front facing at the neck edge (see page 71).

Flat and stand collars

Collars are a decorative addition to a garment neckline and come in many shapes; we shall be focusing on flat and stand collars, which are popular and easy to make. Flat collars add a touch of innocent femininity and are suitable for blouses, dresses, and children's clothes; the stand collar often indicates an eastern influence and is sometimes called a Mandarin collar.

Flat collar

Flat collars appear from the neckline to lie flat against the garment, because the neck edge of the collar (the inner curve) follows the shape of the neckline. Flat collars may be made up as one unit that fits the neckline—usually on a front-opening garment—or as two units if the collar is split at the front and back—common if there is a back opening.

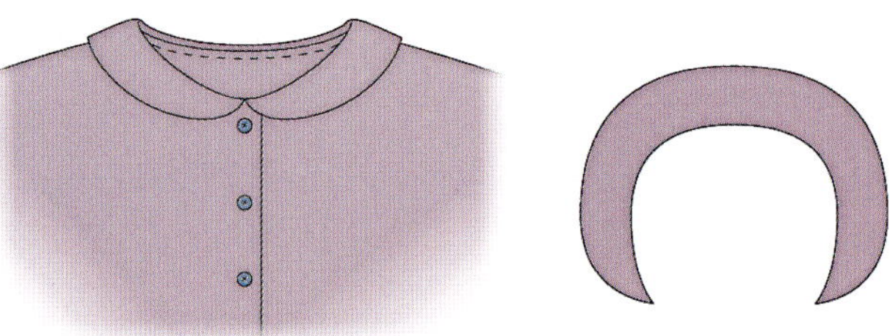

A flat collar is easy to make and attach. If the garment has a front opening, it is made in one part; if it has a center back zipper, it is split into two parts.

Attaching a flat collar

The following illustrations show how to attach a one-piece collar, but if you have a two-piece collar each unit is made in the same way. Before you begin, staystitch the neck edge of the garment (see page 141), and make up, press, and neaten all seams and darts that intersect the neckline. Any zippers that open at a neckline should also be inserted before the collar is applied to the garment.

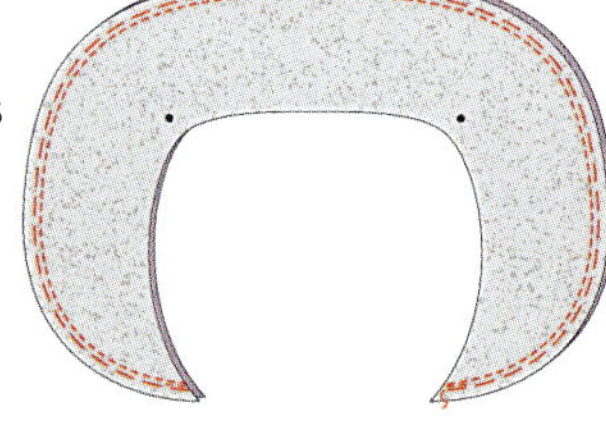

1 Apply interfacing to the wrong side of the top collar (see page 134). With right sides together and raw edges level, pin and baste (tack) the top collar to the under collar, leaving the neck edge open. Machine stitch the pieces together, reverse stitching to start and finish. Trim and layer the seam allowances, trimming across any corners and notching or snipping curved seam allowances (see page 43).

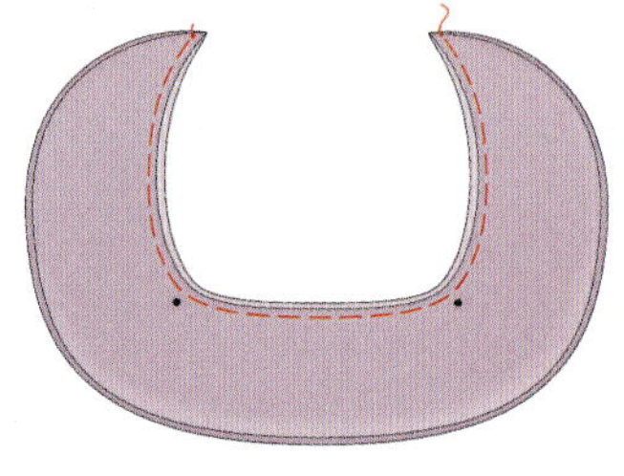

2 Turn the collar right side out and tease out any corners. Press the collar, rolling the seam slightly to the underside. Pin and baste (tack) the collar neck edges together, matching the corresponding pattern markings. If you are making a two-part collar, repeat steps 1 and 2 with the remaining collar pieces.

Center front

3 With raw edges level and right sides uppermost, pin and baste (tack) the collar or collars to the neckline edge, matching corresponding pattern markings and the ends of the collar to the center front (and/or center back) at the neckline seam; bear in mind that the center front collar ends may overlap slightly within the seam allowance on a back-opening garment.

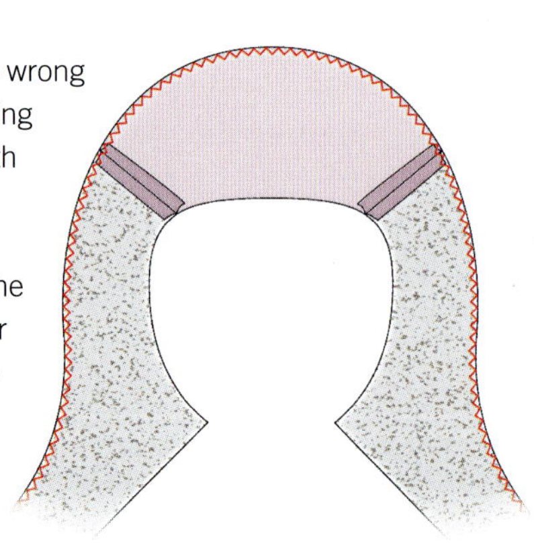

4 Apply interfacing to the wrong side of the appropriate facing pieces (see page 134). With right sides together, pin, baste (tack), and machine stitch the front facings to the back facing at the shoulder seams, reverse stitching to start and finish. Press the seams open, then neaten the outer edge of the joined facings.

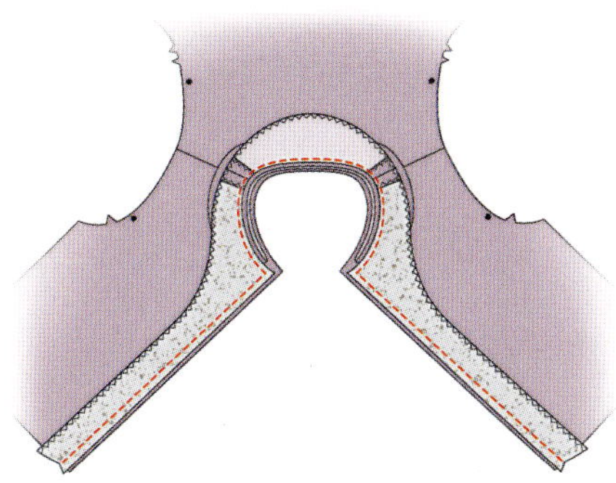

5 For a front-faced opening: With the right sides together, pin and baste (tack) the joined facings to the collar and the garment at the neck and front edges, matching the pattern markings, shoulder seams, and front hem edges. Stitch the pieces together, working around the neckline from one hem edge to the other, pivoting your work at the corners, sandwiching the collar in place, and reverse stitching to start and finish. Trim, layer, and clip the seam allowances (see page 43). Turn the facing to the right side and tease out the front corners.

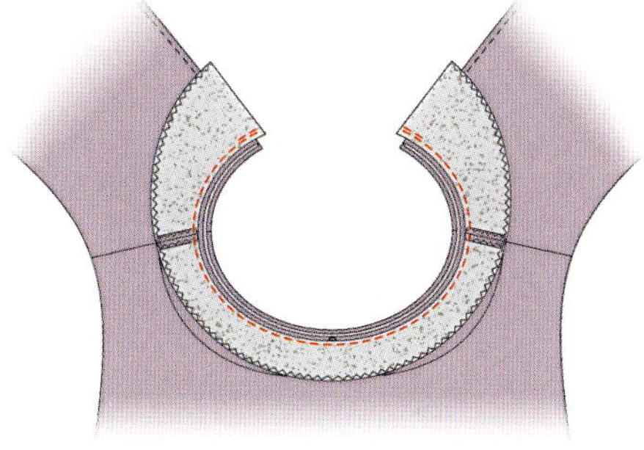

6 For a back-zipper opening: To attach the joined facings and trim the seam allowances, follow step 5, omitting references to the front hem edges; make sure that the back facing ends extend the depth of the seam allowance at the back-opening edges, and check that the ends of the neck seamline align when the zipper is closed.

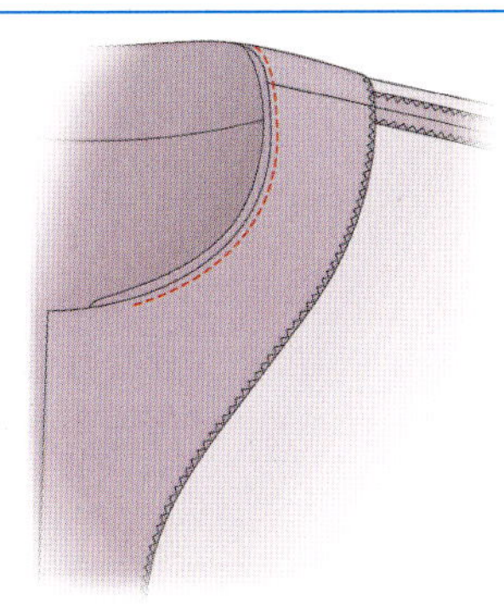

7 With the facing right side up, understitch the seam allowances to the facing close to the neck seamline (see page 51), stitching as far around the neckline as possible. Press the facing to the inside of the garment, rolling the front opening edges slightly to the inside on a front-opening garment. Slip hem the neatened outer edges of the facing to the shoulder seams (see page 91). For a back-zipper opening, turn under the back facing ends, slip hem them to the zipper tape (see page 91), and attach hooks and eyes to the facing (see page 72).

Stand collar

The stand collar is at the opposite end of the spectrum to a flat collar, as it extends up from the neck seamline. There are two types of stand collar: the plain band or Mandarin collar, or the turned-down collar, sometimes known as a turtle neck. The main difference between the two is the depth, the second being twice as wide, to turn back on itself.

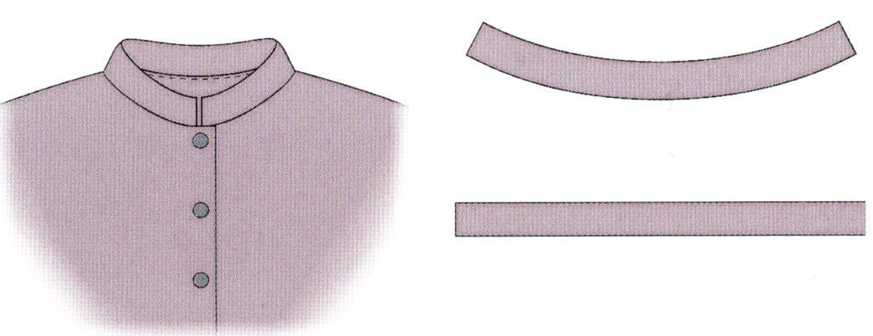

Stand collars can be straight and made of one piece, or cut on a curve and made of two pieces; a two-piece collar sits close to the neck, whereas a one-piece stands away.

Attaching a stand collar Attach a stand collar in the same way as a flat collar. Before you begin, staystitch the neck edge of the garment (see page 140), and make up, press, and neaten all seams and darts that intersect the neckline. Any zippers that open at a neckline should also be inserted before the collar is applied.

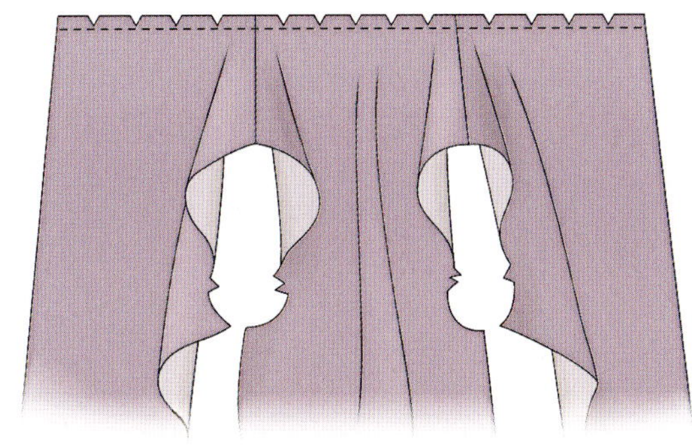

Refer to steps 1–7 of Attaching a flat collar, but clip into the neckline seam allowances of the garment to allow you to "straighten" out the seamline (see page 43) before basting (tacking) the collar in place; this will make it easier to stitch the pieces together.

Needle, thread, and stitch length selection

This is a quick reference guide to the recommended thread, needle, and stitch length combinations for most basic home-sewing jobs.

Fabric	Machine needle	Thread	Stitch length
Woven fabrics, either man-made or natural fibers, such as linen, cotton, wool, velvet, and chiffon	Normal sharp-point needle, size 12 (80)	Polyester thread	10–11 stitches to the inch (2.5 cm)
Woven fabrics, natural fibers only, such as cotton, linen, wool, and velvet	Normal sharp-point needle, size 12 (80)	Cotton or poly/cotton thread	10–11 stitches to the inch (2.5 cm)
Fine woven fabrics, natural fibers only, such as silk, silk velvet, chiffon, and wool	Normal sharp-point needle, size 10 (70)	Silk or polyester thread	12 stitches to the inch (2.5 cm)
Fine knitted fabrics, made from man-made, silk, cotton, or wool fibers	Fine ball-point needle, size 10 (70)	Polyester thread	11 stitches to the inch (2.5 cm)
Heavy knitted fabrics, made from man-made or natural fibers, such as jersey or fleece	Medium ball-point needle, size 12–14 (80–90)	Polyester thread	9–10 stitches to the inch (2.5 cm)
Dense fabrics such as twill, denim, heavy linen, and canvas	Extra fine-point or jeans needle, size 12–14 (80–90)	Heavy-duty polyester thread, or linen twist	6–7 stitches to the inch (2.5 cm)
Leather, suede, imitation leathers and suede, and plastics	Wedge-point (leather) needle, size 14–16 (90–100)	Heavy-duty polyester thread, or linen twist	6 stitches to the inch (2.5 cm)

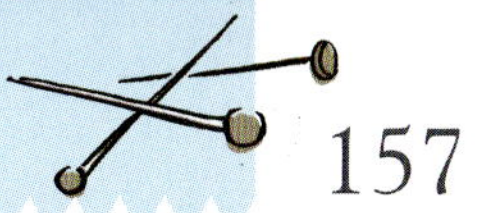

Looking after your sewing machine

Like any other machine, your sewing machine will require some regular maintenance in order to keep it running smoothly. Every machine normally comes with an accessories box that contains all the equipment you need, such as oil, screwdrivers, and a cleaning brush. Regular cleaning of all the sliding parts is essential so that dust and lint do not accumulate. By following these simple steps every few weeks, you will help prolong the life of your machine and have a much more enjoyable sewing experience.

Cleaning away dust and lint

1 Unplug your machine and remove the needle, thread spool, bobbin case, and bobbin.

2 Remove any dust and lint from the exterior of your machine casing and any exposed parts with a soft lint-free cloth. For any stubborn dirty marks, use a dampened cloth and mild detergent.

3 Using the small lint brush, remove lint from all the thread guides.

4 Unscrew and remove your needleplate (refer to your instruction manual for details of how to do this) and, using the brush, remove lint from the feed dogs and the back of the needleplate. Replace the needleplate.

5 Using the brush, remove lint from around and in the bobbin case; for lint that has got packed under and around the bobbin housing, use a pair of tweezers.

6 Replace your needle with a new one; you are now ready to start to sew again.

TIPS

- If your machine does not have a lint brush, use a soft, dry, small paintbrush as a substitute.
- Look out for cans of compressed air, which you can use to blow away lint from the moving parts, rather than using a brush.

Oiling your machine

Over-oiling a motor is unwise; one or two drops twice a year should be sufficient, placed in the oiling points indicated for your machine. (Check your instruction manual to find out where these are.) However, some new electronic and computerized models never need oiling at all, so please check your manual to find out whether yours is one of these types.

Useful advice

- When your machine is not in use, cover it up, so as not to attract excess dust. If your machine does not have a cover use an old sheet or a piece of cotton cloth to protect it.
- Take care of your mains power cable and plug and have them repaired at the first sign of any damage or wear.

Glossary

Appliqué: One piece of fabric stitched to another in a decorative manner (*see* page 83).
Backstitch: A strong hand stitch with double stitching on the wrong side (*see* page 48).
Basting: A means of temporarily holding two layers of fabric together for stitching; known as tacking in the UK (*see* page 38).
Bias: The diagonal grain of a fabric, at 45° to the lengthwise and crosswise grain of the fabric (*see* page 32). Bias-cut fabric drapes well.
Bias binding: Narrow folded strips of fabric cut on the bias; can be home made or purchased ready made. Used to neaten raw edges (*see* page 54).
Binding: A method of finishing off a raw edge by wrapping it with a strip of bias binding (*see* page 55).
Blanket stitch: A stitch worked by hand along a raw or finished edge of fabric to decorate or neaten it (*see* page 49).
Blind-hem stitch: Tiny hand stitches used to attach one piece of fabric to another, by hand or machine (*see* page 90).
Bobbin: The round holder beneath the needle plate on a sewing machine, onto which thread is wound (*see* page 14).
Button shank: The stem between a button and the fabric to which is it attached, which can be part of the button or constructed with thread (*see* page 66).
Casing: A tunnel of fabric created by parallel lines of stitching, through which elastic, drawstring, or curtain wire is threaded (*see* page 124).
Center line: Vertical center of a bodice, skirt, or yoke section of a garment; marked on the relevant pattern pieces.
Contour dart: Also known as a double-pointed dart, used to give shape at the waist of a garment (*see* page 133).
Crosswise grain: The direction of the widthwise (weft) threads on the fabric, running from selvage to selvage (*see* page 32).
Cutting line: Solid or broken lines printed on a pattern piece, used as a guide for cutting (*see* page 113).
Dart: Tapered, stitched fold of fabric, used to shape fabric around contours of the body (*see* page 132).
Dressmaker's carbon paper: Paper available in a number of colors, used with a tracing wheel to transfer pattern markings to fabric.
Ease: Distribution of fullness without the formation of gathers (*see* page 146).
Edge stitch: Worked on the right side of an item, close to the finished edge, seam, or edge of a fold (*see* page 51).
Facing: A layer of fabric positioned on the inside of a garment and used to finish off raw edges—for example, at a neckline, waist edge, front, or back jacket opening; it can be interfaced for weight (*see* page 92).
Fibers: Natural or man-made filaments from which yarns are spun; the yarns are then made into a variety of fabrics (*see* page 24).
Flat-fell seam: A strong, hardwearing, self-enclosed seam (*see* page 89).
French seam: A self-enclosed seam traditionally used on sheer and silk fabrics (*see* page 89).
Gathering: Decorative bunches of fabric created by sewing two parallel rows of loose stitches and then pulling them up (*see* page 144).
Grain: The lengthwise and crosswise direction of threads in a woven fabric (*see* page 32).
Grainline: Line that follows the grain of a fabric (*see* page 113).
Heading tape: A fabric tape containing loops for inserting curtain hooks for the purpose of hanging (*see* page 97).
Hem: The neatened lower edge of an item–for example, thebottom of a garment or curtain (*see* pages 45 and 90).
Hem allowance: The amount of fabric allowed for turning under to make a hem.
Herringbone stitch: A hand-worked hemming stitch used to join the edges of interfacing or facings inside an item (*see* page 49).
Hook-and-eye fastener: A two-piece metal fastener (*see* page 72).
Hook-and-loop fastener: A two-part tape fastening consisting of a "hook" side and a "loop" side; when pressed together, the two pieces grip each other (*see* page 73).
Integrated or self-facing: Used at a straight garment edge, this type of facing is cut as one with the garment, and then folded to the inside.
Interfacing: Specially designed fabric placed between the garment and the facing to give support; it can be iron-on or sewn-in (*see* page 134).
Interlining: A layer of fabric placed between the lining and garment fabric to add warmth and bulk (*see* page 135).
Lapped seam: Used on non-frayable fabrics, as a flat way to join seams (*see* page 137).
Layering: Trimming fabric layers at seam allowances to reduce bulk (*see* page 43).
Lengthwise grain: The direction of the lengthwise (warp) threads on a woven fabric, which lie parallel to the selvages (*see* page 32).
Lining: An underlying fabric layer used to give a luxurious, neat finish to an item (*see* page 135).
Lockstitch: A stitch made by a sewing machine, where the upper and lower threads "lock" together to form stitches (*see* page 12).
Machine foot: Also referred to as a presser foot, a part of a sewing machine that is lowered onto fabric to hold it in place on the needle plate during stitching (*see* page 20).
Mitered corner: A diagonal seam formed at a corner where two hems meet—for example, at the base of a curtain (*see* page 93).
Mock French seam: Used as for a French seam, but on curved fabric edges (*see* page 89).
Nap: Raised pile surface of a fabric, or a printed design pointing in one direction (*see* page 34).
Notch: An outward or inward-facing V-shaped mark, indicating alignment with another piece for seaming (*see* page 113).
Notion: An item other than fabric needed to complete a project, such as a button, zipper, or elastic. Known in the UK as haberdashery.
Overcast stitch: A hand stitch used to neaten raw fabric edges (*see* page 49).
Paper-backed adhesive web: An adhesive web with a paper backing; the glue is activated by a hot iron and is used to bond two layer of fabric together (*see* page 83).
Pinking shears: A cutting tool with serrated blades used on fray-resistant fabrics to neaten a seam allowance with a zigzag finish.
Piping: A trim made out of bias binding and cord, used to edge garments and soft furnishings (*see* page 82).
Pivoting: A technique used to stitch around sharp corners (*see* page 42).
Plain weave: Basic flat finished fabric, where the warp and weft yarns interweave alternately (*see* page 26).
Pleat: An even fold of fabric, often partially stitched down, used to take in fullness (*see* page 146).
Pocket flap: A piece of fabric that folds down to cover the opening of a pocket (*see* page 58).
Prick stitch: Small, spaced hand stitches used for invisibly inserting a zipper (*see* page 48).
Raw edge: The cut edge of fabric,

which requires to be neatened to stop fraying (*see* page 44).
Reverse stitch: Straight machine stitching that is worked backward for a short distance at the beginning and end of a seam to secure the threads (*see* page 40).
Running stitch: A hand stitch used for seaming or gathering (*see* page 48).
Seam allowance: The amount of fabric allowed for on a pattern where sections of an item are to be joined together with a seam.
Seam guide: Lines marked on the needle plate, or an adjustable attachment used as a guide for sewing straight seams (*see* page 41).
Seamline: Line designated for stitching the seam, generally 5/8 in. (1.5 cm) from the raw edge.
Seam ripper: A hooked cutting tool used to open or undo seams and slit buttonholes (*see* page 23).
Snap fasteners: Also known as press studs, these two-part fasteners are used as a lightweight hidden fastener (see page 71).
Snap-fastener tape: Two tapes with a row of corresponding snap fasteners (*see* page 73).
Stay stitching: Straight machine stitches worked just inside the seamline to strengthen it and prevent it from stretching and breaking (*see* page 141).
Straight stitch: Plain machine stitch, used for most sewing applications (*see* page 18).
Self-enclosed seam: A seam in which the raw edges are enclosed to form a neat finish (*see* page 88).
Selvage: The finished edge on a woven fabric, which runs parallel to the warp (lengthwise) threads (*see* page 26); selvedge in the UK.
Slipstitch: A hand-worked hemming stitch used to attach a folded fabric edge to another layer (*see* page 49).
Stitch tension: On a sewing machine, this dial controls the degree of tightness or looseness of the top and bobbin threads when interlocking to make a stitch (*see* page 19).
Straight grain: *See* Grainline.
Tacking: *See* Basting.
Tailor's chalk: Used to mark fabric; easily removed by brushing (*see* page 22).
Topstitching: A row of straight stitches worked on the right side of an item for a decorative effect (*see* page 50).
Tracing wheel: A tool used in conjunction with dressmaker's carbon paper to transfer pattern markings (*see* page 23).
Tuck: A stitched fold of fabric formed along the straight grain to take in fullness (*see* page 149).
Twill-weave: Diagonally patterned weave on a woven fabric (*see* page 26).
Underlining: A layer of fabric cut to the same shape as and placed beneath the garment fabric before seams are joined, used mainly on tailored garments (*see* page 135).
Waistband: A band of stiffened fabric attached to a waist edge of a garment to give it a neat stable finish (*see* page 142).
Warp: The lengthwise threads or yarns of a woven fabric (*see* page 26).
Weft: Threads or yarns that run across the width of the fabric, interlacing with the warp yarns (*see* page 26).
Zigzag stitch: A machine stitch used to neaten, secure seamed edges, and make buttonholes. The width and length of the stitch can be altered (*see* page18).
Zipper: A widely used fastening consisting of two tapes carrying specially shaped teeth that lock together, available in different types, weights, and lengths (*see* page 78).

Index

Author's acknowledgments

Many thanks to all the people who helped to make this book possible—I couldn't have done it without you.

Particular thanks go to Jan Dabbous, a very special and dedicated friend, without whose help this book would never have come together during my very hectic working schedule. Thanks also go to Beryl Miller, a brilliant seamstress, for making up some of the projects in record time for our photo shoots.

To Sarah Hoggett for tirelessly working through my copy to make grammatical sense and Stephen Dew for his sterling work in producing the step-by-step illustrations. To Gillian Haslam and publisher Cindy Richards, without whose encouragement the book wouldn't have seen the light of day!

And finally, thanks go to everyone who has lent and supplied items for the book: The Eternal Maker (www.eternalmaker.com) for the cushions, scarf, apron, bag, and Roman blind fabrics, and giant rickrack braid; Dots n Stripes (www.dotsnstripes.co.uk) for the girl's pinafore dress fabrics and spotty ribbons; The Cloth House (www.clothhouse.com) for the pants, skirt and blouse fabrics; and Janome UK (www.janome.co.uk) for the sewing machine, model number 5255.